DWELLING ON THE THRESHOLD

I'm a Dweller on the Threshold
And I'm waiting at the door,
And I'm standing in the darkness,
I don't want to wait no more.

—VAN MORRISON

DWELLING
ON THE THRESHOLD
Critical Essays on Modern Legal Thought

■

ALLAN C. HUTCHINSON
LL.B. (Hons.), LL.M.
Barrister of Gray's Inn
Associate Professor of Law
Osgoode Hall Law School
York University

1988

THE CARSWELL COMPANY LIMITED
Toronto ▪ Calgary ▪ Vancouver

SWEET & MAXWELL LIMITED
London

Canadian Cataloguing in Publication Data

Hutchinson, Allan C.
    Dwelling on the threshold

Bibliography: p.
ISBN 0-459-30561-1

1. Law — History and criticism. 2. Law and
politics 3. Law — Philosophy. I. Title.

K235.H87   1988   340'.1   C88-093166-3

Sweet & Maxwell Limited   ISBN 0-421-40050-1

CONTENTS

PREFACE

The nice thing about a preface is that it gives me the chance to get in the last word first. But, before I tell you what I really intended the book to say and not to say, I want to begin by thanking all those people who made it possible and enjoyable for me to write it. Some had a direct influence on the substance of my views; others had a more indirect, but no less important effect. As this collection of essays tries to argue and show, any individual project draws life from its intellectual and intimate context. It is truly the product of many people's ideas, criticism, encouragement and affection. While I considered leaving them all unnamed in order to protect their innocence, the need for some convenient scapegoats proved irresistible.

Jane, Katie, Emily and Rachel loved me enough to provide all the distractions and demands of family life that anyone could realistically expect. Grey Denham first fired me up with the jurisprudential passion and Andrew Ashworth made me get serious. Duncan Kennedy turned that earnestness to Critical advantage, Hans Mohr gave me the confidence to be playful and Harry Glasbeek set an example of political integrity. Patrick Monahan, Derek Morgan, Andrew Petter and John Wakefield were and still are co-authors from whom I have learned so much about scholarship and friendship. Garry Watson put his faith in me, John McCamus was an always supportive Dean, Mary Jane Mossman shared her feminist insights and Harry Arthurs continues to be a strong influence. Gail Kenny organised me and my work in an enviable way: Corinne Doan saw the project through. An exceptional group of researchers—Joanne Boulding, Lynda Covello, Barry Ennis, Pino DiEmedio, Michael Gottheil, Michael Kanter, Gretchen Kewley, Greg Ljubic, Larry Ritchie and Kevin Whitaker—endured my eccentric ways and saved me from even greater embarrassments and errors. And, finally, the multitude of people, including friends, colleagues and "enemies", who took the time to read my work and give me the benefit of their criticisms.

As the title of the book suggests, these essays dwell on the threshold of modern legal thought. They are intended to occupy a narrow ledge of criticism and, as with all such positions, they run the considerable risk of succumbing to the secure comforts of traditional jurisprudence or straying too far into the wilderness of political irrelevance. In keeping with my critical ambition, I have tried to examine various dimensions of the legal enterprise and to explore more than one jurisdictional exemplar of its condition. Most importantly—for me, at least—I have taken seriously the idea that, in order to say different things about law, it is necessary to say them differently as well. By jolting readers' traditional expectations about the style and presentation of academic argument, the hope is that they will become more sensitive and responsive to critical challenges to received jurisprudential wisdom.

If there is a connecting thread to these essays, it is in the basic belief that law and its study is inescapably political in scope and substance. Legal theorists must begin to take responsibility for all, both good and bad, that is done in the name of the law: there is no position of political innocence. Too often, the cool and unsmiling face of juristic reason has been conveniently averted from circumstances of social injustice. If, at times, I tend to paint in colours that are too uniformly dark and depressing, it will at least serve as a cautionary counterpoint to the suspect optimism of most traditional theorists. After all, the pessimist is only a better-informed optimist. Also, my opposition to the Rule of Law must be placed in political perspective. If it is intended to mean being against arbitrary or tyrannical government, then the Rule of Law has my unreserved support. If, however, it is shorthand for a particular brand of liberal individualism, then I am unalterably opposed to it. My radical challenge is not to law per se, but to its present ideological structure and social consequences.

In trying to resolve the mysteries of law and legal thinking, I have called in aid a whole range of different scholarly insights and disciplinary methodologies. Notwithstanding Pope's admonition that "a little learning is a dang'rous thing," I have preferred the risks of intoxication from "shallow draughts" at "the Pierian spring" to a safer, but less rewarding regimen of intellectual abstinence. While I cannot even pretend to have achieved any final resolution of jurisprudence's perennial riddles, I do hope to have contributed a more relevant and revealing agenda of questions to be asked and answered about the politics of law. I will be more than content if, as Adrienne Rich puts it, from "these words, these whispers, conversations," an occasional and modest truth "breaks moist and green".

This collection is a mix of old and new essays. However, those pieces previously published have been substantially revised and re-worked. I am grateful to the *American Bar Foundation Research Journal*, *Buffalo Law Review*, *California Law Review*, *Modern Law Review*, *New York University Law Review*, *Osgoode Hall Law Journal*, *Southern California Law Review* and *Yale Law Journal* for permission to use material that first appeared in their publications. Also, with characteristic generosity, Derek Morgan and Andrew Petter allowed me to rewrite and include papers that we had originally co-authored. Finally, for the convenience of reviewers, if I am so blessed, I have left in a number of glaring inconsistencies and blatant contradictions.

1

IN TRAINING

(*A crisp autumn day. On a train bound for anywhere. Robert is sitting by the window. Opposite him, across a table, sits Charles. Next to him is Rachel. The rest of the car is sparsely peopled. The journey is scheduled to take about three hours. For the first forty-five minutes, Robert has been gazing out of the window; Charles has been dozing off after finishing his newspaper; and Rachel is seemingly immersed in reading a weighty tome.*)

ROBERT
  (*to no one in particular*) That scene is pure Vivaldi.

  (*There is no response. Charles awakes rather abruptly but quickly strikes a more dignified pose. Rachel seems oblivious to Robert's announcement.*)

ROBERT
  (*a couple of minutes later*) Pure Vivaldi! Perhaps a hint of Pachelbel. Don't you think so?

CHARLES
  (*preceded by a nervous cough*) It certainly is a nice sight.

ROBERT
  (*directed at Rachel*) Don't you think those trees are sheer poetry?

RACHEL
  (*after a slight pause*) Well, you certainly mix your metaphors. First

music, then poetry. Yes, it is a stunning view. But isn't it all a matter of taste? Vivaldi for you. Maybe Wagner to another. Or Madonna for some.

ROBERT

Hold on. Hold on. You can't simply lump Vivaldi, Wagner, and Madonna together. That's to soil the sublime with the ridiculous. Vivaldi managed to capture the harmony and majesty of autumnal nature. He wasn't simply pandering to adolescent fancies. He captured a slice of the infinite. William Blake knew what he was about:

> To see a World in a Grain of Sand
> And a Heaven in a Wild Flower,
> Hold Infinity in the palm of your hand
> And Eternity in an hour.

First, you glimpse the trees in the music and then you recognize the music in the trees. You have to connect with nature. Separate the profound and the popular. Caviar isn't pablum.

RACHEL

Oh, I don't know. Of course, poetry is powerful and can touch the heart. But its appeal is to the emotional, not the intellectual. It's more soul-stew than food for thought. The harmony of nature is in our heads, if anywhere.

ROBERT

Oh, come on now.

RACHEL

No, really. You seem to want to create an exclusive club of aesthetes. You want your world to be the only world. That's *subjective*.

CHARLES

(*with another nervous cough*) You know what they say: "Beauty is in the eye of the Beholder." But, leaving aside poetry, I recently heard a joke—well, a humorous tale really—that your conversation reminds me of. While on a visit to New York, a rich oil sheikh—are there any poor ones?—was given a private performance of a Mahler symphony. At the end of the concert, he was asked if he wished for an encore. Without hesitation, he requested a repeat performance of the first part. The orchestra began to replay the first movement, but the sheikh said "No, no; the first part." After a while, the distinguished conductor realized that it was the tune-up that he had enjoyed most. There's no accounting for taste!

(Charles effects a hearty, if hollow, laugh; Rachel and Robert smile. Rachel returns to her book; Robert looks back out of the window; and Charles goes off to get a coffee. Robert picks up Charles' newspaper and begins to read it. It is the Toronto Globe and Mail, June 15, 1985, and is open at the Books section.

Developments that have in recent years undermined both these theories are the growing sophistication of linguistic and semiotic analysis and, more important, the growing conviction among theorists that all human belief, especially esthetic belief, is socially constructed—that there are no absolute critical standards, only ones that meet the needs of particular communities at particular times. This is particularly well demonstrated in *Lyric Poetry: Beyond New Criticism.*

Among literary beliefs now suspect are the New Criticism's conviction that unity is essential to art (recent deconstructive criticism sees disunity, contradiction and disjunction as equally powerful); thematic criticism's conviction of the referentiality of literature to the culture in which it was created (many linguistic critics argue that powerful writing gains this power from play among its own elements, from containing subtextual patterns or hypograms, or from self-referentiality); the new Criticism's insistence on the autonomy of the literary work (recent critics often see the work as interacting not only with the history of meaning carried by its individual words but with other texts it invokes or resembles); thematic criticism's faith in literature as individual expression (contemporary marxist criticism holds that writing, like the individual human being, is socially conditioned, that the self-expression theory is no more than a sub-fantasy of the bourgeois belief in the free-acting citizen); the New Criticism's assumption of the existence of distinct literary genres (much contemporary criticism holds that genres are arbitrary distinctions that mask the overwhelming similarities all literary works share as fabrications of language, or "writing") . . .

A major disappointment in the book, however, is how uninteresting most of the essays are as texts. Despite their espousal of "new new" critical theory, few of them transcend the discursive conventions of earlier criticisms. Given the collapse of genre theory, assumed at least by semiotic and Marxist criticism, distinctions between criticism and fiction, poetry and drama can no longer hold. Not only is each work of criticism in part "fictive" and in part "poetic," it is obliged to compete with poetry, fiction, drama and biography as writing. Its claim to be read can no longer be based on its referentiality to other work; it must be based on its materiality, on the power of its intrinsic qualities as text. In their sequential arguments and dependence on the texts, the majority of these essays—like most book reviews, including this one—are old criticism.

Robert puts the newspaper down. After another few minutes, Charles returns.)

CHARLES
It's getting very warm and stuffy in here. Would anyone mind if I opened the window? The windows are drenched with condensation.

(Rachel and Robert make agreeable gestures.)

CHARLES
Now that's interesting. Look at that window.

(The window on the other side of the compartment is covered with condensation. There are, however, small patches of glass that remain relatively dry.).

ROBERT

(*summoning up some interest*) Hm, it seems to spell "SON." At least, if you look at it with a sympathetic eye.

CHARLES

I suppose it does. I wonder why someone would have written that there.

(Rachel looks up from her book and snatches a quick glance at the window.)

RACHEL

Well, maybe you're a bit quick to jump to conclusions? There are lots of ways to look at things other than in our own self-image.

ROBERT

(*indignantly*) What do you mean?

CHARLES

(*defensively*) Yes, the word is there for all to see.

RACHEL

There's no there there until you put there there.

ROBERT

Very cute.

RACHEL

It might not be an English word. It could be French or Swedish or Welsh. It might not be a word at all. After all, it's just a set of traces that we recognize as an alphabetical notation.

CHARLES

Maybe you have a point there. It might be some special code used by a secret sect. Decoding is encoding, and all that. Chinese and Arabic are nothing more than scribble to me. I wouldn't be able to tell a Chinese proverb from modern art. (*Charles laughs.*) I remember *Jabberwocky:*

> 'Twas brillig, and the slithy toves
> Did gyre and gimble in the wabe:
> All mimsy were the borogoves,
> And the mome raths outgrabe.

ROBERT

Well, even so, we can settle any dispute by reference to its origin. Surely, the real meaning of any sign is determined by the sign-maker?

RACHEL

I'm not so sure. In your cherished world of classical music, the best interpretation is not necessarily the one intended by the composer.

CHARLES

Some self-styled purists hanker after some mystical recreation of the composer's mental performance. But most musical buffs seem happy to agree to disagree on the best interpretation of a work.

RACHEL

Some relish the idiosyncratic arrangement, let alone interpretation.

CHARLES

Yes, what about Glenn Gould's rendition of the *Goldberg Variations* by Bach?

ROBERT

(*a little fazed*) Well, that's as may be, but he still plays the same notes. But language is quite different. Its quality is more fixed.

CHARLES

Oh, I don't know. I've seen renditions of Shakespeare's *Richard III* which bear only a passing resemblance to each other even though the words are the same. Delivery and nuance are crucial.

RACHEL

What you see as the word on the window might not be written by a human hand. The markings might be coincidental.

ROBERT

(*sarcastically*) A subtle combination of meteorological elements and technological artifacts leaving residual traces of dryness on a pool of moisture which miraculously arrange themselves to sketch the word "SON," no doubt?

RACHEL

I suppose you could say the invisible, but literate and English hand of nature.

CHARLES

(*preceded by a nervous laugh*) It might have been done by a baby or some insect wending its haphazard way across the window. Who knows? I've often scribbled cryptic notes for myself and, then, when I go back to read them, I can't remember what I meant.

ROBERT

Sure, but isn't all of this a little farfetched? In a rare instance, those fanciful explanations may be true. But in a run-of-the-mill situation, it's obvious from the context what those "markings," as you put it, mean. When you see a sign at the foot of an escalator saying Dogs Must Be Carried, you don't run off and look for a dog to carry.

CHARLES

And if you choose to sit in a smoking compartment on a train, you don't have to spend the whole journey puffing on a cigarette.

(*They all laugh.*)

RACHEL

Perhaps. But doesn't your comment make the point? Doesn't the exception prove the rule? It's our understandings and expectations that give a situation meaning. One might attribute all kinds of mystical significance to those particular words in that particular setting. Freud said something like "In the beginning, words and magic were one and the same thing."

CHARLES

If he did, it's probably one of the few magic things that the psychobabbler did say.

ROBERT

Let me ask you then; is there anyone or anything that does warrant your approval?

RACHEL

Well . . .

CHARLES

(*interjecting*) Look. Since we opened the window, the condensation has cleared. The "word" (*Charles makes the customary gesticulations*) has disappeared. Our discussion seems to have become purely academic. Of course, not that being academic is completely useless.

RACHEL

(*laughingly*) Perhaps not entirely useless. Ornaments, not props of society. Anyway, the clear window may still hold a message for us. An empty space can be full of meaning.

CHARLES

Yes. I know that I could feel the lack of a tooth when I had it extracted.

RACHEL

See. It all depends on your expectations. Or, at least, the society's expectations. To a computer, a blank signal is an important feature of its instructional language.

CHARLES

A blank sheet of paper can speak volumes, especially if you put a picture frame around it and place it in an art gallery.

(*Charles gives another hearty laugh.*)

ROBERT

But that's as ridiculous as your Madonna stuff. Even if some trendy people wish to group Madonna with Vivaldi or an empty sheet of paper with a Van Gogh landscape, there is no reason for the rest of us to accept such ephemeral standards. It's simply bad art. Next you'll be telling me that John Cage's *4'33"* is a musical composition of the highest quality. In that magnificient opus, there were precisely four minutes and thirty-three seconds of pure silence. Cage was generous enough to suggest that our minds and our environment would provide the music.

CHARLES

That's a good one. But I'm not so sure that there isn't something to the idea that silence can be meaningful. In one of Arthur Conan Doyle's tales, Inspector Gregory asks Sherlock Holmes whether there is anything Holmes wishes to mention. Holmes refers to the curious incident of the dog in the night. "But the dog did nothing," a surprised Inspector Gregory replies. With characteristic understatement, Holmes delivers the punch line, "That was the curious incident."

(*This exchange of views is followed by a considerable, and perhaps fitting, period of silence. Rachel returns to her tome; Robert falls asleep; and Charles removes a book from his case, opens it at the bookmark, and begins to read it. The book is John Fowles'* Mantissa.)

. . . tapping one extended forefinger with the other.

"Serious modern fiction has only one subject; the difficulty of writing serious modern fiction. First, it has fully accepted that it is only fiction, can only be fiction, will never be anything but fiction, and therefore has no business at all tampering with real life or reality. Right?"

He waits. She nods meekly.

"Second. The natural consequence of this is that writing *about* fiction has become a far more important matter than writing fiction itself. It's one of the best ways you can tell the true novelist nowadays. He's not going to waste his time over the messy garage-mechanic drudge of assembling stories and characters on paper."

She looks up. "But—"

"Yes, all right. Obviously he has at some point to write something, just to show how irrelevant and unnecessary the actual writing part of it is. But that's all." He starts tying his tie. "I'm putting this in the simplest terms for you. Are you with me so far?"

She nods. He ties his tie.

"Third, and most important. At the creative level there is in any case no connection whatever between author and text. They are two entirely separate things. Nothing, but nothing, is to be inferred or deduced from one to another, and in either direction. The deconstructivists have proved that beyond a shadow of doubt. The author's role is purely fortuitous and agential. He has no more significant a status than the bookshop assistant or the librarian who hands the text *qua* object to the reader."

"Why do writers still put their names on the title page, Miles?" She looks timidly up. "I'm only asking."

"Because most of them are like you. Quite incredibly behind the times. And hair-raisingly vain. Most of them are still under the positively medieval illusion that they write their own books."

"I honestly didn't realize."

"If you want story, character, suspense, description, all that antiquated nonsense from pre-modernist times, then go to the cinema. Or read comics. You do not come to a serious modern writer. Like me."

"No, Miles."

He realizes something has gone wrong with the knot of his tie; and rather irritatedly pulls it apart, then starts the tying again.

"Our one priority now is mode of discourse, function of discourse, status of discourse. Its metaphoricality, its disconnectedness, its total ateleological self-containedness."

"Yes, Miles."

"I know you thought you were half teasing just now, but I consider it symptomatic of your ridiculously . . .

Charles puts his book down and gazes into the middle distance for a couple of minutes.)

CHARLES

You know, one thing my experience in law school taught me is that there is always a happy medium, if you'll excuse the pun. (*Charles laughs.*) We used to say that you only get run over in the middle of the road. I think that words have a central core of meaning, even if they are a little fuzzy around the edges. Whatever else it might mean, the word "SON" applies to someone's male child. Sure, there'll be an ongoing disagreement over whether it includes illegitimate, adopted, stepchildren or the like, but these are peripheral questions.

ROBERT

(*sleepily*) What about a daughter who has a sex change? Is he or she then a son, daughter, both or neither?

CHARLES

Good point. I suppose it depends on why a decision is needed. And, of course, on changing social mores.

RACHEL

You don't give up easily on the idea that there must be some kernel of objective truth, do you? Anyway, in legalese, I'm sure it's possible for "SON" to include women as well, isn't it?

CHARLES

Well, actually, it does. If I remember correctly, the Interpretation Act stipulates that "male" includes "female," unless there's some contrary intention.

RACHEL

Women become equal only by being treated as men. The whole of our language forces us into a male way of thinking.

CHARLES

It's a man-made language!

RACHEL

I know it's a cliché, but we are such prisoners of our language. Our horizons are so limited. We're so myopic. So resigned. We go through life in dark glasses.

ROBERT

Spare us the angst. I know who you do approve of. You're a Humpty Dumpty academic—"words are what you want them to mean." Or, at least, you'd like words to be what you choose them to mean. Nursery rhymes are not your style, though. James Joyce is more your cup of tea: "And wordloosed over seven seas crowdblast in cellelleneteuto slavezendlatinsoundscript." Such pretension. Stream of consciousness. Tell me about it!

CHARLES

What you say sounds refined and sophisticated, but isn't it all hot air? Give me some specifics.

RACHEL

Take that so-called word "SON." Try to imagine a world where the division between men and women is abandoned. There, giving birth will not be women's work.

CHARLES

I suppose we already have the technological means to revolutionize the whole way we conceive children. More's the pity.

RACHEL

And think about raising children. Imagine parenting as a general social responsibility. The word "SON" might become meaningless or, at least its usage would have to be radically transformed. Your kernel of truth would disintegrate.

ROBERT
Now, that is scary. You'll have us all spouting Orwell's "Newspeak" soon. Ignorance is Strength, War is Peace. All that totalitarian gibberish.

RACHEL
But isn't our language—"Oldspeak"—just as distorted by our present values and beliefs? The whole notion of "children" is a fairly modern idea. Up until the past couple of hundred years, people were just adults or infants. The word and idea of children brought into play a whole set of duties and responsibilities that previously didn't exist. And . . .

CHARLES
Quite a speech. But I'm a man—sorry, person—of this world—here and now, not there and then. I have to dirty my hands, as it were, and operate in the hurly-burly of people's affairs. Isn't your cynicism a luxury? To me, it sounds like a counsel of despair. We need standards. Without some certainty, we'd have anarchy and tyranny. Words, at least, offer us some solid foundation in a shifting world. A port in the storm.

(*Before Rachel can answer, several youths enter the compartment and sit across from Rachel, Robert and Charles. They have a large radio with them, playing at full blast. The music fills the compartment and their senses.*)

The youths leave the compartment and the music fades away. The conversation seems to have come to an end. Rachel goes back to reading her weighty tome.).

. . . are all tellers of tales. Our lives are a struggle to imagine and enact the best stories we can. These stories run from the sublime to the ridiculous, the ecstatic to the elegaic, the hopeful to the fearful and the marvellous to the mundane. Only in our fantasies are we anywhere near free to indulge our dramatic imaginings to their fullest: even then we are not entirely free for we must dream within the historical experience of our life stories. In life, we are thrust into a work-in-progress. It is a sprawling performance with countless acts and a profusion of scenes, often being performed simultaneously and repeatedly. Reality becomes congruent with these enactments of the habitual stories and stock tales of the community.[21] To the extent that we are able to write and enact our own lives, we must begin with and respond to the dramatic plot in which we find ourselves. The story of my life can never be disentangled from the community's story in which my story develops and gains significance. While we can never be free of the past or of our communal connections, we need not become slavish adherents to their perceived weight and hold. The future of the past is our present and continuing responsibility. The past has passed and was what it was, but it is up to us to decide what it will become. In accepting the past of pastness, we must also recognize its presence.[22]

For many, life will be exhausted in playing out the stories of others, cameo roles on a stage and in a script not of their making. At best, these enlisted thespians will have to live their stories before they can tell them. As an old African proverb has it, "until the lions have their historians, tales of hunting will always glorify the hunter". It is in this sense that people make their own history, but not under conditions of their own making.[23] We cannot abandon history nor dispossess ourselves of its dramatic heirlooms. We cannot create afresh our autobiographies. At best, we must play our given roles until we have the capacity and confidence to re-create ourselves and re-make our world. The narrative used or constructed to relate our lives is integral to our experience and self-understanding of that life. As our lives unfold, we revise the story of our own past. In moving forward, what we look back at often changes shape and emphasis. My youth, and my experience of it, is not the same as it was then and will not remain the same as I grow older.

Facts, theories and interpretations are twisted into a thread of historical narrative that can never be fully disentangled. History and life can only be re-told; they can never be exhibited in their pristine untoldness. There is nothing beyond history and narrative, but more history and narrative. It is not that everything is without meaning, but that everything already has meaning *for us*. Moreover, as the language of narrative reconstruction is a collective property, this crucial act of history-making is a social phenomenon. It is the force of present concerns—the contemporary sense of relevance and regimen—that energizes and orders the past because the past is as chaotic and jumbled as the present. As we

---

21 *See* A. MACINTYRE, AFTER VIRTUE 204–225 (2d ed. 1984).

22 Eliot, *Tradition and the Individual Talent* in SELECTED ESSAYS, 1917–1922 (1932).

23 Marx, *The Eighteenth Brumaire of Louis Bonaparte* in MARX AND ENGLES: BASIC WRITINGS ON POLITICS AND PHILOSOPHY 320 (L. Feuer ed. 1959).

shape the past, it re-shapes us and our efforts to understand that past; "history is the wake of a mobile mind falling in and out of love with the things it detaches by its attachment."[24] Historical discourse signifies rather than follows "reality". History-as-narrative is a specialized genre:

> The great intellectual advantage of telling stories is that it does not rationalize the irrationality of actual experience and of history. . . . All our conflicts are preserved in all their inconclusiveness. . . . It is often said that literature is not life; but though that seems obvious, it does not really matter much. . . . Although the rules of evidence clearly mark a history off from a novel, the difference is one of degree, and its biographical elements are often psychologically less plausible than the work of a great novelist.[25]

We are never not in a story. History and human action only take on meaning and intelligibility within their narrative context and dramatic settings. There are many stories being imagined and enacted, but we can only listen to them and comprehend them within the vernacular contexts of other stories. Our conversations about these narratives are themselves located and scripted in deeper stories which determine their moral force and epistemological validity. There is no truth nor knowledge outside the dramatic context and idiom of history. All conversations occur within history. Human knowledge is a *human* enterprise. From the available narrative resources, we are able to shape and shade the possibilities and parameters of our own identities. Also, the anthology of communal folktales tells us how we expect, predict or assume others will act. Stories are so powerful and pervasive that they not only lay out a path for us to follow, but also provide the familiar crop of dramatic devices and rhetorical strategies for comprehending and altering the story. It is these dramatic practices and narrative procedures that allow us to perceive, understand, act, criticize and change in a mutually intelligible manner.

By simultaneously empowering certain modes of action and foreclosing others, narrative holds us in a grip that is as powerful as force of arms. Through the interweaving plots and intricate sub-plots of the different narratives, people inhabit different worlds; their understandings of the world and their normative response to it are substantially at odds. One of the most colourful illustrations of "different-worldliness" is offered by Jorge Luis Borge.[26] He quotes from a Chinese encyclopedia, entitled *Celestial Emporium of Benevolent Knowledge*, which divides ani-

---

24 Hartman, *History Writing as Answerable Style* in NEW DIRECTIONS IN LITERARY HISTORY 100 (R. Cohen ed. 1974).
25 J. SHKLAR, ORDINARY VICES 230 (1984).
26 Borges, *The Analytical Language of John Wilkins* in BORGES: A READER (1981).

mals into (a) those that belong to the Emperor, (b) embalmed ones, (c) those that are trained, (d) suckling pigs, (e) mermaids, (f) fabulous ones, (g) stray dogs, (h) those that are included in this classification, (i) frenzied, (j) innumerable ones, (k) those drawn with a very fine camel's hair brush, (l) others, (m) those that have just broken a flower vase, (n) those that resemble flies from a distance. As Michel Foucault observes, "the wonderment of this taxonomy" is not only "the exotic charm of another system of thought," but "the limitation of our own, the stark impossibility of thinking *that*."[27]

"The law" is a potent and institutional story. It is one of the privileged ways society defines itself and presents the world to itself.[28] The life of the law is not logic nor experience, but a narrative way of world-making. The styling, staging and phrasing of the law structure the world in particular and partial ways. Being normative in nature, law is a way of social imagining and has a distinct theory of its own relations to a larger nomos. Like all tales, legal stories gain meaning and significance from the selective emphasis of certain features of our always complex and frequently ambiguous experience. As a narrative, legal stories favour some aspects of our experience at the expense of others, thereby empowering some individuals and disenfranchising others. Most importantly, it is the stories themselves that come to comprise the reality of our experience. In this sense, legal stories mediate our engagement in the world and with others: they provide the possibilities and parameters for our own self-definition and understanding.

As a partially intelligible description of and mutual prescription for action, legal stories predispose their writers, actors and audience to certain interpretive choices and social stances. Courts make many telling contributions to social life. Indeed, their major function as a state-sanctioned agency for dispute resolution is to render an ending to the stalled tales of conflicting persons. Located and sustained by historical conditions and circumstances, the dramatic performance of the law is socially imposed and, what is often overlooked, psychologically assumed by individual actors and members of the audience. It is often forgotten that law is a story and, like all stories, can be rescripted. The struggle to control meaning and, therefore, the conditions for communal life is fought anew each day. Existing legal plots and scenarios are only compel-

---

27 M. FOUCAULT, THE ORDER OF THINGS xv (1970).
28 For similar approaches, see Cover, *The Supreme Court, 1982 Term—Foreword: Nomos and Narrative*, 97 HARV. L. REV. 4 (1983); Dalton, *An Essay in the Deconstruction of Contract Doctrine*, 94 YALE L.J. 997 (1985); Lopez, *Lay Lawyering*, 32 UCLA L. REV. 1 (1984).

ling insofar as they are constantly reinforced through daily use and re-hearsal. The Rule of Law is a cherished and resilient icon.

Legal language shapes those social encounters that fall within its reach. As disputes move into the magnetic field of law, they are 'trans-lated' into the received argot. In this way, legal discourse enforces the canons of relevance and rationality that it generates for its self-serving purposes. This encoding process changes and thereby screens out many disputes.[29] To partake of law's special privileges and prizes, speakers must become proficient in its idioms and nuances; those who do not are dep-rived of a voice and are therefore rendered powerless. In this way, the powerful manage to survive by assuming a discourse of justice. To under-stand law-power and its pervasiveness, it is necessary to engage in an analysis of its discursive operations as much as to study the decisional outcomes of that discourse. Its success is premised on its prowess at in-filtrating and traumatizing other discursive domains. Political debate is dominated by the legal ideolect and, in providing its vocabulary and mind-set, law pervades politics in a much more profound way than is commonly understood.

As a privileged mode of world-making, legal discourse constructs and presents a story that is not about the world, but *of* the world. Even the most prosaic of judicial statements hide and rely upon a host of metaphysical assumptions and ideological commitments. For example, a recent torts opinion offered a fairly uncontroversial summary of the law:

> A man on the beach is not legally bound to plunge into the sea when he can foresee that a swimmer might drown. In *Jaensch* v. *Coffey* (1984), 54 A.L.R. 417, Deane J. observed (at 439) that "the common law has neither recognised fault in the conduct of the feasting Dives nor embraced the embarrassing moral percep-tion that he who has failed to feed the man dying of hunger has truly killed him."[30]

For most lawyers, this is an accessible and unremarkable statement. Yet, the layperson will have trouble making even superficial sense of it: its classical allusions and coded references mystify as well as illuminate. Sup-posing that the reader got beyond/behind these stylistic quirks, the whole text is resonant with underlying values and images. Some of the

---

29 *See* Galanter, *Reading the Landscape of Disputes: What We Know and Don't Know (And Think We Know) About Our Allegedly Contentious and Litigious Society*, 31 UCLA L. REV. 4, 18–20 (1983).

30 *Sutherland Shire Council* v. *Heyman* (1985), 60 A.L.R. 1, 41 (H.C. Aust.), per Brennan J.

questions it silently provokes and answers include: Are there only dying men and male samaritans?; Are women only made visible by their invisibility?; Is this not only a man-inhabited world, but a man-made one?; Do individuals/men stand alone?; Are they "naturally" self-regarding?; Are they social creatures or social creators or both?; Do they have responsibilities or feelings to others:? Is there an unfolding of life that occurs "naturally"?: Are omission and commission distinguishable?; Would other-regarding persons have any use for such a distinction?; Is hunger a fact of life?; Is feasting?; Who will be "embarrassed"?; The starving man?; and so on. The text suggests and actually gives particular answers to these queries. Further, in phrasing the statements in the way they are, the judicial speaker clearly imagines himself as a potential rescuer. He does not associate himself with the drowning or starving person: he is above the fray. How different might things be if judges occasionally saw themselves in the water or the gutter?

Another related and staple feature of modern legal language is rights-talk.[31] The law insists on characterizing social interaction as occasions for the exercise or breach of legal rights. When one individual charges another with "breaching" their "contract," their interactions have been forced into a particular linguistic and, therefore, ideological straitjacket. By speaking this form of legalese, they have adopted a very partial idiom and have abandoned other ways of describing their shared experience. For example, what lawyers term a contract may alternatively be experienced as an act of shared trust and commitment or as an honorable undertaking. They have given an objective existence to abstract rights-talk; they have treated it and experienced it as a thing to be grasped and wielded. Moreover, litigants bring into play a whole paraphernalia of expectations about their future dealings together. In effect, they create for themselves a distinct past and future scenario for their experience. Discourse works a practical and significant exercise of power.

A less obvious, but more unsettling version of power's insidious operation through legal discourse is the recent movement in the United States to establish a constitutionally entrenched set of welfare rights to housing, food and the like. This is a continuing episode that highlights the thin or nonexistent line between a genuine concern for others and a coercive interference with their lives. Though the courts have not gone so far as to acknowledge such substantive rights, they have imposed procedural standards for the administration of government-provided be-

---

31 *See* Hutchinson and Monahan, *The "Rights" Stuff: Roberto Unger and Beyond*, 62 TEX. L. REV. 1477, 1479–1491 (1984).

nefits.[32] Of course, this offers some much needed relief and protection for the have-nots. The long-term effects of such a trend, however, are less benign: the pastoral pose of the state has a dark and powerful side.[33] Although the "welfare state" relieves people of much of the anxiety and suffering born of the struggle to keep body and soul together, it engenders debilitating feelings of alienation and loss of self-respect in those it supports. As individuals come to rely directly on state charity for their basic sustenance, they become enmeshed even further in the thick web of dependence and power. Rights-talk will have extended its dominion— but in filling the stomach, we eviscerate the person.

This situation points up an important dilemma for and warning to those who want to bring about a radical change in social conditions. Rights-talk is the pervasive conversational idiom of modern society; it is the sophisticated voice of institutional resources. It is difficult not to participate in that conversation in any attempt to challenge existing arrangements and improve the lot of people. But to join that conversation poses a grave risk of being co-opted and becoming vulnerable to takeover. To speak in the voice of rights is to play the game in the establishment's home park, with its equipment, and in accordance with its rules. Moreover, as the ludic metaphor suggests, rights-based language is a male-created idiolect and is inimical to feminist ambitions.[34] Accordingly, traditional rights litigation must comprise a limited strategy in any radical practice of law. The challenge to power must be made on a wider, more popular front. . . .

(*Three people enter the compartment. Rachel is momentarily distracted.*)

FIRST PERSON
Is this Wembley?

SECOND PERSON
No, it's Thursday.

THIRD PERSON:
So am I. Let's go get a drink.

(*The three people leave the compartment. Rachel goes back to her reading.*).

---

32 *See Re Singh* (1985), 17 D.L.R. (4th) 422 (S.C.C.), and *Goldberg* v. *Kelly*, 397 U.S. 254 (1970).

33 Foucault, *On Governmentality*, 6 IDEOLOGY AND CONSCIOUSNESS 5 (1979).

34 C. GILLIGAN, IN A DIFFERENT VOICE 128–150 (1982).

. . . If law is a story, writing about law is a meta-story or a story about a story. Operating at different levels and from different perspectives, academics tell stories about the legal story, the way it develops and changes, the roles and responsibilities of the dramatis pesonae, and the like. Themselves located in history, they perceive their primary task to be both exegetical and editorial. As exegetes, they clarify and explain the obscurities and mysteries of the law story, especially as told by its judicial authors. Different schools of interpretation have formed and there is heated debate over their validity and value. The performance of this exegetical function inevitably collapses into a more creative editorial exercise. Academics reorganize, rework and recreate judicial and legislative texts. In so doing, they often embellish, enrich, ennoble or enfeeble the primary texts. This is not an occasion for surprise or censure for "decoding is always another form for encoding"—*traduttore, traditore*.[57] Occasionally, academic translators attain such prominence that the judicial or legislative story-tellers officially re-script the legal drama and incorporate their telling insights. However, as one of the foremost interpreters of law, academics possess and exercise considerable power. At the considerable risk of overestimating academic influence, there is some truth to the fact that "madmen in authority, who hear voices in the air, are distilling their frenzy from some academic scribbler a few years back."[58] In short, their stories are not *about* the world, but *of* the world.

One form of legal discourse that has become prominent in recent years is "law and economics". Its supporters have sought to replace "mushy" humanistic theorizing with the 'hard' analytical framework of economics. Surfacing when objectivity was seemingly slipping from the desperate grasp of judicial theorists,[59] law and economics was a timely and welcome voice. Claiming to be scientific, law and economics profits from the prestige of *science*, which arises from its idolatrous image as the dispassionate search for timeless truths through objectively valid methods of inquiry; "when *science* speaks—or rather when its spokesmen (and they generally are men) speak in the name of science—let no dog bark."[60] Yet *science*, like any story, has social determinants and functions.

---

57 *See* Calabresi, *Thoughts on the Future of Economics in Legal Education*, 33 J. LEG. ED. 359, 364 ("To translate from one language to another is to betray. That is the translation, and the betrayal, of an Italian saying: *Traduttore, traditore*").

58 J.M. KEYNES, THE GENERAL THEORY OF EMPLOYMENT INTEREST AND MONEY 383–384 (1936).

59 *See* Hutchinson and Monahan, *Law, Politics, and the Critical Legal Scholars: The Unfolding Drama of American Legal Thought*, 36 STAN. L. REV. 199, 213–219 (1984).

60 R. LEWONTIN, S. ROSE AND L. KAMIN, NOT IN OUR GENES: BIOLOGY, IDEOLOGY AND HUMAN NATURE 31 (1984).

The Olympian image of scientists as standing astride of nature and grappling with it so as to pin down its secret truths disguises the extent to which scientists are part of and contributors to that nature. In short, the "science story" has no particular epistemological clout, except insofar as we give it any.

The law and economics story is a form of worldmaking that has achieved a high and undeserved political status in the world of legal theory. It has become an officially sanctioned conversation stopper. As such, it is not so much wrong as simplistic. Law and economics emphasizes certain aspects of our present social situation—in particular, bargaining over scarce resources in a market-based economy—and forces the rest of our rich and chaotic experience into this model's limited narrative framework. It either reduces, and therefore redefines, values like love, charity and solidarity to a monetary credit or simply ignores them. Although its guru, Richard Posner, concedes that law and economics is unrealistic, this is not considered to be fatal. It is claimed to be an unavoidable consequence of a scientific approach that there must be an abstraction from the welter of experience if a theory is to have predictive force. Indeed, Posner asserts that, not only is economics a science of rational behaviour that can be set over against ethics or ideology, but that his theory's simplicity is a sign of its strength; the less nuanced a theory, the more hypotheses it is likely to yield.[61]

The imperial practitioners of the law and economics model claim to render irrelevant or marginal all other legal tales. Its ambition and appeal lie in its inflated promise to deliver right answers, but this promise merely confers a spurious legitimacy on a very ideological tale.[62] For the law and economics fabulist, life is a market, and all human relations consist of commodity exchanges. The law and economics world is populated by rational, risk-neutral, perfectly informed egoists who voluntarily maximize their stable preferences under conditions of relative scarcity. Such heroic figures inhabit only the pages of the *Journal of Legal Studies*. Even its more modest incarnation, this "economic creature" represents a narrow facet of our complex selves and social lives. We are either and only producers or consumers: social worth becomes exclusively synonomous with exchange value.

Even if the market could achieve an equilibrium of supply and demand, the resulting allocation of resources would still have to be defended as socially just on independent ideological or ethical grounds.

---

61 *See* Posner, *Some Uses and Abuses of Economics in Law,* 46 U. CHI. L. REV. 281, 281–287 (1979) and, generally, ECONOMIC ANALYSIS OF LAW (3d ed. 1986).

62 *See* Mcgonigle, *The Tribune and The Tribe: Toward a Natural Law of The Market/Legal State,* 13 ECOLOGY L.Q. 233, 278–283 (1986).

What about the effect of the existing distribution of resources and entitlements on the particular allocation of decision? What about information being allocated through the market? What about "wealth effects" (i.e., persons tend to value a good more if they already own it than if they want to own it)? For instance, some Hicks–Kaldor disciples want to equate *actual* compensation for those who lose from a Pareto optimal move with *hypothetical* compensation under a different test for efficiency; the decision whether to pay actual compensation is considered a "political" question which is independent of efficiency considerations.[63] Moreover, the "law and economics" tale ignores completely the extent to which we become the characters of our stories and to which our society shifts to reflect the new dramatic plot. For instance, scarcity is, at least in part, as much a function of the market as its pre-condition. Also, our preferences do not stand outside the market ideology, but are constructed and installed by it. That is, legal rules, premised on a world of profit maximizers, force people to act as the model predicts they would. We become the productive/consumptive actors of the market script, choreographed to the cold music of the cash register.

Appropriately, however, the moral bankruptcy of law and economics can be brought home in a short story. A couple of years ago, I attended a seminar which was devoted to an overview of economic jurisprudence. The paper began with a hypothetical. Imagine that a car driver rounds a sharp curve and finds that it is impossible to avoid hitting and most likely killing one of the two obstacles on the road—one is a newborn Haitian baby girl and the other is Lassie (the real thing!). Notice the dog has a human persona and the child is "barely human". In his opening remarks, the author stated that "if this problem seems at first blush an 'easy' one, it is not so at all".[64] Although the paper concluded by making the "right" choice, its very positing of such a hypothetical as raising an ethical dilemma says much about law and economics. Like any world-making narrative, it not only provides answers, but dictates the problems to be answered and the mind-set that is to be brought to bear. It does not simply view and react to the world in partial ways, but it begins to constitute and present the world in its own image. Consequently, notwithstanding its technical indeterminacies and shortcomings, the power of law and economics lies in its success at becoming part of the world. By re-interpreting the world, it changes more than our ways of relating to the world; it is a way of being in the world. Any

---

63 *See* D. MCCLOSKEY, THE RHETORIC OF ECONOMICS 43 (1985).
64 Krauss, *Good as Gold?: An Overview of Economic Jurisprudence* 1, October 1983, University of Toronto Law and Economics Workshop Series (WSVI–4).

successful attempt to oust law and economics from its contemporary primacy must understand and dislodge it as a way of world-making by re-making another world.

As the legal economists so readily and sadly reveal, lawyers fall prey to the hegemonic impulse to treat their stories as either the only story or, at least, the story of stories. The legal raconteurs claim for their tales an authority and objectivity that overwhelms and trivializes other stories. More than most languages, law has managed to suppress the contingent character of social history. By institutionalizing an entrenched set of social values, legal discourse has succeeded, at least partially, to contain the dynamism of history-making and, in the process, has persuaded people of the "naturalness" and "necessity" of current social arrangements. However, while the intellectual categories and rhetorical tropes of legal discourse do provide a superficially coherent image of the world, it is so fragile and shallow that it can offer no real repose. It merely papers over the endemic cracks and contradictions of contemporary life. Consequently, its authority and appeal as a privileged and heeded voice of society is illusory. The discursive categories of the law are neither determinate nor dispositive. Although they do not sanction and produce a detailed set of social prescriptions and consequences, they do stake out the venue, weapons and strategies for political struggle. As such, law is a formidable obstacle to any real social change; for the way we think about ourselves and the limits of our situation is an integral component of any engaged attempt to change the world.

For there to be any effective challenge to the status quo, there has to be a concerted effort to tackle the paralyzing operation of legal discourse. As the reach of law and lawyers extends, the variety and richness of discursive resources at society's disposal are diminished. Being controlled by so-called experts, legal stories impoverish the opportunities for people to experience first-mouth the demands and responsibilities of narrative reconstruction. Those committed to change must stem the tide of law-talk by multiplying and enriching the occasions for people to exercise the prerogatives of democratic citizenship. While it will not be enough simply to outtalk the privileged voices of law, it will help to open up the constituting conversations of social life and personal development. As a partial and liberating antidote, a hermeneutical account of the "law" and "jurisprudential stories" might help to exhibit the relations of power that sustain, dictate and benefit from their historical recounting and privileging. Through examining contemporary legal practice and jurisprudential debate, the ambition will be to demonstrate the need to debunk the elite fables of the law and to democratize the crucial responsibility of storytelling and re-telling, worldmaking and re-making.

Although we cannot move to a narrative ground above or beyond history and politics, we can salvage or create a space within which individuals can contribute to the constantly changing process of history-making. "Law stories" and other stories have ill-defined edges. Although they often overlap, there are pockets and folds in which the storyline is faint, garbled or ambiguous. Traditional theorizing tries vainly to grout these irrepressible cracks and contradictions. In contrast, the social critic must seek out and inhabit these wrinkles between history's and language's past and their future unfolding. This is essential for the success of any radical restructuring of social and intellectual life.

All stories, and especially legal tales, constitute a language of power. Within the contingent space between their customary accent and its evolving dialect, people might be better able to engage their history dialectically and to actualize their imaginative potential. Of course, by their contingent nature, these sites of narrative pockets and opportunities for storytelling will be constantly shifting. But, emboldened, we must cultivate a brogue that can give expression to the inarticulate speech of the heart. Already heard, but stifled and emarginated, the language of civic virtue and the story of democratic egalitarianism must be nurtured. An idiom of popular power could be developed, along with an accessible thesaurus of public empowerment to replace the elite lexicon of law. Yet, to achieve this state of affairs, we must not only enhance and extend the constitutional conversation, we must also quieten certain voices. For instance, lawyers will have to adopt a more humble tone and speak sotto voce, if at all. Also,. . . .

(Rachel puts down her tome. The train has pulled into a station. She notices a man writing on the outside of the window. She catches the attention of Robert and Charles. With some effort, they are able to read it.).

Many read but few see the writing on the wall.

2

About Formalism

(including some notes on what Deconstruction
might and might not be about)

*"The convoluted wording of legalisms grew up around the necessity to hide from
ourselves the violence we intend toward each other."*—FRANK HERBERT[1]

A year or so ago, a swimming meet took place at the University of
Toronto. Most of the races proceeded as planned. But, at the end of one
race, there was a challenge to the winner of the race. The appropriate
group of officials convened. The deliberations were lengthy and tense.
After much argument and poring over the rules, a decision was announced: the winner had been disqualified and the second swimmer was
acclaimed the victor. The referee took the unusual course of offering a
brief justification of the committee's decision—"the rules were clear
('The winner is the first swimmer to touch the side of the pool with both
hands') and, if this regrettable outcome is to be avoided in the future, it
will be necessary to change the rules". The winning swimmer had only
one arm.

This episode offers many insights. An interesting and revealing observation, but one that I will not pursue here, is the hold that rule-formalism has on the public imagination: it is not only a feature of the legal
mentality.[2] When thrust into the role of decision-maker, an assumed re-

---

1 F. HERBERT, DUNE MESSIAH 183 (1969).
2 See J. SHKLAR, LEGALISM (2d ed. 1986).

sponsibility is to take the rules very seriously. They are felt to place a very real constraint on the type and range of permissible decisions that can be made. While each of the officials most likely wanted to circumvent the rule and reach a "fairer" result, they seemed to believe that the moral force of following the rules laid down took precedence over their own moral intuitions, no matter how strongly held or shared. The rules existed and operated as a palpable check on their official power. To ignore the rules would be to indulge in "palm-tree justice" with all its attendant dangers; the long-term benefits of rule-following outweighed any temporary costs. While obviously disappointed, the winner would understand the predicament and solution of the committee.

While I will not explore the extent or force of this rule-formalism in quasi-legal or extra-legal settings, I do intend to explore its operation in the legal community. The immediate response from lawyers will be that, although there may be a few Neanderthals still around who subscribe to such a slot-machine version of rule-formalism, such an unsophisticated and mechanical version of decision-making cannot be foisted on today's lawyers—"we are all realists now" is the chorused response.[3] They argue that, while rules are dominant and deserving of close respect, they are necessarily open-textured. In "hard cases", when the facts fall within their penumbral margins, the rules will give unclear guidance. It will be necessary to consult the more general maxims and broad principles that stand behind the rules. In combination, these norms provide a more coherent scheme for resolving disputes in a flexible and just fashion. For these lawyers, rules are bare bricks that have to be laid in accordance with the architectural plans of the whole legal order.

When the swimming rules were made, the possibility of a one-armed swimmer was clearly not in the rule-makers' contemplation. One solution is to assume that, if they were confronted with such a situation, the rule-makers would agree that there was an implicit qualification or exception to the rule. Another solution is to ignore these counter-factual speculations and to read the rule against the existing body of equitable principles that inhere within the legal order. The moral structure of the common law demands that "each person can only do the best they can and no more; they cannot be expected to do the impossible". In light of this maxim, the rule is illuminated to read that "the winner is the first swimmer to touch the side of the pool *with as many hands as they have*". Such an interpretation and application of rules not only makes sense and does justice in the particular circumstances, but is consistent with the

---

3 *See* W. TWINING, KARL LLEWELLYN AND THE REALIST MOVEMENT 382 (1973).

officials' general responsibility to resolve the dispute in accordance with the laws of swimming and not their own personal code of morality.

Yet, for all this so-called sophistication and sensitivity, modern lawyers remain enthusiastic practitioners of a pervasive formalism: enthusiastic in that their power and prestige is dependent for legitimacy upon it and pervasive in that their professional lives are thoroughly dominated by its demands. However, their's is not a crude rule-formalism; that represents only a sub-species of a grander genus.[4] While they draw upon the full range of doctrinal materials, modern lawyers rest their claims to authority on the two major components of formalism: that there is a defensible and workable distinction between legal reasoning and open ideological debate and that such legal reasoning itself represent a defensible and workable scheme of social justice. In this sense, although appearing to be at odds, the reasoning of the swimming officials and the critical response of modern lawyers are fundamentally the same; the latter is simply operating at a higher and more abstract level of formalism than the former.

First, both recognize and consider realizeable the responsibility of the decision-maker to eschew personal preference and to be guided by the dispositive force of the law: each defers to and feels bound by the appropriate legal norm. In a liberal democracy, the compulsion to reason within a closed system of premises is thought to guarantee the enduring integrity of the law and to insulate lawyers from ideological controversy. In both instances, it is "the law" that resolves the dispute and not "the lawyer".

Secondly, both defend any decision by reference to an implicit vision of social justice. The swimming officials look to a standard of formal justice or legality: society will work best when people can rely on an established and uniformly applied set of general norms that act as a skeleton for each person to flesh out with their own substantive muscle. To avoid arbitrary government, it is especially important that officials entrusted with decision-making power strictly adhere to the declared rules until they are publicly changed. On the other hand, modern lawyers adopt a more substantive vision of social justice. As well as being sceptical about the actual possibility of performing a thoroughly formal and value-free application of rules, they maintain that such an ideal compromises the decision-maker's responsibility rather than fulfils it. Justice can be frustrated by the blind application of individual rules; each person is entitled to a decision in line with the overall scheme of justice that the

---

4 *See* R. UNGER, THE CRITICAL LEGAL STUDIES MOVEMENT 5–42 (1986).

total body of rules embodies. In this way, legal reasoning and decision-making is claimed to satisfy the political need for decisional objectivity and the popular demand for social equity. Of course, the difference between these two approaches is not trivial and it does result in a considerably divergent set of decisions. Nonetheless, both share the same general theoretical justification for their account and the decisions it preserves. That justification is the worth and efficacy of formalism—an attitude and a technique of reasoning that is separate from political haggling, expresses a coherent and neutral blueprint for human relations and, as such, is deserving of institutional allegiance and obedience.

Throughout this book, I attack the plausibility of formalism and reject its legitimacy. My ambition is to prise legal thought from the *vice*-like grip of this unfortunate tendency and to suggest other ways of thinking about and performing the legal project. In different approaches and styles, the essays look at the detailed assumptions, practical operations and systemic consequences of formalism. The central thrust of my critique is to reveal its theoretical untenability and political partiality. Throughout, I will insist that the crime is not ideology, but the silence that hides it. The ambition is to combine philosophical critique with ideological commitment and to develop a style of jurisprudential praxis that transforms the present performance and possibilities of legal theory and practice.

In this essay, I will attempt to sketch out the deep premises and commitments of my own theoretical position. Although often implicit and frequently denied, everyone has to have some theoretical beliefs about the nature of human existence and social life. Without such rudimentary beliefs, daily existence would be profoundly meaningless and incomprehensible. The only difference between "a person without a philosophy and someone with a philosophy is that the latter knows what [his or her] philosophy is."[5] By emphasising this, my aim is not to make jurisprudence even more abstruse or arcane. My rationale for subjecting the reader to the rarified environment of metaphysical debate is concrete and practical. Immersion in epistemology and ontology is only justified if it can lead to an improved understanding of our present predicament. By exploring the theoretical basis of contemporary jurisprudential practice, it might be possible to redirect and redeploy the massive energy and resources invested in the legal project. Informed by a fresh theoretical self-appreciation, law and legal theory might develop a

---

5 F.S.C. NORTHROP, THE COMPLEXITY OF LEGAL AND ETHICAL EXPERIENCE 6 (1959).

greater relevance and a rigour in the struggle to achieve social justice. There is nothing so practical and so necessary as good theory. Without the ability to theorise a problem, we are destined to reinscribe its debilitating pattern within the fabric of any proposed solution. In theorising about practice, we practice theory. Theory can never free itself from practice nor practice escape theory. They are the flip sides of the philosophical coin.

★   ★   ★   ★   ★

As troubling a condition as formalism is, it is only a symptom of a much more profound malaise. The villain of the piece is the Rationalist tradition which has dominated our thinking (and our thinking about thinking) for so long.[6] We have never managed to shake off the effects of the Platonic contagion. Indeed, so accustomed have we become to its presence that we consider its metaphysical malady to be the natural and proper condition of human endeavour and thought. This is all the more debilitating because it is venerated as the universal solvent for social conflict and moral disharmony. As the embodiment of rational wisdom and thinking, law has not suprisingly come to occupy a sacred position in this culture and its thinking; the Rule of Law is venerated, even by many on the political left, as an "unqualified human good."[7]

Resuscitated in the 17th and 18th centuries by Descartes, Kant, Locke, and others, it is now more commonly and conveniently referred to as the Enlightenment Project. It is the attempt to escape our finitude and its thoroughly contingent contexts and to establish a body of principles that are unconditionally valid for all persons at all times. Philosophy saw and still sees the road to respectability and success in the faithful epidopterists, the challenge was, armed with a small number of rudimentary insights into human nature, to capture the precious and eternal butterflies of Truth and Justice as they flitted through history, to press them flat in the heavy tomes of philosophical learning and to exhibit them for people's temporary gratification and edification. In this way, although history is always on the move, we might better be able to distill

---

6 Apart from the other sources directly referred to, this chapter is heavily influenced by the work of R. RORTY, PHILOSOPHY AND THE MIRROR OF NATURE (1979), A. MACINTYRE, AFTER VIRTUE (2d ed. 1984). N. GOODMAN, WAYS OF WORLDMAKING (1978) and R. BERNSTEIN, BEYOND OBJECTIVISM AND RELATIVISM (1983).

7 E.P. THOMPSON, WHIGS AND HUNTERS: THE ORIGINS OF THE BLACK ACT 265 (1978).

its enduring essence and withstand its continuing vicissitudes.

To understand what would otherwise be another intellectual indulgence, it is necessary to appreciate the belief and ambition of such a tradition. It is founded on the notion that, in order to command any moral authority or intellectual allegiance, there must be a solid epistemological foundation on which to build moral theory. Without such a base, people cannot be expected to live in and be bound by its ethical maxims. In a world in which the voice of God no longer commanded the necessary attention or respect, some alternative ground or origin of authority had to be established for obedience to be expected or enforced. Without an objective grounding, knowledge and truth would become prey to a radical scepticism, behind which lurks the spectre of social chaos and tyranny. As Kant put it: ·

> [This domain of pure understanding] is an island, enclosed by nature itself within unalterable limits, It is the land of truth—enchanting name!—surrounded by a wide and stormy ocean, the native home of illusion, where many a fog bank and many a swiftly melting iceberg give the deceptive appearance of farther shores, deluding the adventurous seafarer ever anew with empty hopes, and engaging him in enterprises which he can never abandon and yet is unable to carry to contemplation.[8]

Separate from myth and religion, human reason must and can transcend vulgar political debate and ideological struggle. For the rationalist, the solution lies in letting Nature speak for itself. Although it might speak in an unrecognizable tongue, its utterances will be translated and popularized by the philosophical cyphers.

Despite its regular incantation that "the life of the law has not been logic, but experience",[9] modern legal scholarship remains firmly within the rationalist tradition. Abstract reflection is given priority over experiential engagement. Human reason remains the touchstone for valid knowledge about ourselves, our socio-historical situation and the legal order. Law is still packaged and promoted as a scientific study. Although the Kelsenian search for methodological purity is exceptional,[10] the rationalist dream retains a tenacious hold on the juristic imagination. More often implicit, Posner's work is devoted to discovering the knowable rationality of the observable world:

---

8 I. KANT, CRITIQUE OF PURE REASON 257 (N. Smith trans. 1929).

9 O.W. HOLMES, THE COMMON LAW 1 (1881).

10 See H. KELSEN, WHAT IS JUSTICE? 266–287 (1960).

> As biology is to the living organisms, astronomy to the stars, or economics to the price system, so should legal studies be to the legal system: an endeavour to make precise, objective and systematic observations of how the legal system operates in fact and to discover and explain the recurrent patterns in the observations—the "laws" of the system.[11]

Many thought that legal rationalism/formalism had been laid to rest by the realist critique of the 1920s and 1930s; Posner and others were engaged in a morbid form of intellectual necrophilia. However, realism was, at best, only an interlude in the long-running drama of legal formalism. At its height, realism toppled the regnant rule-formalism only to pave a better path to a full political realization of the formalist ideal. Ideologically and practically wedded to the reform programme of New Deal liberalism in the United States, the realists effected a pragmatic shift of institutional focus rather than a thoroughgoing rejection of formalism: they wanted to replace judge-dominated legal science with bureaucracy-wielded policy science. As such, realism's attacks were never intended to amount to more than a palace revolution. Smothering the truly radical insights and implications of the Realist critique, contemporary scholars have served up a thin gruel of neo-formalism and returned it (for it was never expunged, but only relocated) to the adjudicative arena.

While any faith in a crude reliance on some mechanical algorithm has been abandoned, there is still a fervent commitment and aspiration to the possibility of developing a theory of legal interpretation that is built around an impersonal and determinate application of immanent rationality. As Ronald Dworkin puts it, "law . . . is deeply and thoroughly political . . . , [b]ut not a matter of personal or partisan politics".[12] The task of scholars is to uncover the political morality that runs deep within the common law. To do that, theorists have begun to step outside the legal arena and to search for formal allies in other disciplines. The role of this inter-disciplinary study is not to supplant legal reasoning nor to provide a substitute for legal wisdom, but to locate and understand better the formal threads that tie together the legal blanket in which society is wrapped. Like Coke, they all reaffirm their urgent and traditional belief that "the artificial reason and judgment of law . . . requires long study and experience." As always, Truth only reveals itself to the

---

11 *An Afterword*, 1 J. LEGAL STUD. 437 (1972). For one of the most extreme versions of rationalism in modern scholarship, see Rudden, *Notes towards a Grammar of Property*, [1980] CONV. 325.

12 R. DWORKIN, A MATTER OF PRINCIPLE 146 (1985).

initiated few and remains forever elusive to those unlearned in professional ritual and acumen: it is truly an *acquired* taste.

In delving into the foreign fields of other scholarly disciplines, the hope remained constant. There was no desire to open up the legal project to the subversive messages of some of those toiling in the anthropological or sociological soil of radical study. The objective of this extra-legal adventure was to complete the rationalist programme of the legal order, not to undermine its validity or success. Like their illustrious ancestors, modern jurists craved "a language which can receive no gloss, requires no interpretation, cannot be distanced, cannot be sneered at by later generations."[13] This dalliance has taken many different forms, but each has sought the same goal. Many have found refuge and relief in departments of economics and have affected the language of the market and efficiency. Others have retreated to the traditional sanctums of moral and political theory and have revived the flagging spirits of natural rights. Still others have turned to the study of language itself to fulfil their rationalist ambitions.

In each of these disciplines, lawyers have received a warm welcome and found kindred scholars engaged in the same high-minded calling. Yet, within these temporary havens, there exists the same crises of rationalist faith and confidence. Jurists seem to have jumped the legal ship and boarded other scholarly vessels only to find that these are shipping sceptical water at much the same rate and that the crews are also in the process of abandoning ship. Indeed, the whole scholarly enterprise seems to be shipwrecked or, at least, foundering on the icebergs of radical doubt. The concerted struggle is to keep the rationalist flotilla afloat; survival rather than progress toward the promised land has become the immediate aim.

HISTORY AND PHILOSOPHY

"Can we actually 'know' the universe? My God, it's hard enough finding your way around Chinatown."—WOODY ALLEN[14]

Although a little damaged and dented, the rationalist dream of discovering one explanation of everything for all time in one uniform and uncontradictable theory still continues to inspire and inform the scholarly

---

13 Rorty, *Deconstruction and Circumvention*, 11 CRIT. INQ. 1 at 5 (1984).
14 Allen, *My Philosophy* in GETTING EVEN 28 (1972).

project. Theories have been discredited and abandoned, but the problem continues to be, so the story goes, with the theorists; the search for a 'foundational' system of thought remains as abiding and as elusive as ever. Human frailty and fallibility are the culprits rather than some fundamental flaw in the project itself. Truth and Knowledge are not only our destiny, but the lodestars which illuminate and guide our journey. History is something we must rise above and control rather than succumb to or be controlled by. For the rationalist, freedom and fulfilment are the children of reason and it is our highest responsibility to save them from the chaotic contingency of history.

In recent years, there has been a radical and eclectic assault upon Western metaphysics. While operating on many different fronts, the attack is loosely unified in its shared objective of explicating the intimate and crucial relation between philosophy and history. The central thrust is that there is no position of theoretical innocence or political neutrality. In effect, there is no privileged ground for philosophers to stand or build on. Kant's fabled island of Truth is one more foggy iceberg and the voyages of discovery in its name are cruel flights of fancy. We must abandon this whole metaphysical metaphor which has dominated the theoretical imagination for far too long. The maps and charts of the rationalist navigators are reflections of their own intuitions and ideals; philosophers mistake personal preference for universal insight. History can be hidden, but it can never be excluded. By asking us to look beyond the horizon to a rational paradise, the hope is that we might not notice or mind the oppressive conditions of the present; conditions that were once introduced and justified in the name of reason itself. Yet nothing will appear or be discovered (like Truth, Knowledge or some other illusion) to rescue us from ourselves or the inescapable responsibility to make our present into a better past for the future. The footprint we will find on the shores of that fateful island of Truth will be our own.

Directed towards its evasion and transcendence, philosophy is grounded in historical circumstance. Theories are produced in specific socio-historical situations and help to generate a particular version of history: "the teaching of method is nothing other than the teaching of a certain kind of history."[15] Human reason and language are the prized possessions of a social heritage and they cannot divest themselves of their history so as to reach an ahistorical or metalinguistic truth. Philosophy

---

15 This quotation is from page 61 of the original typescript of an article, *Epistemological Crises, Dramatic Narrative and the Philosophy of Science*, published in abbreviated form in 60 MONIST 453 (1977), and quoted in Bernstein, *supra*, note 6, at 57.

can never amount to more than a stylised genre of story-telling and, like all literary genres, is beholden to its historical milieu for its substance and form. Unless we decree it to be so, philosophy has no privileged status above other modes of discursive practice. For all its huff-and-puff, philosophy can never attain that cherished independence from contingent considerations; it is destined to live and die, flourish and perish at the hands of historical circumstance. It is not so much that Minerva's owl flies at dusk, but that it is another stuffed artifact of Western culture.

The history of philosophy is philosophy *tout court*.[16] To understand a philosophical proposal and its career, it is important to appreciate its historical context; it can only begin to make sense in terms of an agenda of pressing issues, the methodologies on offer, the bounds of political propriety and the like. To put it crudely, philosophers begin and end with their own prejudices as understood within the larger social context of available values. By a circuitous process of reasoning, they strive to bestow universal validity on contingent preference: "having thought from Z to A, [they] pose as thinking from A to Z."[17] A good example of this is the work of John Rawls.[18] Much of the phenomenal success of his theory of justice can best be appreciated through even a rudimentary understanding of the American situation in the 1960s and 1970s. A stylish and sustained account, it is a thinly disguised and cosmetically spruced-up theoretical version of the Democratic Party ticket. It derived from and spoke into a developing political setting. It travels from a distinctly historical Z to an imperfectly metaphysical A and, affecting a convenient amnesia, makes a supposedly path-breaking trip from A to Z. Yet the journey through the abstractions of the original position and behind the veil of ignorance ends in the very place that it began—safe at home in the heartland of the liberal establishment. It is an elaborate and histori-cally-specific piece of political narrative.

The critical upshot of this argument (i.e., the inextricable relation of philosophy and history) is that modes of thinking and discourse are themselves revealed as contingent. The great systems of philosophy and styles of theorising about the human condition are not fixed nor immut-able. The Enlightenment is a phase, albeit an extended and durable one. It originated and was allowed to mature at a particular time and served certain interests. The historical introduction and search for the ahistorical foundations of Truth and Knowledge resulted in the freezing of existing

---

16 *See* PHILOSOPHY IN HISTORY (R. Rorty et al. eds. 1984).
17 K. BURKE, THE PHILOSOPHY OF LITERARY FORM 383 (3d ed. 1973).
18 A THEORY OF JUSTICE (1971).

patterns of social relations and insulated them against the warm winds of history. It tended to legitimate an established distribution of power by conferring upon it a spurious, but respected ontological status: it is little more than ethnocentrism, elevated to a more general level of abstraction and turned out in the uniform of rational respectability.

Detached reason does not offer improved access to historical reality nor establish independent standards for its identification or evaluation, but acts as a trusted "means for fixing up the world for utilitarian ends."[19] Importantly, this epistemological strategy has not only informed political theory and practice, but it has constrained and dimmed our appreciation of the historical imperative itself; it has worked to persuade us to turn a deaf ear to its subversive message. So effective has it been that it makes the imagining and performance of an alternate way of thinking *unthinkable* except by a massive act of will. The difficulty of learning is as naught compared to the Sisyphean task of unlearning.

In a world where history cannot be sidestepped or bracketed, any claims to offer an objective analysis or value-free judgment of any social practice immediately become suspect. The critical challenge is to expose the vested interests and values that thrive behind this philosophical front. The approximation of a nonsituated viewpoint or a lack of point of view is only plausible because a particular point of view is so widespread and pervasive. A truth that claims to be independent reproduces its dependent sources. As Catherine MacKinnon sums it up, "objectivity, as the epistemological stance of which objectification is the social process, creates the reality it apprehends by defining as knowledge the reality it creates through its way of apprehending it."[20] For her, the objective way of thinking is inscribed with a male point of view; or, perhaps even more strongly, that the idea of objectivity *is* male thinking. Knowledge and gender are not mutually exclusive categories: the metaphysical commitments of male-stream scholarship operate to conceal the man-made and man-serving construction of reality by making women's experience and standpoint invisible or, at best, trivial.[21]

---

19 Nietzsche, as quoted in R. RORTY, THE CONSEQUENCES OF PRAGMATISM 205 (1982).
20 MacKinnon, *Feminism, Marxism, Method, and the State: Toward Feminist Jurisprudence*, 7 SIGNS 635, 636 (1983). *See also*, Olsen, *The Family and The Market: A Study of Ideology and Law Reform*, 96 HARV. L. REV. 1497 (1983).
21 For a succinct account of this disagreement, see Held, *Feminism and Epistemology: Recent Work on the Connection Between Gender and Knowledge*, 14 PHIL. & PUBL. AFFS. 296 (1985). For an excellent account of this male inscription in Canadian legal scholarship, see Lahey, . . . *Until Women Themselves Have Told All That They Have To Tell* . . . , 23 OSGOODE HALL L.J. 519 (1986).

This assertion of the deep nexus between philosophy and politics is nicely and graphically illustrated again in the writing of John Rawls and modern liberal theory generally. Behind the veil of ignorance, individuals are supposedly stripped down to their bare moral selves without knowledge of their wealth, natural assets or conception of the good life. This is so that they will not be tempted to make choices that might work to their own advantage.[22] Significantly, Rawls makes no mention of gender or reproductive capacities. As such matters have played such a decisive role in the organisation of societies to date and will continue to do so in any foreseeable society, although not hopefully in the same way and with the same consequences, silence on gender and reproductive capacity is at best suspicious and at worst oppressive; it smacks of an "objective" world in which everyone is a man and in which the interests of men are equated with the "universal" interests of humankind. Would women choose the same principles of justice as men? Would men choose the same principles if reproductive roles and capacities were reversed?

Liberal theory posits individuals as rational and self-interested agents. Moral autonomy is the primary value: each individual is to be free to determine their own particular idea of the good life and not have one forced on them by the state. The problem is that in modern society, as presently constituted, women do not pursue the same goals as men.[23] Insofar as many women tend to eschew the aims of self-reliance and competition in favour of greater cooperation and mutual support, women become either irrational or nonhuman in a liberal theory that emphasises the capacity for robust and self-sustaining isolation. In liberal society, women face a demeaning dilemma. They must become men if they are to share in the fruits of liberal equality in the workplace. By contrast, if women want to enjoy the pleasures of parenthood, they cannot do so (as men can) and remain autonomous individuals. Instead, they must be prepared to be economically dependent, usually on a man or sometimes the state. As such, their dependence both removes their right to be treated as autonomous beings within liberal theory and simultaneously confers on them a second-class status.

---

22 *See supra*, note 18, at 136–150.
23 These arguments are drawn from a talk and unpublished paper by Jan Crosthwaite of Monash University, Australia. I am grateful to her for her permission to use her ideas and arguments. *See* Feminist Criticism of Liberalism [unpublished August 1986]. It should be said that my project is not necessarily her's. Also, I do not make any claim here that those qualities associated with or attributed to women in contemporary society are in some way universal or absolute. See C. GILLIGAN, IN A DIFFERENT VOICE (1982) and Menkel-Meadow, *Portia in a Different Voice: Speculations on a Woman's Lawyering Process*, 1 BERKELEY WOMEN'S L.J. 29 (1985).

For women to want a domestic life and a public career is to be written off by liberalism as being greedy and ungrateful—to want their cake and eat it too. In the guise of objectivity and abstract justice, liberal theory and practice reinforce and reiterate the discriminating logic of the male bread-winner and the female child-raiser. They inculcate the very values, roles and prejudices that they claim to be neutral toward. As such, liberal philosophy is implicated in and supportive of the historical and discriminatory status quo and its perpetuation. Its partial and dichotomous way of viewing and constituting the world has effectively stalled attempts to reform our personal and social existence in anything but a piecemeal and relatively superficial way.

THE DECONSTRUCTIVE RESPONSE

The diverse demands for the abandonment and denial of the Enlightenment Project is often collectively referred to as "deconstruction". Much heard and read about in the law schools, this troubling tendency has received the usual range of responses designed to neutralise its subversive potential. While some have castigated it as an unwelcome and unhelpful foreign import, others have sought to defuse it by making it synonomous with any unconventional attack on legal theory and practice. Without wishing to pretend that there is some canonical description of deconstruction or to turn it into one more dogmatic philosophy (the irony of which is not lost on me), I will offer some general comments on the deconstructive genre and make a short defence of a particular version of it.[24]

Deconstruction is an enigmatic approach that glories in its own slipperiness for its intellectual cogency and appeal. From the outset, it must be understood that it is not a philosophy, but a theoretical strategy for displacing traditional philosophy: a deconstructionist "is a bad son demolishing beyond hope of repair the machine of Western metaphysics."[25] It is not intended to realize the metaphysical dream by some other means or to locate some new source of Truth or Knowledge. It is a rigorous

---

24 Apart from those works expressly referred to, I have benefitted from J. CULLER, ON DECONSTRUCTION: THEORY AND CRITICISM AFTER STRUCTURALISM (1983); C. NORRIS, DECONSTRUCTION: THEORY AND PRACTICE (1982): David Kennedy, International Legal Structures [unpublished July 1982]; and Hoy, *Jacques Derrida* in THE RETURN OF GRAND THEORY IN THE HUMAN SCIENCES (Q. Skinner ed. 1986).
25 Miller, *The Critic as Host* in DECONSTRUCTION AND CRITICISM 251 (1979).

and uncompromising onslaught on such thinking. As its mentor, Jacques Derrida, puts it, "there is no such thing as truth in itself. But only a surfeit of it. Even if it should be for me, truth is plural."[26] Indeed, deconstruction does not exempt itself from its own critical manoeuvring. Its sensitivity and openness to its own deconstruction reinforces its potency.

For deconstruction, referentiality and meaning are not so much non-existent as profoundly problematic. The attempt to demonstrate and defend any theory of embodied meaning is ruthlessly revealed as leading down the blind alley of foundational thought. No interpretation is right or wrong and no mode of linguistic signification can achieve interpretive hegemony. It is not that deconstruction erases meaning or denies intentionality, but that it perpetually defers and de-centres them and so deprives them of any privileged or original authority. It foils any orderly attempt to progress to final knowledge or recover correct meaning by its insistence that "all discourse—including its own—forever remains both belated and precipitous with respect to the textual practice it attempts to comprehend."[27] Deconstructive critique celebrates and revels in the polysemic quality of texts; it does not lament or work to contain it. By denying philosophical closure, it is a strategy without finality. Yet deconstruction is not randomly or wantonly destructive. It de-constructs the constructs of philosophy to better reveal their constructedness. Moreover, deconstruction proceeds by taking such constructs seriously and works to collapse them from within.

To understand and control the world, metaphysical thinking employs a set of enabling distinctions that are treated as natural and obvious, such as objective/subjective, reason/emotion or mind/body. This means that it must not only explain the precise and stable relation between these oppositions, but also find a way of talking about them that is itself precise and stable. It claims to do this by privileging one over the other and granting epistemological authority to it. Deconstruction goes behind these hierarchical dichotomies and shows that they have a history and are far from natural or obvious. Operating from inside the traditional paradigm, deconstruction unravels and lays bare the contradictory, inescapable and warring forces that both constitute and confound the common sense meaning of words and texts. A good example of this is the gender distinction of male/female and the historical privileging of one over the other. Moreover, these duplicitous dualities cannot be sustained. The unprivileged "other" disrupts and undermines its privileged partner;

---

26 SPURS: NIETZSCHE'S STYLE 103 (B. Harlow trans. 1979).
27 Johnson, *Introduction* in J. DERRIDA, DISSEMINATION xxxiii (1981).

while it is a necessary contrast, it is also a contradiction. So interrelated are each that the one not only makes the other possible, but contributes to its negation: "neither/nor, that is, *simultaneously* either *or*."[28] In short, what is excluded is implicated in and is essential to what is included: philosophy depends on the very history that it is at pains to deny.

The metaphysical dream of providing a complete and unassailable explanation of everything for all time is doomed to failure by its own lights. It must exclude to be intelligible, but, in so doing, it renders itself incomplete. For instance, at the heart of the Enlightenment Project is the central and weighted distinction between absolute knowledge and radical doubt. Yet each one is only understandable in relation to the other. Radical doubt is both the friend and enemy of absolute knowledge; each is the pre-condition and most serious threat to the other. Absolute knowledge is built on the fear of radical doubt and, at the same time, committed to its displacement. As such, rationalism can only succeed by pulling the rug from under its own feet. It must deny the very conditions of its own possibility: "And now what shall become of us without any barbarians? / Those people were a kind of solution."[29] Importantly, however, the deconstructive technique is not intended to simply reverse the hierarchical order and place, for instance, community over individual or woman over man in terms of epistemological authority. It is to be understood as rejecting entirely the dichotomous way of thinking about and acting in the world. Irrationalists, like Paul Feyerabend, remain trapped within the very system they revile and claim to reject.[30] A studied irrationality in which "anything goes" is the mirror image of the despised rationality; it is guilty of the same reductionistic and totalising tendency.

As powerful as this Derridean strain of deconstruction is, it is not without its own shortcomings. The main problem is that it deconstructs the existing rational and irrational "constructs" only to leave itself still inhabiting the same metaphysical territory as those deconstructed. Although Derrida shows the rationalistic dream to be a nightmare, he continues deep in a metaphysical sleep. For deconstructionists like Derrida, the text is all—*il n'y a pas de hors-texte*.[31] History and all other *contexts* are secondary and similarly unclosable. Derrida pushes the hermeneutic belief in the relation between knowledge and historical contexts of under-

28 J. DERRIDA, POSITIONS 43 (A. Bass trans. 1981).
29 Cavafy, *Expecting The Bomb* in THE COMPLETE POEMS OF CAVAFY 19 (R. Dalven trans. 1976).
30 *See* P. FEYERABEND, AGAINST METHOD (1975).
31 OF GRAMMATOLOGY 158 (G. Spivak trans. 1974).

standing to (or beyond) its limits by showing how every context is itself limitless. The text becomes both the source of knowledge and its disguise and what is present necessarily depends on what is absent: meaning is enclosed within a perfect hall of textual mirrors.

What Derrida begins by discrediting and deconstructing, he ultimately reinforces and confirms. Deconstruction needs metaphysics as much as its proponents; it has no relevance or purchase without it. Like those he assails, Derrida is a slave to the mastery of the metaphysical metaphor. He condemns himself and his followers to the endless task of tilting at figurative windmills of the mind or, in Kantian imagery,[32] to showing each freshly-discovered archipelago of Truth to be one more stream of foggy icebergs. As Richard Rorty so beautifully puts it, metaphysical construction and deconstruction only survive in the form of self-parody:

> The attempt to find a closed and total vocabulary produced lots of great binary oppositions which poets and essayists and novelists then proceeded to use as tropes. But one can use a trope perfectly well without taking seriously its claim to be part of such a vocabulary. One does not need to see it as deconstructing itself, as committing suicide, in order to escape its baleful and totalizing influence. Concepts like causality, originality, intelligibility, literalness, and the like are no more dangerous, and no more suicidal, than sunsets or blackbirds. It is not their fault that in another country, long ago, they were believed to have magical powers.[33]

Although deconstruction has been put to work in the very metaphysical process it was intended to disrupt and dislodge, it can be salvaged without defusing its thoroughly subversive message. The intoxicating freedom of deconstruction is bought at the too high price of political inconsequence. The challenge is to reintroduce the liberating dynamic of history and to politicise the polysemic quality of texts and interpretive practice. Infused with the radical energy of historical contingency and political signification, deconstruction can emerge better able to carry through on its critical agenda. By trapping meaning in a web of inter-textuality, Derridean deconstruction cuts off interpretation from its vital political and historical dimensions. Meaning and knowledge must be loosed from its metaphysical moorings and relocated in the political docks.

This is not to maintain that there is some final or true meaning or some final or true context of understanding. Nor does it reduce the need

---

32 *Supra* note 8.
33 Rorty, *supra*, note 13, at 20–21.

to indict and detail the duplicity of philosophers' plans to "divide and conquer". But it does demand a recognition that such inquiries are not enough on their own and that knowledge and meaning involve a historical taking of sides. The deconstructive critique of embodied meaning does not require the conclusion that all texts are meaningless. On the contrary, it puts language and texts up for political grabs or, to be more accurate, makes it "open to interested appropriation."[34] It is the task of criticism to note the meaning actually ascribed to texts, to identify the historical determinants of the meaning-giving exercise, to draw out the social practices that the text reflects and reworks, and to uncover the relations of power that produce and benefit from this textual knowledge. In short, the text must be placed within its historical context so as to re-establish its genetic affiliations with institutions, classes, professionals, and the like.[35] However, although texts are produced by, and must be correlated with, those forces, they must not be reduced to them. To reduce text-making to the traces of historical forces is as much a distortion as it is to confine it to some ahistorically isolated cell of metaphysical activity.

How does all this affect the performance and critique of legal thinking and practice, in particular its continuing formalist foundations? It is the main ambition and burden of this book to answer that question in a variety of settings and with a selection of strategies for an alternative style of lawyering. However, although the preceding discussion should have pointed in the relevant direction, it seems appropriate at this stage to adumbrate some of its more important themes and substantial implications:

(a) In *all* its manifold forms, lawyering is profoundly political. The practice of law, the study of law and the study of the study of law (including this one) can never be carried out in an apolitical or ahistorical way. There is no position of political neutrality or historical detachment; the defence of neutrality and detachment is itself historically and politically situated. We can only act and think within a set of beliefs that are unavoidably partial and selective about the nature of truth, knowledge, meaning, individuality, etc.

(b) Language and discourse are social entities. Like all language, legal discourse is not a way of talking about or acting in a world independent

---

34 F. LENTRICCHIA, CRITICISM AND SOCIAL CHANGE 81 (1983).
35 This view of deconstruction is based on the work of Michael Foucault. *See infra* ch. 9.

of it, but a way of constituting that world. It does not so much describe reality as inscribe a particular form of reality in the world. By speaking a language, we are implicated in its values and commitments. It is the silent police of the mind. As a medium of power, it thrives on an ignorant dependence and perpetuates established centres of power.

(c) Legal interpretation is not a matter of formal logic and imminent rationality, but is an elaborate exercise in operational logic and functional rationalisation. The Rule of Law is a sham; the esoteric and convoluted nature of legal doctrine is an accommodating screen to obscure its indeterminacy and the inescapable element of judicial choice. Traditional lawyering is a clumsy and repetitive series of bootstrap arguments and legal discourse is only a stylized version of political discourse. Legal rules can, but never must lead to any particular result. Determinacy and indeterminacy are locked in an unfathomable historical embrace. Beneath the patina of legalistic jargon, law and judicial decision-making are neither separate nor separable from disputes about the kind of world we want to live in.

(d) This is not tantamount to suggesting that doctrinal development is autonomous from the status quo-oriented prejudices of ideological debate: there is a deep logic and structure to law that broadly reflects the contradictory relations of modern hierarchical society. There exists doctrinal indeterminacy with an ideological slant. The judicial Emperor, clothed and coiffured in appropriately legitimate and voguish garb by the scholarly rag trade, chooses and acts to preserve the propertied interest of vested white and male power.

(e) These claims of indeterminacy and contradiction do not simply go to legal doctrine and theorizing; they go to the very heart of traditional political theory and practice. Doctrinal indeterminacy is a localized illustration of the bankruptcy of that theory and practice. The ailing corpus of black-letter legal theory cannot be made good by injecting a dose of black-letter political theory. As in the legal sphere, political debate is open-ended and unclosable. It exhausts itself in an agonized struggle for the ever elusive Archimedean point outside history and society from which to mediate conflicting interests and sustain a position of normative equilibrium. There is no available metatheory. Political decisions and social arrangements can never be objectively justified and always amount to contingent choices. This does not mean that they are arbitrary for they follow the general pattern of established interests.

(f) All critique must recognise the operation of law as ideology. The Rule of Law lends to existing social structures the appearance of legitimacy and inevitability; it transforms the contingency of social history into a fixed set of structural arrangements and ideological commitments. Far from being built on the hard rock of historical necessity, the status quo and its legal footings are sited on the shifting sands of social contingency. This insight is both critical and constructive. Not only does it expose the illusory and fraudulent claims of traditional scholarship, but it also clears the ground for different and transformative ways of thinking about law and society. By laying bare the rhetorical status of law, it becomes possible to subvert law's philosophical and political authority. In a world in which law plays such an important role in structuring the routine practices of social life, the need to understand the historicity and ideology of the lawyer's way of thinking about and acting in the world is so important to that world's critique and improvement.

THE TRADITIONAL REJOINDER

Beneath its calm and confident facade, the contemporary world of academic study is characterized by self-doubt and confusion. Jurisprudential discourse is fragmented and discordant. Legal thinkers no longer speak "*ex cathedra*, but with a babble of voices".[36] Scholars are acutely self-conscious about the very nature of the scholarly enterprise. There is particular concern over the status of theorizing and the standard for its evaluation. There is more heat than light generated and any light tends as much to blind with its brilliance as illuminate with its clarity. While this confusion and occasional desperation is partially revealed in the traditional rejoinder to the deconstructive challenge, there tends to be the concerted and understandable effort to resist the effects, real or imagined, of deconstruction; it has occasioned a temporary closing of ranks. While the most extreme response is to condemn deconstructors as intellectual terrorists who must be banished from the law schools,[37] general hostility has taken more subtle and sophisticated forms. Most interestingly, the different strategies have tended to reinforce and reveal the extent to which traditional scholarship remains thoroughly committed to the Enlightenment Project.

There are four basic responses to deconstruction. Each is closely related and can be helpfully described within the Kantian trope.[38] The first

---

36 L.P. SULLIVAN, HANDBOOK OF THE LAW OF ANTITRUST 6 (1977).

37 *See* Posner, *The Present Situation in Legal Scholarship*, 90 YALE L.J. 1113 at 1127–1128 (1981) and Carrington, *Of Law and The River*, 34 J. LEGAL ED. 227 (1984).

38 The reliance on conceptual tropes or metaphors is a major feature of human life. As a particular style of narrative, it is one of the ways through which we give meaning

and most populous group of scholars have ostensibly shifted their epis-temological ground. They claim to be content to inhabit the sandy beaches of the island of Truth and to spend most of their time paddling in the shallows of the sceptical sea. Another bunch have announced that they have given up on ever sighting the fabled island and have begun to cultivate and rejoice in an aquatic form of life. A third group have refused to take to the water at all for fear of drowning in its skeptical storms. They have redoubled their efforts to locate dry land, even if it means having to make do with flitting from one swiftly melting iceberg to another. Finally, a growing number of scholars have accepted that we might well be adrift on the sceptical sea, but that this dire piece of infor-mation must be kept from the passengers of the legal lifeboat or else panic might ensue and everyone be drowned. In short, while fools may be easily separated from their money, lawyers remain closely attached to their metaphysical assumptions and ambitions.

The first group of beachcombers display a philosophical sophistica-tion and willingness to change metaphorical tack that belies their conser-vative instincts and stubbornness. In a post-Kuhnian world, the search for absolutes is considered passé. The newly-received wisdom is that all theorizing contains an "arbitrary element, compounded of personal and historical accident."[39] It is accepted that scholarship can be neither en-tirely divorced from raw data nor fully insulated from a "meta-physical theory". The belief in science as a purely objective and impersonal study has been discredited. Any theory partakes of an irreducible subjective and personal component; "scientific knowledge, like language, is intrin-sically the common property of a group or else nothing at all."[40] In mak-ing this concession, though, modern scholarship has not succumbed to

---

to the world. We live in and through metaphors; they do not reflect the world as much as constitute the world. See G. LAKOFF AND M. JOHNSON, METAPHORS WE LIVE BY (1980), and P. RICOEUR, THE RULE OF METAPHOR (1981). The danger is that, in recognising this, we will take them too seriously; see Rorty, supra note 33. In respecting their centrality to human thought and action, we must not forget that metaphors are characterised by their historicity, selectivity, multiplicity and contradictoriness; see supra pp. 10–17. For an elegant example of metaphorical thinking about law, see Auden, Law Like Love in THE COLLECTED POETRY OF W.H. AUDEN 74–76 (1945).

39 T. KUHN, THE STRUCTURE OF SCIENTIFIC REVOLUTIONS 4 (2d ed. 1970).

40 Id. at 210. Kuhn's assault has met with stiff opposition. See CRITICISM AND THE GROWTH OF KNOWLEDGE (I. Lakotos and A. Musgrave eds. 1970). One problem, as Kuhn himself has conceded, is that his text "can be too nearly all things to all people." T. KUHN, ESSENTIAL TENSION: SELECTED STUDIES IN SCIENTIFIC TRADITION AND CHANGE 293 (1977).

an abject scepticism. Legal, literary and political theory unite in their efforts to ground the critical act in something more than personal whim or caprice. Jurists still strive to demonstrate that judging is neither discretionary nor wholly mechanical and that legal materials combine to provide a coherent and just agenda for social justice. Along with literary theorists, they seek to show how interpretation is generated through the reader's encounter with the text. In this confrontation, the reader completes, but does not exclusively control, meaning.[41]

The modern challenge, according to these scholars, is to embrace and ground a belief in the relativity of truth, while, at the same time, staving off a threatened helter-skelter into the nihilistic deep. Academic debate whether based on textual criticism, legal construction or political decision-making centres on the nature and location of that constraint. Indeed, Bruce Ackerman argues that the whole liberal tradition "is best understood as precisely such an effort to define and justify broad constraints on power talk."[42] The goal is to acknowledge the plurality of values, but avoid a sophisticated solipsism. Contemporary scholarship scrambles to colonize a precarious beachhead between the ground of objective truth and the ocean of radical subjectivism.

For such scholars, the Enlightenment Project has been revised, but not rejected. The problem is that, as Hegel put it, "when philosophy paints its grey in grey then has a shape of life grown old."[43] Such beachcombers are neither philosophical fish nor fowl. Although they imagine themselves standing bravely in the surf, with the sceptical waves threatening to wash them away at any moment, they pursue the same dream of wanting to plant their feet on the island of Truth. The fact that it is a precarious and unsatisfactory position is considered preferable to the alternative. Of course, for such surf-dwellers, the only possible alternative is to push out onto the stormy seas where survival is presumed to be the only objective—and of the fittest and the mightiest at that. But such a scenario is as self-serving as it it mistaken. No less than the firm clay inland, the beach is part of the island of Truth: a place where particular preference is dignified with universal significance and foisted on a stupified mass. The choice is not, like Hobson's, between a dangerous relativism and a comforting objectivity. There are other metaphors for living to explore and other stores to tell and enact. These scholars have

---

41 The leading examples of this are to be found in the work of Ronald Dworkin and James Boyd White. *See infra*, chs. 3 and 5.
42 B. ACKERMAN, SOCIAL JUSTICE IN THE LIBERAL STATE 10 (1980).
43 G. W. F. HEGEL, PHILOSOPHY OF RIGHT 13 (T.M. Knox trans. 1952).

made a bare shift of residence, but are still citizens within the geographic republic of the imagined island of Truth.

Another group have plunged into the icy waters and celebrated an interpretive life on the ocean waves. Indulging their vast freedom and relying on a pseudo-deconstructive line of criticism, they posit the judge as an ideologue-at-large who is a conscious and unrestrained manipulator of an independently given set of legal materials; doctrinal knowledge and history comprise the residual traces of the unbounded free-play of the judicial mind.[44] Interpretation is viewed as inescapably creative and personal. In contrast to formalism, this tendency thinks of the text not as a photograph, but as a mirror; the interpreter does not search for some external truth or meaning, but sees reflected her own prejudices and convictions. The interpreter becomes the interpretation. The Nietzschean Superjudge is rampant and the Anti-Formalist is regnant.

Although eschewing any reliance on or search for absolute truth, these scholars remain haunted by Pilate's question, "What is truth?" They cannot escape or discard the logocentric urge for objective and original meaning. "Man" remains the source of history and meaning; truth and knowledge are produced by the individual mind operating upon independent experience. In effect, unable to imagine anything other than individuals as the privileged affixers of meaning, they have sought to deradicalize deconstruction by simply locating it at one extreme of the objectivistic/subjectivistic spectrum of textual interpretation. It is little more than a liberal eclecticism which privileges the individual consciousness and allows it to drift free of social and historical practices. Indeed, in their obsession with "interpretive validity", critics have enlisted deconstruction in the battle over interpreting particular texts. Domesticated and neutralized, it has been reduced to a tamed dogma of textual nihilism. It has been put to work within the very metaphysical process that it is intended to disrupt.

Of course, there are many occasions of overt manipulation and Machiavellian scheming, but the judge is located within a context of professional commitments and interpretive allegiances. Indeed, it was Nietzsche himself who insisted that "the 'subject' is not something given, it is something added and invented and projected behind what there is. . . . Even [the interpreter] . . . is invention, hypothesis."[45] If

---

44 The best example of this is to be found in the work of Sanford Levinson. *See infra*, ch. 5. More enigmatic illustrations can be found in the work of Sherry, *Selective Judicial Activism in the Equal Protection Context: Democracy, Distrust and Deconstruction*, 734 GEO. L.J. 89 (1984) and Husson, *Expanding the Legal Vocabulary: The Challenge Posed by the Deconstruction and Defense of Law*, 95 YALE L.J. 969 (1986).

45 F. NIETZSCHE, THE WILL TO POWER 481 (W. Kaufmann ed. 1967).

formalists take legal doctrine too seriously, these nihilists do not take it seriously enough. Lawyers are shaped by legal doctrine as they re-shape it; each interacts and is implicated in the other. As we use language, we are used by it. Discursive practices manipulate as well as themselves being manipulated by those who function within them; structural determinism or naive humanism is not a viable option. The deconstructive response takes seriously the felt boundedness of legal interpretation. The operation of legal discourse is treated as a special form of social activity, but only to demonstrate its historicity. Deconstruction acknowledges that things are a certain way, but insists that they need not stay that way nor have to be that way. As such, it does not claim to provide a more reliable interpretation of particular cases or offer a more useful body of interpretive rules. It is concerned with the phenomenological and historical task of exploring the nature and possibilities of interpretation itself. It is a systematic analysis that attempts to understand the mediation of past meaning through present understanding and future aims.

The third group are those who are so frightened of the incoming sceptical tide that they have chosen to resist the siren call of those who ride it. For them, it is better to exhaust oneself in the heroic pursuit for "bounded objectivity" than it is to succumb to the nihilistic charms of the sea-monsters. In a world in which there is "absolute freedom to create a metaphysics of justice fashioned out of a private vision of moral reality,"[46] the spectre of this "deepest and darkest of all nihilisms"[47] threatens the collective life of society. Such pervasive scepticism, it is argued, engenders a moral vacuity which crude political forces vie to fill. For these scholars, law becomes nothing more than a lamentable mask behind which hides the ugly face of brute power.

The problems with this response, apart from its obvious alarmist screech, are many. For instance, why is public morality preferable per se to personal morality and where are these reviled nihilists who want to submerge us in a flood of unmitigated oppression? As Clifford Geertz argues, "there may be some genuine nihilist out there, along Rodeo Drive or around Times Square, but I doubt very many have become such as a result of an excessive sensitivity to the claims of other cul-

---

46 Patterson, *Interpretation in Law - Toward a Reconstruction of the Current Debate*, 29 VILL. L. REV. 671, 679 (1984).

47 Fiss, *Objectivity and Interpretation*, 34 STAN. L. REV. 739, 745 (1982). Fiss' response to this dilemma is to posit the existence of a set of disciplining rules which are sanctioned by the extant interpretive community of lawyers. But this seems to beg the very question he intends to answer: what is the source and nature of that community's authority? *See* Hutchinson and Monahan, *The "Rights" Stuff: Roberto Unger and Beyond*, 62 TEX. L. REV. 1477, 1506–1507 (1984).

tures . . . Anti-relativism has largely concocted the anxiety it lives from."[48] Moreover, CLS writers, the present black sheep of the legal fold and putative "nihilists", are more interested in questions of personal liberation and social justice than most of their traditional counterparts. The true nihilist is that strange fish which not only believes in the need for rational foundations if a theory is to command moral authority, but also refuses to accept that the discovery or laying of such foundations is possible. For all their supposed craziness, as deconstructors do not believe in the former, their acceptance of the latter is of an entirely different order and consequence.[49]

These observations lead to a deeper problem with these scare-mongers. Nihilism is only threatening or comprehensible for those who maintain that objective truth and rational knowledge are required for moral action and authority. It is only troublesome to those who continue to believe in the worth of the Enlightenment Project. The nihilistic deep is a construct of that project. If the Enlightenment Project is abandoned, the association of nihilism with moral despair will also be rejected. Like the proverbial horse and carriage, objective truth and subjective value go together; one is part of the other. The suggestion that we cannot have meaning is ludicrous. Determinacy and indeterminacy are polarities on the plane of praxis. While theory struggles to disentangle them, our existential condition means that we must constantly experience both. History will not stand still long enough to fix their contingent relationship. Meaning can only come through us. While our lives may have no absolute aim, we can give them one ourselves. The mythic comfort of transcendental absolutes – either/neither objectivism or/nor relativism – is cold and dangerous. The focus of critical energy must move to how we establish meaning in a chaotic world rather than continue to look for meaning through an immanent examination of the "world" itself. For us, as historical beings, to crave an ahistorical ideal is a denial of our humanity.

---

48 Geertz, *Anti-Anti-relativism* [unpublished, 1983] quoted in D. MCCLOSKEY, THE RHETORIC OF ECONOMICS 40 (1985).

49 Singer, *The Player and the Cards: Nihilism and Legal Theory*, 94 YALE L.J. 1 (1984). John Stick criticises Singer's so-called "nihilism"; *see* Stick, *Can Nihilism be Pragmatic?*, 100 HARV. L. REV. 332 (1986). Without entering the ins-and-outs of that particular skirmish, I believe that what I offer is something of a Rortyianesque analysis. I do not let my philosophic commitments paralyse my political imagination; I emphasise its radical potential rather than its conservative possibilities. Nor do I, as Stock seems to suggest writers like me must do, join the liberal ranks; that is, unless, as often appears to be the case, liberalism is expanded to incorporate any proposal for social justice. *Id*. at 401.

In abandoning that search, "we are not left with nothingness but with our affirmative ability to speak about human beings in a human voice . . . and to focus on the truly important ethical task . . . : the development of a praxis oriented to the creation of dialogic communities and new forms of democratic solidarity."[50]

Finally, a small, but influential group exists, claiming to recognise and accept the mythic quality of the Island of Truth. Though related to those who have opted for an aquatic existence, these die-hards prefer to embrace the nautical life and to perpetuate the myth of objectivity. Apparently disabused of the possibility of objective values, if not the urge to search for them, they insist that a continuing belief in them is "a natural . . . [and] useful fiction".[51] Without such beliefs, people might succumb to a sense of purposelessness and moral decay. Accordingly, it is the responsibility of the "intelligent" and the "enlightened" to hide this from others and to shoulder the heavy burden of defining objective morality for the greater good of society as a whole. In legal matters, this means that a lingering belief in the possibility of formalism is to be preserved for expediency's sake and as an instrument for implementing moral values. Disguise will protect people from moral despair and place a necessary check on the power of the morality-makers: "paddling across the Rubicon [dividing legislative and judicial territory] by individuals in disguise who will be sent back if they proclaim themselves is very different from the bridging of the river by an army in uniforms and with brass bands playing."[52]

Even if this response is taken at face value and not as a subtle strategy of confession-and-avoidance, it is perhaps the least satisfactory of responses to the deconstructive challenge. It remains trapped within the geographical confines of traditional epistemology; the only alternative to objective values, or a belief in them, is a desultory surrender to moral vacuity. But, unlike some other responses, it compounds the problem by deceiving people with a huge ethical confidence-trick and justifying it in the name of morality itself. Furthermore, this brazen lack of candour and touted selfless devotion to communal well-being smacks of the most patronizing and superior form of moral oppression. It represents an intel-

---

50 Cornell, *Toward a Modern/Postmodern Reconstruction of Ethics*, 133 U. PA. L. REV. 291, 378 (1985).
51 J. MACKIE, ETHICS: INVENTING RIGHT AND WRONG 239 (1977).
52 P. DEVLIN, THE JUDGE 12 (1979). *See also*, Wilson, *The Morality of Formalism*, 33 UCLA L. REV. 431 (1986) and Atiyah, *Judges and Policy*, 15 ISRAEL L. REV. 346 (1980).

lectual elitism that insists that "the best knows best", insults the moral capacity of each person and ensures that such capacity atrophies through lack of use. Its practitioners embody the worst of traditional theorizing and practice. On their ship of "fools", moral slavery or political mutiny are the only options.

Even the less tyrannical members of its crew mistake the force of the deconstructive critique as they imagine themselves modifying it. For instance, Kenny Hegland concludes his ill-directed attack on deconstruction by making an apparent plea for moderation and cooperation: "articulate deconstructionists, instead of blithely denying the existence of the [legal] mountain with tiresome epistemology, might better devote their obvious talents to making it more habitable."[53] Like so many of his traditional colleagues, he misses the whole point of the deconstructive project. In ways that are only joyful in their dedication to and hope for a better future, deconstruction is devoted to revealing the constructedness of the "mountain" and to suggesting how we might re-construct more humble and accommodating habitats beyond the shadow of any legal range. Hegland is left neither halfway up nor down the mountain of traditional theory, suspended on a never-never ledge between the shifting ground of history and the receding peaks of transcendent truth. His perilous predicament symbolizes the lasting plight and unfulfilled promise of traditional theory.

IN LIEU OF A CONCLUSION

The major thrust of this essay has been to identify and criticise the tendency to try and give meaning and authority to our lives by looking for something beyond ourselves and our finite context that will authenticate them. By deploying an ubiquitous Reason, it is hoped to escape the painful burden of taking responsibility for present conditions and future actions. Moreover, by bidding us to lift our heads and look to the hills, it romanticises the philosophical enterprise and persuades us to accept our domination with gratitude.[54] In law, this attitude has manifested itself in the enduring attachment to formalism with its appeal to the value and possibility of objective and just decision-making. Without such foundations, formalists imply that social and legal life will collapse into the *bellum omnium contra omnes*.

---

53 Hegland, *Goodbye to Deconstruction*, 58 S. CAL. L. REV. 1203, 1221 (1985).
54 *See* Gabel, *Taking Rights Seriously (Book Review)*, 91 HARV. L. REV. 302 (1977).

This bleak vision of social life is a construction of the very system of thinking and practice that claims to be its salvation. There is nothing above, beyond or aside of history than more history. Any claim to escape our finitude reinscribes in the world the very historical attitudes from which it pretends to detach itself; it dignifies contingent concerns with universal significance. Objectivity is little more than "the way we do things around here". Instead of repressing its impulse, we have capitulated to the insistent urge to turn philosophy into PHILOSOPHY. We have been unable to resist the fatal attraction of TRUTH and KNOWLEDGE and to be content with various truths and differing knowledges. It is not so much that there is no rationality—a ridiculous idea. There is no RATIONALITY, but a historical multiplicity of rationalities.

Of course, the need for and worth of reflecting on and thinking about our lives and its possibilities is indisputable. But we must be involved in such pursuits to understand better the worlds we have made and can re-make for ourselves than to search vainly for some absolute essence of the human condition. Knowledge is not so much reflected by reality as reality is generated by knowledge. The Enlightenment Project is beyond repair and must be junked. The self-image of the philosopher as a trader in eternal verities must be abandoned. The whole theoretical endeavour must undergo a radical reappraisal and re-orientation. Philosophy (of law) will cease to be a task of refined description and re-description, but will become an engaged project of deconstruction and reconstruction. (Legal) hermenuetics will replace epistemology. Attention will shift to the rhetorical techniques of knowledge-making. The theorist (of law) will not mimic the metaphysical lepidopterist,[55] but will work to open up the essential and continuing dialogue of world-(re)making.

For many, this plea for a rethinking and reworking of jurisprudential study will signify a capitulation to a "dark fatalism which bids [people] regard themselves as the sport of fate, their conditions beyond curing, their lot one to endure."[56] On the contrary. We would gain much more than we would lose: empowerment might replace resignation. By giving up on the possibility of finding lasting Truth through the transcendent methods of Philosophy, we might pay more attention to the present sacrifices made in the name of future salvation. The Hitlers of this world did what they did in the name of absolute knowledge. My challenge to such inhumanity is no less real or justified because I do not march under

---

55 *See supra*, p. 27.
56 J. HERTZLER, THE HISTORY OF UTOPIAN THOUGHT 259–260 (1965).

the banner of Truth. Indeed, those who do must do so in the company of such vile demagogues, albeit in an entirely opposite direction. Moreover, even if we could possess such Truth, what exactly would we do with it: Truth is surely much less important than the life it makes possible.

To traffic in disillusionment is not to indulge in a cheerless cynicism. It throws back the veil of philosophical ignorance to reveal that, as we have made what we have, we can remake it: we can only unmake by remaking for we can never not be in a historical world. Authority or legitimacy is not a condition for action nor is it the gift of Philosophy, Science or History. It is the result of people coming together in history to establish the terms for collective world-making and remaking and for which they are willing to take responsibility. Ethical proof is not the signal for action; moral accountability of the actor must become its premise and its consequence. People might combine in the production of truth and knowledge and cease to be the objects of study. We can only illuminate our own way into the dark by the clarity of our commitment and engagement. Rather than sight and pursue an imaginary light at the end of the historical tunnel—it will only be the thief's torch anyway—, we must look to each other: "what matters is our loyalty to other human beings clinging together against the dark, not our hope of getting things right."[57]

Any attempt at social reconstruction must work at the levels of both ideas and practice. It is ultimately counter-productive to demolish theories, if we leave in place the general system of thinking that supports them. Deconstruction must strike at the deep roots of consciousness that condition and shape the psychic, theoretical and practical possibilities and parameters of social life:

> To tear down a factory or to revolt against a government because it is a system is to attack effects rather than causes; and as long as the attack is upon effects only, no change is possible. The true system, the real system, is our present construction of systematic thought itself, and if a factory is torn down but the rationality that produced it is left standing, then the rationality will simply produce another factory. If a revolution destroys a systematic government, but the systematic patterns of thought that produced the government are left intact, then those patterns will repeat themselves in the succeeding government. There's so much talk about the system and so little understanding.[58]

---

57 R. RORTY, THE CONSEQUENCES OF PRAGMATISM 166 (1982). This conclusion is heavily influenced by the ideas and arguments contained in this collection of essays.
58 R. PIRSIG, ZEN AND THE ART OF MOTORCYCLE MAINTENANCE: AN INQUIRY INTO VALUES (1974).

This undertaking is a daunting prospect. For it is in the nature of the task that we can only understand a general system of thought through our efforts to change it, but we can only change it through our efforts to understand it.[59] The workings of law and lawyers is a good place to begin this simultaneous effort of understanding and change. While legal thought and practice is a symptom of a much deeper malaise, they are its most prestigious and prominent manifestations and they have direct and identifiable effects on social life. When Einstein commented that "whoever undertakes to set [himself or herself] up as a judge in the field of Truth and Knowledge is shipwrecked by the laughter of the gods,"[60] he failed to realize that lawyers thought such mirth was the distant echo of their own risible satisfaction at a job well done. Lawyerliness is still thought next to godliness. The challenge is to replace legal hubris with popular humility.

★   ★   ★   ★   ★

As I started with a story about racing, it seems fitting—not Rational or Right, simply fitting—to close with some thoughts on that story. Or, more precisely, to offer some random musings that aim to capture some of this chapter's themes and, to coin a phrase or mint a metaphor, give them some "cash value":

(a) The idea of a Race offers a revealing metaphor for contemporary life and for thinking about that life. Philosophers of all shades have long depicted life as being a race. In the early days, we used to think that we knew what the destination was, but simply had to work out ways to get there. When we lost faith in our ability to know the destination with any certainty, we began to think that the race would be won when we could locate the destination. We would get there by finding where "there" was. Today we are much less sanguine. We will seem to think of ourselves as involved in a race, but are no longer sure whether there is any destination at all. Some philosophers seem content to equip us with sufficient amounts of metaphysical stamina, analytical dash and ethical agility so that we can each run our own race to the destination of our own choosing. The contemporary challenge is to keep the race going.[61]

(b) The comparison of life to a race has, of course, a very important

---

59 *See* R. UNGER, KNOWLEDGE AND POLITICS 107–118 (1975).
60 A. EINSTEIN, IDEAS AND OPINIONS 38 (1973).
61 *See* J. CARSE, FINITE AND INFINITE GAMES (1986).

place in our social psyche. Thomas Hobbes used it as a powerful and brutal metaphor for his description of and prescription for society. As such, it deserves quoting at length:

> But this race we must suppose to have no other goal, nor other garland, but being foremost; and in it:
>
> To endeavour, is appetite.
> To be remiss, is sensuality.
> To consider them behind, is glory.
> To consider them before, humility.
> To lose ground with looking back, vain glory.
> To be holden, hatred.
> To turn back, repentance.
> To be in breath, hope.
> To be weary, despair.
> To endeavour to overtake the next, emulation.
> To supplant or overthrow, envy.
> To resolve to break through a stop foreseen, courage.
> To break through a sudden stop, anger.
> To break through with ease, magnanimity.
> To lose ground by little hindrances, pusillanimity.
> To fall on the sudden, is disposition to weep.
> To see another fall, disposition to laugh.
> To see one out-gone whom we would not, is pity.
> To see one out-go we would not, is indignation.
> To hold fast by another, is to love.
> To carry him on that so holdeth, is charity.
> To hurt one's-self for haste, is shame.
> Continually to be out-gone, is misery.
> Continually to out-go the next before, is felicity.
> And to forsake the course, is to die.[62]

(c) We tend to live our lives as though in a race. We emphasize the qualities of competitiveness and convince ourselves that there are natural winners and losers. The market is seen as a vast stadium in which we all compete for scarce trophies and prizes, with victory going to the dedicated and the innovative. Further, by imagining life to be a race, we prepare ourselves and our children to be racers and, in the process, let our non-racing qualities atrophy. The agenda of pressing problems and solutions are dictated by the existential marathon. For instance, the problems of inequality become matters to be resolved by an adjustment of starting points; each individual is thought to have a right to "an equal

---

62 T. HOBBES, THE ELEMENTS OF LAW 47–48 (F. Tonnies ed. 1969).

starting place"[63] in life's race. Gary Wills had the measure of what a mess this metaphor is:

> For where, when one gets down to it, is the starting line? Does a man begin the race at birth? Or when he enters school? Or when he enters the work force? When he attempts to open a business of his own? Or is the starting place at each one of these points. And if so, then why not all the intermediate points as well? And how does one correlate this man's starting line (or lines) with the staggered, endlessly multiplied starting lines of every other individual? How do we manage the endless stopping of the race involved in starting it so often? One second after the gun has sounded, new athletes pop up all over the field, the field itself changes shape, and we must call everybody in, to line them up once more. We never even get to surmise where, in this science fiction world of continual starting and racing, the finish line might be. Or rather, the staggered infinite lines for each runner.[64]

(d) The whole idea of "starting" and "finishing" is misleading because most people spend their lives running, but do not succeed in getting anywhere; they run on much the same inherited spot. Also, it seems to be the case that, not only do we not seem to know where we are going until we get there, we do not know where we have been until we have left there. T.S. Eliot is eloquently to the point:

> What we call the beginning is often the end
> And to make an end is to make a beginning.
> The end is where we start from.[65]

(e) This whole notion of the race draws upon a very masculine imagery. It conjures up notions of the noble and solitary savage who, through a reliance on his own independent skills and perserverance, manages to hurdle the fences of life and come through triumphant; other people are reduced to the threatening status of rival contenders. This imagery not only distorts the fact that a large section of society—women—are expected to sit out the race and selflessly devote themselves to nurturing the competitors, but it depicts the values of a cultivated self-reliance as superior to the virtues of mutual support and collaboration. Life is a race run by men and for men; women have to become men to take part and share in its victories.

---

63 Ackerman, *supra* note 42 at 204–205.
64 G. WILLS, NIXON AGONISTES 224 (1969).
65 *Little Gidding*, part v in THE COLLECTED POEMS OF T.S. ELIOT, 1909–62 (1963).

(f) The problem that arose in deciding who should win the swimming meet is in no way resolved if we give up thinking in a formalistic manner. What it does do, however, is allow us to recognize the nature of the decision-making we must engage in. If we accept that there is no solution beyond ourselves, we must look to ourselves and take responsibility for any decision we make. We must recognize that the whole notion of swimming and racing is a construct of our own; there is no absolute sense in which we can talk about the essence of swimming, racing or winning. Values do not give meaning to our lives, but our lives give meaning to values. The participants in the race must be prepared to debate and to decide upon the appropriate standards for their mutual engagement and to take responsibility for those values. There is no need to be cavalier about the past or any received understandings; they can act as a baseline from which to operate. But our perceived freedom will be tempered by responsibility to ourselves, both individually and collectively.

It may well be that the view that the one-armed swimmer should win because he touched the pool with as many arms as he had will prevail. But this will not be because it represents some intrinsic principle of the "rules of swimming" or some general maxim of moral action. It will be because we have determined that the values that our decision represents and embodies are the values that we would want ourselves and others to be bound by and respected. Other swimmers and other racers at other times might reach a different decision, but this ought not to be cause for concern or regret. We respect the past not by an unthinking reliance on its decisions, but by taking a critical stance towards them and so nurturing a tradition of constructive engagement in which it is not the decisions themselves that bind us, but the willingness to debate and honour the decisions that *we* make. It might well be that the tradition will be more honoured in the breach than in its continued observance.

(g) Although the later essays in this collection suggest a way to act upon the reconstructive potential of deconstruction, an initial response is to abandon the Kantian trope for thinking and to imagine other metaphors for informing and joining the practice of theory and the theorising of practice. If we are still to think of the human "race", we should emphasise the human and not the race. There are other metaphors that we can employ that will give us a better image of ourselves and a greater aspiration for ourselves. Instead of thinking of ourselves as competitors in a race, we could think of ourselves as a nomadic tribe. In suggesting this, I should emphasise at the outset that I am not making a ridiculous proposal that we take up a life in the desert, but only that we think about our lives in the metaphorical context of a nomadic tribe.

(h) Out on the beginningless and endless tracts of sand, we are wandering through social history. Like the desert itself, we are always on the move. The desert offers us a place to live, but obliges us to respect its shifting character. It provides a temporary, but real firmness rather than a hard, but illusive grounding. Our journey has no destination; if anything, the journey is the destination. However, unlike in a race, we are not caught in a frenetic steeplechase in which to stop is to fall behind, lose or be trampled on. We move from one resting place to another. We set up temporary shelters, but make no attempt to create fortresses which will later become prisons for our own confinement. These encampments allow us to rest, but most importantly to savour the fullness of life. We will engage in a cooperative and collaborative life-style because we will have to rely upon one another to weather the storms and droughts of life.

As part of this communal existence, we will have to cooperate with the desert for in moving through it, we shape the desert as it shapes us. We will retain a critical respect for past wanderings and assume the commitment to preserve the nomadic spirit for future generations. We will live for today, not in the sense of plundering the future nor of ignoring the past but in taking advantage of the opportunities for reconstruction and reorientation that the nomadic life offers us. We would be temporary stewards of the desert and our nomadic tradition. Yet, in upholding that tradition, we would not be obliged or expected to follow particular customs. We respect them better when, in the face of an ever-changing desert, we act imaginatively and creatively to supplement and revise those customary ways in the greater spirit of the nomadic tradition. Further, by participating in the protean process of history-making, people might cultivate a refined sense of responsible loyalty to others who inhabit the historical spaces of past, present and future. Within such a life and ways of thinking about life, freedom and constraint are not thought of as polar opposites or relentless rivals; they become part and parcel of the very act of living. Being constantly renegotiated and reworked in the daily routines of existence, they would be interwoven into the fabric of social action and experienced simultaneously.

3

Indiana Dworkin and Law's Empire

"A new look at ancient problems of judicial romance, philosophical mystery, and academic adventure."—SOCRATES

"Join our Local Hero in this soaring spectacle through the exotic terrain of Modern Thought. Each confrontation more amazing and intriguing than the last."—THE MID-ATLANTIC

"Set to an exciting tempo of incisive writing, you can share the forgotten experience of Empire-building and marvel at the Palace of Principle."—THE OLD REPUBLIC

"An enchanting performance—it will leave you breathless."—JOHN LOCKE

OPENING CREDITS

Law's Empire
Written, directed, and acted by
Ronald Dworkin.
Produced and distributed by
Harvard University Press
Release date: 1986
Running time: 470 pages
Price of Admission: $20.00

I. THE STORY SO FAR (OR JURISPRUDENTIAL ENCOUNTERS OF EARLIER KINDS)

"Movies are dreams. They're daydreams you often get bad grades over when not concentrating on school work. You grow up being a daydreamer like I did and some day you take those daydreams and turn them into . . . something."—STEVEN SPIELBERG[1]

Indiana Dworkin needs little introduction. He is a juristic adventurer of international fortune and fame. Full of cosmopolitan dash and derring-do, Indy never shirks nor ducks a challenge. He is a Man for All Legal Seasons. He thrives on and searches out opportunities to risk his professorial neck in crusades to slay academic dragons or to rescue philosophical damsels in distress. He is the classic hero who, armed only with the "bull-whip" of his wit and courage, defends Law's Empire against the intellectual barbarians who work for its demise and the forces of legal evil that covet its moral prestige. In his own version of The Greatest Legal Story Ever Told, Indy finds himself in a procession of tight corners, close calls, and near-misses which he manages to survive by dint of his own ingenuity and imagination. With a knowing wink and deceptive ease, he reassures us that "I'm making this up as I go." But, not only does he survive these escapades unscathed, he manages to come through a stronger and better person for it, stronger in his conviction about Law's potential and better in his ability to justify its Empire. With each assault on its authority and citadels, Law's Empire is buttressed and its dominion extended. While others exhaust themselves in the hopeless search for the jurisprudential grail, Indiana Dworkin leaps to the defense of existing virtues. All his adventures end at the same place that they began—safe at home in the Palace of Principle.

Law's Empire[2] is Indiana Dworkin's first full-length feature film and, like his earlier efforts, is bound to be a massive box-office success. It is an action-packed, stand-'em-up-knock-'em-down extravaganza. Those earlier works, *Taking Rights Seriously*[3] and *A Matter of Principle,*[4] were collections of short videos, little more than a sparsely edited "The Best of. . . ." Yet, although not essential to the viewer's enjoyment or under-

---

1 T. CRAWLEY, THE STEVEN SPIELBERG STORY 105 (1983).
2 R. DWORKIN, LAW'S EMPIRE (1986) [hereinafter by page number only].
3 R. DWORKIN, TAKING RIGHTS SERIOUSLY (1977) [hereinafter TAKING RIGHTS SERIOUSLY].
4 R. DWORKIN, A MATTER OF PRINCIPLE (1985) [hereinafter A MATTER OF PRINCIPLE].

standing, a familiarity with the Dworkin genre will enhance the viewer's experience and encourage a critical perspective.

Dworkin captured the public imagination with *Taking Rights Seriously*. Although his dreams of Empire can be detected in that work, Dworkin's immediate project was to topple the positivist regime and its utilitarian ethic and to dislodge H.L.A. Hart, its reluctant juristic proconsul, with a naturalist putsch. Dworkin laid the ground for future imperialism in *Taking Rights Seriously*, but more importantly, Indy performed sufficiently well in these early shorts to establish himself as The Man Who Would Be King and to give warning to all the other aspiring usurpers that he was the one to watch and beat. The significance of these early works must not be overlooked. Reworking the craft and insights of earlier American juristic moguls like Roscoe Pound, Benjamin Cardozo, Alexander Bickel, and Lon Fuller, Indiana Dworkin revived the flagging energies of political jurisprudence and brought his Technicolor touch to the often drab and dreary world of legal theorizing. Yet he dazzled, but only to deceive. Behind the gloss is the usual collection of hackneyed ideas and dull apologetics.

In *A Matter of Principle*, Indiana Dworkin consolidated his position and went in search of further adventures and scrapes. He was not short of offers or opportunities; the gauntlet always lay at his feet. Operating on many different fronts, he honed his critical skills and perfected his patented method of turning the debilitating attack to his own advantage. Combining careful preparation with ruthless technique, he located his antagonists' Achilles' heels and tricked them into shooting themselves in the foot. In particular, he engaged and claimed victory over the growing menace of the Literary Fish[5] and the Utility Monster.[6] Typically, in these altercations, Indy discovered new and interesting facets of his own political psyche and intellect; he developed the qualities of "equal concern and respect" and the charm of "the chain novel."[7] Further, after apparently defeating his enemies, he did not leave their critical carcasses to be picked over by the circling vultures of future juristic infatuation. Like the "gentleman of fortune" he is, he extended his hand to the vanquished and enlisted them, suitably reformed and healed, as foot soldiers in Law's Empire. As well as engaging in these titanic struggles, Dworkin took time out to chastise and correct the mistakes of the Empire's judicial ambassadors who had strayed, albeit in good faith, from the imperial path

---

5 *See, e.g.*, Fish, *Working on the Chain Gang*, 60 TEX L. REV. 551 (1982).

6 *See, e.g.*, Posner, *The Ethical and Political Basis of the Efficiency Norm in Common Law Adjudication*, 8 HOFSTRA L. REV. 487 (1980).

7 *See* A MATTER OF PRINCIPLE, *supra* note 4, at 158–162.

on issues of reverse discrimination, pornography, and free speech. After all was done, the Palace of Principle took on a more finished, if more baroque, appearance and cast its long shadow over the relatively squalid huts and habitats of power politics.

II. THE MAIN FEATURE

A. OLD FRIENDS AND OLD ENEMIES

In *Law's Empire*, Indiana Dworkin offers us a modern epic. If it is a narrative of high jurisprudential adventure, it is also a tale of moral accounting and philosophical proselytizing. It bids us to lift our heads from the trough of mundane legal practice and to gaze upon a juristic splendor that, with will and nerve, could be ours to share. Its appeal is both intellectual and inspirational. No matter how menial or limited our legal task, we must all engage in and become part of the noble enterprise of legal philosophy; lawyers are always philosophers because "[j]urisprudence is the. . . . silent prologue to any decision at law."[40] In this spirit, the key to Dworkin's directorial success has been his cinematographic insistence that "in jurisprudence detail is more illuminating than range."[397] He foregoes sweeping vistas and instead indulges us in a series of in-depth portraits. A past master of the theoretical fade-in/fade-out and the flashback/cross-cutting techniques, Dworkin has in *Law's Empire* produced the film for modernist times—slick, sophisticated, but at the same time, resonant with classical motifs.

While there is no shortage of new academic thrills and spills, there are many familiar antics and amusements to satisfy the Dworkin buff. The old favorites of "articulate consistency,"[8] "right answer,"[9] and "aesthetic hypothesis,"[10] not only are back in action, but have moved to front and center in the jurisprudential spotlight, costumed in more formal battledress. To make way for them, "hard cases"[11] and the "rules/principles distinction,"[12] have been abandoned; decorated for gallantry in early campaigns, they are now unsuited to the rigors of more modern legal warfare. Yet many will be delighted or pained to learn that Hercules lives

---

8 TAKING RIGHTS SERIOUSLY, *supra* note 3, at 87–88.
9 A MATTER OF PRINCIPLE, *supra* note 4, at 119–145.
10 *Id.* at 149–154.
11 TAKING RIGHTS SERIOUSLY, *supra* note 3, at 81–130.
12 *Id.* at 22–28.

to fight another day, his appetite and ability to solve the most vexing of judicial conundrums undiminished. As Indy's trusted sidekick and judicial alter ego, this character of "superhuman skills, learning, patience, and acumen"[13] is an academic one-of-a-kind, something of a cross between Mr. Spock of Star Trek fame and Edgar Bergen's ingratiating dummy, Charlie MacCarthy. His singular talent is to reveal "the hidden structure of . . . judgments"[265] that eludes lesser morals. He responds to Indy's assignments with a flexing of his mental muscles and a brief, but respectful "Okey-doke." Not only is Hercules an awesome paragon, with his breadth and depth of legal wisdom, but he embodies a commitment and loyalty that we would all do well to emulate. If we dedicate ourselves to serving Law's Empire, we too can become fulfilled citizens in a just and rewarding communal life. As imperial acolytes, when the going gets tough, we can rely on the tough Indiana Dworkin and the incomparable Hercules to get us going.

The production opens with some quick-fire footage that reminds us that what judges do matters, for to understand legal argument is to know ourselves better: "No department of state is more important than our courts, and none is so thoroughly misunderstood by the governed."[11] After this anguished cry of the frustrated and responsibility-laden leader, Dworkin reminisces about and relives the triumphs of more simple days. He assails the Plain-Facters who hold the law to be a morality-independent matter of historical fact. Wearing the contemporary mask of conventional sense and sculpted from the stone of Hartian positivism[14] or Finnisian naturalism,[15] these anachronistic figures make mischief by a dogged use of the "semantic sting." [45–6] Although Dworkin presents it as little more than a logical dodge, this argument holds that reasoned debate is possible only when parties share an interpretive horizon that contains substantially common definitions of terms. Those who have fallen prey to the semantic sting's "great mischief" thus place all argument into three categories: arguments about the logical consequences of agreed premises; arguments about the borderline meanings of generally agreed upon definition; and futile discussions based on divergent definitions. Because those who deliver the semantic sting believe that, whatever else it might be, "Law . . . is not a grotesque joke,"[44] they reject the suggestion that legal arguments fall into the third category. As a result, they waste their

13 TAKING RIGHTS SERIOUSLY, *supra* note 3, at 105.
14 H. HART, THE CONCEPT OF LAW (1961).
15 J. FINNIS, NATURAL LAW AND NATURAL RIGHTS (1980).

time searching for the generally accepted, but forever elusive, premises which must buttress legal discourse.

Although the Plain-Facters' view commands considerable support, it is disposed of with a minimum of fuss. To Hercules, the Hartians, Finnisians, and other victims of the semantic sting fail to capture the dynamic tension of the interpretive dimension in law. Unlike Michaelangelo's *Pieta*, with its unique artistry, their works are static and empirical monuments whose accounts fail both as descriptions of how judges struggle to fill the legal gaps and as prescriptions of how judges should fill such gaps. Where there are complex and subtle disagreements of a theoretical and evaluative nature, these dolmens see only mechanical and empirical disagreements; "we are marked as [their] target by too crude a picture of what disagreement is or must be like."[46]

B. JURISPRUDENTIAL ARMAGEDDON

In effect, Indy uses these Plain-Facters as sparring partners to warm up for the more demanding struggle ahead. All interpretations take part in the ideological fray; there can be no position of moral neutrality or political fence-sitting. The real villains of the piece and threats to Law's Empire are those who have seen the interpretive light, but not its best light. Whereas some have been blinded by its intensity, others have mistaken its source and direction and still others have become enthralled by its kaleidoscopic refractions and optical illusions. In confronting these rogue interpreters, Dworkin follows a familiar strategy in engineering their downfall. Having divided them, he seeks to conquer by engaging them in an enervating game of jurisprudential cut-and-thrust. After being made to stumble over their own flaws and faults, Indy allows them to surrender in the face of his withering intellectual artistry. By way of insurance, he makes sure that he entices these competitors onto the labyrinthine territory of some cannily chosen legal set-pieces: *Riggs v. Palmer*,[16] *Tennessee Valley Authority v. Hill*,[17] *McLoughlin v. O'Brian*,[18] and *Brown v. Board of Education*.[19]

---

16 115 N.Y. 506, 22 N.E. 188 (1889) (when statute of wills is silent, common law proscribes murderer's inheriting from victim).

17 437 U.S. 153 (1978) (snail darter case; appropriations may not be used to modify or repeal environmental legislation by implication).

18 [1983] 1 A.C. 410 (plaintiff received damages after learning about accident to family members and visiting hospital, despite previous rule that generally denied recovery for nervous shock).

19 347 U.S. 483 (1954).

For Dworkin, interpretation is a constructive affair. The raw data often do not determine the ascription of value; they allow a variety of interpretations and demand an assortment of value judgments. Thus, it "is a matter of imposing purpose on an object or practice in order to make of it the best possible example of the form or genre to which it is taken to belong."[52] The challenge in understanding this dynamic interaction between object and purpose is not to retrieve some original purpose or authorial intention, because the primacy of this task can only be a consequence of prior interpretive convictions about what counts as the thing to be interpreted, the extent of fit with those data required by any suggested justification, and a body of substantive beliefs about the kinds of justifications that show the data in the best light. Although the nature of the first two convictions must be roughly shared within the relevant community, the third must be relatively independent or else it might not be possible to "distinguish interpretation from invention."[68] Fortunately, there is "a fairly uncontroversial preinterpretive identification of the domain of law."[92] Although there is more debate about the appropriate convictions of "fit" and "substance," Indy holds that there is a sufficiently abstract and uncontroversial "description of the point of law most legal theorists accept so that their arguments take place on the plateau it furnishes":[93]

> Governments have goals: they aim to make the nations they govern prosperous or powerful or religious or eminent; they also aim to remain in power. They use the collective force they monopolize to these and other ends. . . . [T]he most abstract and fundamental point of legal practice is to guide and constrain the power of government in the following way. Law insists that force not be used or withheld . . . no matter how beneficial or noble these ends, except as licensed or required by individual rights and responsibilities flowing from past political decisions about when collective force is justified.
>
> The law of a community on this account is the scheme of rights and responsibilities that meet that complex standard: they license coercion because they flow from past decisions of the right sort. They are therefore "legal" rights and responsibilities.[93]

On this "plateau," Dworkin scripts and restages the pitched battles of contemporary jurisprudence. Three contending forces of juristic wisdom are pitted against one another in a deadly struggle for control of Law's Empire: Conventionalism, Legal Pragmatism, and Law as Integrity. In short, Conventionalism insists that legal rights and responsibilities can be recognized only when there exists explicit consistency with past decisions, and that "when the force of convention is spent judges must find some wholly forward-looking ground of decision."[95] In contrast, Pragmatism is more skeptical; it maintains that consistency with past decisions has no intrinsic value in deciding what is best for the community's future, but may be relied upon for strategic or expedient reasons. Law as Integrity brings together Conventionalism and Pragmatism, as Dworkin suggests, in a novel and convincing blend. It goes beyond explicit consistency with the legal past by looking to "the principles of personal and political morality the explicit decisions presuppose by way of justification."[96] Legal integrity offers more than the appeal of predictability and procedural equity "by securing a kind of equality among citizens that makes their community more genuine and improves its moral justification for exercising the political power it does."[97] Law as Integrity supplements the stiffness of Conventionalism by taming the wildness of Pragmatism. In this titanic encounter, there is never any doubt about the outcome for, we all know, nothing and no one could resist Law as Integrity once Indy and Hercules throw their lot in with it. The production's intellectual excitement and moral satisfaction come from the bravado and sheer elan with which our heroes vanquish Law as Integrity's seemingly invincible and mighty opponents.

Marching under the banner of "Law is Law," Conventionalism is an essentially backward-looking movement; it insists that legal rights are the product of existing legal conventions and nothing more. When novel cases arise and conventions are incomplete, there are no legal rights to be enforced, but only a strong judicial discretion to engage in forward-looking justification. Although Jules Coleman,[20] David Lyons,[21] and Philip Soper[22] number among the conventionalist ranks, Indy gives this popular approach short shrift. Teasing them into the maze of Elmer and his friends, he defeats them with one of Hamlet's favored tactics: "I must be cruel only to be kind. . . . For 'tis the sport to have the engineer / Hoist with his own petard, and't shall go hard / But I will delve one yard below their mines / And blow them at the moon."[23] Paradoxically, Indy demonstrates that conventionalists "pay *more* attention to so-called conventional sources of law like statutes and precedents than conventionalism allows them to do."[130] Legal practice shows that judges, in novel cases, do not abandon or make strategic resort to the law. Instead, they struggle to extrapolate from it by way of principled consistency rather than precedential convention. Furthermore, even if conven-

---

20 Coleman, *Negative and Positive Positivism*, 11 J. LEGAL STUD. 139 (1982).
21 Lyons, *Principles, Positivism, and Legal Theory* (Book Review), 87 YALE L.J. 415 (1977).
22 Soper, *Legal Theory and the Obligation of a Judge: The Hart/Dworkin Dispute*, 75 MICH. L. REV. 473 (1976).
23 W. SHAKESPEARE, HAMLET, act III, scene iv, lines 180, 208–211.

tionalism did fit legal practice, it does not provide a decent justification for it. Its alleged virtues of protecting settled expectations and facilitating social coordination are fraudulently preserved, for predictability is but one ingredient, competing primarily with flexibility, in a richer mix of political qualities. Conventionalism prevents the judge from making that balance by insisting on too rigid a view of past legal practice "because any relaxation would inevitably involve the defeat of publicly encouraged expectation."[150] In short, Indy wins by demonstrating that Conventionalism is really a misguided form of Law as Integrity and can never prosper until it recognizes that and comes over to Indy's side.

Having dispensed with Conventionalism, Indy turns to the forward-looking Pragmatists. Committed to liberation "from the dead hand of the past and the fetish of consistency,"[151] Pragmatists decide what is best for the community. As reference to past decisions is by way of strategy and not principle, judges should deviate from clear, but bad precedent. Again, Indy lures his adversaries into his chosen set-pieces and exposes the pragmatists' descriptive and prescriptive flaws. To gain descriptive credibility, they would have to support the claim that, in difficult cases, judges "who worry about problematical statutes and precedents . . . [practice] some unmotivated form of deception."[159] As a prescriptive matter, they defeat themselves. By failing "to take legal rights seriously . . . as trumps over . . . the best future properly understood,"[160] they leap off the "plateau" of jurisprudential conflict to their scholarly deaths. But, instead of letting the Pragmatists join earlier generations of legal lemmings in the canyon of failed theories below, Indy invites them to play a high-stakes game of Political Virtue on his "Solomonic checkerboard."[184] By planning a symbolic embarrassment for the earnest Pragmatists, Dworkin hopes to attract even more recruits for Law's Empire: it is a contest of pure Carrollian magic.

Imagine a debate on abortion. The antagonists are implacably opposed. To break the impasse, abortion is made illegal for pregnant women born in even years, but not for those born in odd years. Dworkin shows that the Pragmatist ought to be attracted to this "checkerboard solution" as both sides would prefer it to total defeat. Yet, while some compromises might be acceptable, such as only allowing abortion after rape, this checkerboard solution is unprincipled and, therefore, wrong: "each point of view must be allowed a voice in the process of deliberation but . . . the collective decision must nevertheless aim to settle on some coherent principle . . . [and any] compromise must be . . . about which scheme of justice to adopt rather than a compromised scheme of justice."[179] The Pragmatists' cry that the state may be acting in an unprincipled way, although the individual legislator may be faithful to a coherent personal morality, is seized upon by Indy as a fatal opening through which to deliver his jurisprudential coup de grâce. Law as Integrity "takes the community itself as a moral agent."[187] Indeed, political legitimacy is not to be secured in social contracts and the like, but in "fraternity, community, and their attendant obligations."[206] Law as integrity is the organic bond of any political association that goes beyond bare similarity of interest and aspires to fraternal status. Although people have no need to love each other, as "this would mean the extinction not the universality of love,"[215] they must recognize that group obligations are special, that they are personal and not owed to the group as a whole, that each member must be concerned for the well-being of others, and that that concern must be equal for all members.

What does this mean for political practice and organization? Indy's answer is predictably predictable. Dismissing the possibility of "community as a matter of circumstance and as a matter of rules,"[210] he champions "the community of principle":

> [M]embers of a genuine political community . . . accept that they are governed by common principles, not just by rules hammered out in political compromise. Politics . . . is a theater of debate about which principles the community should adopt as a system . . . not the different story . . . in which each person tries to plant the flag of his convictions over as large a domain of power or rules as possible. . . . So each member accepts that others have rights and that he has duties flowing from that scheme, even though these have never been formally identified or declared. . . . [T]hese obligations arise from the historical fact that his community had adopted that scheme, which is then special to it, not the assumption that he would have chosen it were the choice entirely his. In short, each accepts political integrity as a distinct political ideal and treats the general acceptance of that ideal, even among people who otherwise disagree about political morality, as constitutive of political community.[211].

With his typical feel for realpolitik, Dworkin concedes that integrity might not hold much sway in a political community that was "abstract and timeless" and "perfectly just and fair."[216] But it does represent the best interpretation of "a morally pluralistic society."[213] Accordingly, Indy's Janus-faced Law as Integrity puts paid to the challenge of the backward-looking Conventionalists and the forward-looking Pragmatists. He defeats both by becoming both. All that now remains for Dworkin and Hercules to do is to complete the rout by revealing the detailed route through the doctrinal maze of Elmer and his friends to the Palace of Principle and, by so doing, to enhance the power of Law's Empire. They give us a sneak preview of "the unfolding political narrative"[225] that is contemporary legal practice.

C. THROUGH THE MAZE

Reflecting the lawyer's cultivated disregard of history, Law as Integrity does not seek to recapture the legal past, but to reconstruct it for the present as "a single unified novel that is the best it can be."[224] In this way, judges are "novelists with epics in mind."[409] Interweaving textual engagement with political judgment, Indy dispatches Hercules on a series of doctrinal excursions. His first voyage of discovery is through the tortious terrain of the *McLoughlin* Challenge. After an arduous tour, Hercules completes his labors by declaring that the best interpretation of the emotional damage cases is that compensation is available if emotional injury is "directly caused by careless driving and foreseeable by a reasonably thoughtful motorist."[258] Yet, and this is crucial, the key to the doctrinal chest is not the choice of the right answer, but the cultivation and adoption of the correct interpretive attitude: "Law's empire is defined by . . . an interpretive, self-reflective attitude addressed to politics in the broadest sense."[413] A different decision is unremarkable provided that the judges were "trying to find, in some coherent set of principles about people's rights and duties, the best constructive interpretation of the political structure and legal doctrine of their community."[255]

Having laid out the required interpretive mind-set of those who serve Law's Empire, Dworkin proceeds to lead us along the common law, statutory, and constitutional pathways of the imperial labyrinth that legal integrity has illuminated. He begins by dealing with the economic approach to the common law; his critical moves are well-known and well-rehearsed.[24] Although meeting a reasonable threshold of doctrinal fit, the justification of wealth as a cherished value is indefensible as an ethic for social or personal morality. However, with characteristic theoretical thrift, Indy argues that market-simulating behavior is defensible from a more egalitarian perspective. Although there is no general duty for people to act always to increase communal happiness, is there not, he asks, "a duty to take others' interests as of equal importance . . . when abstract legal rights conflict?"[246] From the variety of equality theories on offer, Dworkin opts for "equality of resources"—not a constant levelling of resources, but a continuing effort to compensate the less talented beyond what their market transactions produce. This "fits our legal and moral practices no worse [than any other] and is better in abstract moral theory."[301] Consequently, if rights conflict, we should forego our plans when the damage to overall life-plans will be less than

---

24 *See* A MATTER OF PRINCIPLE, *supra* note 4, at 237–289.

the damage to others'. Furthermore, if resources are fairly evenly divided, damage is to be assessed by "comparative financial harm,"[306] the monetary amount each would be prepared to pay the other not to carry on with her plans.

Although a direct repair to equality is appropriate in common law cases, it becomes less so in conflicts arising under statutory schemes. Armed with a whole host of assumptions about the legislative process, Dworkin has Hercules wend his way through the fragile environment of the *Snail Darter* Clash. As an intellectual diversion, Hermes makes a cameo appearance as the mythic hero of those who seek to interpret a statute by discovering the communicative will of the legislators. Hermes is "just as patient" as Hercules and *"almost* as clever."[317] [emphasis added] Their encounter is rather tedious and contrived, however, for Hermes is in fact "Hercules' twin,"[337] albeit an inferior relation who can only make something of himself if he emulates the Herculean exemplar. The upholding of Law as Integrity means that "Hercules interprets not just the statute's text but its life, the process that begins before it becomes law and extends far beyond that moment. He aims to make the best he can of this continuing story, and his interpretation therefore changes as the story develops."[348]

Finally, Dworkin permits Hercules to lead us across the Olympian range of the Constitution and back home to the heartland of Law's Empire. Our training in the statutory foothills of Law as Integrity has prepared us well for this climb and its more rarified philosophical atmosphere. As the Constitution is the foundational law, its interpretation must both fit the most basic institutional arrangements of political power and be justified by abstract political theory. In the climb to the interpretive summit, Indy and Hercules clamber over the exhausted bodies of earlier failed expeditions, like those of the active/passive and liberal/conservative interpretation theories. The last obstacle to be surmounted is the *Brown* Saga. After much huffing and puffing, Hercules declares that, although the Constitution does not mandate a singular conception of equality, "it insists that each state recognize certain rights qualifying any collective justification it uses."[382] Read in the best light of contemporary legal practice, state-imposed racial discrimination is unconstitutional. Moreover, legal integrity suggests a justifying principle of "banned sources" that can make sense of the Fourteenth Amendment generally: "people have a right . . . that preferences that are rooted in some form of prejudice against one group can never count in favor of a policy that includes the disadvantage of that group."[384] Bringing together popular conviction, national tradition, and philosophical sophistication,

Hercules interprets the Constitution as the "parent and guardian of democracy."[399] The summit has been reached, the principled pilgrimage is at an end and Indy's moral mission is almost complete.

Atop the constitutional Olympus, Law's Empire stands before us in all its principled majesty and splendor. Yet, as if this magnificent sight were not enough to sate the head and heart, there stands behind it a "mysterious image" of "present law gradually transforming itself into its own purer ambition."[400] Indeed, Indy's epic ends fittingly with a rush of unparalleled jurisprudential aestheticism, a touch of the Dworkinian divine. Unconstrained by commitments of institutional arrangements and normative conceptions, pure legal integrity escapes its earthly bounds and realizes the vision of social justice that is adopted only in part at present. The Palace of Principle stands in the shadow of this metaphysical Mecca. Indy's preeminent place in this perfect pantheon of jurisprudential greats is assured:

> The courts are the capitals of law's empire, and judges are its princes, but not its seers and prophets. It falls to philosophers, if they are willing, to work out law's ambitions for itself, the purer form of law within and beyond the law we have.
>
> . . . .
>
> So utopian legal politics is . . . law still. . . . But the dreams are competitive, the visions are different, choices must be made. . . . No coherent program may take hold for long enough among enough people; we may be left in the hands of law's cunning after all. . . . But philosophers are part of law's story even then . . . for their arguments . . . remind the profession of the pressure of law beyond law, that the imperatives of integrity always challenge today's law with the possibilities of tomorrow's, that every decision in a hard case is a vote for one of law's dreams. [407, 409–10]

III. THE REVIEWS

*"[T]he trouble with serious film criticism today is
that it is too serious."*—DWIGHT MACDONALD[25]

THE UNSEEING EYE
(from *The Journal of Film Optics*)

. . . William Shakespeare was always a man (men?) ahead of his time.

---

25 D. MACDONALD, ON MOVIES 25 (1969).

He would have had the measure of Dworkin and his fellow juristic directors:

> "The lunatic, the lover, and the poet,
> Are of imagination all compact: . . .
> And, as imagination bodies forth
> The forms of things unknown, the poet's pen
> Turns them to shapes, and gives to airy nothing
> A local habitation and a name.
> Such tricks hath strong imagination."[26]

The "lunatic" guild of traditional juristic film-makers presents us with a bewildering array of "strong" and "tricky" images and ideas. Yet, for all their differences, they share much more than meets the eye. Their practice of their craft coheres, not in the range of their visual presentations, but in the fixity and focus of their stare. Like many of his colleagues, Dworkin gazes at the world and misses much of its sensual resonance and historical complexity: an eclectic balance of the senses is sacrificed to the hegemony of rational sight.

The jurisprudential gaze is simply one of many ways of confronting and understanding the world. Sight seems most immediate and simultaneous and, therefore, most neutral and reliable. In modern times, the power of the eye has withered almost all in its gaze. In the popular mind, the power and prestige of science is dependent on the extent to which we celebrate the epistemological primacy of sight—"seeing is believing." Much scientific wisdom has it that, if only we look hard enough and in the right places, the universe will reveal its secrets to us; the unblinking eye will illuminate dark corners of existence. The use of such stratagems as "double blinds" to counteract prejudice works to underline, not modify, the reliance on the visual method. Clearly, the Cartesian icon still holds contemporary society in its spell. The "objective observer" is the doorkeeper at the temple of scientific truth. Within such a culture, the attainment of knowledge is a clinical and voyeuristic activity.

Yet, in all this, the politics of seeing are overlooked or ignored. Vision is deformed by interest and perspective; there is no image that is not pre-censored. What we believe is not what we perceive and what we perceive is not what we see; we see with much more than our eyes. When we "look and see" more happens than the passive physical connection between light waves and optic nerves. To "look and see" involves a

---

26 W. SHAKESPEARE, A MIDSUMMER NIGHT'S DREAM, act V, scene i, lines 7–8, 14–18.

whole apparatus of mental images, intellectual habits, social assumptions, imaginary constructs, and, often, a wilful act of attention. The "male" stare of the Dworkinian eye distorts the world in at least two ways: it objectifies and desensitizes the world of personal relations and it places part of the world out of sight.

The eye sees, but it does not always understand. By honing our visual skills at the expense of our other senses, we lose in intimacy and engagement what we gain in detachment. The rational eye divests people of their history and their experience: it breeds estrangement and alienation. Yet this lack of involvement in the rich emotions of life enables a distanced control. By freezing and fixing the fluidity of social life, the staring eye is better able to control it. The words of Susan Sontag highlight the shared ideological shortcomings of photography and jurisprudence: "Through photographs, the world becomes a series of unrelated, freestanding particles. . . . The camera makes reality atomic, manageable, and opaque. . . . [T]he habit of photographic seeing—of looking at reality as an array of potential photographs—creates estrangement from, rather than union with, nature."[27] In Dworkin's world, there are no settled relations, bonds of dependency, nor lasting ties. It is the moral terrain of middleclass America, where a comfortable isolation is interrupted by occasional confrontations that are quickly defused, before life returns quickly to normal. It is a robust world in which people stand alone and only form alliances to further their own interests. Indeed, Indy himself represents the epitome of the good imperial citizen: an independent and decisive spirit who has the moral courage and foresight to know what integrity demands. In short, *he* is the Man of Principle.

The other way that the jurisprudential stare affects the representation of the world is through its artful filtering out of certain images and interests. For, as we all know, a way of seeing is always a way of not seeing: sight and blindness are simultaneously present. Jurisprudential cinema is the drama of the visible and the invisible. It is often the silences that speak most and the spaces that reveal most. Indeed, for thirty percent of the time that a film is on the screen, the screen is blank. So it is with *Law's Empire*. It is an almost exclusively male affair; Dworkin's metaphysical commitments conceal the man-made and man-serving construction of reality by making women's experience and standpoint unseen or trivial. In *Law's Empire*, women are best represented when they are absent. Those women who do make it to the silver screen are stereotypically "female." In his romp through the jurisprudential jungle,

---

27 S. SONTAG, ON PHOTOGRAPHY 22–23, 97 (1977).

Indy encounters only five women: the distressed and nervous Mrs. McLoughlin,[24] the dimwitted Senator Smith,[321] the rebellious daughter,[205] and Lear's daughters, the savage Goneril and the treacherous Regan.[15] Law's Empire is a male bastion in which women must become "as important as men"[204] to be recognized as its citizens.

In a paradoxical sense, Law's Empire is a land of the blind in which the one-eyed lawyer has become king. Because people are reduced to principled dependence, the ability of lawyers to see principles has given them power. Yet the jurisprudential gaze is uniocular; it not only fails to see that there are many different scenes to shoot, locations from which to film, and cameras to use, but it also uses the glassy stare of ahistorical reason to the exclusion of other ways of being in and reacting to the world. The project of radical jurisprudence must be one "of jamming the theoretical machinery itself, of suspending its pretension to the production of truth and of meaning that are excessively [uniocular]."[28] It must strive to open up our thoughts to the manifold other ways of experiencing and living in the world.

Rather than focus exclusively on the relating individuals, attention must shift to include the more subtle, sustaining, and often elusive character of the relation itself. We must explore and expand the rich and rewarding possibilities of intersubjective experiences. An acceptance of intersubjectivity helps us to come to terms with our vulnerability to and dependence on others, our commitment to and responsibility for others. By viewing the individual self as constituted in and through intersubjective experience, the notions of autonomy and solidarity can be differently and more fruitfully understood; criticism and commitment, innovation and connection can be mutually supportive. By emphasizing intersubjectivity, we can better avoid the over-socialized fate that an unrelieved communitarianism promises and the splendid anomie that a full-bloodied liberalism has effected.[29]

THROUGH THE LENS BESTLY
(from Film Community)

. . . Dworkin's directorial style is self-confessedly of the "best light" school of jurisprudential cinematography. He takes very seriously the idea that "interpretation strives to make an object the best it can be."[53] He not only adopts this as a narrative injunction, but also pro-

---

28 L. IRIGARAY, SPECULUM OF THE OTHER WOMAN 78 (1985).
29 See supra ch. 9.

jects this preference onto Indy such that his juristic credo demands "the best justification of legal practice as a whole."[152] Filmed through a battery of rose-tinted lenses and filters, *Law's Empire* has a surreal and sentimental gloss. Dworkin's art does not mimic legal life, but idolizes and fantasizes it as an almost perfected project of human endeavor. Of course, all filming requires cameras to be situated somewhere and operated by some directing eye. Yet, while the "worst light" school of jurisprudential cinematography is excessively bleak and pessimistic in its imagery and symbolism, the "best light" approach wants to see many more silk purses than sows' ears. Its optimism is contrived and ultimately self-defeating.

While many think of the U.S.A. as becoming ever more the United States of Anomie, Dworkin gazes upon it and represents it as a United States of Association. Where others see despair and isolation in American political and social life, Dworkin sees an enviable community of personal contentment and social solidarity. Dworkin manages to effect a spiritual aestheticism in a world of moral asceticism. Indeed, Law's Empire is portrayed as a civic community of fraternal responsibility, a moral agency of principled proportions. Bonded together by the political virtue of integrity, Law's Empire is "a special form of community, special in a way that promotes its moral authority to assume and deploy a monopoly of coercive force."[188] Yet, no matter how lyrical or rhapsodic the quality of Dworkin's political cinematography, it is simply impossible to ignore experience sufficiently to give credence to this fraternal imagery. As Dworkin says of other communal tropes, it "rings hollow as an expression of fraternity."[212]

The fraternal essence of Law's Empire is the existence of associative obligations. "Bare" geographic or genetic communities can become "true" communities if they meet the institutional and personal conditions of equal concern for each individual.[30] In a style redolent with MacIntyrean motifs,[31] Dworkin blends traditional social practices with principles of justice to establish a just community. However, even Dworkin's "true"community is a pale and anemic shadow of its full-bloodied ideal. It is little more than an aggregate of self-interested individuals who band together to facilitate the pursuit of their own life projects—a relation of strategic convenience and opportunism rather than mutual commitment and support. Stripped of its visual rhetoric, it amounts to the very Lockean social contract of the conditional kind that Dworkin is at pains to discredit and disclaim. People are bound in associative arrangements that

---

30 *See supra*, p. 66.
31 A. MACINTYRE, AFTER VIRTUE (2d ed. 1984).

are "contingent on reciprocity." [198] I need only count others as friends if and so long as they extend the same concern to me. Moreover, I am morally free to act as I choose so long as I do not interfere with others' similar rights; I need only consider others' interests when our rights compete or our projects overlap. Indeed, Dworkin's metric of comparative financial harm—I should forgo my plans when the amount others would be prepared to pay me not to continue would be greater than that I am prepared to pay others not to continue with theirs—is premised on exactly the kind of moral accounting that communal aspirations, if they are to be meaningful, must aim to resist: "If I forgo an opportunity in one case, because the relative loss to you would be greater, this should be entered to my credit in a moral ledger against the next decision I (or you) have to make." [306]

This moral discourse of costs and benefits is surely anathema to the citizen committed to the community. It is the language of economic transactions and not of personal relations. It makes morality into a matter of quantitative dealings and not qualitative experiences. The "moral ledger" reveals an ethical bankruptcy that must be compensated for and not embraced by a communal mode of social life; the standard of a community's moral well-being is not measured by its balance of moral trade. In the "bare" community of moral ledgers, any possibility of nurturing warm habits of the heart is lost in the cool calculations of the head. Moral accounting is the language of impoverishment and not empowerment. Within Law's Empire, communal and interpersonal relations are haunted by Emerson's chilling protest; "Then, again, do not tell me, as a good man did to-day, of my obligation to put all poor men in good situations. Are they *my* poor?"[32]

Not only does *Law's Empire* transact in a devalued moral coinage, but it is also profoundly elitist and undemocratic. Under the ostensibly liberating tutelage of principle, there functions a subtle regime of oppression. Despite paying lip-service to "a theater of debate,"[24] Law's Empire is about accepting and assuming political obligations and not about participating in the making of them. Rationality and expertise are the political order of the day. Imperial citizenship is about "fidelity to a scheme of principle each citizen has a responsibility to *identify*"[190] (emphasis added) and "sensing and exploring what these principles *require*."[188] (emphasis added) This, of course, should come as no surprise, for empires are not known for their popularist concerns and participatory initiatives. In Law's Empire, judges have been elevated to the rank of

---

32 R.W. EMERSON, *Self-Reliance*, in ESSAYS AND LECTURES 262 (1983).

moral prophets and philosopher monarchs. For citizens, politics has become a spectator sport. Yet, philosophy has no monopoly on truth and justice; its privilege is contrived and invalid. Our images of justice should not be the philosopher's gift, but should be produced through the sweat of our democratic brows. In that way, they are likely to be valued more.

Law's Empire is an unadulterated form of oligarchic politics. Its stunted character of public discourse confirms Rousseau's dictum that, without robust debate and active citizens, below the rulers (i.e., Indy and Hercules) there is nothing but debased slaves.[33] A community worthy of its name is not based on a set of abstract commitments to universal principles, but is grounded in the experience of interpersonal relations and ties. It is more of an emotional and shared existence than a disembodied and cognitive enterprise of rule by judicial proconsuls. Abstract knowledge is second- or third-hand; the abstract gossip of philosophical experts is no substitute for the engaged conversation of ordinary citizens. Principled discourse represents one small part of the dramatic dialogue that composes communal life and politics. Individuals are products of their social contexts, not ahistorical entities of given preferences. As such, people must be encouraged to participate in and revise the social context through which their preferences are cultivated and questioned. As Richard Rorty so wonderfully put it, "persons have dignity not as internal luminescences, but because they share in contrast-effects."[34] Politics is legitimated by participation and not principle.

The oppression and transparency of Dworkin's conception of community is beautifully captured in the plaintive scenes between father and daughter; "Does a daughter have an obligation to defer to her father's wishes in cultures that give parents power to choose spouses for daughters but not their sons?"[204] In a few short frames, Dworkin inadvertently captures the oppressive power relations that characterize Law's Empire; the familial setting is the wider political environment writ small, the private is the public. Assuming that in such cultures it is possible that "*women are as important as men,*"[204] Dworkin explores whether such an "isolated" act of paternalism can place strong obligations on a daughter. Dworkin concludes that in such circumstances, "a daughter who marries against her father's wishes . . . has something to regret. She owes him at least an accounting, and perhaps an apology, and should in other ways strive to continue her standing as a member of the commu-

---

33 J.J. ROUSSEAU, THE SOCIAL CONTRACT, bk. II (G. Cole trans. 1950).
34 Rorty, *Postmodernist Bourgeois Liberalism*, in HERMENEUTICS AND PRAXIS 218 (R. Hollinger ed. 1985).

nity she otherwise has a duty to honor."[205] Surely little needs to be said about the powerful and destructive dynamic at work; it is oppression of women masquerading as traditional honor. What does her father owe her? How is he treating her as an equal? Duty is assumed through mutual connections and not imposed in the name of principle.

Yet, despite its offensiveness, this familial cameo is not aberrational. In Law's Empire, political life is organized as a grand national seminar. Evoking traditional jurisprudential symbolism à la Rostow,[35] Dworkin casts judges as republican schoolmasters. Deciding upon the agenda and appropriate principles of justice in the cloistered atmosphere of the faculty common room, they transmit these values to the masses. Education becomes an alienating exercise in the rote learning of principled values; any attempt to encourage participation in or questioning of the formation or wisdom of these values is deplored. Education becomes the heart and muscle of social control and imperial conformity. The cult of the teacher/father-figure serves to foster an inegalitarian sense of cognitive and moral superiority. This is not the stuff of the civic good life, but the hierarchical caste of empire. In a true community, all imperial trappings would be banished. Political knowledge would become a matter of practical, popular, and interrelational judgment that works to recast the world in its own developing and experimental image. Dworkinian philosophers would be exiled, for "*[g]enuine philosophers are . . . commanders and legislators*: they say, '*thus it shall* be. . . . ' "[36] Democracy abhors such politics.

OFF THE PLATEAU
(from *The Lizard*)

. . . The least satisfying encounter in Indy's adventure is the encounter that never takes place—his jurisprudential stand-off with the Glinsk. These are a modern and eclectic bunch of academics (a.k.a. The Crits) who maintain, so Dworkin thinks, a global internal scepticism toward Law's Empire. They deny the possibility of a coherent and unified interpretation of legal practice. Over the past decade, they have generated a rich and radical body of tribal literature. The story they tell is vast and varied. Its textual heart lies in the historical insistence that legal reasoning is not only indeterminate and contradictory, but serves to sustain political hierarchy and social domination. To avoid a genuine locking

---

35 *See* Rostow, *The Democratic Character of Judicial Review*, 66 HARV. L. REV. 193, 208. (1952)

36 F. NIETZSCHE, BEYOND GOOD AND EVIL #211.

of juristic horns, Indy relies on the full range of his rhetorical skills.

As a prelude to being conquered, the Glinsk are first divided by a classic piece of Dworkinian obscurantism. Without bothering to identify any real-life sceptics and without reference to scepticism's own intellectual traditions, Indy distinguishes the Glinsk from the non-metaphysical Extskeps who make the external and disengaged claims that do not challenge the conduct of interpretation, but merely reject its epistemological validity.[76–56] In effect, Indy confers on the Glinsk the status of official opposition. Yet his distinctions are crude and contrived; they do not respect the intellectual or genealogical self-understanding of the Sceptical Nation. The Glinsk and the Extskeps are not genetically pure, but interbreed in many complex ways. It is typical of Indy's imperial anthropology that he classifies and comprehends all others in accordance with his own philosophical and epistemological lights. Conveniently forgetting his own critical injunction that "there is no position of interpretive neutrality," he stands outside the sceptical tradition and imposes his own political predispositions on their tribal traditions. Indy fails to extend that interpretive generosity he demands others extend to him. He refuses "to make of it the best possible example of the form or genre to which it is taken to belong."[52] As a story of contradiction and ideology, he does not read it in its best light by interpreting it as a tale of coherence and idealism. If only he were anything approaching consistent, Indy would find that his interpretive weapons cut both ways.

Having converted the Glinsk into an interesting instance of scholarly counter-culture, he proceeds to patronize them. Indy confesses that "[t]heir work is useful to Hercules, and he would neglect it at his peril," [273] but he concludes, without actually examining any arguments, that they "have so far been spectacular and even embarrassing failures."[274] Indy's style is philosophical debate by fiat, a matter of imperial decree rather than engaged argument. He pats the Glinsk collectively on the head and tells them to come back when they have grown up. He suggests that the Glinsk have struggled to demonstrate only that a flawed account of law fits as well as a smoother one; he argues that "[n]othing is easier or more pointless."[274] The task of jurisprudential manhood, according to Indy, is to "show that the flawed and contradictory account is the only one available."[274] This is exactly the task that The Glinsk have undertaken and accomplished. Indy's decision to note rather than face them is not an act of colonial superiority, but a gesture of jurisprudential cowardice. Indy may be the present king of the jurisprudential castle, but the dirty rascals are already inside the gates.

Even assuming that Dworkin was prepared to face the Critical challenge, he has stage-managed his enactment of the jurisprudential armageddon so well that The Crits would fare no better than the Conventionalist or Pragmatist forces. The "plateau" of conflict[37] is situated in a theoretical environment and at a level of philosophical abstraction that preempts their participation. Indeed, it is this very kind of apolitical theorizing, with its loaded epistemological standards and reduced hermeneutic horizons, that the Critical project is most at pains to deconstruct and reject.[38] With its conditions of "individual right" and "past decisions of the right sort," to expect The Crits to agree to such a venue is like asking a fish to swim in a pool of oil so that it will swim faster and with less resistance than in water. . . .

A WICKED WEAKNESS
(from *The Popular Press*)

. . . the flashbacks to the horrible days of Nazi Germany and Civil War America are particularly disturbing. The "too wicked" scenes of institutionalized slavery and anti-semitism are brutally graphic. Yet Dworkin's technique and its theoretical underpinnings are at their weakest and most exposed in these moments. Although still on the side of the gods, Hercules shows that he might be human, all too human, and Indy seems uncharacteristically stumped.

The central question is whether wicked legal systems generate legal rights and whether judges must enforce such rights. Did slave owners have the right to the return of their escaped slaves? Did a judge have to confiscate the property of Jews at the request of Aryans? Hercules is sorely troubled by these cases; not simply because he finds them intolerable, but because legal integrity seems to warrant their answer in the affirmative. A good faith reading of the library of legal materials points to the existence of such rights. Yet, although Hercules seems to have met his Waterloo, Indy slips him another distinction that allows him to elude such an ignominious end:

> A full political theory of law . . . includes at least two main parts; it speaks to both the *grounds* of law—circumstances in which particular propositions of law should be taken to be sound or true—and to the *force* of law—the relative power of any true proposition of law to justify coercion in different sorts of exceptional circumstance. . . .

. . . .

---

37 *See supra*, p. 63.
38 *See infra*, ch. 2 and Hutchinson, *Introduction*, in CRITICAL LEGAL STUDIES (A. Hutchinson ed. 1987).

> . . . Philosophies of law are . . . usually unbalanced theories of law: they
> are mainly about the grounds and almost silent about the force of law.[110–11]
>
> . . . .
>
> If a judge's own sense of justice condemned [the grounds of law] as deeply
> immoral . . . , he would have to consider whether he should actually enforce
> it . . . , or whether he should lie and say that this was not the law after all, or
> whether he should resign. The principle of integrity in adjudication, therefore,
> does not necessarily have the last word about how the coercive power of the state
> should be used. But it does have the first word, and normally there is nothing
> to add to what it says.[219]

Yet, Hercules (and, therefore, Indy) may have won this particular
battle, yet lost the legal war. The escape turns out to have been bought
at too high a price—to be a Pyrrhic victory. Shaved so thin, the transparent legal integrity will be of little use in future skirmishes. The "judge's
own sense of justice" is regnant. This means that judges are unconstrained by past judicial and legislative decisions if they consider them
sufficiently wicked. But wickedness is a notoriously contested concept;
one judge's iniquity is another's equity. In circumstances that are not "exceptional," the primacy of the judge's conscience is not fatal because "the
principle of integrity" will provide the necessary institutional constraint.
But, in "exceptional circumstances," the judge's "own sense of justice"
will be irresistibly paramount. Indeed, contrary to Indy's later statements, the dreaded Marxist or fascist (or feminist or Crit or whoever)
would "qualify for the [jurisprudential] contest."[408] Furthermore, the
threshold requirement of "exceptional circumstance" operates as no
check at all, as it would be logically impossible to ask "the principle of
integrity" to determine the conditions of its own applicability. Accordingly, on a showing of wickedness, a judge is free to "lie," "resign," or
"refuse to enforce the law."

Recall the anguish of the *McLoughlin* Challenge.[39] Suppose a judge
believed that any system that did not provide full compensation for all
victims of misfortune in all circumstances was wicked because failing to
compensate would be to treat people's lives as mere commodities to be
traded in the market of accidents. Or imagine a judge who believed that
no one should ever be required to compensate another for injury unless
it was deliberately caused because to do otherwise would be to curtail
people's liberty. In his "morally pluralistic society,"[213] Dworkin has little comeback against such judges. He must rely on the fact that "legal
argument takes place on a plateau of rough consensus." [108–09] When

---

39 *See supra*, p. 62.

that fragile consensus breaks down, Law's Empire will begin to crumble. The imperial foundations, supposedly formed from the hard rock of principle, will be revealed to rest upon the shifting sands of ideological consensus. Dworkin's complacency about that consensus is born of a splendid isolation from popular movements. He depends on the moral inertia of the undifferentiated political center and the tyranny of the familiar; "no one really thinks the law wicked or its authors tyrants."[111] Sez who? Has Dworkin spoken to many women, gays, blacks, or Indians recently? *Law's Empire* deals with the deprived and disadvantaged in society by simply pretending that they do not exist—*Qu'ils mangent de la brioche.*

CHEAP SHOTS
(from *The Hollywood Times*)

. . . it is an old trick of pornographic film producers to announce at the beginning of their celluloid creation that "this is not a pornographic film." This, of course, has all the subtlety of waving a red rag at a bull, and none but the complicit or gullible are convinced. *Law's Empire* is far from the seedy world of the porn merchants. Yet Dworkin employs a similar tactic of avoidance, albeit in more sophisticated style. In the opening scenes, Dworkin explains that his project "centers on formal adjudication, on judges in black robes, but these are not the only or even the most important actors in the legal drama."[111] As in the pornographic film trade, judicial fetishism is no less a fetish because it is dignified with euphemistic garb. The whole work is an indulgent exercise in judge-watching. The momentary parade of "legislators, policemen, district attorneys, welfare officers, schoolboard chairmen . . . bankers and managers and union officers"[12] merely serves to emphasize their complete absence from Indy's adventures and to highlight the judicial center of Law's Empire.

From these opening moments, the production hardly ever moves beyond escapist fantasy: Law's Empire is a travelogue through the intellectual landscape of Dworkin's jurisprudential mind. His psychic opponents bear little resemblance to their real-world counterparts. Indeed, Dworkin concedes that the juristic dissidents are little more than fragments of his own fertile imagination. While "each [deliberately constructed conception of legal practice] captures themes and ideas prominent in that literature," the conceptions "are not meant precisely to match the 'schools' of jurisprudence . . . and perhaps no legal philosopher would defend [them] exactly as I describe [them]."[12] Although his motives might be honorable, the result of Dworkin's effort is a massive act of condescension and arrogance. Dworkin offers his reconstituted versions of legal thought as "more illuminating than the stale battles of the texts."[94] Yet is is difficult to escape the conclusion that he "constructs" and "illuminates" his adversaries only to defeat them more easily. It is a tempting, but illegitimate technique.

As in the musicals of the 1930s, Dworkin seems to be hoping that Indy will lure back many of the scholarly discontents to the legal fold with his own modernist brand of jurisprudential romance. In a cleverly cast and lavishly choreographed production, the insouciant Hercules steals the show with his effortless combination of urbane philosophical charm and rough-house skills of realpolitik. Yet, when you have seen one Indiana video, you have seen them all; the intended mythic massage for the bruised judicial ego is in danger of becoming a gratuitous pummelling. The appeal of Indy's bootstrap trickery is decidedly short-lived and ultimately self-defeating. The constant effort to inject the vivid colors of heroic adventure into the dreariness of daily life in contemporary society defeats itself by heightening future expectations and existing frustrations. Dramatic tension turns to tedium and what Dworkinian lawyers consider brilliant becomes merely boring; there is a limit to the fascination of watching lawyers roll up the stone of Sisyphus by dint of the paring and parsing of endless tomes of law reports and philosophical treatises. The identification of principles in the soil of parochial facts is not the mark of the critical thinker, but the obsession of the formalistic gardener. While the achievement of turning this task into an elevated art form is not to be underrated, its credibility and value are beginning to wear extremely thin.

HARPOON'S INDEX*

It matters how judges decide cases. [1]

No department of state is more important than our courts. . . . [11]

The United States is a more just society than it would have been had its constitutional rights been left to the conscience of majoritarian institutions. [356]

[T]he social revolution that [Brown] announced was both national and foundational.

The courts developed a distinct jurisprudence of racial integration, neither entirely successful nor entirely coherent, but nevertheless largely a credit to law. [391]

---

* For index sources, see Appendix.

Percentage of black children who live below the poverty line: 47.3

Percentage of non-black Americans who say that there should be a law against interracial marriage: 28.

Percentage of non-black Americans who say that blacks "should not push themselves where they are not wanted": 58.

Chance that a white male in the U.S. will be murdered in a given year: 1 in 9927.

Change that a black male in the U.S. will be murdered in a given year: 1 in 1539.

Percentage of black high school graduates over 16 who are unemployed: 18.3.

Percentage of white high school dropouts under 25 who are unemployed: 15.2.

Percentage of blacks unemployed in 1984: 17.2

Percentage of whites unemployed in 1984: 7.2

Percentage increase in ratio of black to white unemployment rates between 1965 and 1984: 20.

Percentage of elected officials who were black in 1985: 1.2.

Earnings of black families as a percentage of earnings of white families: 56.

Percentage of black families below poverty level: 32.4.

Percentage of white families at poverty level: 9.7.

Ratio of male black children dying in first year of life to male white children dying in first year of life: 1.8 to 1.

Percentage of persons in New Orleans who are black: 50.

Percentage of qualified applicants for police in New Orleans who are black: 40.

Percentage of police officers in New Orleans who are black: 2.

Chance of an American being in state prison on any given day: 1 in 800.

Chance of a black male American being in state prison on any given day: 1 in 33.

Median income for all black families in 1983: $14,506.

Median income for all white families in 1983: $25,757.

Median income of black families as a percentage of that of white families in 1970: 61.

Median income of black families as a percentage of that of white families in 1983: 56.

Percentage increase in black unemployment rate from 1972–1982: 82.

Percentage increase in white unemployment rate from 1972–1982: 69.

★　★　★　★　★

Dear Editor,

Your stark listing of data does not refute or conclusively confound Professor Dworkin's claims. However, it does present a formidable challenge and counterpoint to the typical lawyer's empirical naivete (or arrogance) that Dworkin's extravagant statements reflect. With almost no supporting evidence, lawyers make the most sweeping and smug claims for the instrumental impact and efficacy of adjudication; when the courts speak, the world not only sits up and listens, but changes in line with judicial expectations. The small amount of evidence available strongly suggests the contrary view that litigation and adjudication are of marginal importance to global change. Revealing how Dworkin slides over a controversial issue, the cited data cast the gauntlet firmly at his feet and challenge him to support his intuitive and admittedly widely shared claims. While judge-made law is a formidable mode of discursive action and rhetorical ordering, its instrumentality is suspect; see Hutchinson, *Charter Litigation and Social Change: Legal Battles and Social Wars* in CHARTER LITIGATION (R. Sharpe ed. 1987).

For instance, the literature on *Brown* is sizeable and casts severe doubt on the usual lawyerly view that the Supreme Court's decision was a major victory in the continuing battle against American racism. Although there has been improvement, racism persists in more subtle, indirect and ostensibly non-racial ways; see Pettigrew, 37 RUTGERS L. REV. 673 (1985). To put it another way, if *Brown* had been decided differently, would the unfolding of events have been much changed? Dworkin must confront this question.

The attempt to isolate and assess the impact of the courts is notoriously difficult. It is plainly ridiculous to abstract the courts from American history and to point to the mixed performance of the remaining branches of government. The evidence from other countries without constitutional review suggests that, without the Supreme Court, those other branches would take up much of the slack. Moreover, the performance of the legislative branch has been by no means as bad as is often thought and, over time, stands up easily to comparison with the Supreme Court's contribution to American life. Also, even with its vaunted Constitution and judicial review, the United States has no better, and often a worse, record of dealing with the central problems of social injustice, like poverty and racism, than other comparable countries such as Canada, Australia, and the United Kingdom. Indeed, at certain crucial junctures in American history, like the abolition of slavery and the New Deal, the Supreme Court has hindered rather than facilitated change.

It is a very sad comment on traditional jurisprudence, as championed by Dworkin, that its adherents are content with and so need to go beyond the most sweeping of unfounded generalizations; it puts their heralded virtues of rigor and sophistication into harsh perspective. Their only inadequate and pathetic response recalls a line from Chekhov: "[E]verything is peaceful and quiet and only mute statistics protest."

Yours truly,
Charles Hutchins

4

THE RISE AND RUSE OF ADMINISTRATIVE LAW AND SCHOLARSHIP

For many members of the legal community, the single achievement of the past two decades has been the rise of administrative law. The 1964 decision of *Ridge* v. *Baldwin*[1] has been hailed as a "milestone in the history of judicial pronouncements"[2] and the birthdate of the revival of administrative law in England.[3] Roused from their slumbers, the judicial Rip

---

1 [1964] A.C. 40. The immediate reaction to this decision was very cool; see A.L. Goodhart (1964), 80 L.Q.R. 105 and A.W. Bradley, [1964] C.L.J. 83.
2 Lord Guest, *The Executive and The Judiciary*, [1973] JUR. REV. 113, 116. For a more sanguine view, see JUSTICE/ALL SOULS DISCUSSION PAPER, REVIEW OF ADMINISTRATIVE LAW (1981).
3 For an account of its earlier life dating back to the 1800s, see Arthurs, *Jonah and the Whale: The Appearance, Disappearance and Reappearance of Administrative Law*, 30 U. TORONTO L.J. 225 (1980). For instance, in 1888, Maitland noted that: "If you take up a modern volume of the reports of the Queen's Bench division, you will find that about half the cases reported have to do with rules of administrative law; I mean with such matters as local rating, the powers of local boards, the granting of licences for various trades and professions, the Public Health Acts, the Education Acts, and so forth." CONSTITUTIONAL HISTORY OF ENGLAND 505 (1955). For an account of even earlier developments, see E. HENDERSON, THE FOUNDATIONS OF ADMINISTRATIVE LAW: CERTIORARI AND MANDAMUS IN THE SEVENTEENTH CENTURY (1963).

Van Winkles have taken the State to task and imposed a strenuous regime of administrative legality. In the slipstream of this judicial activity, there has been a corresponding surge of academic interest and output. While other regions of the common law atrophy and die in the statutory swath, administrative law and scholarship is pronounced healthy and thriving. After 21 years, administrative law has come of age; the best is yet to come. Against such an exciting and optimistic backdrop, I present a more realistic scenario, presently depressing but potentially exciting. I argue that the doctrine of judicial review of administrative action is quantitatively insignificant and qualitatively indeterminate. As such, I unashamedly pick up the gauntlet thrown down by Patrick McAuslan and accept his challenge to carry out an ideological analysis of the current system and to experiment with new theories of administrative law. It is a self-conscious attempt "to live dangerously, to chance [my] arm and philosophise."[4]

The rise of administrative law and scholarship is a ruse. For all the ballyhoo, the impact of the law on the administrative process is marginal. The rhetoric is far removed from the reality. The importance of administrative law lies in its ideological rather than its instrumental function. Administrative law and scholarship facilitate and legitimate administrative power whose exercise and abuse they purportedly exist to constrain and eradicate. Indeed, administrtive law has an impoverished scope and meaning. It is treated as the body of judicial doctrine to govern the relationship between state and citizen; the actual law and practice of governmental regulation is largely ignored. Moreover, insofar as the supposed need and justification for judicial review is premised on democratic inertia or indifference and legislative impotence or overwork, attention must switch to these institutional evils. The reform and revitalisation of the democratic organs of government must be adopted and pursued. An ounce of democratic prevention is better than a pound of judicial cure. The vast institutional and intellectual resources invested in administrative law and scholarship must be redeployed.

Of course, to criticise administrative law and to advocate the abolition of judicial review is not to approve of maladministration. As presently constituted, administrative agencies and tribunals are little more democratic than the courts. Yet, a commitment to criticism represents a constructive step towards an effective control of the administrative pro-

---

4 *Administrative Law and Administrative Theory: The Dismal Performance of Administrative Laywers,* 9 CAMBRIAN L. REV. 40, 41 (1978). *See also,* M. Loughlin, *Beyond Complacency,* 46 M.L.R. 666 (1983).

cess. The courts are constitutionally and democratically incapable of acting as a "bridle for [the administrative] Leviathan."[5] The proclaimed revival of judicial review is, at best, wishful thinking by academic commentators and judges. Also, a troubling paradox lies at the heart of this resurgent activity. The aim and rationale of judicial intervention in the administrative process is to avoid a monopoly of power with its tendency to corrupt and curtail individual freedom. Yet, in so doing, the judges open themselves to the charge that this reinforces their own monopolistic position and unchecked power.

Sadly, as so often, legal academics have allowed themselves, unwittingly or otherwise, to be used as ideological apologists, identifying political impartiality and conceptual coherence in the jumble of decisions. As loyal exegetes, they recognise an appropriate and realisable role for the courts in supervising the legality of administrative acts, while leaving their substantive merits to political modes of control. Yet, there is developing a powerful critique of this traditional scholarship. In this sense, I do not make any claims to originality or novelty.[6] However, I do adopt a different methodology which offers a more structured, sustained and cogent account of the workings of administrative law and the legal process generally. As such, it is an exercise in Critical scholarship. Whereas other critics retain a lingering faith in the potential efficacy of judicial review, suitably reformed and reconstituted, this essay suggests that the retention of any form of judicial review cannot be justified if our democratic commitments and ambitions are to be taken seriously.

It is the burden of this essay to substantiate these claims which will appear extravagant, and perhaps offensive, to many. There are four sections. First, the theoretical foundations of the critique will be sketched and the problematic relation between the individual and the State introduced. Secondly, an analysis of the courts' handling of administrative disputes is offered. This section forms the bulk of the essay and touches upon different aspects of the judicial process, including its doctrinal indeterminacy and its practical marginality. Although far from exclusive, there is a strong focus on the saga of London's "Fares Fair" scheme. Thirdly, a critical survey of the burgeoning scholarly literature is presented which focuses upon its theoretical reductionism, its practical naivety and its constructive inadequacies. Finally, I suggest new democratic paths to be cut and followed.[7]

---

5 Harvey, *The Rule of Law in Historical Perspective*, 59 Mich. L. Rev. 487, 491 (1961).

6 *See, e.g.*, Prosser, *Toward a Critical Public Law*, 9 Brit. J. of Law & Soc. 1 (1982).

7 The alternative basis and options for a more thorough democratic mode of life are canvassed in chapter 9.

I. LAW, STATE AND THE INDIVIDUAL: THE CONTRADICTION OF LEGAL DOCTRINE

A. A CRITICAL PROLEGOMENA

Traditional political theory and practice has been devoted to containing the corrosive messages of social contradiction and historical contingency. Along with legal theory, it has sought to deny two fundamental and related ideas. First, there is no natural or necessary form of social life. Existing social arrangements can lay no claim to objective or universal validity. They represent nothing more than temporary and historical solutions to the problems of human interaction. There is no one true, enduring and ahistorical form of social existence. Secondly, this historical contingency feeds upon the contradiction in contemporary social life between the individual and the community.[8] *Both* individualists and communitarians insist that there exists a mere conflict which can be rationally resolved and the resulting solution be possessed of objective moral force. Yet, there is actually a contradiction between individual choice and collective control. They are antithetical concepts and defy compromise or mediation. Interaction with others is both necessary to and incompatible with freedom. Communal control protects and facilitates individual freedom as well as threatens to overwhelm it.[9] In crude terms, whereas communitarianism sacrifices the individual to the collective will, liberalism worships the individual at the expense of the collective good. An individual is more than an automatic functionary of some holistic society and less than an obsessive egoist in an alienated world.

The universe of legal discourse is profoundly and complexly implicated in this political struggle. The enterprise of adjudication and legal scholarship serves to clothe social arrangements with the essential garments of legitimacy. Judges and scholars contribute to the prevailing ideology or mind-set which insists that the present organisation of society is not only rational and just, but necessary and inevitable. Moreover, the construction of elaborate schemes of legal rights and entitlements

---

8 Although often characterised as a dilemma of modern liberalism, this contradiction troubled much earlier thought; see Berlin, *The Originality of Machiavelli* in AGAINST THE CURRENT 45–79 (1980) and Dumont, *A Modified View of Our Origins: The Christian Beginnings of Modern Individualism*, 12 RELIGION 1 (1982). Notwithstanding this, my focus is upon modern liberal society.

9 *See* Kennedy, *The Structure of Blackstone's Commentaries*, 28 BUFFALO L. REV. 205 (1979).

from available legal materials helps to justify the status quo and erect formidable barriers to social change. In this way, law is an ideological force and presence. It offers a plausible description of the world and a convenient prescription for action. The challenge is to expose the actual workings of law in society, to discover the process by which contradictions in the world are denied and to understand the way in which the status quo is presented as a natural, rather than a contingent, state of affairs.

Although hierarchy and domination are rife within society, the ideal of governance according to the Rule of Law masks these offensive facts. By pretending that legal outcomes are the product of apolitical and neutral modes of argument rather than the imposed preferences of an arbitrary hierarchy, the Rule of Law contributes to the transformation of an illegitimate world of social disorder into a legitimate world of legal right.[10] Legal thought operates as an intellectual tool for the suppression of historical contingency and the denial of social contradiction. It helps to obscure the fundamental truth that everything is in the irresistible process of becoming and not being. Modern legal thought offers itself as a timeless way of understanding *and* conquering the world.

Nevertheless, the universe of legal discourse does not provide a true mirror-image of the socio-political culture. There is an element of distortion. In Kuhnian terms, the proliferation of "anomalies" makes untenable the establishment and defence of a crude and direct causal nexus between the material conditions of social life and its legal superstructure.[11] While the extant legal materials are constitutive of a social system and sustain *in part* the existing hierarchy, it is fanciful to suggest that a "capitalistic" social system, able to weather the storms of welfare statism and industrial nationalisation, necessitates a particular regime of detailed legal rules.[12] Consequently, the law is not simply an institutional instrument at the disposal of the ruling class. It possesses a considerable degree of "relative autonomy." The historical consciousness reigns, but does not govern absolutely. The need for legitimation is so strong that it may best serve the dominant groups in society to encourage or permit some decisions which benefit the dominated. Indeed, legal ideology must convince the dominant as much as the dominated of the justness of the status quo. As E.P. Thompson concludes:

---

10 On the relation between the Rule of Law and democracy, see Hutchinson and Monahan, *Democracy and the Rule of Law* in THE RULE OF LAW: IDEAL OR IDEOLOGY (A. Hutchinson and P. Monahan eds. 1987).

11 *See* T. KUHN, THE STRUCTURE OF SCIENTIFIC REVOLUTIONS (2d ed. 1970).

12 *See* M. WEBER, LAW IN ECONOMY AND SOCIETY (1954).

> The rhetoric and the rules of a society are something a great deal more than a shame. In the same moment they may modify, in profound ways, the behaviour of the powerful, and mystify the powerless. They may disguise the true realities of power, but, at the same time they may curb that power and check its intrusions.[13]

The law is like a dog on a long leash. Although it will ultimately follow the lead of its political master, it has considerable range of movement. It can wander from the chosen path and cause considerable damage and frustration.

Accordingly, the outcome of struggles within the legal arena are not dictated solely by the whims of the dominant hierarchy. Legal doctrine does not conform to any simple logic and is unified only by its enduring indeterminacy; there exists "a permanent disequilibrium of doctrine."[14] With imagination and industry, legal materials can be organised so as to support radically inconsistent positions. Indeed, most modern legal theorists have conceded that "law . . . is deeply and thoroughly political," but they contrive to insist that it is "not a matter of personal or partisan politics."[15] Abandoning the high ground of formalism, they search for a "background theory" which shows the legal data in their best light as precepts of political morality. Yet the very diversity of theories offered undermines the enterprise. Insofar as it is possible to defend a variety of plausible theories, no one proposal can lay claim to exclusivity or universality.[16] Meaningful interpretation is only possible where there *already* exists a commitment to a shared set of values. However, as in the political domain, the legal territory is a locus of conflict. There is a pervasive matrix of contradictory forces which prevents the establishment of a sufficiently full tradition of shared understandings. The indeterminacy of legal doctrine finds its energy and power in the antithetical modalities of individual and community. This deep logic of contradiction sustains and ensures an inescapable scheme of doctrinal indeterminacy. It is indeterminate, but not incoherently so. Doctrine can be consistently converted into its own opposite self-image.

---

13 Whigs and Hunters: The Origins of The Black Act 260–265 (1978).
14 Unger, *The Critical Legal Studies Movement*, 96 Harv. L. Rev. 561 at 574 (1983). The following arguments represent a condensed version of a much fuller thesis, see Hutchinson and Monahan, *The "Rights" Stuff: Roberto Unger and Beyond*, 62 Tex. L. Rev. 1477 (1984).
15 R. Dworkin, A Matter of Principle 146 (1984).
16 For instance, Dworkin identifies a "rights-based" thread, whereas Posner unearths an "efficiency criterion; see Law's Empire (1986) and The Economics of Justice (1980).

B. THE ADMINISTRATIVE STATE AND ITS CITIZENS

The courts are a venue for the unending struggle between competing world-visions. Although fundamentally contradictory, they are believed in and espoused at the same time. In mistakenly viewing these visions as capable of compromise or mediation, judges and lawyers are not active participants in some vast Machiavellian plot; they are conscientious players in an irresistible and ceaseless game of social chess. The problem lies not so much in their self-imposed, although rarely realised, utopian ambition, but in the hopelessness of making anything more than intuitive, ad hoc guesses at the desirability of any particular social arrangement. The judge and legal scholar cannot evade the role of social visionary. The dialectical tension between individualism and communitarianism generates competing legal principles that march in pairs throughout the law. While the doctrinal manifestations of one vision may temporarily gain the upper hand and the whole areas of doctrine appear uncontroversial, the insoluble quality of the contradiction guarantees that renewed struggle is always close at hand. The alternate vision can be contained, but can never be obliterated. There is no logical or natural point at which one vision ends and the other begins. At every turn, commitments must be made and re-made.

The esoteric and convoluted nature of legal discourse is the direct consequence of the need to obscure this inescapable element of judicial choice. Rather than "arbitrate conflict through the impartial elaboration of a mechanical legal analytic,"[17] the judge is a political and creative actor. To judge is to take sides. The evolution of legal doctrine comprises an unending series of fragile and makeshift compromises between contradictory ideals. Importantly, there is no meta-theory available for determinate guidance. Legal discourse is nothing more than a stylised version of political discourse. The question is not "when, if at all, should judges step into the political arena?"[18] but what they should do there, for they are never not in the political arena.

Legal materials comprise a repository of technical resources by which to naturalise and universalise the temporary structures that interrupt the flow of social history. Yet, the analysis is not nihilistic. It treats legal doctrine seriously. Law is not a jumble of unintelligible materials, but is shaped by the deep and contradictory structure that informs con-

---

17 Livingston, *Round and Round The Bramble Bush: From Legal Realism to Critical Scholarship*, 95 HARV. L. REV. 1669 at 1670 (1982).

18 Jones, *Should Judges Be Politicians? The English Experience*, 57 IND. L.J. 221 (1982).

temporary hierarchical society. The vitality and history of the common law can be traced to the continuous oscillation between competing social visions. This dialectical drama is most openly played out in the arena of administrative law where social concerns and individual interests collide head-on. As one prominent commentator notes, the challenge is "to balance action taken on behalf of the public at large against the interests of a single individual whose rights . . . may be affected by the exercise of the public power."[19]

As abstract and ahistorical visions, individualism and communitarianism represent highly stylised ends of an ideological spectrum.[20] Individualism represents a world consisting of independent and self-sufficient persons who confidently draw up and robustly pursue their own life-plans. Values and tastes are relative and personal; individuals seek to maximise their own preferences. While there is the possibility of a common good, it will never be more than a passing coincidence of private ends. The legal system supports such a regime by protecting private property, enforcing bargains and creating autonomous spheres of action which are policed by an active judiciary. At the other extreme, communitarianism comprises a world made up of dependent and connected persons. Recognising the vulnerability of individuals, it encourages greater solidarity and unity. There exists a central belief in the possibility of communal values and the capacity to know a common good that cannot be known alone. The legal system contributes to such a regime by reinforcing a common morality, regulating the distribution of resources and encouraging judicial deference to legislative decision.[21]

---

19 WADE AND PHILLIPS' CONSTITUTIONAL AND ADMINISTRATIVE LAWS 57–58 (9th ed. A.W. Bradley 1977). A very similar point is made by Hartley and Griffith; see GOVERNMENT AND LAW 334 (2d ed. 1981).
20 See Kennedy, Form and Substance in Private Law Adjudication, 89 HARV. L. REV. 1685 (1976).
21 The "individualist" regime is distinct from pure egotism in that it demands respect for the rights of others. It simply states that it is legitimate for individuals to prefer their own interests over those of others and they have no obligation to share the benefits of their efforts. It can be roughly equated with classical libertarianism. While based on the work of Hobbes and Locke, its more recent advocates are A.V. DICEY, LECTURES ON THE RELATION BETWEEN LAW AND PUBLIC OPINION IN ENGLAND DURING THE NINETEENTH CENTURY (1905), F. HAYEK, LAW, LEGISLATION AND LIBERTY (1969), and R. NOZICK, ANARCHY, STATE AND UTOPIA (1974). The "communitarian" regime is distinct from pure selflessness in that it does not expect a complete denial of one's own interests. It simply states that it is illegitimate to make a sharp distinction between one's own interests and the interests of others. Its advocates include K. MARX, ECONOMIC AND PHILOSOPHIC MANUSCRIPTS OF 1884 (D. Struick ed. 1964), and M. SANDEL, LIBERALISM AND THE LIMITS OF JUSTICE (1984).

However, each vision represents only a partial and incomplete depiction of social life and its possibilities. Neither is reliable or realisable as an exclusive basis for social organisation. Oscillating between freedom *from* and freedom *through* dependence on others, one vision is the antithesis of the other. Yet there can be no synthesis for each is the consequence of the other and any attempt to expunge one serves ultimately to reinforce it: they are "partners as well as antagonists".[22] Individualism must depend upon some "nightwatchman State" to guarantee the conditions for effective individual achievement. Similarly, communitarianism must acknowledge some claims of individuals to their own tastes and preferences. Whereas one tends to libertarian anarchism, the other pushes to state totalitarianism. If individualism encourages indifference to others, communitarianism countenances intolerance of others. While both a pure atomism and holism are unworkable and indefensible, they provide the binary context for social decision-making. However, once the viability of the spectral extremes is denied, the slide into indeterminancy and *ad hockery* is ensured. Moreover, "the mock rationality of the debate conceals the arbitrariness of the will and power at work in its resolution."[23]

An actual example will clarify this argument. A persistent problem for administrative lawyers is to determine the circumstances in which an individual is entitled to an administrative hearing. Traditional legal scholars are obliged by their own jurisprudential premises to claim that there is some neutral calculus which generates a coherent and consistent doctrine of "hearings." But the actual practice repudiates the theory.[24] In extreme terms, there exists a stark choice between "no hearing" and a "full hearing." These options crudely reproduce the basic contradiction.[25] A "no hearing" doctrine pulls towards the communitarian pole with its

---

22 A. MACINTYRE, AFTER VIRTUE 33 (2d ed. 1985).

23 *Id.* at 66.

24 *See, e.g.,* Wade, *infra* note 117, at 439–451; Garner, *infra* note 118, at 139–144; and Evans, *infra* note 112, at 163–179. This analysis, of course, can be replicated throughout administrative law doctrine. An obvious example is the extent to which discretion can be exercised in line with a fixed policy or on a case-by-case basis. For a traditional review of this area, see Molot, 18 McGILL L.J. 310 (1972) and Galligan, [1976] P.L. 332, 346–355.

25 Paradoxically, in contemporary society and its political practices, the communitarian-minded might well prefer the apparently individualistic position. In reality, the "communal" decision may well be exercised for the benefit of certain individual interests; see *supra,* p. 120. It has to be remembered that the communitarian vision is an *ideal* and assumes that "communal" decisions are made by a sincere and *representative* administrative agency. This is not the case today.

implicit assumptions that the public good outweighs individual interests and that decisions are best made in terms of community solidarity. A "full hearing" doctrine, while accepting that the public good might be preferred over individual rights, maintains that individuals ought to be given the fullest opportunity to defend and argue their own individual claims. Insofar as traditional legal thought is premised on the necessary and realisable reconciliation of the competing interest of individuals and community, it would be the negation of its very *raison d'etre* to opt completely for either extreme. Doctrine vacillates. Neither legal logicians nor policy analysts can provide objective guidance as to where doctrine ought to position itself along the continuum.

While the dominant principle in contemporary doctrine favours a "full hearing,"[26] there exists a counter-principle which concedes that "no hearing" is justified in certain circumstances.[27] However, once a valid communitarian component is admitted, it must be arbitrarily held in check or else it will consume the whole doctrine. At any time, the discrete legal pieces could be rearranged into a completely different doctrinal jigsaw. Determinacy is contrived, superficial and ephemeral. The still waters of legal doctrine run deep and dangerous. The apparent calm is continuously being disturbed. So much so that surface determinacy must give way to deep indeterminacy. Ever present, the doctrinal struggle most clearly manifests itself in "instances of exemplary difficulty"[28], recalcitrant cases where the tension between contradictory forces and its previous suppression become so volatile that the temporary calm of doctrine is shattered.

C. SUBSTANCE AND SYMBOL

It is often said that Britain has become a socialist state. As early as 1905, Dicey opined that the years from 1865 to 1900 were a "period of collectivism".[29] While it is true that Britain has added the trappings of a welfare state, society remains founded upon the individualistic institu-

---

26 *See Breen* v. *Amalgamated Engineering Union*, [1971] 1 All E.R. 1148.

27 *See McInnes* v. *Onslow Fane*, [1978] 1 W.L.R. 1520. *See also* de Smith, *infra*, note 37, at 179.

28 Unger, *supra* note 14, at 633–634.

29 Dicey, *supra* note 21, at 64. Later he conceded that the delegation of power was "inevitable," but "such a transference of authority saps the foundation of [the] rule of law"; see *The Development of Administrative Law in England*, 31 L.Q.R. 148, 150 (1915).

tions of private property and private enterprise. Notwithstanding the demise of laissez-faire capitalism, British society is dominated by the commitment to industrial profitability.[30] There is a large public sector, subject to governmental regulation, but the vast amount of wealth and power is still wielded by private interests. In retrospect, the move from a market economy toward a more mixed economy occurred to avert crisis and to enable the continued expansion of private capital accumulation.[31] The governmental apparatus has fallen captive to large-scale business corporations which are, in turn, controlled by a small coterie of privileged individuals. The creation of a large public sector has facilitated the concentration of economic power as much as its redistribution. While benefiting many, the welfare state has acted as a prop for beleaguered private centres of economic and political domination; it is premised on a continuing belief in the justice and efficacy of a market economy as long as everyone can have access. Any loss in autonomy is considered to be adequately compensated for by greater material gains. Moreover, the expansion of the regulatory state has served to divert attention away from the private sector. It has enabled "the citadels of private power [to remain] insulated from the risks of party-political conflict."[32]

Although Parliament has been the builder of the regulatory state, the Executive has been the architect. Moreover, Parliament has sub-contracted out most of the work. There exists a mammoth administrative apparatus to implement, monitor and enforce the legion activities of government. Originally a creature of legislative enactment, the administrative process has taken on an institutional life of its own. This development has profoundly affected the balance and allocation of power within the British system of governance. Agencies and tribunals manage the nation's business in accordance with governmental policies, conceived by the Executive and rubber-stamped by an obedient Parliament. Few aspects of people's lives from before the cradle to beyond the coffin are unaffected by the state. Ostensibly, acting in the public good, the state is protector, dispenser of social services, industrial manager, economic controller and arbitrator.[33] Throughout the century, there has been a

---

30 *See* R. Miliband, The State in Capitalist Society: An Analysis of the Western System of Power (1969), and N. Poulantzas, State, Power, Socialism (1979).
31 *See* J. O'Connor, Fiscal Crisis of the State (1974), and T. Benn, Arguments for Democracy (1982).
32 Unger, *supra* note 14, at 589.
33 W. Friedmann, Law in a Changing Society 378–383 (1964).

marked shift in the governmental centre of gravity. Although private interest remains the life force, the public process of administration has become "the pulse of the modern legal order".[34] Administrators not only make far more law than legislators, but they resolve far more disputes than judges.

The legal process has played a major role in distorting this state of affairs. There is a marked discrepancy between the actual practice of the administrative process and the picture painted of it by legal doctrine. This ideological function of the law is of paramount importance.[35] Also, in responding to the establishment of the administrative process as the fulcrum of modern governmental power, the courts have been dually motivated. First, they have sought to reassert their own waning institutional power and to confirm their essential relevance to the control of allegedly illegitimate power. Some involvement with the burgeoning administrative activities of the state seemed appropriate. However, secondly, they have been very concerned to justify their own exercise of power and to adopt a stance that befits their perceived constitutional responsibilities. In short, they insist that "judicial review is concerned, not with a decision, but with the decision-making process."[36] Their achievement has been mixed. As an ideological exercise, they have been successful in persuading people of their constitutional propriety and effectiveness. As a matter of practical effect, they have been less successful.

D. THE RHETORIC OF JUDICIAL REVIEW

Although the contemporary history and development of judicial review is fascinating reading,[37] it is its present status and ambit that is more important. A doctrinal model of the objectives and limits of judicial review can be constructed from recent judicial statements. Relying on particular decisions in a sparing way, the model offered is a composite picture; much of the ideology is implicitly assumed rather than expressly stated. It must be emphasised that this model is not intended to be an account of what the courts do, but only of *what they say they do*.

---

34 Galligan, *Judicial Review and the Textbook Writers*, 2 OXF. J. OF LEG. ST. 257 at 258 (1982).

35 *See infra* pp. 121–123.

36 *Chief Constable of the North Wales Police* v. *Evans*, [1982] 2 All E.R. 141 at 180, per Lord Brightman.

37 *See* DE SMITH'S JUDICIAL REVIEW OF ADMINISTRATIVE ACTION 3–35 (4th ed., 1980, John Evans), and P. CRAIG, ADMINISTRATIVE LAW 57–88 (1983).

The doctrinal model of judicial review centres upon two important issues; the appropriate division and exercise of governmental power. Not surprisingly, the dominance of the individualistic vision is marked. Within society, people are assumed to be constantly at odds and band together to form a government. Compromise is considered preferable to the oppressive uncertainty of unrestrained struggle. The limited duty of the government is to enact a body of norms through which to regulate the social interaction of its atomistic citizens. To enforce, interpret and apply these norms, a judicial branch of government must be established.[38] However, problems of democratic legitimacy arise. This constitutional dilemma of decision-making is overcome by resort to the basic dichotomy between values and facts. Whereas values are considered personal, subjective and arbitrary, facts are taken to be homogeneous, objective and orderly. The legislature is presumed to operate in the unstable realm of values and has the responsibility to enact laws designed to achieve a substantively just compromise between competing values. However, once its decisions are translated into a set of rules, there is a clear shift from the realm of values to the domain of facts. The Machiavellian world is left behind and the constitutional Rubicon is crossed. Expressed as a rule, the legislative compromise of values is converted into fact and becomes amenable to scientific interpretation and application; "[t]he sovereignty of Parliament runs in tandem with the rule of objective law."[39]

In this way, the fundamental democratic demands of popular consensus, as sought in the legislative process, and technical rationality, as embodied in the judicial process, are claimed to be satisfied. Arguments of law and morality are rendered mutually exclusive and the neutral application of rules insulates judges from political controversy.[40] The compulsion to reason within a closed system of premises guarantees the enduring integrity of the constitutional compact. Within this constitutional scenario, administrative agencies only exist as the "executory amanuenses of the legislative will."[41] However, overwhelmed and overcommitted, the legislature must delegate massive authority to avoid a total paralysis of government. Inevitably, this delegation becomes an ab-

---

38 See *Duport Steel Ltd.* v. *Sirs*, [1980] 1 All E.R. 529 at 551, per Lord Scarman.
39 See *Black-Clawson International Ltd.* v. *Papierwerke Waldorf-Aschaffenburg A.G.*, [1975] A.C. 591 at 645, per Lord Simon.
40 See *supra* note 38.
41 Stewart, *The Reformation of American Adminstrative Law*, 88 HARV. L. REV. 1669 at 1706 (1975).

dication of power. Accordingly, the courts step in to take up the democratic slack. They perform a constraining function and act as the policing agents of the legislature. With suitable constitutional deference, judges resist the temptation to second-guess the exercise of administrative discretion.[42] It is a matter of formal process and not substantive decision. The courts act as frontier guards between the spheres of state action and citizen activity. As such, there exists "a fluctuating frontier war between the judges and the executive."[43] Legislators are the cartographers and legislative enactments are the boundary markers. Indeed, the ambit, if not the source, of the judicial policing power is also conferred and confined by legislation.

To guard against the temptation to establish themselves as independent power centres, judges claim to adjudicate disputes between the State and its citizens by the rigorous and faithful implementation of legislative intent. Neutrality and objectivity are preserved by casting statutory interpretation as an exercise in linguistic analysis. Judges search not for what the legislature intended, but the true meaning of the words used.[44] The legislative expression of the political compromise is treated as a certain fact whose proper application can and must be determinatively effected through an impersonal and apolitical set of interpretive techniques. Furthermore, it is presumed that, unless Parliament states to the contrary, administrative discretion is subject to the existing common law rules. The essential quality of their involvement is neatly captured by Lawton L.J. and Lord Bridge:

> In the United Kingdom . . . policy is determined by ministers within the legal framework set out by Parliament. Judges have nothing to do with either policy making or the carrying out of policy. Their function is to decide whether a minister has acted within the powers given him by statute or the common law. If he is declared by a court, after due process of law, to have acted outside his powers, he must stop doing what he has done until Parliament gives him the powers he wants. In a case such as this, I regard myself as a referee. I can blow my judicial whistle when the ball goes out of play; but when the game restarts I must neither take part in it nor tell the players how to play.[45]
>
> It ought not to need emphasis that the appeal has nothing whatever to do with

---

42 *See* Lord Hailsham, *Evans, supra* note 36, at 1158–1161.
43 Lord Scarman, *Public Administration and The Courts*, 57 PUBL. ADM. 1 at 2 (1979). *See also*, *R. v. Boundary Commission for England; Ex parte Gateshead Borough Council and others*, [1983] 1 All E.R. 1099, per Lord Donaldson.
44 *Supra* note 39 at 613, per Lord Reid.
45 *Laker Airways Ltd. v. Department of Trade*, [1977] 2 W.L.R. 235 at 267.

the political wisdom or unwisdom, propriety or impropriety of the decisions impugned. The respondents have throughout disclaimed any intention to challenge the decisions as being "unreasonable" in the *Wednesbury* sense. Even such a challenge does not, on a proper understanding, involve the courts in making any political decision. But we are still further removed from the political arena when, as in the instant case, the decision turns exclusively on the interpretation of statutes. The GLC was created by statute, has been abolished by statute and throughout its life had no power to act otherwise than as authorised by statute. The only questions arising in this appeal are whether the several proposed grants were grants which any Act of Parliament authorised the GLC to make.[46]

In this way, the judges claim to underwrite their constitutional power, transcend vulgar political debate and still make a valid contribution to the continued efficacy of the basic compact between the State and its citizens. Importantly, they claim to do so within the bounds of constitutional propriety. Yet, the rhetoric of judicial review is not substantiated by its performance. The judicial achievement falls hopelessly short of its ambition. Indeed, the ambition is futile. With the best will, the promise could not be performed. It is the burden of the next section to support these claims.

II. The Administrative Process and the Courts

A. The Ideology of Statutory Interpretation

In performing its self-acclaimed role as a constitutional police force, the judiciary promotes an image of impartial obedience and servitude, faithfully adopting a deferential posture to the will of Parliament. Indeed, the cornerstone of administrative law has been the notion of *ultra vires*. The judicial task is intended to exhaust itself in ensuring that the administrative process operates within the legislatively ordained parameters of permissible conduct. Although not the exclusive device of containment, administrative law is primarily a matter of statutory interpretation. Accordingly, this section will demonstrate that statutory interpretation is not a technical and objective activity, but is inescapably creative and political. Although this characteristic can be disguised or obscured, it can never be side-stepped nor eradicated. Moreover, the indeterminancy of those politics will be constantly revealed.

---

46 *Westminster C.C.* v. *G.L.C.*, [1986] 2 All E.R. 278 at 281.

In subtle and revealing contrast to their defence of judicial review as constitutionally-mandated posture of deference to the legislature, the courts' justification of their techniques of statutory interpretation is premised on a marked scepticism toward legislative wisdom. Indeed, the judicial struggle to enforce or enfeeble statutes is at the heart of the legal process; the tension between the common law and statute has energised constitutional law. Within the doctrinal canon, the common law is portrayed as a vast and intricate landscape, carved out with enduring patience over time. Statutes are treated as unsightly man-made structures that disturb the natural beauty and harmony of the common law. The need for legislative intervention is begrudgingly acknowledged, but never fully accepted. Whereas legislation is identified as a temporary structure for accommodating transient economic and political interest groups, the common law is presented as the embodiment of impartial rationality. Its life force is not cold logic, but a living experience that has been cultivated in the greenhouses of constitutional history. That history has consisted of a continual, shifting conflict between King and Commons, Parliament and Privy Council, statute and prerogative order, and legislature and executive. Law is considered older and more venerable than legislation: it represents a taught tradition of ideals and principles into which legislation intrudes.[47] In short, Pollock's characterization of this judicial attitude remains pertinent today: "Parliament generally changes the law for the worse and the business of the judges is to keep the mischief of its interference within the narrowest possible bounds."[48]

The problems with this stance are many. Against the more general challenge to the simplistic linguistic assumptions and operational practices that underlie and constitute contemporary lawyering,[49] there are more traditional objections. The "naturalistic" attitude begs the basic issue by assuming that statutory enactments appear as temporary blights on the legal landscape, but never become part of that landscape. It insists that legislative intrusions can be filtered out to leave a full and life-like

---

47 *See* Pound, *Common Law and Legislation* (1908), 21 HARV. L. REV. 385, and Hayek, *supra* note 21. These ideas are explored further in Hutchinson and Morgan, *The Semiology of Statutes*, 21 HARV. J. ON LEGIS. 583 (1984).

48 F. POLLOCK, ESSAYS IN JURISPRUDENCE AND ETHICS 85 (1882). Good examples of this attitude can be found in the writings of P. DEVLIN, THE JUDGE 14 (1979), and LORD SCARMAN, ENGLISH LAW—THE NEW DIMENSION 3 (1974). Also, a similar shadow hangs over the work of modern formalists like Richard Posner and Ronald Dworkin. See *supra* note 16.

49 See *supra* chapter 5.

picture of the common law. Beneath the concrete pathways of legislation, there is still said to thrive the natural countryside of the common law. Yet this picture resides only in the lawyer's nostalgic mind. For at least a century, we have lived in the Age of Statutes.[50] To believe anything less is indefensible and exposes the reactionary values that motivate such beliefs. So long as the courts cast themselves as the apparent dumb sideshow on the political stage, the inevitable ideological nature of the meaning-giving enterprise means that they run the risk of being as duplicitous as those villains they regularly condemn and disavow.

Although the courts insist that statutory interpretation can be effected apolitically, they nonetheless claim that the power to interpret statutes is pivotal. It is the courts' construction of legislative words and not the words themselves that is law. Not only is the extent of that power extremely limited, but the claimed existence of such a power sits uneasily with their presentation of statutory interpretation as a technical exercise in linguistic analysis. Whichever one of the great triumvirate of approaches, "literal", "golden" or "mischief", is used or whether a more general purposive approach is adopted,[51] the courts "are seeking not what Parliament meant but the true meaning of what they said."[52] By drawing a marked distinction between the legislative and the interpretive function, the courts hope to legitimate their power. But this is little more than a constitutional pose. At a general level, it can be observed that words do not interpret themselves and that the analysis of language is not a value-free exercise; the creation and interpretation of meaning are not distinct. Discourse is a prism through which the meanings of words

---

50 *See* Hutchinson and Morgan, *Calabresian Sunset: Statutes in the Shade*, 82 COLUM. L. REV. 1752, 1753–1756 (1982).

51 There is no settled group of methodological principles used, but simply a plethora of judicial dicta of varying weight, age and uniformity; *see* W. TWINING AND D. MIERS, HOW TO DO THINGS WITH RULES 334 (2d ed. 1982), and R. CROSS, STATUTORY INTERPRETATION 42 (1976). Nonetheless, many basic textbooks devote considerable space to the elaboration of the famous triumvirate of Literal, Golden and Mischief Rules, along with a series of presumptions and canons of construction; *see* WALKER AND WALKER, THE ENGLISH LEGAL SYSTEM 99–122 (5th ed. 1980). However, some writers now argue that the great triumvirate have coalesced into a general "purposive" approach; *see* D. LLOYD, INTRODUCTION TO JURISPRUDENCE 865 (4th ed. 1979), and E. DRIEDGER, THE CONSTRUCTION OF STATUTES 67 (1974). Yet, despite the apparent liberalisation, this purpose is, according to conventional wisdom, to be gleaned from the words of the statute. A particularly trenchant statement of judicial practice is made by Lord Salmon in *Johnson* v. *Moreton*, [1980] A.C. 37 at 50.

52 *Duport Steel Ltd., supra*, note 38, at 613, per Lord Reid.

are refracted in many colours and hues. Yet the prism is not natural nor fixed; it is manufactured and held in place by political actors and forces.

For instance, the courts' handling of so-called "gaps" in a statutory scheme is contradictory and inconsistent.[53] Taking a strict stance, the court will treat the statutory text as exhaustive and strike out a claim as revealing no legal cause of action. In so doing, the court will have flouted reality by acknowledging that it cannot generate a solution to the inevitable batch of "unforeseen" cases. Further, if a liberal stance is taken, the court will recognise the existence of a "gap" and seek to fill the legislative silence. To do this, the court will have to resort to considerations extraneous to the text of the statute. Moreover, the initial recognition of a gap is premised on the assumption that the statutory text is not an exhaustive expression of the sovereign will of parliament. Adopting either a strict or liberal position, the traditional approach is incomplete and inconsistent.[54]

B. THE JUDICIAL OUSTER OF PRIVATIVE CLAUSES

The transparency and duplicity of statutory interpretation is vividly revealed in the judicial handling of privative clauses. The rationale for judicial review is said to be the constitutional and democratic need to regulate and resist the monopolisation and arbitrariness of State power. Yet there is discernible within the cases a less subtle and less commendable sub-plot. In checking bureaucratic power, the courts have extended their own constitutional power. This self-aggrandising tendency is revealed in their interpretative handling of "ouster clauses". According to judicial rhetoric, the courts are the willing servants of the legislative master.[55] With Tennyson's *Light Brigade*, the judiciary proudly proclaim that

---

53 The established view of the handling of the so-called *casus omissus* is that "if a gap is disclosed, the remedy lies in an amending Act." To do otherwise would amount to "a naked usurpation of the legislative function under the thin disguise of interpretation"; see *Magor and St. Mellons Rural District Council* v. *Newport Corporation*, [1952] A.C. 189 at 191. Although stated in less extravagant terms, the House of Lords has recently reaffirmed this conviction; see *James Buchanan & Co. Ltd.* v. *Babco Forwarding and Shipping (U.K.) Ltd.*, [1978] A.C. 141; and *Nothman* v. *London Borough of Barnet*, [1979] 1 All E.R. 142. Nonetheless, the courts have been prepared to assume the authority to fill gaps in several cases; see, *e.g.*, *Williams* v. *Williams*, [1979] P. 271.

54 *See generally,* Stewart and Sunstein, *Public Programs and Private Rights*, 95 HARV. L. REV. 1195 at 1229–1231 (1982).

55 For a selection of private clauses and their treatment by the courts, see de Smith, *supra* note 37, at 357–376, and Garner, *infra* note 118, at 175–192.

"ours is not to reason why, ours is but to do and die." Consequently, provided it expresses itself clearly, the legislature is reasonably entitled to expect that the judges will respect its wish to have them stay off the administrative turf. The courts have confounded such expectations. Indeed, they have launched a counter-offensive. The privative clause is to legislative-judicial relations

> what the Maginot Line was to military tactics: a virtually impregnable legislative project of defence, designed to protect the [adminstrative process] from frontal assault. And now it has suffered the same fate. It has been outflanked by a judicial panzer attack, a virtual constitutional blitzkrieg.[56]

As a general observation, the courts have construed preclusive provisions so as to limit, rather than debar, judicial involvement in the control of administrative action. While feigning deference to legislative intent, the courts' power to review on jurisdictional grounds remains intact in spite of repeated legislative protestations and no matter how sweeping or encyclopedic the clause. It is characterised as "a straightforward problem of statutory interpretation."[57] In the acclaimed decision of *Anisminic*,[58] the House of Lords held that a statutory provision that "the determination by the [Foreign Compensation] commission of any application made to them . . . shall not be called in question in any court of law" did not oust the supervisory jurisdiction of the courts. The courts have managed to achieve such "straightforward" interpretations by the familiar device of interpretative presumptions. The basic force of this position is that any *error* of law puts the tribunal outside its jurisdiction and places it within the supervisory jurisdiction of the courts. Although Lord Diplock concedes that Parliament can deprive the courts of all power, the present judicial disposition to privative clauses makes that merely a theoretical rather than a practical possibility.[59]

---

56 H.W. Arthurs, Protection Against Judicial Review (unpublished, 1982). The enactment of the Tribunals and Inquiries Act 1957 is often cited as providing legislative endorsement for this restrictive interpretation. Apart from giving approval to the adoption of vague generalities like fairness, impartiality and openness in administrative adjudication, it expressly nullified privative clauses in almost all statutes extant in 1957. Yet, surely, this decision to wipe the slate clean supports the view that henceforth any privative clause enacted by Parliament was to be taken very seriously and given full effect. For a forceful and cogent critique of the Franks Report, see Griffith, *Tribunals and Inquiries*, 22 M.L.R. 125 (1959).
57 *Re Racal Communications*, [1980] 2 All E.R. 634 at 646, per Lord Scarman.
58 [1969] 2 A.C. 147.
59 *See Racal, supra* note 57, at 638–639, per Lord Diplock. Indeed, Craig goes so far as to say Parliament is "powerless"; *supra* note 37, at 524.

This disingenuousness undermines the whole constitutional compact which the courts claim to uphold and enforce. By adhering to a linguistic approach to statutory interpretation and hedging it with defensive presumptions, the courts manage to constrain and dictate the terms of Parliament's legislative competence. They impose a constitutional and linguistic strait-jacket on the legislature. The message from the judges to the legislators rings loud and clear—"Use a particular verbal formula if you want us to even consider implementing your decisions. Even then, nothing is guaranteed. Otherwise, you run the risk of having a different set of legal consequences occur than you bargained for." Accordingly, the general approach to statutory interpretation, especially when applied to privative clauses, severely confines and often subverts the wishes of Parliament. The rhetoric may be of constitutional partners, but the reality is of constitutional competitors. While pretending to be a bulwark against the usurpation of political power, the judicial process usurps the legislative function. The ghost of Lord Coke is alive and well; it stalks and haunts the corridors of legislative and administrative power.

C. THE POLITICS OF JUDICIAL POLICING

The recent fiasco over the Greater London Council's "Fares Fair" scheme emphasises the creative dimension of statutory interpretation.[60] Under the harsh glare of media-fuelled public interest, the rhetoric of judicial review was represented and indicted in microcosm. It was an ironic version of judicial trial by political ordeal. The facts are too notorious to warrant detailed repetition. After a successful election campaign, the Labour-controlled G.L.C. instructed the London Transport Executive (L.T.E.) to reduce bus and tube fares by 25 per cent. The cost was to be financed by a supplementary levy on the ratepayers. As a result of the new fares scheme, the Government reduced its block grant to the G.L.C. This effectively doubled the cost of the reduction in fares and a supplementary rate precept was issued to all 32 London boroughs. Bromley L.B.C. sought to quash the imposition of the supplementary rate and restrain the G.L.C. from continuing with the new fares scheme. Although the Divisional Court rejected Bromley L.B.C.'s application on the ground that the G.L.C.'s action lay at the margin of what is permissible, the Court of Appeal found for Bromley L.B.C. and held the pre-

---

60 *See Bromley L.B.C.* v. *Greater London Council*, [1982] 2 W.L.R. 62. For a rhetorical analysis of this case, see Goodrich, *Law and Language*, 11 J. OF LAW & SOC'Y 173 at 191–200 (1984).

cept to be null and void. In a unanimous decision, the House of Lords upheld the decision of the Court of Appeal. The thrust of the courts' decisions was that the Transport (London) Act 1969 did not empower the G.L.C. to finance a reduction in fares by a supplementary precept. Although the G.L.C. had broad policy and grant-making power over the L.T.E., it was under a duty to promote the provision of integrated, efficient and economic transport services for Greater London.

For the House of Lords, the central issue was legality: was the decision of the G.L.C. within the limited powers that the statute had conferred upon it? This question of *ultra vires* could be disposed of by ascertaining the "proper",[61] "true",[62] or "correct"[63] meaning of "economic". Although the court conceded that the Act was drafted in "opaque and elliptical language", evidenced "a lack of clarity",[64] was "vague, possibly with design"[65] and, in particular, that the term "economic" was "chameleon-like",[66] the Law Lords sought to attach a precise meaning to "economic". Moreover, the interpretative process was to be "looked at objectively".[67] For instance, Lords Wilberforce and Diplock recognised that the subsidisation of public transport from public funds and its treatment as a social service raised grave and important issues of transport policy, but remained adamant that it was "a matter of political controversy . . . [which the court] must scrupulously refrain from entering."[68] In their own terms, the Law Lords were insufficiently scrupulous. To ignore the debate over whether transport is a social service supports the view that it is not a social service. There is no neutral ground. Moreover, failure to inquire into Parliament's contribution to the debate casts an even greater air of unreality over the attempt at statutory interpretation. Although not conclusive of legislative intent,[69] Richard Marsh, then Minister of Transport, in moving the second reading of the Bill, gave a strong indication of Parliament's stance on the G.L.C.'s policy and grant-making power:

---

61 *Id.* at 109, per Lord Keith.
62 *Id.* at 114, 117, 120, per Lord Scarman, and 108, per Lord Diplock.
63 *Id.* at 127 and 128, per Lord Brandon.
64 *Id.* at 101, per Lord Diplock.
65 *Id.* at 94, per Lord Wilberforce.
66 *Id.* at 118, per Lord Scarman.
67 *Id.* at 100, per Lord Diplock.
68 *Id.* at 97, per Lord Wilberforce, and also 196, per Lord Diplock.
69 The difficulties of discovering legislative intent have been thoroughly documented; see Dickerson, *Statutory Interpretation: A Peek into the Mind of a Legislator*, 50 IND. L.J. 206 (1975).

> This is very important, because if the Council wishes the executive to do some-
> thing that will cause it to fall short of its financial targets, it will itself have to
> take financial responsibility for it. The Council might wish, for example, the
> executive to run a series of services at a loss for social or planning reasons. It
> might wish to keep fares down at a time when costs are rising and there is no
> scope for economies. It is free to do so. But it has to bear the cost.[70]

Rather than face the issue of transport policy squarely and openly, the Law Lords decided that "the only *safe* course is to try to understand the contemporary language."[71] In so doing, they concluded that the "economic" restraint on the G.L.C. meant that it must act in accordance with ordinary business principles; transport was to be run as a cost-effective business enterprise.[72] While transport need not operate at a profit, it did demand that the G.L.C. must seek to avoid loss and, certainly, not adopt a policy of loss-making. Lord Scarman left no room for doubt when he said that the "reduction was adopted not because any higher fare level was impracticable but as an object of social and transport policy. It was not a reluctant yielding to *economic necessity*, but a policy preference. In so doing, the G.L.C. abandoned business principles. That was . . . wrong in law."[73] By placing such a limited definition on "economic", the House was not only delivering a slap in the face to local democracy, but was confirming a very clear vision of society. The decision represents a clear political preference in favour of the ethic of private enterprise over that of collective consumption.[74] Yet, for present purposes, the existence of choice is more important than the nature of the choice made.

The meaning of "economic necessity" is far from self-evident. Indeed, it is ludicrous to suggest that it has *one* "true" or "correct" meaning. Necessity is a dubious concept at best and, when qualified by "economic", becomes vacuous, "nonsense on stilts".[75] There is a vast literature on the "economic" operation of public services and nationalised industries. Whether such organisations should seek to break

---

70 H.C. Deb., Vol. 775, col. 1247. For a succinct history of the Act, see (1983), 99 L.Q.R. 605 at 615–630.
71 *Supra* note 60, at 97, per Lord Wilberforce (emphasis added).
72 *Id.* at 95–96, per Lord Wilberforce, 110–111, per Lord Keith, 119–121, per Lord Scarman, and 127–129, per Lord Brandon.
73 *Id.* at 123, per Lord Scarman.
74 *See* M. CASTELLS, THE URBAN QUESTION 454–462 (1977), and P. DUNLEAVY, URBAN POLITICAL ANALYSIS 42–52 (1980).
75 Bentham, *Anarchical Fallacies* in THE WORKS OF JEREMY BENTHAM 501 (J. Bowring ed. 1843).

even, maximise profit, price discriminate, marginal cost price or whatever is moot. At its broadest, "economic" can refer to any decision that concerns the distribution or allocation of resources. In a narrow sense, it can be argued that, as it is not politically or logistically feasible to charge private road users a realistic cost for the congestion they cause, subsidised public transport is the next best "economic" policy to reduce congestion and its costs.[76] Also, the extent of the subsidisation by G.L.C. is very low when compared to the annual investment by other municipalities in their transportation network.[77] Accordingly, the decision to construe "economic" as meaning "commercially viable" is by no means inevitable or rationally necessary. Moreover, even if it was conceded to be the relevant standard, nothing necessarily flows from that in evaluating any particular situation.[78] It represents a choice. It does not flow inextricably from the words of the statute, but demands a judicial interlocutor. The interpretative process is not mechanical or objective, but creative and normative.

Before examining the determinants of that judicial choice, there is a more subtle and, in a sense, more profound objection to the practice of judicial review and statutory interpretation generally. Under the traditional model, individual interests and preferences are in constant flux. Therefore, parliamentary rule-making occurs under conditions of uncertainty; a statutory enactment is based on a series of probabilistic assessments about its impact which in turn depends upon its interaction with other rules of law and their application to factual situations. Yet, by definition, although the legal element in this projected scenario will remain fixed, the non-legal elements will be continually changing. In such volatile circumstances, it will be extremely difficult to arrive at *any* just compromise of conflicting interests, however temporary or makeshift. The task of striking a just compromise effective over time will be practically

---

76 *See* J. Buchanan, Traffic in Towns (1963); C. Sharp, Transport Economics (1973); A. Grey, Urban Fares Policy (1975); and C.A. Nash, Economics of Public Transport (1982).

77 For instance, G.L.C.'s investment of £93M represents about 15% of the annual investment by New York on the city's subway system. Indeed, the Americans seem to accept that public transport is a social and community responsibility; see U.S. Dept. of Transportation, A Study of Urban Mass Transportation Needs and Financing (1974). For a general view, see Morris, *Should We Subsidize Public Transport?*, 54 Pol. Q. 392 (1983).

78 *See* Kennedy, *Cost-Benefit Analysis of Entitlement Problems: A Critique*, 33 Stan L. Rev. 387 (1981), and Heller, *Is the Charitable Exemption from Property Taxation An Easy Case? General Concerns About Legal Economics and Jurisprudence* in Essays on the Law and Economics of Local Governments 183 (D. Rubinfeld ed. 1979).

and theoretically impossible. Further, this unpredictable interplay of facts and values will not only inhibit the implementation of the original compromise, but will inadvertently bring into play a whole new group of generative forces which will support an entirely different and "unconsented to" compromise. This means that the judges create, through their decisions in particular cases, "the situation from which will emerge an as yet indeterminate constellation of legal forces."[79]

In this way, judges contribute to the future enactments of Parliament. Their decisions will have a redistributive impact likely to be different to that intended by Parliament and these will influence the political struggle whose institutional venue is, of course, Parliament. This is exactly what happened in the aftermath of the *Bromley* case. Although the decision favoured its position and policies, the Government has removed future doubt and successfully introduced a new Transport Act which imposes stringent controls on locally subsidised public transport.[80] Consequently, as a contributor to legislative resources and a creator of the private interests which effectively constrain and dictate the legislative pronouncements of Parliament, judges cannot treat statutes "as an external objective factor validating whatever [they] may choose to do".[81] Judges are political actors and must justify their contribution to the legal process rather than rely on their activities being justified by it. As such, judges shoulder the heavy burden of political responsibility.

D. THE SOCIAL VISIONS OF JUDICIAL REVIEW

The law of judicial review is one doctrinal venue for the struggle over the terms and conditions of social life. Doctrinal principles are little more than historic plots on the legal graph which describe the contingent resolution of the dialectical tension between competing social visions. However, individual decisions are selective and amount to only fragmentary snatches of a more organic vision of social life. In any particular case, the outcome may be confused or uncertain and it will often be

---

79 Kennedy, *Legal Formality*, 2 J. LEGAL STUD. 351, 385 (1973).
80 The Transport Act 1983 repeals ss. 7 and 11 and replaces them with a provision that imposes a common and simplified version of the financial duty: "2(1) An Executive shall so perform their functions as to ensure so far as practicable that the combined revenues of the Executive and any subsidiaries of theirs for any accounting period are not less than sufficient to meet their combined charges property chargeable to revenue account in that period." For a discussion of the changes, see Loughlin, *Public Transport Subsidy, Local Government and the Courts*, 132 N.L.J. 283 (1983).
81 *Supra* note 79, at 386.

difficult to estimate which social vision has prevailed. In others, the decision may clearly represent the victory of one vision over another. Yet, over the long or medium haul, there will exist competing trends and conflicting themes. In the shifting sands of legal doctrine, pockets of stability appear, but they are quickly disrupted by the swirling winds of litigation. Again, G.L.C.'s "Fares Fair" scheme offers a clear glimpse of this doctrinal indeterminacy. Few argue that *Bromley* was not a political decision.[82] Moreover, it can be easily exposed as a blatant attempt to frustrate the socialist ambitions of an elected local authority. Harold Laski's observation over 50 years ago in the wake of *Roberts v. Hopwood*[83] remains painfully pertinent:

> The test of reasonableness is, of course, one that it is seldom easy to apply in a court of law. For . . . it tempts the judge to believe that he is simply finding the law when in fact he is really testing and rejecting other men's views by the light of his own. . . . The [G.L.C.] is a body of persons chosen to carry out certain functions, and each way, ultimately, expresses a philosophy of life. . . . The [G.L.C.'s] theory of what is "reasonable" in the exercise of discretion is, even though affirmed by its constituents, seemingly inadmissible if it does not square with the economic preconceptions of the House of Lords . . . [The judges] are in the exercise of their functions, enacting into law a system of social philosophy; it is inevitable, accordingly, that they should be judged by the social philosophy they enact. . . . It is an easy step from the [*Bromley*] judgment to the conclusion that the House of Lords is, in entire good faith, the unconscious servant of a single class in the community.[84]

The self-imposed task for the court was to determine whether the actions of the G.L.C. were "reasonable".[85] Although the House of Lords

---

82 But see Kerr L.J., *infra*, note 87. He argues forcefully that any suggestion that the House of Lords' decision was politically motivated was "total rubbish."
83 [1925] A.C. 578.
84 H. Laski, Studies in Law And Politics 208–221 (1932).
85 See *Associated Provincial Picture Houses* v. *Wednesbury Corporation*, [1948] 1 K.B. 223 at 229–230, per Lord Greene. It is worth quoting Lord Greene in full because the intended narrowness of this inquiry highlights the interpreted width of the test applied in *Bromley*:

> It is true the discretion must be exercised reasonably. Now what does that mean? Lawyers familiar with the phraseology commonly used in relation to exercise of statutory discretions often use the word "unreasonable" in a rather comprehensive sense. It has frequently been used and is frequently used as a general description of the things that must be done. For instance, a person entrusted with a discretion must, so to speak, direct himself properly in law. He must call his own attention to the matters which he is bound to consider. He must exclude from his consideration matters which are irrelevant to what he has to consider. If he does not obey these rules, he may truly be said, and

sought to balance the interests of ratepayers and transport users, its reliance on a purely formal analytic ignored their substantive inequalities.
The House argued that, as they represented 40 per cent of the electorate
and provided the major source of G.L.C. rates revenue, the interests of
ratepayers acted as a legitimate check on G.L.C. programmes.
Moreover, as most of the transport users were not ratepayers, G.L.C.
had failed to give sufficient prominence to the ratepayers' interests. On
a head-counting basis, the House's conclusion seems sound and even defensible. However, it assumes, without inquiry, that all ratepayers are
conservative; that they do not want their money spent on public transport and that less rates is *always* better than more rates. Moreover, the
decision to attribute electors, ratepayers and transport users with equal
formal status is a choice and not a given. It is part of the legal order and
not the natural order of things. As over 60 per cent of the rates are collected from commercial sources, the interests of corporate entities are
given equal or greater weight than the electoral or travelling public. Accordingly, in the same way that G.L.C. made a choice to prefer transport
users over commercial interests, *Bromley* represents a contrary preference. Indeed, as entry to the class of ratepayers is based exclusively on
ownership of private property, the decision clearly favours the advantaged members of society over the less advantaged. In visionary terms,
Bromley signifies a famous success for the supporters of individualism
with its emphasis on free enterprise.

For many, *Bromley* offers cogent evidence for the ideological bias of
judicial review.[86] Not only does it undermine any lingering claims about
judicial neutrality, but it is brandished as incontrovertible proof of their

---

often is said, to be acting "unreasonably". Similarly, there may be something
so absurd that no sensible person could ever dream that it lay within the powers of the authority. Warrington L.J. in *Short* v. *Poole Corporation* gave the
example of the red-haired teacher, dismissed because she had red hair. That
is unreasonable in one sense. In another sense it is taking into consideration
extraneous matters. It is so unreasonable that it might almost be described as
being done in bad faith; and, in fact, all these things run into one another.
He also went on to say: It is true to say that, if a decision on a competent
matter is so unreasonable that no reasonable authority could ever have come
to it then the courts can interfere.
Would this mean that, if all authorities followed the G.L.C. example on fares, they
would all be acting unreasonably (i.e., all authorities are unreasonable)?

86 *See, e.g.*, Griffiths, *Fares Fair or Fiduciary Foul?*, [1982] CAMB. L.J. 216; Note, 98
L.Q.R. 177 (1982); and Griffith, *The Law Lords and the G.L.C.*, Marxism Today,
February 1982, p. 29.

reactionary politics. Yet, such rejoicing or mourning is premature. No sooner had the dust been kicked up, let alone settled, than along came another gust of litigation.[87] Undeterred by its setback in *Bromley*, G.L.C. resolved to put into operation an alternative plan. It directed L.T.E. to reduce fares by 25 per cent; the 17 per cent increase in the deficit on L.T.E.'s revenue account was to be made good by a grant from G.L.C. Naturally, L.T.E. doubted the legality of this, so G.L.C. sought various declarations from the Divisional Court to validate its proposed scheme. While strenuously claiming to uphold and follow *Bromley*, the court held that the "new" scheme was lawful. This *volte-face* came as much of a shock to G.L.C., albeit a pleasant one, as to the legal establishment. The attempt to weave the two decisions, *both* explicitly based on a *true* construction of the 1969 Act, into the conceptual or ideological fabric will surely test the ingenuity and dexterity of the most gifted legal scholar or judge.

The central thrust of the Divisional Court's judgment in *Ex parte G.L.C.* seems to be that, whereas, in *Bromley*, G.L.C. has arbitrarily proceeded to put their election promise into effect, the alternative plan had been arrived at after an informed and considered balancing of the transport users' and ratepayers' interests. Although the 1969 Act can reasonably bear such an interpretation, the decision attaches an extremely generous meaning to *Bromley*. For most commentators, the ratio of *Bromley* is found in its "breakeven" and "commercially viable" requirements.[88] Indeed, the Law Lords expressly refer to the actual policy decision and not just the process of decision-making as being unreasonable. In the light of such comparisons, the indeterminacy of legal doctrine seems manifest. If *Bromley* marks a success for individualism, *Ex parte G.L.C.* scores an equally famous victory for communitarianism or, at least, for the forces of anti-individualism. It seeks to promote the interests of the public at large over discrete segments of it. Moreover, it shows that the dust of visionary conflict never settles. It is constantly blown around by the cross-currents of social struggle.

An equally compelling illustration of the doctrinal indeterminacy of judicial review is *Tameside*,[89] another politically high profile decision.

---

87 *See R. v. London Transport Executive; Ex parte Greater London Council*, [1983] 2 All E.R. 262.
88 *See, e.g.*, Comment, 146 Loc. Govt. Rev. 37 (1982), Bull, 13 Vict. U. of Well. L. Rev. 193 (1983), and Note, 98 L.Q.R. 177 (1983).
89 [1976] 3 W.L.R. 641.

Satisfied that he was acting unreasonably, the Secretary of the State sought an order of mandamus to force implementation of a comprehensive school system, earlier approved by him, but later postponed by the local authority. The House of Lords held that his opinion of reasonableness was insufficient *per se* to justify intervention; there must be a sufficient factual basis for him to decide that no reasonable authority would postpone such plans. For many, the decision was another thinly disguised attempt to maintain the status quo and frustrate efforts to introduce an educational system based on a more egalitarian model. Yet, less than a year later, the Court of Appeal reached an entirely contrary result. In *Smith*[90] the local authority sought to change the grammar schools into comprehensives. A group of parents at one grammar school sought to restrain the move. They obtained an interlocutory injunction from Megarry V.-C., but it was discharged on appeal. The local authority had not misused their power, which they exercised in an informed and considered way. In such matters, the court held that it was fitting that the interests of the whole community prevail over the views of a discrete group of individuals.[91]

Clearly, the two decisions pull in opposite directions; each tacitly sanctions a different scheme of arrangements. Although each case involved a separate statutory provision,[92] both cases were disposed of on the basis of the "reasonable" exercise of discretion. This standard is sufficiently broad to embrace a wide range of applications. Such a reconciliation of *Tameside* and *Smith* must concede the political nature of the judicial task. Also, the argument that the courts simply protected the prevailing political preferences, as expressed in the local democratic process, against private or governmental interference is extremely difficult to sustain in light of the views stated in *Bromley* on the marginal weight to be given to electoral preferences.[93] Indeed, the conflicting views over the impact of local elections on an authority's activities gives further support to the "indeterminacy thesis."

---

90 [1978] 1 All E.R. 411. *See also North Yorkshire County Council* v. *Secretary of State for Education and Science*, The Times, October 20, 1978.

91 *Id.* at 422, per Browne L.J.

92 Whereas *Tameside* concerned s. 68 of the Education Act 1944 which empowered the Secretary of State to intervene if a local education authority acted "unreasonably," *Smith* involved s. 8(1) of the same Act which obliged the local education authority to provide sufficient schools "in number, character and equipment."

93 *See supra* note 60, at 107–109, per Lord Diplock, and 129, per Lord Brandon. *See also Norwich C.C.* v. *Secretary of State for the Environment*, [1982] 1 All E.R. 737.

Finally, one more illustration can be drawn from the field of immigration law. It remains a sad, but undeniable fact that, except in times of economic expansion, immigrants have not been the favoured children of the politico-economic establishment. It is startling, therefore, that at a time of economic recession and legislative tightening of immigration controls, the courts seem to be taking a strong stand against the State in favour of what many would consider to be the most undeserving of characters, the illegal immigrant. I say *seem to be* because the performance of the courts in a line of cases ending with *Khawaja*[94] evidences further the inherent indeterminacy of legal doctrine. The central question was the proper role of the courts when the State detains people as illegal entrants and intends to deport them. More specifically, is the courts' function to determine simply whether there was sufficient evidence on which immigration officers could reasonably reach their decisions or whether their decisions are actually justified on the evidence? In less than a decade, the courts have embraced all possible solutions. As Lord Bridge noted, this is "a matter of high constitutional principle affecting the liberty of the subject and the delineation of the respective functions of the executive and the judiciary."[95]

Beginning in 1974 with *Azam*,[96] it was held that the courts should review the factual basis on which a finding that a person is an "illegal entrant" is made and set it aside if it is not justified by the evidence. This amounts to a "precedent fact" theory of review. However, by 1978 in *Hussain*,[97] the courts had moved to a "reasonable grounds" approach which favoured the State. This test was formally approved by the House of Lords in 1980 in *Zamir*.[98] Yet, early in 1983, the Law Lords experienced a complete change of heart. In *Khawaja*, they held unanimously that the courts' function was to examine the actual evidence on which the immigration officer's finding was made. Stressing that the liberty of individuals was at stake and expressly departing from *Zamir*, the House decided that reasonableness was an inappropriate standard of review. Where executive authority is tied to the precedent establishment of a objective fact, the courts must determine whether the precedent requirement has been met.

---

94 [1984] A.C. 74.
95 *Id.* at 125.
96 [1974] A.C. 18.
97 [1978] 1 W.L.R. 700.
98 [1980] A.C. 930. *See also Choudary*, [1978] 1 W.L.R. 1177 (C.A.) and *Eqbal*, [1979] 1 Q.B. 264 (C.A.)

In Lord Scarman's words, "liberty is at stake: that is . . . a grave matter . . . [and] the reviewing court will therefore require to be satisfied that the facts which are required for the justification of the restraint put upon liberty do exist."[99]

This line of immigration cases underlines most of the major points made in this section. First, not only is the rhetoric of judicial review removed from its actual practice, the rhetoric itself is often inconsistent and contradictory. Far from fulfilling a limited policing function, the courts have assumed the responsibility, as Lord Wilberforce puts it, "to see whether [the finding] was properly reached, not only as a matter of procedure, but also in substance and in law."[100] Secondly, in performing that substantive inquiry, the courts do not consistently favour the interests of the dominant groups in society. Although taking a pro-individualistic position, the protection of illegal immigrants is not usually considered to be supportive of a conservative ideology. Thirdly, judicial indecision subverts the claim that there is a coherent conceptual pattern imprinted on the judicial fabric. The only perceivable "pattern" is the constant oscillation between competing social visions, fragmentedly portrayed and vaguely grasped. The indeterminacy is inevitable and represents an irrepressible dimension of the political condition. Judges and scholars cannot avoid being institutional brokers for competing social ideals. But they do deserve to be castigated for their efforts to deny the contingent character of social arrangements, to wrap it in a pseudo-scientific cloak of mystification and to pretend that the present organisation of society is rational, necessary and just. The sustained efforts of administrative lawyers "make a particular scheme of the possible and desirable forms of human association stand in place of the indefinite possibilities of human connection."[101]

E. THE MARGINALITY OF JUDICIAL REVIEW

As a necessary corollary of assuming the management of the nation's business, the State has established a pervasive network of administrative agencies to carry out its decisions and plans. Indeed, a major reason for the creation of such a bureaucratic enterprise was dissatisfaction with the courts' performance. There were doubts about their capacity and willing-

---

99 *Supra* note 94, at 113.
100 *Id.* at 101.
101 Unger, *supra*, note 14, at 579.

ness to handle effectively the problems of collective consumption, especially when their traditional forte and preference was for the protection of individual rights.[102] Also, the selective, but systematic attempt to withdraw vast areas of administrative competence from the judges through the enactment of privative clauses is indicative of this trend.[103] Moreover, a crude analysis and comparison of judicial and administrative statistics provides ample support for the marginal operation of judicial review.

Apart from other administrative bodies, there are about 2,000 separate tribunals. Calculating *very* conservatively, there are over a million administrative decisions made annually. However, only a minute fraction of those decisions is reviewed by the courts. Although there has been an increase in applications for judicial review, the ratio of applications for judicial review of administrative decisions remains insignificant. Further, no more than 25 per cent of the handful of applications are successful.[104] Also, a successful application only means that a decision will be set aside or quashed; it does not guarantee a favourable decision the second time around. A litigant may win the legal battle, but lose the administrative war. Nevertheless, while the resort to judicial review is a remote possibility, the spectre of judicial intervention might have an exhortatory and intimidating effect. Mindful of its possible invocation, the administrative process will remedy its practices to conform to the doctrinal dictates of judicial review. Such an argument places great and unjustified faith in the instrumental effect of law.

Like it or not, litigation and adjudication are of marginal importance and have limited success in changing society.[105] Legal doctrine is "best

---

102 See McAuslan, *Administrative Law, Collective Consumption and Judicial Policy*, 45 M.L.R. 1 (1983).

103 See *supra*, pp. 102–104.

104 These figures are drawn from the *Civil Judicial Statistics*. While they are an uncertain and imprecise guide, Evans uses these figures to support his view about the "striking" growth in judicial review. He also argues that "the qualitative record . . . is more impressive than the quantitative"; *supra* note 37, at 31.

	1968	1971	1974	1977	1979	1980
Applications	87	227	160	376	410	491
Orders Granted	24	36	52	29	71	121

A similar non-instrumental critique is made by C. Harlow and T. Rawlings, see Law and Administration 256–283 (1984).

105 This is a bold and controversial claim. I have defended it at length elsewhere. See Hutchinson, *Charter Litigation and Social Change: Legal Battles and Social Wars* in Charter Litigation 357 (R. Sharpe ed. 1986).

understood as belonging to the transhistorical discourse of a peculiar fellowship of specialists, those charged with resolving those minor problems that are occasionally tossed to the courts."[106] For instance, in America, judicial attempts to curb and control the conduct of the police failed to improve its practices and, in some instances, actually encouraged police perjury.[107] At best, the direct effect of legal rules on public officials is problematic and the limited amount of available research suggests that the impact of law is as likely to be indirect and unintended as direct and intended. The Canadian experience is that the corrective and inhibiting influences of judicial decisions on administrative behaviour ought not to be taken for granted at all.[108] Finance is a more effective and important tool of control than adjudication: regulatory intervention is far superior to judicial pronouncements. The chances of success are greatest where a "negative order"—one requiring somebody to refrain from action—is sought against a non-bureaucratic entity in a discrete dispute and which can be implemented by a simple, non-policy directive. The most intransigent situations are those that involve a policy dispute of a continuing nature with a large bureaucratic organization, public or private, and which requires compliance by ground-level, frontline officials, such as the police, immigration officers or welfare officials.[109]

There will, of course, be the landmark cases, such as *Bromley* and *Tameside*, which loom large in the public consciousness. Although these are of syumbolic value, their importance must not be underrated. The widespread attention devoted to such celebrated instances underlines the potent and subtle "educative" force of the law. As Douglas Hay has so pertinently observed, "ideologies do not rest on realities, however, but on appearances."[110] *Bromley* and *Tameside* have not improved the lot of the sickly in National Health Service hospitals, the homeless on the council housing waiting list, the destitute at the Supplementary Benefit offices or the consumer of public utilities.[111] Such landmark cases are simply

---

106 Gordon, *Critical Legal Histories*, 36 STAN. L. REV. 57 at 89 (1984).

107 *See* Oaks, *Studying the Exclusionary Rule in Search and Seizure*, 37 U. CHI. L. REV. 665 (1970), and *Bivens*, 403 U.S. 388 (1971).

108 *See Angus, The Individual and the Bureaucracy: Judicial Review—Do We Need It?* (1974), 20 McGILL L.J. 177. *See also*, Page, *Legal Analysis of Economic Policy—2*, 9 J. OF LAW & SOC'Y 225 at 246–248 (1982).

109 *See* J. HANDLER, SOCIAL MOVEMENTS AND THE LEGAL SYSTEM 232–233 (1978).

110 *Property, Authority and Criminal Law* in ALBION'S FATAL TREE 36 (1975).

111 *See* McAuslan, *supra*, note 102, at 5.

isolated instances presented as evidence of the courts' continuing and pivotal involvement in the control of the administration. These infrequent outbursts should not be mistaken for a continuing and productive dialogue. Indeed, even the immediate effect of *Bromley* was minimal; the G.L.C. achieved its general object of reduced fares. In the immigration field, even a traditional scholar like John Evans has conceded that, although it is not "a complete irrelevance," judicial review has little effect on the administrative process; initial dispositions survive procedural correction, subsequent rule changes nullify judicial intervention, no effective modification of impugned administrative behaviour occurs and there is continued ignorance by political applicants of legal rights.[112] As Bridges put it, "immigration appeals were a perfect legal buffer, enabling the state to maintain a liberal image while pursuing essentially illiberal policies."[113] Accordingly, judicial review is of marginal "quantitative" significance.

III. THE RAG TRADE OF ADMINISTRATIVE LAW SCHOLARSHIP

A. THE CONCEPTUAL CLOTHIERS

In the wake of the revived judicial interest in the administrative process, the academic community has greeted enthusiastically the refreshed sources of raw judicial material. Sadly, but predictably, most legal scholars have acted with intellectual deference; they have been happy to follow rather than lead the judges. As such, they have made no real contribution to the debate over the pressing problems of the administrative process. With good cause, the performance and record of most administrative scholars have been assessed as "dismal."[114] They have deliberately set their sights low. Conceiving of their role as being "to expound the black-letter rules of law in such a way as to reveal *coherence*,"[115] they seem to

---

112 J. EVANS, IMMIGRATION LAW 412 (2d ed. 1985).

113 Bridges, *Legality and Immigration Control*, 2 BRIT. J. OF LAW & SOC'Y 221 at 224 (1975).

114 McAuslan, *supra* note 4, at 48. For a powerful and critical assessment of modern scholarship, see Harlow and Rawlings, *supra* note 104.

115 Simmonds, *The Changing Face of Private Law: Doctrinal Categories and the Regulatory State*, 2 LEG. ST. 257, 258 (1982).

relish their self-appointed role as bespoke tailors to the Emperor. Using the available judicial data, they have spun a whole invisible wardrobe of co-ordinated and voguish garments. In the process, they have convinced themselves that the clothes are real and that the Emperor is not naked. This craftsmanship has been given the jurisprudential seal of approval by the master couturier, Ronald Dworkin. He is adamant that "the judge must show the facts of history in the best light he can, and this means that he must not show that history as unprincipled chaos."[116]

In the search for coherence, there have evolved two main camps, the "conceptualists" and the "ideologists." The former is by far the most populous, but there are important divisions among their ranks. The conceptualists are united in their attempt to construct and defend a corpus of doctrinal principles, which coalesce to form an effective, fair and objective restraint on State action. This doctrine is claimed to be non-political in origin and objective. At one extreme is a "classical group," headed by H. W. R. Wade[117] and J. F. Garner.[118] Both fit judicial review into a very simple constitutional design. Parliament delegates power to administrative bodies which are accountable both legally and politically. While the substantive policies and merits of any decision are political issues, the courts ensure that delegated power is not abused or misused. However, this does not mean a complete subservience to the legislative will. The courts' constitutional responsibility is to provide "adequate safeguards for the reasonable interests of the individual."[119] For both writers, parliamentary sovereignty is a guiding principle of the English constitution.

Another principle is adherence to the Rule of Law. Of Diceyian origin, the Rule of Law has become a legal-cultural artifact. It embraces three intertwined principles; due process, equality before the law and judicial involvement.[120] As Wade observes, the judges have sought to "preserve a deeper constitutional logic than that of mere literal obedience to Parliament."[121] The Rule of Law operates as a bulwark against the powerful engines of State running amok.[122] Moreover, Wade insists that the existing doctrine of judicial review is devoid of political content or

---

116 See Dworkin, *'Natural' Law Revisited*, 34 U. FLA. L. REV. 165, 169 (1982) and N. MACCORMICK, LEGAL REASONING AND LEGAL THEORY 106–107 (1978).
117 ADMINISTRATIVE LAW (5th ed. 1983).
118 ADMINISTRATIVE LAW (5th ed. 1979).
119 *Id.* at 20.
120 For a trenchant criticism of this precept, see Arthurs, *Rethinking Administrative Law: A Slightly Dicey Business,* 17 OSGOODE HALL L.J. 1 (1979).
121 Wade, *supra* note 117, at 573.
122 *Id.* at 5.

colouring; it represents a neutral and necessary protection of the individual against the abuse of State power.[123] The fact that the revival of judicial activity coincides with the increased growth of the modern regulatory state is presumably both appropriate and necessary. Further, such political conservatism tends to result in judicial activism.

A more enlightened form of "conceptualist" scholarship has arisen recently. Although de Smith rejects the simplistic "classical" approach and concedes that judicial review is "inevitably sporadic and peripheral,"[124] he has little constructive to offer in its place. At bottom, he suggests that the courts must maintain standards of formal legality and leave substantive control to political forums.[125] Whereas Wade and Garner experience no doubts over the appropriateness of such foundational premises, de Smith endures some crisis of confidence. Yet he seems insufficiently disturbed to reject such premises entirely. He even goes so far as to argue that "the degree of unity in the principles traceable in the law of judicial review has been underestimated."[126] For de Smith, the need to maintain legitimacy is prior to the need to develop a more sophisticated, less constrained response to the administrative regime of the collectivist state. Similarly, John Evans, while recognising that "judges tend institutionally to conservatism," maintains that "it is the constitutional duty of the courts to give effect to the plain meaning of legislative enactments even though this may result in great hardship or injustice to individuals."[127] Despite their troubled consciences, de Smith and Evans defer to what they view as the inevitable. Their progressive sympathies are stifled by their adherence to the traditional ideology which conceives of judges as impotent captives of a workable formalism.

Such scholarly endeavours fail on two clear counts; they do not provide a convincing account of existing judicial practice nor do they offer a satisfactory blueprint for future judicial activity. There is ample evidence within the case law to demonstrate judicial interference with the substantive aspects of administrative decisions. Indeed, the possibility of performing a purely formal policing function is not available.[128] Secondly, as a strategy for reform, the "classical" theory is not only ideologically partisan, but fails to preserve its thinly disguised political preferences. Insofar as it advocates the application of the common law rules

---

123 *Id.* at 24.
124 de Smith, *supra* note 37, at 1.
125 *Id.* at 30–34 and 279.
126 *Id.* at 66–67.
127 *Supra* note 112, at 421 and 424.
128 *See supra*, pp. 99–114.

of private law, it often sanctions the courts' application of the more conservative brake of the common law to the more liberal accelerator of
legislation. Whereas modern legislation tends to be regulatory and partially communitarian, the common law remains largely individualistic
and pathological.[129] At other times, of course, the common law—itself a
blend of competing visionary elements—can be used to the excesses of
reactionary legislative zeal. Nevertheless, the courts' general commitment to individual autonomy in today's urban and technological world
is misplaced and benefits the privileged few to the detriment of the common many.

As such, the "classical" approach stymies the potential, but restricted, impact of legislation; "the corollary of this judicial deregulation
is a vision of laissez-faire individualism as the embodiment of a 'natural
order' . . . that protects individuals from the pervasiveness, inexplicabil-
ity and uncertainty of regulatory law."[130] Notwithstanding its commitment to and dependence on a minimal state, the "classical" weapons are
plainly inadequate for the task and a truly "classical" model of judicial
review may actually facilitate the spread of the bureaucratic state. While
the emphasis upon process and form may result in the protection of individual interests in the occasional dispute, individual interests cannot be
effectively protected without resort to substantive precepts. Moreover,
the historical facts tell a very different tale. During the supposed revival
of administrative law, the administrative process has gone from strength
to strength. On the macro-level, the impact of judicial review is difficult
to detect.[131] On the micro-level, mindful that judicial dealings with the
administrative process are pathological, the increased number of applications for judicial review by individuals indicates that all is not what it is
made out to be.

Recently, a "neo-classical" approach has begun to gain attention.
Recognising the simplism of the earlier work, it still maintains that it is
feasible to construct an adequte model of judicial review without the
courts being thrown into the political malestrom of policy-making. For
instance, D.J. Galligan suggests that this can be achieved by courts demanding that administrators meet the standards of rational decision-

---

129 This seemingly pro-communitarian appearance must not be mistaken for its more
  pro-individualistic reality: see *supra*, pp. 92–94. For a more general critique of the
  Rule of Law, see Hutchinson and Monahan, *supra*, note 10.
130 Note, *Intent, Clear Statements and the Common Law: Statutory Interpretation in the
  Supreme Court*, 95 HARV. L. REV. 892 at 411 (1982).
131 *See supra*, pp. 114–117.

making; "a condition of the legitimacy and justifiability of the exercise of any government power is that decisions be rational and that the power-holder be able to give reasons which both explain and seek to justify its exercise."[132] Each administrative decision must be capable of being located with a wider complex of goals and policies. Paul Craig supports those standards.[133] Further, although he advocates substantive intervention, he explicitly opts out of the search "to find an overarching principle to guide us."[134] Yet, it is not easy to identify or be convinced of the causal link between increased formal rationality and substantive justice. Indeed, it may simply serve to legitimate maladministration. The breadth of the gap that can exist between reasons and action is exemplified by the judicial pronouncements and performance in administrative law. Rationality, like "reasonableness",[135] is never a neutral standard, but represents certain values that themselves need to be justified by more controversial visions of constitutional justice.

B. THE IDEOLOGICAL TAILORS

While the "ideologists" are also engaged in the search for coherence, they insist that the law is in a state of conceptual disarray. The suggestion that there is a subtle, yet meaningful conceptual unity to the case law that meets the dictates of constitutional democracy is dismissed as nothing more than an academic's pipe-dream. Beneath the conceptual chaos, they claim to have unearthed a disturbing ideological coherence. The precise contours of that ideology remain a matter of dispute. For instance, J.A.G. Griffith maintains that the Rule of Law is only another mask for the rule of "conventional, established and settled interests."[136] Far from being a "neutral arbitral force,"[137] the judges are concerned to protect and preserve the existing order. With greater sophistication, Patrick McAuslan detects a similar ideological underpinning. Concentrating on planning law, he argues that the law is devoted to maintaining the existing socio-economic order and to frustrating the redistributive potential of law. In spite of appearances to the contrary, administrative law is a

---

132 *Supra* note 34, at 271.
133 *Supra* note 37, at 49.
134 *Id.* at 55.
135 *See supra*, pp. 109–110.
136 *See* THE POLITICS OF THE JUDICIARY 240 (2d ed. 1981).
137 *See generally*, Devlin, *Judges and Lawmakers*, 39 M.L.R. 1 (1976).

tool "to maintain . . . the existing state of property relations in society,"[138] and evidences "predisposition towards individualism."[139]

Like the conceptualists, the ideologists are guilty of reductionism. While the basic thrust of their arguments is not contested, they ignore and understate the subtle operation of legal doctrine. Although both Griffith and McAuslan concede that the idea of the Rule of Law is not wholly illusory, they appear to have no systemic, but only an ad hoc, explanation for cases like Smith[140] and Khawaja.[141] Yet the frequency and weight of such instances undermine their claim of coherence. The judicial enterprise gravitates between competing ideologies. Apart from ignoring the decisional facts, it is difficult to appreciate why any particular mode of politico-economic organisation requires any given set of rules. Indeed, such a view assumes that law has a direct instrumental effect. The "capitalistic system of society" has weathered the storm of collectivist legislation, welfare statism and industrial nationalisation. It has adapted itself and, arguably, emerged stronger. In the face of such resilience, it is difficult to accept that the "existing order" demands a certain pattern of judicial decisions to guarantee its continued survival. While the abandonment of the regimes of "property" and "contract" would be significant, a different mix of their detailed rules would not. Moreover, even if the whole judicial process was willingly committed to the perpetuation of "capitalism", it is often difficult to know why one particular rule in one particular situation is necessarily demanded. Within the judicial process all is not ideologically black or white; the shades of grey are rampant.

At bottom, English legal scholarship is atheoretical. Like the English philosophical tradition, legal academics tend to be pragmatic and functional. They are extremely suspicious of attempts at grand theorising,[142]

---

138 The Ideologies of Planning Law, 2 URB. L. & POLICY 1, 9 (1979).

139 McAuslan, supra, note 102, at 11.

140 Supra note 90.

141 Supra note 94.

142 As Passmore noted, "the fact that we have to live with is that if most British philosophers are convinced that continental metaphysics is arbitrary, pretentious and mind-destroying, continental philosophers are no less confident that British empiricism is philistine, pedestrian and soul-destroying"; A HUNDRED YEARS OF PHILOSOPHY 459 (1956).

Many seem to share Denning's view, the patron saint of most English academics, that "jurisprudence was too abstract a subject for my liking. All about ideologies, legal norms, 'basic norms', 'ought' and 'is', realism and behaviourism, and goodness knows what else. The jargon of philosophers of law has always been beyond me". See A. DENNING, THE FAMILY STORY 38 (1981).

instinctively inclining toward the practical rather than the philosophical. Although this lends an air of immediacy and direction to their work, it inhibits the development of long-term proposals and critique. Suggestions for reform tend to be piecemeal and incremental. Yet, for there to be real change, there must be a theory of change. For all his critical energy, Professor Griffith has little to offer by way of improvement. He seems content to despair and depose to the inevitable continuance of the judicial and political status quo. Indeed, he seems to believe that the conscious development of a set of general ground rules by parliamentarians and improved drafting[143] will "introduce order and principle into this part of the law."[144] McAuslan's position is less obvious. While he advocates a genuine move toward greater public participation in planning law,[145] he also seems to envisage a residual role for the courts.[146]

IV. The Struggle for Democracy

Legal scholars must redirect their considerable energies and imagination. No matter how efficient the judicial process becomes, it is a marginal activity. To lavish so much time and attention on the courts is to reinforce the mistaken belief that the courts lie at the heart of the legal and political process.[147] Such misdirected activity diverts necessary talents away from the critical scrutiny and improvement of other modes of bureaucratic control.[148] Moreover, the academic preoccupation with judicial review insulates and shields the real sources of bureaucratic maladministration from sustained exposure and eradication. A combination of theory and action is demanded. Without hankering after a nostalgic past that never was, we could do much worse than to act upon the wisdom, intended or otherwise, of Lord Russell in 1898:

---

143 See Griffith, *Constitutional and Administrative Law* in MORE LAW REFORM NOW (P. Archer and A. Martin eds.), 58–59 (1983).

144 See Griffith, Comment, New Society, November 19, 1981, p. 32.

145 *Supra* note 138, at 19–20.

146 *Supra* note 102, at 20.

147 Not all scholars are guilty of this. For example, J. Jowell and M. Partington engage in "applied administrative law"; see WELFARE LAW & POLICY (1979).

148 Very little attention is given by legal academics to the role of parliamentary committees or the parliamentary Commissioner. What attention there is tends to be rather descriptive and uncritical. But see Bradley, *The Role of the Ombudsman in Relation to the Protection of Citizens' Rights*, [1980] CAMB. L.J. 304, and Harlow and Rawlings, *supra* note 104, at 199–226.

[Administrative action] is not unreasonable merely because particular judges may think that it goes further than is prudent or necessary or convenient, or because it is not accompanied by a qualification or an exception which some judges may think ought to be there. Surely it is not too much to say that in matters which directly and mainly concern the people of the county, who have the right to choose those whom they think best fitted to represent them . . ., such representatives may be trusted to understand their own requirements better than judges.[149]

Although such a change in judicial attitude would be commendable, a more profound re-orientation in critical understanding and political sensitivity is demanded. Nothing short of a complete revision of the notion of "state" and "individual" will be sufficient. In place of the supposed opposition between government and governed, a different theory of constitutional arrangements and responsibilities must be nurtured. The focus must shift from an exclusive interest in the operations of public agencies to a more thoroughgoing concern with abuse of power generally. The present pre-occupation with public bureaucracies not only ignores the vast impact of private bodies on the quality of social life, but also tends to legitimate the undemocratic exercise of such power. In effecting this change, legal scholars have a significant role to play. They must grasp the political nettle and work toward a transformation of administrative law and practice. For citizens and scholars alike, it remains true that "self-determination begins at home."[150]

---

149 *Kruse* v. *Johnson*, [1898] 2 Q.B. 91 at 99–100.
150 H. Marcuse, Essay on Liberation 88 (1968).

5

Doing Interpretive Numbers: A Jurisprudential Twosome in Three Parts

Number One: A Whiter Shade of Power

I. A Walk on the White Side

A. White and Words

The linguists, whom one meets everywhere these days, explain that every transaction in our culture—our money and mathematics, our games and gardens, our diet and our sexual activity—is a language; . . . And languages, too, are simply invented systems of exchange, attempts to turn the word into the world, sign into value, script into currency, code into reality. Of course, everywhere . . . there are the politicians and the priests, the ayatollahs and the economists, who will try to explain that reality is what they say it is. Never trust them; trust only the novelists, those deeper bankers who spend their time trying to turn pieces of printed paper into value, but never pretend that the result is anything more than a useful fiction. Of course we need them; for what, after all, is our life but a great dance in which we are all trying to fix the best going rate of exchange, using our minds and our sex, our taste and our clothes. . . .

—MALCOLM BRADBURY[1]

The law is a profession of words; language is its stock-in-trade. Nevertheless, lawyers have shown little sustained interest in the nature of language and its relation to thought and action. Most lawyers rely on a simplistic "functional" understanding of language as a transparent medium for the transmission of ideas and instructions. In skilled hands, it is considered a force for clarity and certainty; in untutored ones, it is a source of confusion and disruption. Like Humpty Dumpty,[2] lawyers maintain that it is simply a question of which is to be master. Referentiality or correspondence is considered both the problem and the solution— if only the world would stay still long enough for us to put the right label on the right things. On such a view, lawyering is an extended exercise in inventory control.

While legal theorists have been more sophisticated, their work has tended to be philosophically oriented.[3] They have been content to ignore the ideological dimensions of language; or, perhaps, they have glimpsed its subversive implications and chosen a discrete averting of their collective gaze as the worse part of scholarly discretion. Yet, it is through language that legal and jurisprudential discourse has operated as a mode of social control. Utilizing a threadbare notion of language, law helps make our social world and defines the role of actors within it. In this way, law becomes a "medium of consciousness for a society, its forms of consciousness externalized."[4]

---

1 M. BRADBURY, RATES OF EXCHANGE 8 (1983).
2 *See* L. CARROLL, *Through the Looking Glass* in THE COMPLETE WORKS OF LEWIS CARROLL 214 (1936).
3 *See, e.g.,* W. BISHIN AND C. STONE, LAW, LANGUAGE AND ETHICS (1972); H.L.A. HART, THE CONCEPT OF LAW (1961); D. MELLINKOFF, THE LANGUAGE OF THE LAW (1963); J. WHITE, THE LEGAL IMAGINATION (1973); Smith, *Law, Language, and Philosophy*, 3 U.B.C. L. REV. 59 (1968); Stone, *From a Language Perspective*, 90 YALE L.J. 1149 (1981). For a powerful critique from a sociological perspective, see Danet, *Language in the Legal Process*, 14 LAW & SOC'Y REV. 445 (1980).
4 G. KRESS AND R. HODGE, LANGUAGE AS IDEOLOGY 13 (1979).

The jurisprudential community has begun to treat the problems of language more critically in the past few years. In their constant efforts to place adjudication on a surer political and philosophical footing, mainstream theorists have plundered other scholarly disciplines. Many have turned to the hard rock of economics. Others, disenchanted with this pseudo-science, have looked for succour to the more refined offerings of literary theory. Like their literary counterparts, legal theorists are concerned with locating meaning in the encounter between reader and text. Proposed solutions run the full gamut from authorial intention through textual objectivity to reader choice and a bewildering series of combinations. Having involved themselves in literary life, jurists have gotten more than they bargained for. Far from facilitating the quest for the jurisprudential grail, their involvement with literary theory has highlighted the shortcomings of mainstream legal theorizing and added further problems for good measure. Nevertheless, many jurists remain undaunted and hope that this engagement will be productive.

The writings of James Boyd White offer a state-of-the-art attempt to enrich legal theory with the insights of modern literary theory. As a professor of law, professor of English, and adjunct professor of classical studies at the University of Michigan, he has (unlike some of us) little trouble avoiding the familiar charge of dilettantism. He offers as sophisticated and eloquent a defense and account of mainstream theorizing as is available. His selections span the whole range of legal, literary, and political offerings; his writing evidences a sustained and intimate experience with these texts. Writing with natural elegance, White manages to be insightful and inciteful. Throughout, his work is energized by an urgent love of literature and law and their liberating potential. His passion and sincerity are palpable. For White, the road to human and political fulfillment is down the way of literature and law. Through "the rhetoric and poetics of law", humanity can make good on itself and constitute a truly egalitarian community.

Of its kind, White's work is a singular and standout achievement: there is very much to admire and learn from his prolific scholarship. Yet for all its polish and erudition, it paradigmatically and powerfully illustrates the ambition and failings of contemporary legal and literary theory. Enslaved to the logocentric desire for objective truth and meaning, White refuses to deal with the political determinants and beneficiaries of language, legal discourse and scholarly endeavour. He flags these crucial matters, but only to ignore and sideline them. Using White's writings as a peg, I will hang on it an essay to explore and expose the ideological foundations and commitments of jurisprudential practice: "criticism and interpretation . . . have a deep and complex relation with politics, the structures of power and social value that organize human life."[5] Linguistic knowledge and interpretive justice are as much the progeny of politics and power as its parents. Although reference will be made to his other work, I will concentrate on his major text, *When Words Lose their Meaning*.[6] Whereas *The Legal Imagination* introduced the difficulties and set the agenda of enquiry, *Heracles' Bow*[7] elaborates on his basic critical themes.

B. THE TEXTUAL CIRCUIT

For White, law and literature comprise a very real common enterprise. Each is nothing more and nothing less than a species of the general activity of claiming meaning for experience and of establishing relations with others in language. Indeed, it is language that is the primary constitutive and constituted force in social life. There is a dialectical relation between language and culture: as language shapes cultural actors, it is being reworked by the cultural drama. With Wittgensteinian wit, White believes that, by imagining and developing a language, we also imagine and develop a form of life: "character and community—and motive, volition, reason, social structure, everything, in short, that makes a culture—are defined and made real in performances of language."[8] Language mediates our experience of the world and is a fundamental kind of social activity. There is no "reality" to break through into beyond language. As such, "language [is] not . . . an apparatus for conceptual elaboration or information exchange, but [is] the living material from which meaning is made in our collective and individual lives."[9]

Building on this dynamic and protean notion of language, White proceeds to describe and practice a way of reading that gives life and significance to legal and literary texts. For him, meaning does not reside in the text, like a fossil embodied in textual rock waiting to be excavated and exhibited in a museum of interpretive history. It comes to life in the cooperative engagement between text and reader; it is a cultural collab-

---

5 Mitchell, *Introduction* to THE POLITICS OF INTERPRETATION 1 (W. Mitchell ed. 1983).

6 WHEN WORDS LOSE THEIR MEANING: CONSTITUTIONS AND RECONSTITUTIONS OF LANGUAGE, CHARACTER AND COMMUNITY (1984) [hereinafter referred to as *Words*].

7 HERACLES' BOW: ESSAYS ON THE RHETORIC AND POETICS OF LAW (1986) [hereinafter referred to as *Bow*].

8 *Words* xi. *See* L. WITTGENSTEIN, PHILOSOPHICAL INVESTIGATIONS 19 (G. Anscombe trans. 1953).

9 *Bow* 126.

oration in which "the writer proposes, but the reader disposes".[10] Nor
is the text an archaeological treasure, but a highly charged source of creative energy in which the author has placed a series of live outlets. Readers
plug in their own cultural experiences, complete the circuit of valoriza-
tion, and produce meaning. For both author and reader, the meaning-
giving enterprise is communal, interactive, experiential and inescapable.
White's version of reading is not an analytic technique, conceptual system nor programmatic solution, but rather a way of being a cultural
actor. Consequently, meaning is reducible to neither the informational
content of the text nor its range of possible logical readings. Instead, it
inheres in the cooperative experience it offers its readers: "reading works
by a perpetual interchange between the person that a text asks you to
become and the other things you are."[11]

White offers "four fundamental questions to organize and inform
the reading process: "How is the world of nature defined and presented
in this language? . . . What social universe is constituted in this discourse, and how can it be understood? . . . What forms and methods of
reasoning are held out here as valid?"[12] By posing and seeking to answer
these questions, the reader will not only better understand the language
of life, but will become a vital participant in the critical construction of
cultural experience.

In addition to providing a structure for the reading process, White
also introduces the interpretive construct of an "ideal reader,"[13] maintaining that a text establishes the characteristics of its own model reader and
invites the reader to take on that identity. In so doing, texts force readers
to consider who they are and whether they wish to become someone
else. For White, the act of reading is a profound exercise in self-education
and improvement, "a lesson in humility."[14] He concedes that the "ideal
reader" of a text will vary from actual reader to reader. Yet he maintains
that this concession does not presage an irresistible slide into the dark
deep of anarchic subjectivism:

> The uncertain reciprocity I describe is often felt to be intolerable, for it seems to
> entail an essential and universal relativism, extending even to our own character

---

10 Hawkes, *Taking It As Read*, 69 Yale Rev. 560, 561 (1980).
11 *Words* 17.
12 *Id.* at 10–12.
13 *Words* 270–73 and *Bow* 90–91. *See* W. Iser, The Act of Reading (1978); W. Iser,
   The Implied Reader (1974); *see also* De Maria, *The Ideal Reader: A Critical Fiction*,
   93 Prog. Mod. Language Ass'n 463 (1978) (exploring emphasis on readers in
   contemporary literary criticism).
14 *Words* 266.

and consciousness. When the resources of a certain kind of thinking run out, a common response is to give up in despair; the disconcerting discovery that the conceptual and logical apparatus of quasi-scientific rationality will not do for the understanding of life or literature or law leads to the announcement that we live in an incoherent and elemental flux in which no reasoning, no meaning, is possible. But to say that there is no meaning or knowledge of one kind is not to deny the possibility of other kinds, and in our actual lives we show that we know how to read and speak, to live with language, texts, and each other, and to do so with considerable confidence. But to do this we must accept the conditions on which we live. When we discover that we have in this world no earth or rock to stand or walk upon but only shifting sea and sky and wind, the mature response is not to lament the loss of fixity but to learn to sail.[15]

Accordingly, White insists that meaning is not simply a function of the whimsical reader or capricious community of readers. While there may not be identity, there will be a "family resemblance" between different readers' "ideal reader". The text remains crucial, "for the meaning is in the original statement and nowhere else."[16]

C. TOWARD CULTURAL CONSTRUCTION

White's work is not simply about the theory of reading. The proof of the theory is in the reading. He devotes his main energies to using his interpretive technique. With enviable range and erudition, he offers a guided tour through some of the great texts of Western civilization. In a series of instructive and resonant readings, he introduces us to the epic world of Homer's *Iliad*, the grand statecraft of Thucydides' *History*, the civilized dialects of Plato's *Gorgias*, the narrative drama of Aeschylus' *Oresteia*, the exhuberant irony of Swift's *A Tale of a Tub*, the didactic eloquence of Johnson's *Rambler Essays*, the gentle humanity of Austen's *Emma*, the fiery rhetoric of Burke's *Reflections*, the historical majesty of Gibbon's *Decline and Fall*, the high-minded fervour of the American *Declaration of Independence*, and the authoritative reasonableness of Chief Justice Marshall in *McCulloch* v. *Maryland*. He probes the culture of each text and teases out the "ideal reader" the text asks us to become. For example, Johnson teaches a language of morality, whereas Austen suggests a language of friendship. It would be an act of great folly and pretension for me to challenge these rich and rewarding readings. Instead, I will deal with his general theory of reading and only join particular issue with his reading of legal texts.

---

15 *Id*. at 277–78. *See also Bow* 40 and 58.
16 *Id*. at 272.

In each of his readings, White concentrates on different aspects of the transformative qualities of texts. The final chapter of *When Words Lose Their Meaning*, "The Possibilities of American Law," displays the full force and workings of the Whitian reading experience. For White, the differences between reading legal and literary texts are largely in emphasis and degree of explicitness. He acknowledges that, whereas the dialectic of cultural reconstruction between the ideal reader that a particular literary text asks us to become and who we already are is necessarily tentative, the reading of a legal text is less conditional: "[I]n its own terms the legal text is authoritative . . . [and law] makes a real social world in a way that a work of literature does not."[17] The difference, however, is consequential rather than quintessential; the structure and character of the reading experience is the same. Like literature, law is another cultural method for individual and collective self-improvement. With refreshing honesty, White portrays adjudication as "no longer the meticulous comparison of precedent against precedent but the large-minded energetic, and perpetual reconstitution of language and the world."[18] Nevertheless, judges are not unfettered ideologues. They must draw upon and use a given set of conversational materials; "[t]he law is a set of social and intellectual practices that have their own reality, force, and significance."[19]

Chief Justice Marshall's seminal opinion in *McCulloch*[20] is offered as

---

17 *Id.* at 270–71. *See also Bow* 238.

18 *Id.* at 359. *See also Bow* 133–36.

19 *Id.* at 273. *See also Bow* 34–35.

20 The achievement of John Marshall in *McCulloch* v. *Maryland*, 17 U.S. (4 Wheat.) 316 (1819), is the subject of mixed views. Some consider his contribution as being the establishment of the Supreme Court as a "bulwark of an identifiable rule of law as distinct from the accommodations of politics," G. HASKINS AND H. JOHNSON, HISTORY OF THE SUPREME COURT OF THE UNITED STATES: FOUNDATIONS OF POWER: JOHN MARSHALL, 1801–1815 at 7 (1981). In a similar vein, Nelson sees him as entrenching a widely shared consensus of values against fleeting majoritarian preferences, see Nelson, *The Eighteenth-Century Background of John Marshall's Constitutional Jurisprudence*, 76 MICH. L. REV. 893, 900–901 (1978); Nelson, *Emulating the Marshall Court: The Applicability of the Rule of Law to Contemporary Constitutional Adjudication* (Book Review), 131 U. PA. L. REV. 489 (1982). A more skeptical assessment is that Marshall engaged in different interpretive strategies, from the textual to the visionary, and illustrated the manipulative and political character of adjudications; see P. BREST AND S. LEVINSON, THE PROCESSES OF CONSTITUTIONAL DECISION-MAKING 35–36, 114 (2d ed. 1983). Moreover, in performing this role, he has been considered to have insulated individualistic values, especially the sanctity of property from legislative encroachment; see Nedelsky, *Confining Democratic Politics: Anti-Federalists, Federalists, and the Constitution* (Book Review), 96 HARV. L. REV. 340, 352–360 (1982). I tend to favour the latter view.

the perfect illustration of White's theory of reading in action. It allows us to enter into a dialectical relation with Marshall himself and also to experience Marshall's own encounter with and reading of the American Constitution. For White, the Constitution, unlike the Declaration of Independence, is not a clarion call to action but "a charter for collective life."[21] Deliberately vague and general, it is not a self-executing document, but requires a committed nation to breath the spirit of just life into it. However, he does claim that it changed "the rhetorical conditions of life."[22] It was for great "constitutional conversationalists," like John Marshall, to lend substance and direction to that rhetorical community.

White seeks to draw out of Marshall's text its "ideal" reader. He highlights the rhetorical strategies used to convince the reader not only that the result was right, even though it seemed at odds with the words and background of the Constitution, but also that the American Supreme Court had the ultimate authority to determine constitutional meaning. Although he employs several argumentative ploys, White concedes that it comes down to the reader's assent and willingness to go along with Marshall: "to make an authoritative culture of argument . . . all rests on the reader's confidence in [pure and disinterested] judicial reasoning."[23] Constitutional interpretation becomes an art that transcends the plain words or commands issuing from some abstract authority. For White, each new case is an invitation to remake the past for the future by redefining the present life and language of the community:

> Like Burke's British Constitution, the Constitution that Marshall expounds must have an internal as well as an external existence, a whole life in the reader's own mind and capacities. Thus the reader becomes for a moment the farmer, the expositor, and the critic of the Constitution; he is to look back to its origins and forward to its construction in the unknown future.[24]

For White, Marshall's opinion introduced a mode of discourse for cultural development. The history of American law has been the seizing of this opportunity to engage in cultural life. Although he does not relate that history, he has no doubt that the triumph of American law has been its insistence on equality, the quality of relations between citizens and state and the success of legal practices as "instruments of liberation."[25] In a Dworkinian move, he depicts the courts as providing a public forum

---

21 *Words* 240.
22 *Id*. at 245.
23 *Id*. at 257.
24 *Id*. at 263.
25 *Bow* 241.

in which the terms of that relation can be debated and declared.[26] In the liberal tradition, White remains agnostic as to the actual decisions reached; he is content with the entrenchment of the rhetorical conditions for cultural regeneration; "the truest meaning of the [judicial] opinion is not its message, but the experience of mind it holds out as a model of legal thought".[27]

White's account is not only a prescription for better organizing legal life, but also a description and defense of much of the actual practice of American law. By locating judicial texts within a larger literary tradition, White reinforces the legitimacy and practice of legal discourse within American life and its primacy as a forum for cultural growth: "the most important [ethical and intellectual] achievement of judicial writing [is] . . . the manifestation in performance of a serious, responsible, and open mind, faithful to the sources of authority external to the self even while contributing to their transformation."[28] The experience of constitutional discourse vindicates and validates his own theory of reading and language. Accordingly, White would presumably deem it right and proper that John Marshall, Felix Frankfurter, and Warren Burger should stand alongside of Homer, Jonathan Swift, and Edmund Burke as cultural giants of the first rank.

II. THE CRITICAL WAGER

A. THE POLITICS OF LITERATURE

Most people would consider it banal to remark that texts are written somewhere by someone at some time and read somewhere by someone at some time. To offer this is an exciting and new foundation for critical inquiry is to run the real risk of being dismissed as trite. Yet mainstream legal and literary theorizing has managed to flourish through a studious avoidance of this insight, contriving to maintain that the production and reception of texts occur in a social vacuum, drained of political and

---

26 *See* R. DWORKIN, A MATTER OF PRINCIPLE 33–71 (1985). *See also*, M. PERRY, THE CONSTITUTION, THE COURTS, AND HUMAN RIGHTS: AN INQUIRY INTO THE LEGITIMACY OF CONSTITUTIONAL POLICYMAKING BY THE JUDICIARY 98 (1982) (discussing dialectical relationship between Biblical metaphors and American morality).

27 *Bow* 118.

28 *Words* 269–270. White denies that he is engaged in a defence of the status quo; see *Bow* xv and 78. My "reading" of his overall text belies that protestation; see *infra*, pp. 140–142.

economic matter.[29] Contemporary theorizing has all but ignored the ideological dimension of language even though all interpretation assumes an entire structure of values. The hard shell of language has a soft ideological underbelly. Everyone makes a critical wager and accepts a package of foundational beliefs and assumptions about reality and nature. Politics is inscribed with language. Authors, readers, and critics exist within a complex web of private and institutional relations and values.[30]

While often paraded as scholarship's highest aspiration and triumph, the constant refusal to historicize represents the tragedy of modern scholarship. To seek to understand a text apart from its socio-political history is not only suspicious, but impossible. It is White's dubious distinction to be a marvelous exemplar of this ahistorical tendency and its ideological significance. After sketching the history of "literature" and the modernist assumptions of literary criticism, I will locate White's theory of reading within contemporary struggles in legal and literary theory, extracting and criticising its ideological content.

The identification of "literature" as a distinct category of texts is relatively recent. Prior to the eighteenth century, poetry and politics were integrated. Reading and writing was an exercise engaged in by small and familiar groups. The actual function of texts depended on the particular socio-economic structure and relations between writer and reader. For instance, it is said that "poetry of the late seventeenth and eighteenth centuries traffics in power."[31] The premodern appreciation of language

---

29 Like scientists, contemporary scholars concede that they have not yet succeeded in making a perfect vacuum. Consequently, the metaphor in the text refers to an interpretive space with most, but not all, of the substantive matter removed. Some quantum physicists maintain that a vacuum represents the most churning space of violent physics: "That nothingness contains all of being." H. PAGELS, THE COSMIC CODE 279 (1982). This hits the literary mark as well.

30 See W. GAIRDNER, THE CRITICAL WAGER: ESSAYS ON CRITICISM AND THE ARCHITECTURE OF IDEOLOGY 3 (1982). This omission is not confined to mainstream theorists, but has been charged against more radical critics, see Said, *Reflections on Recent American "Left" Literary Criticism*, 8 BOUNDARY 2 at 11, 21 (1979).

31 Tomkins, *The Reader in History: The Changing Shape of Literary Response*, in READER-RESPONSE CRITICISM: FROM FORMALISM TO POST STRUCTURALISM 201 at 203 (J. Tompkins ed. 1980). Indeed, one critic has argued that "almost all English Renaissance literature is a literature of patronage." Marotti, *John Donne and the Rewards of Patronage*, in PATRONAGE IN THE RENAISSANCE 207 (G. Lytle and S. Orgel eds. 1981). *See also*, D. JAVITCH, POETRY AND COURTLINESS IN RENAISSANCE ENGLAND (1978) (examining close relationship between court and poetry in Elizabethan England). For a general review, see T. EAGLETON, LITERARY THEORY: AN INTRODUCTION 1–53 (1983).

was as action and not signification. A text was not considered an occasion for interpretation, but an event of engagement, calling for reaction and not reflection. For example, within the Greek bardic tradition, speech was considered a potent force that functioned like magic and drugs.[32] Similarly, Swift's and Johnson's texts were political and promotional texts, intended to shape civic life.[33]

At the end of the eighteenth century, literature began to carve out a territory of its own whose constituency was "not the republic but the republic of letters."[34] With the advent of commercial printing and the relative demise of the patronage system, the literary community burgeoned; writers spoke to a larger, more impersonal and anonymous audience of readers. However, as literature liberated itself from direct political control, literary criticism took on a very different role. Texts became objects of scientific and scholarly analysis rather than political events in their own right. Some declared that great literature was distinguished by its universality and timelessness; criticism was intended to promote "the free play of mind on all subjects . . . , steadily refusing to lend itself to any ulterior, political, practical considerations."[35] Modern literary criticism, even in its Whitian sophistication, still operates within this pseudo-scientific traditions. The text is an object to be interpreted and criticism remains a search for meaning. The central concern and measure of criticism is "interpretative validity." Although frustrated at every turn, critics cannot disabuse themselves of Ruskin's logocentric belief that "[n]othing can atone for the want of truth."[36]

Based on the seminal work of I.A. Richards,[37] New Criticism completed the separation of literature from politics and locked meaning in

---

32 *See* ANCIENT LITERARY CRITICISM: THE PRINCIPAL TEXTS IN NEW TRANSLATIONS 6–8 (D. Russell and M. Winterbottom eds. 1972).

33 *E.g.*, Orwell, *Politics vs. Literature: An Examination of Gulliver's Travels*, POLEMIC, Sept.–Oct. 1946, at 5–21.

34 Crane, *English Neoclassical Criticism*, in CRITICS AND CRITICISM, ANCIENT AND MODERN 376 (R.S. Crane ed. 1952).

35 Arnold, *The Function of Criticism at the Present Time*, in ESSAYS, LITERARY AND CRITICAL 12 (1906). *See, e.g.*, Shelly, *A Defence of Poetry*, in THE GREAT CRITICS, AN ANTHOLOGY OF LITERARY CRITICISM 502 (J. Smith and E. Parks eds. 1951); Wordsworth, *Observations Prefixed to the Second Edition of Lyrical Ballads*, in THE GREAT CRITICS, *supra*, at 563. For an excellent account, see R. WILLIAMS, MARXISM AND LITERATURE 45–54 (1977).

36 J. RUSKIN, 3 THE WORKS OF JOHN RUSKIN 137 (E. Cook and A. Wedderburn eds. 1903).

37 I. A. RICHARDS, PRACTICAL CRITICISM (1929) and PRINCIPLES OF LITERARY CRITICISM (1924).

an objective textual prison. Its ambition was to establish the text itself "as an object of specifically critical judgment."[38] Nevertheless, although democratic and popularist in theory, the practice of New Criticism was elitist. Decried as "a mystery religion without a gospel,"[39] it led to censorship and demagoguery. Like literary buccaneers, they smuggled in personal preferences in the name of textual verities. To their credit, White and similar critics have struggled to release meaning from its confinement in the textual prison-houses of New Criticism so that it can run free in the open fields of liberal pluralism.[40] Those fields, however, are not boundless or uncontoured. White offers his own silent running commentary and erects his own fences.

B. RABBITS REDUX

White and other critics still rely on a prior and independent text which guides readers as they solve the riddles and fill the gaps of the text; "questions [of meaning] . . . have objective answers."[41] In effect, White manages to get his readers and keep his text too. He remains firmly within the modern tradition of text-centered, rhetorical and ahistorical criticism. For such critics, the text exists not only as a physical object of paper and print (or some technological or archaeological equivalent), but, more importantly, as an intellectual record of thoughts and ideas. The tendency to confuse and conflate these two entities is endemic. The radical nature of the shift in location of meaning from text to reader is more apparent than real; it is only significant within the narrow, logocentric and modernist ambitions of "interpretive validity." The status and determinants of the text remain problematic. White does not so much challenge New Criticism as offer an alternative continuation of its project. His is a sustained privileging of a particular form of reading and discursive practice. And, like all such attempts, it reinforces and warrants elite values and interests:

---

38 Wimsatt and Beardsley, *The Affective Fallacy*, in THE VERBAL ICON 22 (W. Wimsatt, Jr. ed. 1954).

39 N. FRYE, ANATOMY OF CRITICISM 14 (1957).

40 Duly acknowledged by White, the central link in this struggle is the work of Wayne Booth, see W. BOOTH, CRITICAL UNDERSTANDING: THE POWER AND LIMITS OF PLURALISM (1979). Interestingly, Booth writes wistfully that "[w]e thus seem to have no Supreme Court in our (literary) republic to determine standards of justice," *id*. at 224.

41 *Words* 6.

The view that a community of readers creates the text by determining its meaning stands things on their heads: for me the text does more to create the community than the other way around. It is with the text that reading starts; and different texts can be shown to create markedly different communities. . . . One [cannot] . . . disregard the independent force of the text. . . . For me, learning to live with a text . . . is a bit like learning to live in a new city. The experience is by necessity somewhat different for everyone who does it. . . . But there are, nonetheless, accounts of [a text], just as there are accounts of Paris or Chicago, that are illuminating and accounts that cannot be right.[42]

Although he characterises writing as a pivotal mode of social action, White fails to consider the historical situation of particular acts of writing and reading. He ignores the socio-economic determinants of the texts he interprets. Indeed, with revealing honesty, he states that "[ideology] has figured largely in battles with which we have nothing to do."[43] To compound this admission, White overlooks the historical specificity of his own interpretive strategies. Rather than remain true to his declared view of language as social action, he reads into his major "transhistorical" texts the basic tenets of liberal pluralism - individual autonomy, formal equality and moral instrumentalism.[44] In this way, by seeming to discover such values embedded in the texts, he naturalizes and universalizes his own partial set of beliefs as the external truths and ideals of cultural life. Like the conjuror, White pulls out of his textual topper only the cultural rabbits he has previously placed there. The critical task is to identify the ideological pedigree of those rabbits and demystify his literary prestidigitation. In short, White's own text confirms Althusser's claim that the practice of reading depends upon a theory of reading which itself has an ideological base.[45]

White recognizes that meaning is not simply found or discovered, but is negotiated and dictated through continuing action. Yet, if meaning is being scripted in the theatre of social action, he does not consider what interests, purposes or resources different actors bring to the performance. While we may all be "readers" of the legal text, very few readings count in the meaning-giving exercise and even fewer readers are "writers". Of those who manage to plug into the energized text, most come up with dead ends rather than live wires.[46] Although White is silent about the

---

42 *Bow* 80 and 90.
43 *Words* 21.
44 *See Words* 18, 24 and 91 and *Bow* 104, 124 and 211.
45 L. ALTHUSSER, FOR MARX 36–39 (B. Brewster trans. 1969).
46 *See supra*, pp. 160–161.

how and *why* of language, there exists, "at the edge of [his] text, the language of ideology, momentarily hidden, but eloquent by its very absence."[47] For instance, White's assumptions about his readers are totally unrealistic; to see equality in the face of gross inequality is disingenuous. White proudly states that "we shall not assume our reader to be a *tabula rasa . . .* but will assume, *what is true of all readers*, that he or she has full competence at the social linguistic practices by which our world is defined."[48] Some "truth"! Some readers!

White's treatment of Homer's *Iliad* illustrates his neglect of the crucial relation between discourse and power. The structure of heroic language and its development in a historically-specific set of social relations—in particular, Homer's depiction of women—demonstrate how "[t]he reflexive elaboration of frames of meaning is characteristically imbalanced in relation to the possession of power. . . . "[49] Homer writes that women are treated as prizes; they bestow honor on the possessor and his household.[50] White identifies this treatment of women as an integral feature of the heroic form, a mode of discourse which he takes as fixed and does not go behind.[51] What does Homer's treatment of women tell us about Greek society? First, as part of a bardic tradition, his text was not written for posterity, but was intended to act as an operative force in the struggle to negotiate meaning in contemporary life. Being constantly retold and performed, it would have had an effect on prevailing relationships between men and women. The categories of "woman" in contemporary Greek life would be appropriately defined and developed. On White's own terms, as the text remakes the culture, the Homeric characterisation of "woman," presenting the subjugation of women as natural and inevitable, would have consequences for the elaboration of that category in Greek society. As a resource presumably controlled by men, the genre of epic poetry becomes social action of the first order and an effective activity of discrimination.

In asking questions about social action from his standpoint "outside

---

47 P. MACHEREY, A THEORY OF LITERARY PRODUCTION 60 (G. Wall trans. 1978).
48 *Bow* 127.
49 A. GIDDENS, NEW RULES OF SOCIOLOGICAL METHOD 113 (1976) (original italicized).
50 HOMER, THE ILIAD 26, 170 (E. Rieu trans. 1969). On the role of Greek women generally, see A. CAMERON AND A. KUHRT, IMAGES OF WOMEN IN ANTIQUITY (1983) and J. ELSHTAIN, PUBLIC MAN, PRIVATE WOMAN: WOMEN IN SOCIAL AND POLITICAL THOUGHT 19–54 (1981).
51 *Words* 24–58.

history," White is caught in a bind. He is committed to accepting the text at face value. When one cannot resort to the grubby facts of social history, one must ignore or deny any distortion between political life and its textual representation. For instance, many women may have contested the image of women as honorific prizes. Yet Homer asks us to adopt or continue his finished categorization of women. To treat the text as a crystallized moment in the unending processing of meaning–negotiation, as White does, is misleading. The text must take its identity and meaning from and be evaluated against the actual dynamics of that process. The ideological function of the text might be downplayed, but it ought not to be overlooked.

White's failure to address the ideology of text-formation prevents him from taking seriously his own assessment of language as social action. The significance of the impact of his omission is compounded by the fact that, throughout the book, he alerts us to the manipulative potential of language. Yet, he perversely chooses to neglect the hierarchical relations of power within which textual activity takes place. Plato's *Gorgias*, however, shows that victory is a matter of power and not of persuasion; Socrates wins over Gorgias by having him agree to his rules of the game.[52] Also, White's description of Johnson's *Rambler* essays is complacent and naive: "he defines a term by showing how it can be combined with others and, in doing so, not only clarifies established meanings (for all the words) but makes possible the new expression of *substantive truths*."[53]

Although White confers interpretative validity on the reader's response, he does not commit himself to a voguish nihilism in which "[l]iterary interpretation becomes a game of tennis played without a net and on a court with no backlines."[54] While recognizing that texts harbor a multiplicity of meanings, White maintains that some meanings are better than others and that his theory of reading can illuminate those meanings. As his books progress, his tolerance wears thin and his dogmatism begins to show. He starts to talk of "proper" and "true" readings and to criticise others whose readings are "a perversion" or "quite wrong."[55] At the end of the book, White completes his task of showing that "the textual community can be understood in ethical and political terms across

---

52 *Words* 102–08.
53 *Id*. 154 (emphasis added).
54 Brooks, *The New Criticism*, 87 Sewanee Rev. 603 at 604 (1979).
55 *Words* 23, 115, 137, 191 and 307.

the whole range of texts we shall read and the genres they exemplify."[56] Like I.A. Richards, White believes that texts have a civilizing mission and inculcate the external values of "beauty and truth and justice."[57] It is in fleshing out those ideals that White reveals and reads into the texts his own preferences and projects. He supplies a barely disguised running commentary for the location of "true" meaning in the pluralistic fields and erects his high liberal fences to contain it.

III. BACK TO THE FUTURE

There are two central themes to the Whitian experience of reading: the idea of human equality and the willingness to be persuaded in political discourse. They are the very core values that comprise the modern version of the procedural republic. "Finding" these themes in different periods of history, diverse types of society, and distinct genres of writing, White concludes that these values are inherently human and represent the best in human nature. Unknowingly, this vast textual tradition has been evoking and celebrating the Rule of Law. Bolstered by the wisdom and authority of the world's great texts, White glorifies the institution of judicial review. Even in Homer's *Iliad* or Thucydides' *History*, he spots an implied support and justification for the Rule of Law based on "equality" and "persuadability".[58] White finds the highest expression of these ideals in the practice of constitutional argument in the liberal democracy of the United States. As such, White effects a colossal exercise in apologetic revisionism:

> [T]he heart of law is what we always knew it was: the open hearing in which one point of view, one construction of language and reality, is tested against another. The multiplicity of readings that the law permits is not its weakness but its strength, for it is this that makes room for different voices and gives a purchase by which culture may be modified in response to the demands of circumstance. It is a method at once for recognizing others, for acknowledging ignorance, and for achieving cultural change.
>
> The central idea of justice, on this view, is a matter not of rules, distributions or correctives but a matter of relations. . . . The essential idea of equality before the law is an equality of speakers, not an equality of distribution or results. . . . [59]

---

56 *Id.* at 18.

57 I.A. RICHARDS, SCIENCE AND POETRY 275 (1926).

58 *Words* 18, 39, 53, 78, 161 and 228 and *Bow* 104, 70 and 124. For a critique of the Rule of Law, see Hutchinson and Monahan, *Democracy and the Rule of Law* in THE RULE OF LAW: IDEAL OR IDEOLOGY (A. Hutchinson and P. Monahan eds. 1986).

59 *Words* 273 and 283.

White's early statement that *When Words Lose Their Meaning* "despite appearances, is really about law from beginning to end"[60] is no small reassurance or idle threat. His whole book is a sophisticated attempt to justify and apologize for the present chaotic practice of adjudication. He revels in the polyglotism of judicial and juristic discourse and sees in its performance the embodiment of civilized and just discourse. His book is a paean to liberal legalism. Like all narratives, it emphasises and privileges some parts of our communal existence at the expense of others. Legal language is one way of forming, living and transforming our social world. It is no more open or neutral than moral or economic language. While presenting itself as an egalitarian forum for the open construction and reconstruction of cultural life, it insulates certain sub-stantive values and constrains that very process. For instance, White's criticism of bureaucracy applies with equal force to adjudication which, after all, is simply another branch of bureaucracy. In condemning its cost-benefit mentality, he recognises that "whatever cannot be talked about in these bureaucratic ways is simply not talked about. Of course all systems of discourse have domains and boundaries, principles of ex-clusion and inclusion; but this kind of bureaucratic talk is unselfconscious about what it excludes. The world it sees is its whole world."[61]

Finally, examining White's book itself as an historical text to be in-terpreted reveals much about White's own pluralism. In his treatment of the *Iliad*, what White does not think is important tells us a great deal about White's own politico-historical context and project. The sounds of silence are meaningful and unmistakable. In stressing the celebration of human equality in the Homeric world, White is only talking about warriors and, at that, only the chief warriors. Equality is respected within a confined community; women, slaves, and rank-and-file soldiers are already defined out of the community.[62] Equality, based on official status, becomes largely artificial. On closer inspection, White's "human equality" is nothing more than formal equality in a society characterised by massive substantive inequality.

---

60 *Id.* at xi.
61 *Bow* 30. The nature of those values and constraints are explored throughout the book. *See supra*, ch. 1.
62 In Greek, *e.g., philos* denoted a limited stock of persons and things which were of special value to their owners and on which their existence depended. Significantly, there was no word for or distinction between persons and things in this category. For a general discussion of the value-structures of Greek society, see A. ADKINS, MORAL VALUES AND POLITICAL BEHAVIOUR IN ANCIENT GREECE (1972).

This definition of equality, of course, parallels the situation in White's and our contemporary society. All citizens are equal before the law, notwithstanding that the material conditions of their lives give rise to severe and pervasive substantive and structural inequality. White has projected the modern ideology of "human pluralism" back on to the ancient *Iliad*. He has translated Anatole France's ironic saw into a political creed: "[T]he majestic equality of the laws, which forbid rich and poor alike to sleep under the bridges, to beg in the streets, and to steal . . . bread."[63]

Number Two:
Gone Fishing

It is impossible to write anything that cannot be misread. Writing is a risky business. To write about writing is doubly jeopardous. So to write about Stanley Fish's writing is simply asking for trouble. Yet anyone who wishes to make a serious and honest contribution to the current "interpretation debate" in jurisprudence must confront Fish's arguments and ideas. After about two decades spent honing and refining his critical project and argumentative techniques on the literary front, he has exploded onto the legal scene like an intellectual firecracker. With irrepressible and mischievious wit, Fish forcefully reminds lawyers that to ask about meaning is to ask about everything.

His critical project is a potent demonstration that there can be no position of theoretical innocence. For Fish, both the theoretical and practical components of the interpretive act have an indivisible political and historical dimension. Both text and reader are products of interpretive practice. In effect, Fish gives a subtle and significant twist to Marx's famous thesis: in interpreting the world, philosophers also change it.[1] Indeed, Fish elevates the critic from "humble servant of texts" to their proud and primary producer.[2] Although he insists that interpretation is and must be anchored in its social setting, his hermeneutic account is stubbornly apolitical and ahistorical in content and illustration. By downplaying the crucial historical relation between power and interpretation,

---

63 A. France, The Red Lily 91 (W. Stephens trans. 1927).
 1 Marx, *Theses on Feuerbach XI* in Marx and Engels: Basic Writings on Politics and Philosophy (L. Feuer ed. 1959).
 2 S. Fish, Is There a Text in this Class? (1980).

Fish has managed to divert jurisprudence down a "conventional" cul-de-sac. In so doing, he has led its practitioners further out of earshot of history's subversive sounds. To locate his theory within concrete historical situations is to reveal that, despite his radical posturing, Fish has produced a profoundly conservative theory of interpretation. He tells a soothing story that extols the virtues of resignation and surrender—"Don't panic! Things are the way they are because they are the way they are."

I. BEYOND THE TEXT

A. FROM SUBSTANCE TO FORM

In the last few years, many legal theorists have turned their attention from the inquiry into *what* the law means to the puzzle of *how* law means.[3] It is not that the earlier inquiry has been satisfactorily resolved, but rather that the theorists seem to have exhausted the possibilities for substantive consensus. Indeed, it was a perception of the polysemous quality of jurisprudential discourse that prompted an expedient retreat to the more abstract yet foundational domain of hermeneutics. Theorists who effected this shift had a twofold hope: to deflect attention from the substantive disarray, especially in constitutional doctrine, that threatened to drown out entirely the voice of scholarly enterprise, and to establish some minimal, shared interpretive ground from which the substantive debate might proceed anew. It was a forlorn hope. Fragmented discourse persists, only its locus has changed. Further, theorists have begun to realize that political questions cannot be divorced from questions about what can count as knowledge. Legal epistemology is the continuation of ideological warfare by other, more esoteric means.

The contemporary interpretive debate has taken place largely on the turf of literary theory. Ronald Dworkin suggested the possible terms for a future engagement in 1977,[4] but a full-scale debate did not take place until the spring of 1982 with the publication in the *Texas Law Review* of a series of polemical essays grappling with the interlocking and contested

---

3 Compare *Symposium: Constitutional Adjudication and Democratic Theory*, 56 N.Y.U. L. REV. 259 (1981) and *Symposium: Judicial Review versus Democracy*, 42 OHIO ST. L.J. 1 (1981) with *Symposium: Law and Literature*, 60 TEX. L. REV. 373 (1982) and *Symposium: Interpretation*, 58 S. CAL. L. REV. 1 (1985) [hereinafter *Symposium: Interpretation*].

4 *No Right Answer?* in LAW, MORALITY AND SOCIETY 58 (P. Hacker and J. Raz eds. 1977).

issues of the autonomy and determinacy of the text, the relevance of authorial intent, and the freedom of the reader.[5] Sanford Levinson fired the opening salvo with his relentless account of radical textual indeterminacy.[6] The main antagonists, however, have been Ronald Dworkin, Owen Fiss, and Stanley Fish. They have taken part in a robust exchange in which each is loath to give the others the last word. The central bone of contention has been the continued validity of textual positivism: to what extent, if any, does the text constrain the interpretation to be placed upon it?

Although Dworkin and Fiss disagree on many matters, they have similar beliefs about the appropriate ambition of any theory of legal interpretation and its necessary theoretical foundations. They reject both a crude textualism in which the text speaks with a clear and single voice and a textual nihilism that celebrates the multiple, anarchic voices of the text. In short, they want to resist any deification of the text without slipping into solipsism. Both Dworkin and Fiss propose interpretive devices that mediate and constrain the encounter between text and reader. Dworkin relies on an artistic analogue to his "soundest theory of law":[7] "an interpretation of a [text] attempts to show which way of reading . . . the text reveals it as the best work of art."[8] He compares adjudication with the enterprise of writing a chain novel: the accumulation of preceding chapters or earlier cases narrows the available choices of a bona fide participant.[9] Fiss relies on a set of disciplining rules and an authoritative interpretive community in which judicial membership is "mandatory."[10] For Fiss, adjudicative legitimacy is not based on the substantive correctness of a decision, but on a bounded objectivity achieved through the use of the extant interpretive rules.

---

5 *Symposium: Interpretation, supra*, note 3.
6 Levinson, *Law as Literature*, 60 Tex. L. Rev. 373 (1982).
7 Taking Rights Seriously 66 (1977).
8 A Matter of Principle 149 (1985).
9 *Id.* at 158–162.
10 Fiss, *Objectivity and Interpretation*, 34 Stan. L. Rev. 739, 746 (1982). Stephen Carter takes a similar line, although he maintains that Fiss's theory is "optimistic but ultimately incomplete." Carter, *Constitutional Adjudication and the Indeterminate Text: A Preliminary Defense of An Imperfect Muddle*, 94 Yale L.J. 821, 835 (1985). Carter argues that "[p]roviding [a clear set of interpretive rules] is probably the most vital task that constitutional theory must perform." *Id.* at 821. Like Fiss, Carter places his faith in the "goodness and ultimately the viability of the American constitutional democracy." *Id.* at 869. He concludes by making an ill-fated attempt to draw a distinction between the more and the less indeterminate parts of the Constitution, suggesting that the interpretive methods used in the latter might be employed to resolve the former. *Id.* at 855–865.

B. THE FISH LINE

Much legal and literary theoretical practice still lingers in the discredited shadow of the New Criticism, the positivistic view in which the text is a self-contained, organic whole whose meaning and unity can be identified and grasped without reference to history or biography.[11] The central thrust of Fish's critique is that any brand of textual positivism, even Levinson's radical version, is misconceived. In Fish's view, lawyers have been allowed to indulge in the general tendency to turn documents into monuments. Indeed, he objects strenuously to the questions Levinson, Dworkin, and Fiss address because they rest on the very presuppositions about the independent nature of the text that Fish is most concerned to overturn. He insists that the text does not announce or present itself, but emerges in the course of interpretive practice: "linguistic and textual facts, rather than being the objects of interpretation, are its products."[12]

Fish argues that this insistence does not make him vulnerable to charges that he embraces the nihilistic bogey of unbridled interpretation. Like the text, the reader does not exist outside a conventional network of interpretive strategies and norms. Both text and reader are always and already situated within a social milieu. Accordingly, meaning is neither the property of a text nor brought to a text by the reader, but is defined by prevailing communal conventions. Given that there is no transcendent algorithm or disinterested rationality, there can only be interested attempts to negotiate and to establish the dominant interpretive strategies.[13] For Fish, meaning is a matter of persuasion, not demonstration. Interpretive knowledge is historically and politically based:

> [I]nterpretation is the only game in town . . . [T]here are no moves that are not moves in the game . . . even the move by which one claims not to be a player . . . [O]ne can neither disrupt the game nor get away from it . . . [T]he stakes are much higher in a persuasion than in a demonstration model, since they include nothing less than the very conditions under which the game in all of is moves . . . will be played . . . [R]ather than being merely a player in the game, [the critic] is a maker and unmaker of its rules.[14]

---

11 For one of the classic examples of New Criticism, *see* C. BROOKS, THE WELL WROUGHT URN (1949).
12 *Supra* note 2, at 9.
13 Fish, *Fish v. Fiss*, 36 STAN L. REV. 1325, 1336–1340 (1984).
14 *Supra* note 2, at 355, 358, 366 and 367.

Shifting his sights more directly to Dworkin and Fiss, Fish charges that, despite their disavowals, they both remain dazzled by the enticing illusion of textual positivism: their sophistication lies only in offering a pluralistic version of it.[15] They persist in believing that the text has some independent, objective, and uninterpreted existence outside its community of interpreters. In short, Fish maintains that Dworkin and Fiss are chasing their own hermeneutical tails, because whatever they are looking for has always been in place and could never not be.

The Fish-Dworkin exchange has developed into a self-styled spat between the "incompetent"[16] and the "confused."[17] Although they vigorously reaffirm their own views, their positions seem to be too close for each other's comfort—or, at least, they seem to share much more than they contest. Much like the confrontation between the Big-Endians and the Small-Endians of Lilliput over the correct way to crack an egg, the Dworkin-Fish "dispute" is a trivial disagreement blown up out of all proportion into a massive and unnecessary falling-out. In contrast, the exchange between Fish and Fiss has been much more good-natured. Fish demonstrates how interpretive rules are unconstraining since they themselves demand interpretation. Consequently, meaning is "a kind of knowledge that informs rules rather than follows from them."[18] Fiss scores some telling points in his rejoinder, emphasizing the interactive nature of rules and practice and showing how Fish trivializes and devalues "the self-conscious and reflective moments" of judicial decision-making.[19] However, he insists on the text's constrained independence and continues to shadowbox with nihilistic specters.[20]

Fish's "conventional" theory is sophisticated and seductive because it presents itself as perfectly self-sufficient and self-serving. By denying the possibility of any metatheory capable of transcending his theory, Fish tries to prevent the grounding of any external critique and thereby to achieve for his theory that privileged status of transcendent certainty he consistently denies to his adversaries. In effect, Fish aspires to trap his critics in a hermeneutical Catch-22. As all interpretation is convention-

---

15 Fish, *supra* note 13, at 1334 (discussing Fiss) and Fish, *Wrong Again*, 62 TEX. L. REV. 299, 309 (1983) (discussing Dworkin).

16 Dworkin, *My Reply to Stanley Fish (and Walter Benn Michaels): Please Don't Talk About Objectivity Anymore* in THE POLITICS OF INTERPRETATION 287 (W. Mitchell ed. 1983) (describing Fish).

17 Fish, *supra* note 15, at 310 (labelling Dworkin).

18 Fish, *supra* note 13, at 1330.

19 Fiss, *Conventionalism*, 58 S. CAL. L. REV. 177 at 191 (1985).

20 Fiss, *The Death of The Law?*, 72 Cornell L. Rev. 1 (1986).

bound, especially the debate over the interpretive conventions themselves, individuals can never escape to some nonconventional ground from which to map the conventional terrain.

In the same way that they cannot escape convention, individuals cannot choose not to have interpretive beliefs. They are the very things that make our engagement in and understanding of the world possible. Enmeshed in a claustrophobic web of interpretive beliefs, Fishian readers can neither know themselves nor put sufficient distance between themselves and their communal contexts to reflect on the prevailing conventions. Even misinterpretation is a form of interpretation. To Hart's claim that the penumbral qualities of vagueness, imprecision and open-texture reside at the edge of settled meaning,[21] Fish would respond that these shadows of uncertainty are produced, controlled and delineated by relevant interpretive conventions. All of this, of course, Fish claims not as a matter of truth, but of "conventional" wisdom.

In his most recent essays, Fish has sought to develop some of the central arguments upon which his thesis depends, as well as to anticipate and deflect criticism. He has concentrated on the process by which changes occur within interpretive practices, specifically the manner in which interpretive beliefs are acquired, discarded, and evaluated. The development of these arguments both fills out Fish's conventional theory of interpretation and exposes the limitations of that theory. His efforts to erect impregnable defenses have been bought at much too high a price.

II. After Bigger Fish

A. A Conventional Response

The "interpretive turn" in modern theorizing has obliged scholars to confront a persistent and profound puzzle: "nothing is more habitual or customary than our ways of speech, and nothing is more continuously invaded by change."[22] We are worked upon and made by history and language, yet, by our interaction with them, we create language and shape history. There is an implicit compact: we live in and change history, but history repays the privilege (or exacts its revenge) by living in and changing us. Articulation of this enigmatic relation is so com-

---

21 H.L.A. Hart, The Concept of Law 125–125 (1961).
22 M. Oakeshott, Rationalism in Politics 64–65 (1962).

monplace as to be almost clichéd. Nevertheless, efforts to understand it constitute the ever-present task of social theory.[23]

Influenced by the French savants, critical theory has dislodged the individual consciousness from its traditional role as the primary source of knowledge and the privileged affixer of meaning. As the significant trends in twentieth century continental theorizing stand in stark contrast to main currents in Anglo-American philosophy, the recent infiltration of continental theory into the Anglo-American tradition has been all the more jarring and perplexing for many. In short, Anglo-American philosophers have preferred positivistic explication to phenomenological critique. Leading continental theorists have been more concerned with evaluating the social dimensions and significance of knowledge, intelligence, and rationality. Anglo-Americans devote their critical energies to answering the question "Is it true?" Continentals, by contrast, focus on the questions "How do social patterns affect our ways of thinking?" and "What are the social effects of our habits of thinking?"[24]

This shift in critical focus has produced a more urgent appreciation of the relation between language and social action. Insofar as the individual consciousness needs to become articulate, it must do so within the social domain of language. Accordingly, we can only express ourselves intelligibly within a *pre-existing* framework of conceptual relations and social practices. However, although words are silent and need individuals to speak for them, language has a social existence that renders pure intentionality by an individual impossible. Self and other combine and contest in the act of making and remaking meaning. It is in this sense that language must be recognized as both the prize of political conflict and the arena in which that conflict takes place. As language and imagination are inextricably linked, the complex interface between individual consciousness and social systems of meaning is the crucial phase of political engagement. It is at this stage that the elemental struggle to control meaning and, therefore, life is won and lost: "[p]ower is a form of explanation and explanation a kind of power."[25]

Although Fish never directly addresses these arguments, he does try to explain the nature of change in interpretive communities. His solution is, however, as predictable as it is incomplete and unconvincing. Fish

23 *See* P. ABRAMS, HISTORICAL SOCIOLOGY x–xiii (1982).
24 *See* PHILOSOPHY IN FRANCE TODAY (A. Montefiore ed. 1983) and Gutting, *Continental Philosophy of Science* in CURRENT RESEARCH IN PHILOSOPHY OF SCIENCE 94–117 (1979).
25 P. SEDERBERG, THE POLITICS OF MEANING x (1984).

insists that "change [or its recognition] is an interpretive fact."[26] Even the most revolutionary onslaught on the status quo must be envisaged and, in a sense, even sanctioned by the prevailing norms, else it would be literally "unintelligible."[27] Hence, each interpretive community contains "a mechanism for its own transformation."[28] Further, in a quintessentially "Fishy" move, he argues that nothing "turns on" his or anyone else's account of the relevant interpretive conventions.[29] Theory, as a generalized scheme to guide or reform practice, is superfluous, for it is always and already "the helpless plaything of the practice it claimed to inform."[30] For Fish, all attempts to construct theories, even purportedly antitheoretical ones, necessarily arise in concrete political settings. Any theory, therefore, "cannot help but borrow its terms and its content from that which it claims to transcend, the mutable world of practice, belief, assumptions, points of view and so forth."[31]

With disarming directness, he underscores the practical impotence of theory by advising anyone who wants to know about the law not to consult Fish, but rather Fiss, who understands better the prevailing legal interpretive norms and practices. But, of course, as Fish does not hesitate to remind us, rightness is internally constructed, not externally given. Fiss's advice would be no more "right" (or "wrong") than his own; it would simply be more conventionally informed and, therefore, conventionally acceptable.[32] Accordingly, Fish's reassuring and thoroughly conservative conclusion is that we should stop worrying about legal epistemology and proceed with "business as usual"—especially as it would be impossible to do anything else anyway.[33]

With characteristic assurance, Fish announces the "conventional" death of the individual. He categorically rejects a naive humanism that holds that individuals are the authors of their own historical fate. Instead, he depicts the self as a "social construct whose operations are delimited by the systems of intelligibility that inform it."[34] Fish's posting of the individual's obituary, however, is premature and greatly exaggerated. If

---

26 Fish, Change 27 (unpublished, November 1985).
27 Fish, *supra* note 2, at 355.
28 Fish, *supra* note 26, at 7.
29 Fish, *supra* note 13, at 1347.
30 Fish, *Consequences*, 11 CRIT. INQ. 433 at 452 (1985).
31 *Id.* at 438.
32 Fish, *supra* note 13, at 1347.
33 *See* Fish, *Anti-Professionalism*, 17 NEW LIT. HIST. 89 at 104 (1985).
34 Fish, *supra* note 2, at 335.

individuals were exclusively and fully determined by their community's conventions and, therefore, nothing more than amanuenses for History's script, their conversation would be superfluous. All individuals would be interpretive clones; there would be no need to communicate. Anything and everything that could be said would already have been heard: anything and everything that could be heard would already have been said. As E.M. Forster so succinctly put it, "a perfectly adjusted organism would be silent."[35] Without the resisting individual, there would be no history.

Of course, Fish would rightly label this challenge to his argument as ridiculous, but, in doing so, must concede that the "conventional" death of individuals has never occurred. Although this concession may seem trivial, it represents the Achilles heel of Fish's critical project. Despite his aim to legislate individuals out of epistemological existence by drowning them in a medium of communal conventions, Fish has paradoxically given them a new lease on epistemological life and facilitated their hermeneutical rehabilitation. His theory only makes sense if individuals are given vast discretion and autonomy. Yet this conclusion not only contradicts the epistemological foundations and aspirations of Fish's project, it runs counter to the dominant stories of our social history. In short, Fish has overlooked the dynamic and formative role of power in creating that history. Fish has replaced the discredited reification of the text with the deification of his own vaunted interpretive conventions. He cannot resist the logocentric urge to offer foundations for truth and meaning.[36] Although he insists on the historical roots of interpretive practice, Fish seems to have devised one more idealistic machine for the suppression of history. He craves divine simplicity where there is only historical complexity.

B. THE POLITICS OF CHANGE

In fortifying his theory and attempting to explain change, Fish has first stretched his defenses so thin and then made them so elaborate that they collapse under their own weight. Indeed, he admits that the mass of conventions comprises "a rather ramshackle structure with little coherence among its various parts."[37] Fish not only concedes that com-

---

35 E.M. FORSTER, A PASSAGE TO INDIA 133 (1924).

36 See supra, ch. 2.

37 Fish, supra note 26, at 10 [quoting with approval T. KUHN, THE STRUCTURE OF SCIENTIFIC REVOLUTIONS 49 (2d ed. 1970)].

munal conventions combine to function as "an engine of change,"[38] he goes so far as to make change his theory's critical motif:

> [E]ven though it is fully articulated and underwritten by a full-fledged philosophy of life complete with an ontology and an epistemology, the code [of interpretive conventions] is not monolithic and self-confirming; it is an entirely flexible instrument for organizing contingent experience in a way that does not preclude but renders inevitable its own modification.[39]

Yet in making this concession, Fish has cast the interpretive net so wide that it ceases to place any meaningful constraints on the interpretive acts of those supposedly trapped within it.

Insofar as the communal code of norms "renders *inevitable* its own modification,"[40] the precise nature of the interpretive constraints is elusive and enigmatic. A prison that contains the whole world is no prison at all. A society's confinement in a particular cell at any given time is illusory and, to that extent, self-imposed. The walls will sooner or later be dismantled and rebuilt elsewhere. Indeed, for Fish, this dismantling and rebuilding is "inevitable." Consequently, although communal conventions circumscribe the available options for interpretive practice, Fish leaves it to individuals to decide on the actual pattern (or chaos) of choices. Far from burying individuals, Fish has reinstated them in their role as the prime and privileged makers of meaning and history. Posing as a radical determinist, he stands revealed as a closet humanist.

An example from literary theory—deconstruction—and an example from legal doctrine—the development of tort law—will help to illustrate and underline these critical objections. The bête noire of modern literary theory is deconstruction. Although defanged by its American practitioners, deconstruction seeks to undermine the entire literary critical project by revealing how the attempt to fix words and texts with stable meaning is a futile exercise. In its relentless challenge to the metaphysical and epistemological assumptions that underpin the traditional task of literary and legal criticism, deconstruction celebrates the polysemic character of textual reading and writing.[41] Yet Fish dismisses this radical tendency as "a programmatic and tendentious focusing of ways of thinking and working that have already come to be regarded as commonplace and or-

---

38 *Id*. at 15.
39 *Id*. at 17.
40 *Id*. (emphasis added).
41 *See supra*, ch. 2.

thodox."[42] Again, Fish's critique is thoroughly ahistorical. In spite of his embracing a "conventional" determinism theoretically capable of explaining why deconstruction surfaced and gained prominence when it did, Fish offers no reason to think that deconstruction could not have surfaced at any time. When taken to its logical (and absurd) conclusion, Fish's theory seems to commit him to the startling view that, if history had unfolded differently, the first literary critics might have been deconstructionists. Yet, without something constructed, it would be extremely difficult to de-construct. In short, Fish's "historical" account lacks any historical substance or credibility.

Another way of illustrating the weaknesses in Fish's theory is to consider the development of tort law. In the twentieth century, Anglo-American society has witnessed a phenomenal increase in the scale and gravity of destruction which modern technology can wreak; the ingenuity of products to cause injury continues apace. To compensate those injured, society relies upon an eclectic combination of private law remedies, collateral insurance benefits and social welfare schemes. Efforts to regulate and deter harmful enterprises and products consist of a mixture of private law incentives, legislative controls and regulatory schemes. The overriding characteristic of accident law is its piecemeal quality. Notwithstanding this, the major focus of academic and judicial attention has been the private law devices of tort and contract. The abiding concern is to organize the common law so as best to optimize accident and safety costs; in other words, to design rules of tort and contract law to deter harmful activities and compensate the victims of such activity. The history of such efforts is a sorry tale.

At the heart of the judicial and jurisprudential task, there lingers the felt need to solve the Millian dilemma; the establishment of some neutral, normative method by which to provide determinate guidance for the choice between individual freedom and collective control.[43] Although often concealed, this central challenge is expressly acknowledged by modern tort scholars.[44] The history of Anglo-American modern accident law is an extended response to this intellectual dilemma: its lesson is that the common law is a defective product. The trend has been towards heightened liability. However, there is no consistent pattern or overall

---

42 Fish, *supra* note 26, at 21.

43 *See* J.S. Mill, Utilitarianism, Liberty and Representative Government 74 (1910).

44 *See*, for example, Prosser and Keeton on Tort 16 (5th ed. 1984); and R. Epstein, Modern Products Liability: Cases and Materials 1 (2d ed. 1982).

logic to the doctrinal patchwork; there still exists a baffling mix of no-liability, negligence and strict liability. Nonetheless, despite the trend to heightened liability, doctrine and scholarship remain essentially indi-vidualistic in character. Accidents are treated as unique and dichotomous rather than probabilistic and continuous. Scholars remain trapped in an interminable discourse between utilitarian- and rights-based theories of liability; each holds individual interests to be the only real interests and each can be used to justify a whole range of liability regimes. Each prop-osal is either too vague and conditional to provide determinate guidance or too detailed and controversial to gain general support. As such, any theory must be judged as simply another contingent method "to make sense of the world and our aspirations".[45]

The common law moves from one doctrinal peak to another through the misty vales of fiction. This results from the deep logic of contradictory relations that underpin contemporary social practice and thought. For instance, the structural design of American accident law pre-*MacPherson*[46] and post-*Greenman*[47] is strikingly similar; the develop-ment of the law has taken place within very specific parameters and in line with a narrow set of formal arguments and alternatives. Each era strives to accommodate competing arguments; "as between two blame-less individuals, the one who caused the damage should pay" and "it is unfair to impose liability where there has been no wrongdoing". Before 1916, the dominant principle favoured private choice and confined liabil-ity to occasions of contractual privity.[48] Yet, there was at work a counter-principle which demanded a set of exceptions, based on the need for public control.[49] Since 1963, the counter-principle has eaten into the prin-ciple and has started to become dominant. Liability is motivated by a concern for public control and is stricter in application. However, the principles of private choice ensure that liability is not absolute and pro-

---

45 Note, *Efficiency and A Rule of "Free Contract": A Critique of Two Models of Law and Economics*, 97 HARV. L. REV. 978, 996 (1984).

46 *MacPherson v. Buick Motor Co.*, 111 N.E. 1050 (1916).

47 *Greenman v. Yuba Products*, 377 P. 2d 897 (1963).

48 *See Winterbottom v. Wright* (1842), 152 E.R. 402. It must be stressed that this rule for product-related injury co-existed with other areas of law that imposed strict liability. *See Limpus v. London General Omnibus Co.* (1862), 1 H. & C. 526 (vicarious liability); *Hutton v. Jones*, [1909] 2 K.B. 44 (defamation); and *Rylands v. Fletcher* (1868), L.R. 3 H.L. 330 (non-natural use of land).

49 The major exceptions, demanding only proof of negligence, were injury from an inherently dangerous product and one known to be dangerous. *See Thomas v. Win-chester*, 6 N.Y. 397 (1852).

vides for a series of causally-based defences.[50] In short, the doctrine contains and has never dispossessed itself of the resources for a reorganization in its own contradictory self-image. This supports the view that doctrinal patterns are a result of contingent choice rather than objective necessity.[51]

Although Fish might not express it in the same way, his theory leads to an interpretation of tort doctrine that closely resembles this "deconstructive" reading of tort history. Although judges claim to be constrained by the extant legal norms, they must negotiate results from among radically contradictory visions of social life. Yet, Fish offers no explanation for the actual choices made. Although legal argument is indeterminate, judicial decisionmaking exhibits an identifiable pattern. In crude terms, legal decisions tend to preserve the status quo and insulate the existing (mal)distribution of power. Of course, this does not mean that every decision is dictated by the needs of established interests. The process is much more subtle and complex; it has its own discursive rationality and constitutive force.[52] Without some account of the dynamics of power and its capacity to channel and constrain individual choice, Fish's project misrepresents the nature and history of interpretive practice. The challenge is to explain the distinct historical ways in which law, language, and power interact to constitute social experience and the individual agents within it[53] and, also, to re-create the continuing negotiations between the socially-situated individual and the individually-constructed society.

---

50 Liability does not follow simply by showing that injury resulted from use of a product. In such circumstances, absolute liability would amount to a full insurance rule, like Workers Compensation. *See* Schwartz, *Understanding Products Liability*, 67 CALIF. L. REV. 435 (1979). Strict liability still demands that there is a product defect. *See Barker* v. *Lull Engineering Co.*, 20 Cal. 3d 413 (1978). Also, there are a number of available defences that go to the plaintiff's product. *See Daly* v. *General Motors Corp.*, 20 Cal. 3d 725 (1978) (comparative negligence); *Shell Oil Co.* v. *Gutierrez*, 119 Ariz. 426 (1978) (product misuse); and *Winnett* v. *Winnett*, 57 Ill. 2d 7 (1978) (proximate cause).

In *Beshada* v. *Johns-Manville Prods. Corp.*, 447 A. 2d 539 (1982), it was held that a state-of-the-art defence was not allowed in a failure to warn case. Although dramatic, the case is explicable on standard notions of responsibility. The defendant is still entitled to rely on the culpable conduct of the plaintiff as a defence. Moreover, it still has to be established that the product was defective. Indeed, in *Beshada*, the court stated that, while products liability was product-based as opposed to conduct-oriented, it has to be decided "whether the product was reasonably safe for its foreseeable purposes." *Id.* at 544.

51 *See supra* ch. 4.

52 *See infra* ch. 9.

53 *See* Tushnet, *Post-Realist Scholarship*, 15 J.S.P.T.L. 20 at 32 (1980).

III. MAKING BOUILLABAISSE

A. A POWERFUL PART

In making these criticisms, I do not intend to fall back into the beckoning arms of a naive humanism by treating individuals as autonomous historical agents. On the contrary, I want to reject such dichotomous thinking. We are neither beyond history nor its helpless playthings. Instead of thinking about the "subject" as either the underwriter or signature of history, we must imagine individuality as both the playwright and player. We act out a script, but, in doing so, we effect a rescripting. As Dru Cornell captures it, "we are part of the story we tell".[54]

In summarizing the difference between my position and Fish's, it is important neither to exaggerate nor to trivialize our disagreement. I have tried to show how Fish's critical project begins by promising to demonstrate how individuals are trapped within and constituted by social conventions, but ends by revealing how those conventions allow (and oblige) individuals to control the whole pace and pattern of historical development. On the other hand, my critical ambition, like Marx's, is to show that, although individuals are not free to write their own history, neither are they hopelessly locked into some indelible historical script: "[People] make their own history, but they do not make it just as they please; they do not make it under circumstances chosen by themselves, but under circumstances directly encountered, given, and transmitted from the past."[55] The struggle to control meaning and, therefore, the conditions for collective life is fought anew every day. Yet that struggle is rigged by the extant protocols of power. Existing practices are sustained to the extent that they are reinforced through regular use. Individuals are reduced from protagonists to puppets. The most urgent undertaking of theorizing is to contribute to the democratization of this hermeneutical struggle. It can do this by chronicling the historical operation of power and enabling us to lessen "the pervasive presence of the status quo in our thoughts, hopes, and actions."[56]

Fish's response to such suggestions is predictable. He criticizes both the political "right" and left" for their futile and "antiprofessional" ef-

---

54 Cornell, *Convention and Critique*, 7 CARDOZO L. REV. 679 at 690 (1986).
55 Marx, *The Eighteenth Brumaire of Louis Bonaparte*, *supra* note 1, at 320.
56 Frug, *The Ideology of Bureaucracy in American Law*, 84 HARV. L. REV. 1276 at 1388 (1984).

forts to locate and rely upon some stripped–down, ahistorical world of essences, a reality independent of convention.[57] In a characteristic move, Fish sets up a loaded and unusual distinction between "professionalism" and "antiprofessionalism." Whereas the latter is held to stand for such thoroughly discredited notions as the disinterested pursuit of lasting truths, the former is associated at bottom with Fish's own "conventional" views. Accordingly, to oppose the reliance on some ahistorical notion of truth is to put oneself in the Fish camp; to oppose the "conventional" view is to be consigned to the anachronistic group who persist in believing in universal truths. Further, by using such a dichotomy, Fish manages to present his own ideas as being at the heart of contemporary literary practice. This dichotomy, however, is both incomplete and misleading. One can reject the ideal of "disinterested inquiry" without adopting Fish's alternative, and one can reject Fish's concept of "professionalism" without pursuing that ideal.

In particular, he chastises Duncan Kennedy and Robert Gordon for groping toward and defending "a form of life—free, independent, acontextual—that cannot be lived."[58] For Fish, the individual self is an asset, completely owned and operated by the community. Yet, Fish offers nothing by way of supporting evidence except the disputed authority and accuracy of his own conventional theory of interpretation. He provides no substantiating historical material for his allegedly historically situated theory. He thus offers nothing but a blatantly bootstrap argument. Moreover, despite his ambition to kill off the individual, Fish's theory succeeds in exaggerating the interpretive performance of the individual in history.

The most fatal failing of Fish's work is that it is shot through with the very either/or thinking that Fish is supposedly devoted to overcoming. He shifts hermeneutic authority from the text/reader to the context. His onslaught on the "individual" serves not only to de-centre it from its traditional position as the privileged affixer of meaning, but to obliterate it entirely from the face of history. In the social struggle, we are either entirely determined by history or stand in transcendent triumph over it. Constraints on thought and action are either illusory or total.

---

57 *See* Fish, *supra* note 33 and Fish, *Profession Despise Thyself,* 10 CRIT. INQ. 349 (1983).
58 Fish, *supra* note 33, at 107. I do not necessarily accept Fish's characterization and criticism of Kennedy and Gordon. Though both admittedly hint at the achievement of some unsituated self, there are clear strands in their writings that suggest a more historically–informed depiction of the individual self. *See, e.g.,* Gordon, *Critical Legal Histories,* 36 STAN. L. REV. 57 (1984) and Kennedy, *Toward a Phenomenology of Adjudication,* in THE RULE OF LAW (A. Hutchinson and P. Monahan eds. 1987).

Fish seems unable or unwilling to understand constraints as real, but tentative and as operative, but provisional: they facilitate as they foreclose meaning.

A high price is exacted for world-making. In order to live, we must generalise and be selective. Yet, in so doing, we necessarily distort, trivialize and overlook: if we do not exclude something, we will have nothing. Sight and blindness are simultaneously experienced. As such, constraint becomes a condition for meaningful freedom:

> If the doors of perception were cleansed every thing would appear to man as it is, infinite.
> For man has closed himself up, till he sees all things thro' narrow chinks of his cavern.[59]

Our caverns are built from the bricks of categorization and the cement of exclusion. In this way, our caverns are both shelters and prisons. They act as welcome havens from the bewildering storms that buffet us through history. But, at the same time, they are *man*-made dungeons whose walls mark off the limits of our world; at best, we can only snatch glimpses of other possible worlds through the bars of our cell-windows. These caverns ensure the possibility and parameters of any world: security cuts both ways. Yet our felt incapacity to imagine different forms of social life to our own has less to do with the limits of "reality" than with the limits of our present world. We re-negotiate the siting and force of these walls as we (con)strain to understand them.

A rigorous account of power can take up the historical slack left by Fish's arguments. Such an analysis must describe the caverns that we have inhabited, the rationalities and truths they have inculcated, and the interests that have thrived in their milieu. In particular, my inquiry will focus on the legal labrynths of these caverns. How does the legal regime of truth and discourse shape the conditions and status of the powerless (and the powerful)? How does the extension of legal discursive practices colonize recalcitrant sectors of social life? How does legal discourse comprise a discrete and constitutive mode of social action, but still be indeterminate and unclosable?

The effect (or design) of Fish's project is to suppress or displace power. Yet the analysis of power is the key to the interpretive lock: "when discourse is responsible for reality and not merely a reflection of

---

59 W. Blake, *The Marriage of Heaven and Hell* in BLAKE: THE COMPLETE WRITINGS 154 (G. Keynes ed. 1966).

it, then whose discourse prevails makes all the difference."[60] Later essays will draw out the inadequacies of traditional analyses of power and suggest a more fruitful approach towards understanding the workings of power and its normative potential for reconstruction. In the remainder of this essay, I will illustrate some of the ways in which the legal protocols of power function by noting the omissions in Fish's account.

B. THE LEGAL WORLD

Legal discourse is a social medium that has been particularly susceptible to power's overtures and infiltration. Yet discourse consists of more than the language spoken; it includes the field of language's operation and the social roles assigned and assumed in its performance. In this sense, some of the most important conventions are those that designate the authoritative voices in the interpretive Babel.[61] An obvious example is revealed in the incident that gave rise to the title of Fish's book, *Is There A Text In This Class?* As Fish recounts the tale, a student asked the teacher on the first day of classes, "Is there a text in this class?" The teacher responded by naming the set textbook. But the student was not satisfied: "no, no . . . I mean in this class do we believe in poems and things, or is it just us?"[62] Fish uses this as a colorful peg on which to hang his account of the pervasive and conventional nature of interpretive practice. But, although he glimpses them, he fails (or refuses) to acknowledge the relations of power that comprise the platform on which the student-teacher exchange takes place. Or, more accurately, he does not explain why this particular convention arises and persists in preference to others, especially its counterconventional twin, which would channel power in the opposite direction.

The need for the student to ask such a question offers a glimpse into the hierarchical and institutional framework in which student and teacher interact. In criticizing a fellow literary critic, Wayne Booth, Fish notes parenthetically that "students always know what they are expected to believe."[63] In this casual remark, he momentarily brings to light the

---

60 Tompkins, *An Introduction to Reader-Response Criticism* in READER-RESPONSE CRITICISM: FROM FORMALISM TO POST-STRUCTURALISM xxv (J. Tompkins ed. 1980).

61 *See* M. SHAPIRO, LANGUAGE AND POLITICAL UNDERSTANDING: THE POLITICS OF DISCURSIVE PRACTICES 150–152 (1981).

62 Fish, *supra* note 2, at 305.

63 *Id.* at 347.

"power-full" conventions that animate and organize interpretive practice. Yet, in his description of the student-teacher exchange, Fish argues
that the student and the teacher were ultimately able to communicate
meaningfully because of "their shared understanding of what could possibly be at stake in a classroom situation."[64] Though these conventions
are clearly shared, they are not consensual: they arise from an uncons-
cionable bargain struck between agents with unequal contracting force
and information. Fish fails to explain why student and teacher do not
share a perfectly converse counterconvention.

As he fails to recognize the pervasive workings of power, Fish must
put his faith in some divine invisible hand. At best, he has hidden rather
than done away with individuals. Also, it is often forgotten that even
though the teacher enjoys "power over" students, she herself is controlled and manipulated by the teacher-student relation. However much she
strives to reduce the hierarchical relation, she will be operating within
it; the temporary reduction of hierarchy is itself an act of hierarchy. The
roles of teacher and student form a grammar of relations that frame any
particular acting out of those roles. Yet, it is only through such constant
challenging of its daily performance that we could ever hope to dislodge
or transform that structure of power.[65]

A glance at life in the law schools reinforces this "interpretation" of
the hierarchical dynamic at work in the educational process.[66] In subtle
and not-so-subtle ways, the competing groups of faculty, bar, *and* students have "established a *modus vivendi* which suits their respective
needs."[67] There has come to exist a sophisticated protocol of power. Indeed, legal education consists largely of exercises to acquire and accept
this potent political etiquette. In a perverse way, "radical" law professors, by virtue of their participation in this system, confer some legitimacy on present arrangements. The challenge is to work the margins so
as to emphasise both the oppressive slant of present arrangements and

---

64 *Id.* at 320. At the end of the book, Fish adds an interesting and revealing postscript
to the story. The teacher replied: "Yes, there *is* a text in this class; what's more, it
has meanings; *and I am going to tell you what they are.*" *Id.* at 371 (emphasis added in
part).

65 Peller, *The Metaphysics of Law*, 73 CAL. L. REV. 1151 at 1278–1279 (1985).

66 The already classic exposition of the politics of legal education is D. KENNEDY,
LEGAL EDUCATION AND THE REPRODUCTION OF HIERARCHY: A POLEMIC
AGAINST THE SYSTEM (1983).

67 Halpern, *On the Politics and Pathology of Legal Education*, 32 J. LEGAL EDUC. 383 at
394 (1982).

its lack of inevitability, and to move towards a transformed style of pedagological practice.

During the first year at law school, students experience a crucial shift in allegiance from the outsider's nonprofessional attitude toward law to the insider's professional understanding of the lexicon. This sense of disorientation is exacerbated by the fact that the teaching experience is rarely uniform; significantly different interpretive norms can be operative in each class. Many, but not all, students soon come to recognize the authoritative voices and to appreciate the benefit of deferring to and, in time, mimicking those voices. Those who never make the transition fall by the legal wayside; those that make it, but who refuse to conform, lead a precarious life in the law school shadows. This transition phase marks a crucial moment in the ideological tuning-up of lawyers and is orchestrated through the prevailing relations of power.

The law school experience serves to highlight another weakness in Fish's theory. Fish contends that there is no interpretive occasion on which one can believe nothing.[68] Indeed, he is right to note that one cannot be in a state of absolute nonbelief; even indifference is a form of belief. Having no belief would only be possible if one could escape one's social milieu which is, of course, impossible. But at times, individuals have more interpretive beliefs than they can possibly deal with; they are in fact meaning-full. This experience will be painfully familiar to most law students and, although we learn to suppress it, to most lawyers.

The law school experience is an example of a more general phenomenon. Legal discourse empowers certain speakers by granting them a license to establish meaning. In this sense, power protects itself by rendering its aspiring usurpers mute or, when it allows them to speak, by putting words in their mouths and depriving their words of significance. Most speakers whistle into the wind, but a small few are privileged to speak with the wind at their backs. For instance, the force and meaning of the statement "You have broken the contract" is far from self-evident. It depends on the appreciation of and immersion in a whole socio-historical context. Much will depend on the identity of the speaker: a statement's "truth value" will increase proportionately with the speaker's authoritative status. In contemporary circumstances, its meaning will change and gain in communal strength depending on whether the speaker is an interested party, an officious bystander, a fledgling

---

68 Fish, *supra* note 2, at 319.

lawyer, a local politician, a law professor, a trial judge, an enacting legislator, or a Supreme Court justice.

The familiar likening of the law to a quasi-religious force, a mystical process replete with arcane incantations, ritual performances and priestly devotees is acutely drawn.[69] The similarity of the potent imagery evoked by the courtroom and the church is not coincidental. When Owen Fiss concludes that "the judge . . . speaks with the authority of the Pope,"[70] he gives the whole game away. The struggle to establish meaning is all about power, divine or otherwise. In the babble of competing idiolects, power ensures that its accent is heard and heeded. As Justice Jackson recognized, "[w]e are not final because we are infallible, but we are infallible only because we are final."[71]

As usual, Fish downplays the radical significance of these examples and critical claims about power. He scoffs at attempts to develop a radical theory explaining power, insisting that theory has no consequences for interpretive practice but only rationalizes changes that have already occurred. A change in substantive beliefs may produce a change in procedural beliefs: "theory is not so much the consequential agent of a change as it is the passive object of an appropriation."[72] Yet Fish concedes that a declaration of theoretical allegiance—for example, a judge declaring herself to be a "noninterpretivist" or a Marxist—might have strategic ramifications in political debate.[73]

Once again, however, Fish has glimpsed an insight but failed to follow through on its full force and effect. Indeed, with typical irony, he opines that, with the exposure of theory's lack of theoretical consequences, "nothing whatsoever will have been gained, and we will have lost any sense that theory is special."[74] But this loss and its revelation would have massive significance for the legal and governmental process: there may be no supreme court of literary criticism, but there is a Supreme Court of law. The constitutional authority and prestige of the judiciary depends on the continuing theoretical belief by the citizenry *and the legal community, including judges,* that judges are not simply ideologues-at-large but are, in some significant sense, constrained by the

---

69 *See* T. ARNOLD, SYMBOLS OF GOVERNMENT 59–62 (1935).
70 Fiss, *supra* note 10, at 755.
71 *Brown* v. *Allen*, 344 U.S. 443 at 540 per Jackson J. (1953).
72 Fish, *supra* note 30, at 451.
73 *Id.* at 446–447.
74 *Id.* at 443.

appropriate legal materials. Fish's critical project exposes that belief as so much pious and wishful thinking.

The main thrust of Fish's argument is that those very constraining materials are not given, but are themselves the products of interpretive practice. Moreover, interpretive practice comprises the interpretive beliefs of its practitioners. According to Fish's theory, judges are not an anarchical gang of subjective interpreters because they are always situated within a community of shared interpretive norms. Yet, the communal code of interpretive directives allows a considerable range of practical movement.[75] Furthermore, judges are conventionally authorized to dictate and change the identity of the prevailing substantive norms of interpretation. In this way, judges rely extensively on theory to preserve, disguise, and enhance their political power. Without some justificatory theoretical apparel, they would stand naked or, perhaps more accurately, their uniforms of official state colours will be revealed for all to see. It is as bespoke tailors to the judicial Emperors that academics have proved most useful.[76] Despite the inventiveness of master couturiers such as Dworkin and Fiss, the attempt to stitch together an entire wardrobe of coordinated and voguish garments has failed. By declining to acknowledge the strength of theory's political consequences, Fish has designed and added his own diaphonous raiment to the Imperial collection.

IV. OFF THE HOOK

Fish's lightning strikes into the jurisprudential heartland have placed its resident experts in a bad light. His critical project has justly exposed the foundational weakness of their continuing dalliance with textual positivism. Yet, for all Fish's pyrotechnics, his argments have tended to impress as much by their rhetorical dazzle as by their intellectual illumination. Along with his adversaries, real and imagined, Fish's "conventional" hermeneutic shares a similar ideological failing: it does not acknowledge the pivotal role of power in the interpretive enterprise or give an adequate account of its historical workings. Fish's vaunted moral and epistemological indifference is almost plausible in the ivory towers of the university, but it is difficult to sustain on the streets of history with its real-life victims and losers.

---

75 *See* K. LLEWELLYN, THE COMMON LAW TRADITION 521–535 (1960).
76 *Supra*, pp. 119–121.

This essay has sought to outline the legal protocols of power that establish texts and their interpretive personnel in their own self-image and self-interest. In so doing, it has reversed Dworkin's hopeful conclusion: politics, art, and law are not so much united in philosophy[77] as art, law, and philosophy are united in politics. It is only by uncovering the hidden systems and rituals of power that determine our most habitual behaviour that individuals can hope to alter the prevailing discourse of truth and justice. Without an understanding and analysis of power, jurisprudence is destined to remain "a darkling plain . . . where ignorant armies clash by night."[78] And, in their encounter, innocent victims will continue to be unintentionally sacrificed at the altar of rationality and rights, needless hostages to intellectual fortune.

NUMBER THREE: TRIBAL NOISES

A couple of Christmases ago, I was introduced to the delights of Trivial Pursuit. One of the first questions I was asked was "What building is often referred to as the eighth Wonder of the World?" The answer which eluded me was "The Houston Astrodome". This "triviality" brought back a feeling that I have long held. As an impressionable and gauche English schoolboy, I envied the natural confidence and egocentricity of Americans. A country so self-assured that, without an apparent trace of irony or self-consciousness, it calls its national baseball championship the "World Series" seemed worthy of my juvenile admiration. I still admire much of the American élan. As a Canadian academic, I am regularly impressed by the verve and vigor of American legal scholarship; it exhibits an enviable intellectual passion and excitement. Yet, no longer a schoolboy, I am increasingly troubled by its parochialism, lack of utility, and irrelevance. While I am not a member of the American tribe, I have been touched by its potent image and vast influence. Taking advantage of my alien status, I offer some critical observations on the theory and practice of American constitutional law.

---

77 Dworkin, *supra* note 8, at 166.
78 M. Arnold, *Dover Beach* in ARNOLD: POETICAL WORKS 212 (1950).

If Ronald Reagan is the tribal chieftain, the members of the American Supreme Court are an elite coterie of tribal elders whose pronouncements are treated with the utmost respect and reverence. In their grandiloquent moments, hacks and historians have venerated these robed stalwarts as "a bevy of Platonic guardians."[1] While the relation between its institutional chatter and the substantive conditions of American life is profoundly problematic,[2] the Court's contribution to the constitutional conversation of America is undisputed and indisputable. The ambition of American constitutional scholarship is to offer some theoretically valid account and justification of this judicial enterprise. As part of the larger project of modern liberalism, lawyers seek to establish the distinctiveness of legal discourse, its constrained objectivity, its just foundations and its pivotal importance for social life. The resonance and relevance of these themes for the Canadian debate over the Charter are too obvious to need labouring.[3] The aim of this essay is to challenge the validity of contemporary constitutional practice as a professional pursuit, a scholarly endeavour and a political aspiration.

Among the clan of American constitutional lawyers, Laurence Tribe is one of the leading and most gifted warriors. With prodigious energy, he has become preeminent in all the legal roles he has assumed. He holds Harvard's only chair in constitutional law, he is a frequent expert witness before Congress, he is a seasoned and successful campaigner at the Supreme Court, and his treatise *American Constitutional Law* won the Coif Award in 1980 for the most outstanding legal writing. His two recent books, *Constitutional Choices* and *God Save This Honorable Court*, reaped a similar harvest of praise. Indeed, the dust-jacket comments by various constitutional celebrities suggest that his constitutional canonization is imminent. I contend that Tribe's work represents the best and the worst of American constitutional culture. To paraphrase Lionel Trilling, the light it gives forth is in part the reflection of a glorious dream and in part the phosphorescence of a living decay.[4] Accordingly, Tribe's writing is a natural focus for critical analysis.

After introducing briefly the context and shape of the general debate in constitutional circles, I will criticise Tribe's transparent attempts to finesse the troublesome question of interpretive commitments. My major argument is that, for all his smooth erudition and apparent origi-

---

1 L. HAND, THE BILL OF RIGHTS 73 (1958).
2 *See* Hutchinson, *Charter Litigation and Social Change* in CHARTER LITIGATION 357 (R. Sharpe ed. 1987).
3 *See infra*, ch. 7.
4 L. TRILLING, THE LIBERAL IMAGINATION 61 (1950).

nality, Tribe is caught within the limited and limiting world of liberal politics and discourse. He presents the same tired set of problems and answers for our edification. His emphasis on "choosing" serves to hide the extent to which liberalism restricts the range and method of choice. In a liberal world, the choices choose us as much as we choose them. I will substantiate these claims by addressing the puzzle of "free speech". I will not engage in a precious cut-and-slicing of legal materials; I am neither trained to do that with American materials nor do I find it a fruitful exercise. Instead, I will explore the political and practical realities of "freedom of the press" so as to illuminate better its structural infirmities. In short, I will discuss three aspects of tribal noise—the scholarly utterances of Laurence Tribe; the doctrinal musings of the courts; and the thunderings of the media.

I. THROUGH THE BLACK HOLE

The ambition to explain the legitimate role and responsibilities of the judiciary within a constitutional democracy has long been the motivation behind most American jurisprudential scholarship. In recent years, the study of legal interprtation has preoccupied jurists. Constitutional scholars have become absorbed in the quest for the hermeneutic grail—namely, the search for an appropriate set of methodological principles for valid interpretation which allows jurists to connect textual properties with ethical intuitions. The plethora of ingenious solutions testifies not only to the fecundity of the juristic imagination, but also to the bankruptcy of traditional legal thought. Between the extremes of an insistence on historical and textual objectivity and a belief in the extra-constitutional authority of a prophetic interpreter, there are a whole host of intermediate positions.[5] For all their apparent diversity, theorists combine and continue in their search for scientifically and politically valid methods of interpretation.[6]

Sadly, even deconstruction has been enlisted in the logocentric struggle for constitutional meaning. Relying on a pseudo-deconstructive line of criticism, Sanford Levinson defends an interpretive mode of legal nihilism. For him, legal language is infinitely manipulable; "[t]here are as many plausible readings of the United States Constitution as there are

---

5 For a thorough account and critique of these offerings, see Brest, *The Fundamental Rights Controversy: The Essential Contradictions of Normative Constitutional Scholarship*, 90 YALE L.J. 1063 (1981).

6 *See supra* pp. 143–144.

versions of *Hamlet*. . . . ""[7] The meaning-giving exercise is reduced to another occasion for the expression of personal prejudice. He maintains that "legal discourse is simply judges and other adjudicators doing what their political and ethical views command,"[8] and confers on John Marshall the dubious distinction of being "the great Nietzschean judge of our tradition."[9] Constitutional interpretation is the unbounded free play of the judicial mind. Yet, like those he is reacting against, Levinson shares the same epistemological commitments and has translated deconstruction into one more interpretive technique.[10] He holds to a foundational faith in individuals as the privileged source of meaning beyond the constraints of their historical and discursive setting. By offering an ahistorical and asocial approach, he fails to take doctrine seriously and thereby blunts the political edge of deconstructive critique. Like a nihilistic cartographer, Levinson offers a doctrinal map without any topographical features or, to be more precise, one that can be filled in with the features of the reader's choice. Doctrinal terrain changes over time, but it is nonsensical to pretend that it has no general shape at any particular time even if that shape cannot be described in detail or is changed in the act of cartographical description.

Tribe is more subtle in his methodological machinations and, in a sense, more persuasive. But his strategy to avoid being trapped in the snares of the interpretive debate is more disingenuous. Like Philip Bobbit,[11] he struggles to present interpretive legitimacy as a product rather than a premise of constitutional practice. Although Tribe insists that his work "does not offer a theory of choice; rather it is an experiment in choosing," he goes on to express his hope that "the whole will . . . add up to more than the sum of its several parts".[12] He explicitly seeks a middle path between those who espouse a resort to some "neutral method" and those who convince themselves that "anything goes." He goes so far as to condemn all legitimating theories as "not simply amusing in their pretensions but, in the end, as dangerous as they are unconvincing".[13] However, it is difficult to avoid the conclusion that Tribe's claims for his own work are just as "dangerous" and "unconvincing": the middle of the road is a hazardous place to be. It is a matter of trite

---

7 Levinson, *Law as Literature*, 60 TEX. L. REV. 373 at 391 (1982).
8 Levinson, *Escaping Liberalism: Easier Said Than Done*, 96 HARV. L. REV. 1466 at 1471 (1983).
9 Levinson, *supra* note 7, at 389.
10 *See supra* ch. 2.
11 P. BOBBITT, CONSTITUTIONAL FATE (1982).
12 L. TRIBE, CONSTITUTIONAL CHOICES viii and ix (1985).
13 *Id.* at 6.

learning that the only difference between those lawyers without an interpretive theory and those with a theory is that the latter know what
their theory is and are better able to reflect upon it.[14] Tribe is much too
sophisticated to be unaware of this. He knows only too well that there
is no position of theoretical innocence. There is nothing beyond politics,
but more politics.

As his work progresses, Tribe loses sight of his modest interpretive
beginnings and gives full rein to his own political instincts. In particular,
he champions the cause of "principled choice" over "instrumental calculation." However, it becomes increasingly unclear how, if at all, these
constraints do or could offer any realistic check on Tribe's own prescriptions for constitutional change and justice. Although Tribe recognizes
that "forces of politics and culture . . . do . . . constrain the constitutional enterprise"[15], he fails to explain the origin, operation, strength,
and character of those forces. It is surely the task of criticism to make
visible the constraints that locate and render the text intelligible. The
challenge is to place the text in its historical context and reestablish its
genetic affiliations with institutions, classes, professionals, and the like.
However, although texts are produced by, and must be correlated with,
those forces, they must not be reduced to them. To reduce textmaking
to the traces of historical forces is as much a distortion as it is to confine
it to some ahistorically isolated cell of human activity.

Tribe acknowledges that "[s]ubstantive perspective, reflecting the
observer's past and context, is inescapable . . . [and] pervasive"[16] but he
chooses to ignore the wisdom of that insight. Professional advocacy collapses into scholarly criticism and hermeneutic sophistication belies
simplistic humanism. Indeed, the whole of *God Save This Honorable
Court* is founded explicitly on the thesis that the law is simply the cumu-
lated opinion of the nine sitting judges who act as almost autonomous
agents in choosing the terms and conditions of social life. *Constitutional
Choices* contents itself with an implicit, but no less important commitment. Tribe seems to suggest that if Americans only select the "right"
justices then constitutional justice will be secure and the fate of the nation
assured.[17] This notion seems dangerously naive. It ignores the very potent

---

14 *See supra* ch. 1.
15 *Supra* note 12, at 4.
16 *Id*. at 7–8.
17 A few years ago, Mark Tushnet's review of Tribe's *American Constitutional Law*
caused a minor furor by suggesting that Tribe was making a grandstand play for
future elevation to the Supreme Court. Although Tushnet was castigated for making
such a tasteless suggestion, any reader of *God Save This Honorable Court* could be
forgiven for thinking Tushnet was right. See Tushnet, *DiaTribe*, 78 MICH L. REV.
694 (1980).

structural and discursive arrangements that shape and manipulate the individuals who function within them. Tribe chooses to overlook the fact that, in the constitutional conversation, we each may speak with our own mouths, but not in the voice or accent of our choosing. As Umberto Eco puts it, "the subject is spoken by language."[18]

Tribe's attempts to finesse an encounter with the black hole of interpretation are transparent. His discussion of recent doctrinal developments is premised on and intended to promote a very partial view of judicial method, function, and performance. Let me emphasize that my criticism is not that it is a partial view, but that he tries to disguise and deny the nature of its partiality in order to avoid having to defend it; ideology is not the crime, but the deafening silence that hides it. For instance, since I met Owen Fiss, Sanford Levinson and Laurence Tribe at the University of Southern California, it would be silly to conclude that they all live in Los Angeles. Similarly, it is equally silly to assume that, since we met to talk about interpretation, we all treat it as an autonomous intellectual pursuit. Just as Fiss, Levinson and Tribe came from and returned to different parts of the United States, so they came to the interpretive discussion from very different political perspectives and returned to their very different political agendas afterwards. They spoke in the interpretive debate with the unmistakable accent of their political home. Indeed, Tribe has committed his own version of the seventh deadly sin—"indulging [scholarly] imperialism, masquerading as modesty."[19] Accordingly, Tribe has backed into the interpretation debate and, as usually happens with such a manoeuvre, has fallen over.

Nevertheless, Tribe's insistence on the "situated" and "engaged" nature of interpretation and decision-making is a step in the right direction. He reminds us, if only to forget it himself, that choice and responsibility for decisions are ours and cannot be ducked by foisting them on the text, the Founding Fathers or some other such device. The fact that we are part of a tradition does not condemn us to a slavish and constant repetition of it: we can work to reject and remake it as we work within it. Tribe glimpses this, but does not recognize, or refuses to pursue, its radical potential. Although he puts forward his choices, conclusions and judgments so as "never to end debate but always to advance it,"[20] he contrives to ensure that that debate proceeds within the same discursive

---

18 U. ECO, SEMIOTICS AND THE PHILOSOPHY OF LANGUAGE 45 (1984).
19 Tribe, *Seven Deadly Sins of Straining the Constitution Through a Pseudo-Scientific Sieve*, 36 HASTINGS L. REV. 155, 170 (1984).
20 *Supra* note 12, at 8.

channels and by the same political dynamic. Any advances will be decidedly liberal in temper and direction. As such, Tribe institutionalises the mysterious paradox of liberal legalism:

> We wish to believe both that our laws come from a necessity beyond our reach, and that they are our own instruments shaping our community to our chosen ends. . . . This leads us to the most tantalizing problem—the mystery—of law in modern society. How retain any belief in the immanence of law, in its superiority to our individual, temporary needs, after we have adopted a wholehearted modern belief in its instrumentality? How continue to believe that something about our law is changeless after we have discovered that it may be infinitely plastic? How believe that in some sense the basic laws of society are given us by God, after we have become convinced that we have given them to ourselves?[21]

II. THE POLITICS OF SPEAKING

A. OPENING SPEECH

The general claims about the troubled character of Tribe's ideological bent can be given body and bite by a more detailed examination of the style and substance of his arguments. I intend to focus on the doctrinal theory and social practice of "free speech." In addition to criticizing Tribe's arguments and scrutinizing his assumptions, I will attempt to demonstrate that existing doctrine is more than "a grab bag of rubrics".[22] As I see it, the conscious (ir)rationality of the legal process rests upon the more fundamental and unconscious "rationality" of the contradictory relations that form the hierarchical society in which we presently live. Although touted by Tribe as "the Constitution's most majestic guarantee,"[23] First Amendment doctrine exemplifies the promise and failing of American constitutional law. Not only is the doctrine confused and confusing, it is also the primary underwriter of privileged power. Moreover, Tribe's criticism is piecemeal and ambivalent; he accepts the operative assumptions of the doctrinal apologists and refuses to recognize the deep structural and systemic infirmities of a judicial republic and its liberal commitments.

First Amendment doctrine seems to consist of an endless process of making, refining, reworking, collapsing, and rejecting doctrinal

---

21 Boorstin, *The Perils of Indwelling Law* in THE RULE OF LAW 76–79 (R.P. Wolff ed. 1971).

22 *Supra* note 12, at 218.

23 L. TRIBE, AMERICAN CONSTITUTIONAL LAW 576 (1978).

categories and distinctions. By the time one has gained a rudimentary understanding of the difference between speech and nonspeech, protected and unprotected speech, political and commercial speech, private and public forums, and the like, the courts have already modified the distinctions and their protean doctrinal infrastructure. The fact that the doctrines are complicated and difficult to grasp is not a problem in itself, but the complexity may signal that things might be rotten in the legal state of America. In short, there is indeterminacy with a political slant: the protection of speech is motivated by and closely connected to the protection of property.

This is not a startling claim, for the Supreme Court itself has acknowledged that there is a "hierarchy of first amendment values."[24] The "haves" have benefited in the supposed campaign to protect the "have-nots". There has been an unholy alliance of doctrinal developments concerning commercial speech,[25] campaign financing,[26] and labour relations[27] that has operated not only to insulate the privileged against government regulation, but also to promote their involvement in political affairs. Further, these modern decisions are not aberrations; they are simply contemporary examples of an established tradition that has been used "to support and legitimize social inequity and injustice, and to mask a lack of real participation and democracy."[28] Although some will argue that the courts have given uncompromising protection to true "political speech," it is clear that the courts have equivocated and relied on fine and spurious distinctions to marginalize such speech.

Two manoeuvres illustrate the thinking and sympathies of the courts. First, when spoken by workers or unions, political speech is classified as labor speech and therefore is placed at a level requiring less protection.[29] Second, the "public forum" component of doctrine has been resurrected. Stressing that the First Amendment was never intended to

---

24 *See Carey* v. *Brown*, 447 U.S. 455, 467 (1980).

25 *Virginia St. Bd. of Pharmacy* v. *Virginia Citizens Consumer Council*, 425 U.S. 748 (1976); and *Central Hudson Gas & Elec. Corp.* v. *Public Serv. Comm'n.*, 447 U.S. 557 (1980).

26 *See Buckley* v. *Valeo*, 424 U.S. 1 (1976); and *First Nat'l Bank of Boston* v. *Bellotti*, 435 U.S. 765 (1978).

27 *See Safeco*, 447 U.S. 616 (1980).

28 Kairys, *Freedom of Speech* in THE POLITICS OF LAW 136 (D. Kairys ed. 1982).

29 *See Minnesota St. Bd. for Community Colleges* v. *Knight*, 104 S. Ct. 1058 (1984); *I.L.A.*, 456 U.S. 212 (1982). For a general discussion of this manoeuvre, see Pope, *The Three-Systems Ladder of First Amendment Values: Two Rungs and a Black Hole*, 11 HASTINGS CONST. L.Q. 189 (1984).

guarantee access to property simply because it is government owned, the Supreme Court has applied only minimal scrutiny to government attempts to regulate speech in anything but the most public places, such as parks and streets. In any other forum, government can restrict speech provided it is reasonable and content-neutral.[30] Indeed, in *Cornelius*, the Court held that fear of controversy was a sufficient ground for regulating speech.[31] The upshot is that property owners can restrict the speech activities of the propertyless, while at the same time amplifying and expanding the opportunities for their own propertied voices.

Tribe, of course, is not insensitive to all of this. He is a trenchant critic of the courts' performance and castigates them for it. He agrees that First Amendment jurisprudence has a "checkered history" and its ostensibly neutral principles "tilt decidedly in the direction of existing concentrations of wealth and influence".[32] He has no truck with the precious exercises of doctrinal categorization in which the Court indulges; "[t]his sort of pigeonholing endangers the pigeon".[33] Yet, for all his critical wit and exposure of the doctrine's economic bias, Tribe still labors under the romantic illusion that, if only we could hit upon the right principles and appoint the right people, all the doctrinal pieces would fall neatly into place and free speech would be assured. He presses forward with his criticism only so far; he pulls back at the very moment that his criticism might begin to do more than scratch the scaly surface of constitutional doctrine. Although directed at a different problem, Noam Chomsky's comment hits the critical mark:

> What is important . . . is the contribution of the harshest critics (within the mainstream) to reinforcing the system of indoctrination, of which they themselves are victims—as is the norm for the educated classes, who are typically the most profoundly indoctrinated and, in a deep sense, the most ignorant group, the victims as well as the purveyors of the doctrines of faith. The great achievement of the critics is to prevent the realization that what is happening today is not some departure from our historical ideals and practice, to be attributed to the personal failings of this or that individual. Rather, it is the systematic expression of the way our institutions function and will continue to function unless impeded by an aroused public that comes to understand their nature and their

---

30 *See United States Postal Serv.* v. *Council of Greenburgh Civic Ass'n,* 453 U.S. 134 (1981); *Widmar* v. *Vincent,* 454 U.S. 263 (1981); *Perry Educ. Ass'n* v. *Perry Local Educators' Ass'n,* 460 U.S. 37 (1982); *Cornelius* v. *NAACP Legal Defense & Educ. Fund,* 105 S. Ct. 3439 (1985).
31 *Cornelius, id.* at 3453–3454.
32 *Supra* note 12, at 188–189.
33 *Id.* at 218.

true history—exactly what our educational institutions must prevent if they are to fulfill *their* function, namely, to serve power and privilege.

A useful rule of thumb is this: If you want to learn something about the propaganda system, have a close look at the critics and their tacit assumptions.[34]

B. JUDICIAL SCHIZOPHRENIA

It would be a particularly uninformed, unsophisticated commentator who did not agree with Tribe that "the Constitution exists in intimate relationship with society as a whole and that the constitutional doctrines . . . are outcomes of a complex interplay among text, history and social forces".[35] Yet he seems content to hide behind this "complex interplay" rather than try to fathom its operating dynamic, its historical structure, and its political significance. To reveal the inadequacy of his attempts at explanation, I will examine a couple of his critical conclusions about First Amendment doctrine and its consequences: that the judicial development of doctrine is "schizophrenic"[36] and that, if current judicial trends continue, "the average citizen's rights of expression and . . . the prospects for realizing free speech values . . . could be seriously threatened".[37]

Tribe seems to think that judicial schizophrenia is a passing affliction that a dose of rational thinking and common sense can remedy. He disregards the possibility that this might be a congenital (and terminal) defect that represents that perennial and inescapable condition of constitutional adjudication. Indeed, the claims of indeterminacy and contradiction do not simply go to legal doctrine and theorizing: they go to the very heart of the entire liberal project of which adjudication is one aspect and of which Tribe is a leading advocate. Doctrinal indeterminacy is but a localized version of a more general political and intellectual problem. Liberalism embraces a host of dualities and is constantly and ceaselessly striving to reconcile these binary opposites, whether they be subjective/objective, public/private, or whatever. Tribe's writing seems to capture that agonized struggle for the ever elusive vantage point outside history and society from which to mediate and sustain a position of normative equilibrium. Tribe's account of recent developments in First Amendment

---

34 Chomsky, *The Manufacture of Consent*, 17 OUR GENERATION 83 at 90–91 (1985).
35 *Supra* note 12, at 192.
36 *Id*. at 195.
37 *Id*. at 198.

doctrine brings to light the unclosable open-endedness of legal doctrine
and the troubled liberal response. In contrast, I prefer to try to reveal the
doctrine's ideological contradictoriness from within (i.e., to deconstruct). In contrast to the liberal theorist, who seems to believe she is
more often than not on solid ground (except for occasional marshy
spots), and the nihilist, who seems to think that we are forever condemned to be awash on a stormy ocean, my view is that the jurist is like
a skater on thin ice: beneath the crystallised doctrinal surface, there are
the icy waters of principled cross-currents and precedential eddies. Determinacy and indeterminacy are locked in an interminable and fluid embrace.

The American doctrine of "free speech" is a microcosm of the challenge and failure of liberal thought; it is an arcane and privileged arena
for the never ending and never endable controversies about the proper
forms of social life. Two themes or principles run through Supreme
Court decisions: "formal neutrality" and "substantive egalitarianism."[38]
The first, and dominant, principle rests on a notion of negative liberty,
like that underlying the decisions in *Buckley*, *Bellotti*, and *Miami Herald*.[39]
This view works from and toward individual self-actualisation. Model-
led on "the marketplace of ideas",[40] individuals must be free from governmental intrusion in their efforts to have others hear their views; the
law is a protective shield. But this dominant tradition has had to graft
on limitations that derive their force from a more positive notion of liberty, as revealed in decisions like *Red Lion* and *Sullivan*.[41] This view looks
more toward collective self-determination. Allowing a more active role
for government, individuals must have more genuine opportunities to
engage in public debate that is "uninhibited, robust and wide-open":[42]
the law is as much an affirmative sword as a protective shield.

---

38 See Denvir, *Justice Brennan, Justice Rehnquist and Free Speech*, 80 N.W.U. L. REV. 285
    (1985) and Fiss, *Free Speech and Social Structure*, 71 IOWA L. REV. 1405 (1986).
39 *Buckley* v. *Valeo*, 424 U.S. 1 (1976) (invalidation of legislation limiting election cam-
    paign expenditure); *Boston* v. *Bellotti*, 435 U.S. 765 (1978) (striking down restrictions
    on political spending by corporations) and *Miami Herald Publishing Co.* v. *Tornillo*,
    418 U.S. 241 (1974) (freedom of the press includes right not to be obliged to publish
    anything).
40 *Abrams* v. *U.S.*, 250 U.S. 616 at 630 per Holmes J. (1919).
41 *Red Lion Broadcasting Co.* v. *FCC*, 395 U.S. 367 (1969) (upholding state regulation
    of broadcasting frequencies) and, *New York Times* v. *Sullivan*, 376 U.S. 254 (1964)
    (constitutional privilege for criticism, even if false, of official conduct).
42 *Sullivan, id.* at 270. For a good illustration of these competing visions, see the major-
    ity and minority opinions in *Posadas*, 1065 S. Ct. 2968 (1986).

As with almost all modern doctrine, each theme not only draws its force and meaning from its juxtaposition to the other theme, but, when push comes to shove, collapses into the other one.[43] For instance, although they lead to very different recommendations and proposals, each principle is united in its attempt to make the market work in a more efficient and equitable manner: the disagreement goes to the nature of that efficiency and equity. Even in *Red Lion*, the Court held that "it is the purpose of the First Amendment to preserve an uninhibited marketplace of ideas in which truth will ultimately prevail, rather than to countenance monopolization of that market, whether it be by the government itself or a private [organisation]."[44] As is true of open ideological debate, legal doctrine is pervaded by competing principles and counter-principles with no metatheory to reconcile them, other than some loose and circular resort to an amorphous "market". Like political choice, doctrinal patterns can never be objectively justified and amount to contingent, if not arbitrary, designs. As the stuff of political controversy, it echoes the fundamental debate over the social visions that are to inspire and guide our struggle towards the good life. Tribe glimpses this, but fails to follow it through: his commitment to the status quo, albeit suitably reformed, prevents him from pursuing his own insights to the point where they demand a radical reappraisal and rejection of the rights-based, market-oriented and individualistic liberal project itself. Tribe could do worse than follow his own earlier advice:

> It should be clear that no satisfactory theory of free speech can presuppose or guarantee the permanent existence of any particular social system. For example, a free speech theory must permit evolution from a society built on the ideals of liberal individualism to a society aspiring to more communitarian visions—just as it must permit evolution from communitarianism to individualism. It is of course possible, and indeed it may be common, to disregard the dangers of excessive parochialism and to design theories slanted toward favored conceptions of society; and surely *some* less than universal social vision must underlie *any* theory of law. But any free speech theory too narrowly conceived must either admit of its own self-destruction, as the evolution triggered by speech itself undermines the social forms the theory presupposes; or it must contain boundaries of a highly troublesome sort: boundaries that proscribe as beyond the pale communicative acts that threaten to transform society beyond the limits of its starting premises.[45]

---

43 This mode of critique is pursued at length elsewhere. *See supra* chs. 2 and 4.

44 *Red Lion, supra* note 41, at 390. For a general discussion, *see* Coase, *The Economics of The First Amendment: The Market for Goods and the Market for Ideas*, 64 AM. ECON. REV. 384 (1974).

45 *Toward a Metatheory of Free Speech*, 10 SW. U.L. REV. 237, 239 (1978).

C. The Fourth Estate

Tribe's other critical conclusion is that if current judicial trends continue, free speech in the United States "could be seriously threatened".[46] The problem with this, of course, is that there is not as much to threaten as is often thought. Only if there is a fundamental shift in our way of thinking about and responding to the institutional maldistribution of speech power can the existing order be seriously threatened. The days of the street-corner orator are gone, we live in a high-tech society in which large corporations have the power to regulate the information pulse of modern political life. First Amendment doctrine fails to recognize that the real impediment to free speech comes more from the private sector than from the state. A.J. Liebling's quip would be amusing if it were not so tragically true: the only person with freedom of the press is the person who can afford to own one. Moreover, the courts' almost pathological insistence on treating huge private bureaucracies as though they were individuals and bestowing human rights on them is a major obstacle to the genuine realization of individual freedom and social justice.

The basic problem in North America is that "whoever controls the image in a world dominated by the mass communication of images ultimately controls that world."[47] Politics has become a matter of spectacle and pesonality rather than of debate and principle. In societies, like the United States, that subscribe to representative democracy and vilify totalitarian practices, the major vehicle of popular control is not violence and coercion but a more subtle process of establishing "the framework for thinkable thought. . . . ; [propaganda] is to democracy what violence is to totalitarianism."[48] Critics like Tribe too conveniently forget that speech is not only a source of knowledge and enlightment, but also of fabrication and indoctrination. The only way to ensure a thorough and open system of communication is to render *all* channels and sources open to democratic participation. Large-scale business enterprises like the mass media must be subjected to the same constitutional principles of popular accountability that we aspire to for state bureaucracies.

In the United States, there is only as much freedom of press as is

---

46 *Supra* note 12, at 198.

47 P. Green, Retrieving Democracy: In Search of Civic Equality 220 (1985).

48 Chomsky, *supra* note 34, at 100 and 106.

necessary to keep its ideal barely plausible and as is compatible with the present distribution of power and property; rocking the boat is permitted as long as it does not jeopardize the existing boat or its traditional course. This is especially evident in the American attitude to the admission of foreign speakers. Thousands have been denied entry visas because of their political beliefs and without any reasons being given or required.[49] Indeed, the United States is the only Western democracy to exclude consistently foreign citizens on ideologial grounds. It has led the Italian satirist Dario Fo to treat his inclusion as a badge of pride and the renowned Mexican novelist Carlos Fuentes to offer his own biting comment:

> experience has taught us all that it is the application of the exclusionary clause that endangers the republic, mocks democracy, demoralizes the true friends of the United States, and offers undeserved aces to the Soviet Union.[50]

The performance and practices of the American media reveal the limitations of the commitment to free speech and the succor that such limitations give the bastions of propertied power and privilege. The primary *raison d'être* of the media is making money (not disseminating news or providing entertainment) and they have been colossally successful.[51] In addition, the leading media corporations have been heavily inflenced by the obsessions of their founders.[52] This tendency to treat "news" as a commodity might be less troublesome if there were not a very marked oligopoly; over 70% of total American circulation is controlled by newspaper chains.[53] Further, to attract advertising, the media have an understandable tendency to emphasize the kind of establishment views attractive to potential advertisers and to "edit out" less congenial views and

---

49 The length and variety of this list of "excludables" is staggering. See Shapiro, *The Excludables*, 11 MOTHER JONES 29 (Jan. 1986). Farley Mowat's exclusion was a recent reminder of this pitiful policy. See F. MOWAT, MY DISCOVERY OF AMERICA (1985).

50 Shapiro, *supra* note 49, at 51.

51 The following comments draw heavily on an excellent essay by my colleague Harry Glasbeek. See Glasbeek, *Entrenchment of Freedom of Speech for the Press—Fettering of Freedom of Speech of the People* in THE COURTS, THE CHARTER AND THE MEDIA. 101 (P. Anisman ed. 1986).

52 *See* D. HALBERSTAM, THE POWERS THAT BE (1979).

53 *See* Helle, *The Impact of Estate Taxes on Independent Daily News: An Illinois Case Study,* 33 DE PAUL L. REV. 323 (1984). For similar figures on the growing concentration in Canada, *see* W. SODERLUND ET AL., MEDIA AND ELECTIONS IN CANADA (1984).

news.[54] News and advertising combine to project a materialistic and individualistic view of the world. This is not to suggest direct intervention or crude censorship by owners in the daily functioning of their media arms. The journalistic knights are not in need of such baronial chastisement. As Tom Wicker put it:

> Now I have great freedom at the *New York Times* as a columnist. I'm not told what to write, and I'm not second guessed at what I do write. But I understand very well that the freedom that I have, unlimited in that sense, is circumscribed within a very well understood area. I'm not going to last around here if I start advocating the violent overthrow of the federal government. I'm not going to last around here if I start advocating socialism. I'm certainly not going to last very long around here if I start advocating Marxist-Leninism. I don't want to do those things, so I don't feel hampered by them. That is because I'm part of the establishment, in that sense. Within that large circle of responsibility that the *Times* grants me, I can be Democrat or Republican. I can be Liberal or Conservative. I can be lots of things, hawk or dove, or whatever. But I know, nobody has to draw that line in the dirt for me, I know where it is, I don't step over it.[55]

Talk of free speech against such a backdrop is fanciful. Indeed, First Amendment doctrine has not only failed to loosen the stranglehold that big business has over speech power; it has also tended to insulate the media from governmental regulation and facilitate their further growth. All of this is thrown into even sharper relief when it is realized that more than 25 million Americans cannot read the warnings on products and an additional 35 million are functionally illiterate. Relative to its socioeconomic status, the United States stands an abysmal 49th of 158 U.N. member states in general literacy levels.[56] In light of all this, Tribe's equivocating conclusions about First Amendment doctrine—a call for a reexamination of principles, recognition of historical and social context, and the exercise of honest choice—offers an extremely weak peg on which to hang the quest for a theory and practice of free speech. This is

---

54 The complicity by the media in suppressing material opposing American support of military and totalitarian regimes has been heavily documented. *See* 1 and 2 N. CHOMSKY AND E. HERMAN, THE POLITICAL ECONOMY OF HUMAN RIGHTS (1979). Without direct encouragement, the media self-censor the news "to serve the important interests that dominate the state and select and suppress facts so as to convey the impression that national policy is well-intentioned or justified." *Id.* at 23. *See, also,* M. PARENTI, INVENTING REALITY (1983).

55 *The Pundits,* on Ideas, CBC-Radio program transcript, at 8–9, May 23, 1984, as quoted in Glasbeek, *supra* note 51, at 107.

56 J. KOZOL, ILLITERATE AMERICA (1984).

nowhere better revealed than in his anguished, but trite observation that "the painful dilemma of *Skokie* might be turned to good use by providing occasions for reexamination of principles and precedents".[57] In many ways, *Skokie* is not a perennial hard case, but a typical, if sharp, example of the predicament of modern liberal theory. In the words of Justice Brandeis, which Tribe is fond of quoting, "the greatest dangers to liberty lurk in insidious encroachment by men of zeal, well-meaning but without understanding."[58]

D. CONSTITUTIONAL WIND

The upshot of my critique of Tribe is that a significant barrier to the establishment of a social order that puts its commitment to the ideal of "free speech" into social practice is the continued existence of the Supreme Court itself. The most obvious reason for this is the lessons for the future provided by its past doctrinal performance: judicial schizophrenia is not a curable affliction but is the continuing and fatal condition of constitutional litigation in the American republic of liberal democracy. Yet, perhaps more significant than this is the fact that the Supreme Court itself, as the pinnacle of constitutional power, is the most effective institutional check on the development of a society in which democratic debates and decisionmaking are at the heart of government. The American, and now the Canadian, community continues to confuse constitutionality with wisdom and judicial review with democratic legitimacy. Judicial review is a pale and perverse substitute for democratic debate and an imperfect conduit for the expression of citizens' views. A reliance on constitutional adjudication dulls the democratic imagination and promotes the atrophy of political consciousness. When the pressing issues of the day are diverted to the judicial forum, free speech is effectively trivialized and marginalized. People are, at best, free to talk and debate, but only the courts are free to decide. The belief that court decisions begin a national conversation is wishful.[59] While the elite few speak with

---

57 *Supra* note 12, at 220. The *Skokie* case was *Collin* v. *Smith*, 578 F.2d 1197 (7th Cir.) (allowing Nazis to march in Skokie where many inhabitants were Jewish and had personal experience of concentration camps).

58 L. TRIBE, GOD SAVE THIS HONORABLE COURT 11 (1985).

59 *See* A. BICKEL, THE SUPREME COURT AND THE IDEA OF PROGRESS 91 (1970). For an extended critique of this possibility, *see* Hutchinson, *supra*, note 2.

the voice of constitutional authority and with the wind of institutional legitimacy and force at their backs, the many must be content to chatter among themselves and to whistle into the constitutional wind.

Yet, in even talking about politics, the citizenry cannot escape the pervasive influence of law. Whatever its instrumental function and efficacy, legal discourse is a particularly potent medium for negotiating and constructing social reality.[60] It is one of the ways society defines itself and presents the world to itself. While the state often relies on crude force or threats to achieve its ends, its strength and long-term viability stem from its successful use of law. Adjudication is vital to the contemporary regime of political life. It does not make anything happen, but it is an essential part of existing arrangements and their continued unhealth. The discursive practices that comprise the language of the law structure the world in particular and partial ways. Rights talk is a rhetorical medium of the most potent kind. Being normative in nature, it is a way of imagining and has a distinct theory of its own relations to a larger nomos.[61] As a rhetorical system of social ordering, it controls the agenda of political controversy as much by dictating the set of questions to be answered as by the answers to be given.

Aided and abetted by scholars like Laurence Tribe, the courts have entrenched themselves at the center of the democratic policy-making process; judges have been elevated to the rank of moral prophets and philosopher kings. For citizens, politics has become a spectator sport. Yet, philosophy and ethics have no monopoly on "truth" and "justice"; its privilege is contrived and invalid. While philosophy ought not to be ignored, we must not be cowed or intimidated by it. Our images of justice should not be like those gifts from a rich and distant aunt that, after their pristine gloss has dulled, result in dependence and resentment. To be valued, our images of justice should be produced through the sweat of our own democratic brows. The ideal democratic polity would not be achieved through the courts, but in spite of them.[62] Values like justice and freedom cannot be defined in some external forum and then forced upon a recalcitrant public. Justice and equality are the products of politics, not its antecedents. In the end, the issue boils down to who

---

60 *See supra* ch. 1.

61 *See* Cover, *Nomos and Narrative*, 98 HARV. L. REV. 4 (1984) and C. GEERTZ, LOCAL KNOWLEDGE: FURTHER ESSAYS IN INTERPRETIVE ANTHROPOLOGY (1984).

62 *See* Hutchinson and Monahan, *Democracy and The Rule of Law* in THE RULE OF LAW: IDEAL OR IDEOLOGY 117–121 (A. Hutchinson and P. Monahan eds. 1987).

should have the responsibility and privilege of making mistakes. As James Bradley Thayer declared:

> The exercise of [the power of the judiciary to disregard unconstitutional legisla-
> tion] . . . is always attended with a serious evil, namely, that the correction of
> legislative mistakes comes from the outside, and the people thus lose the political
> experience, and the moral education and stimulus that comes from fighting the
> question out in the ordinary way, and correcting their own errors.
>   The tendency of a common and easy resort to this great function, now la-
> mentably too common, is to dwarf the political capacity of the people, and to
> deaden its sense of moral responsibility. It is no light thing to do that.[63]

III. CONCLUSION

For all his huff and puff, Tribe is very much part of the American tribe: he is a leading legal shaman. In his temperate criticism of recent constitutional events, he manages to buttress and reinvigorate tribal trad-ition and wisdom about the centrality of courts as forums for democratic debate and instruments of social change. With canny judgment, he makes sure that he never transgresses the bounds of liberal propriety. Like Tom Wicker, he needs no line drawn for him in the political dirt.[64] His ear is well tuned to the rhythms and nuances of the tribal hymns and anthems: "alleviation of the substantive tilt [against redistribution of wealth] . . . need not require a diminution of the protections currently provided to entrenched wealth, *although some diminution might well be sen-sible*".[65] To ensure a more informed feel for the texture and substance of the "political dirt", we should not look to the dreams and aspirations of the tribal elders, but should rather unearth the particular conflicts and inequalities that are mired in it. American soil is not the rich loam of freedom, but the cloying mud of privilege.

Tribe's embrace of contingency and choice is calculated and cont-rived: he merely pays lip service to its liberating potential. He wants to grasp the message of contingency more to smother its radical imperatives than to take them seriously. In grounding and defending his "experiment in choosing," he condemns those commentators and judges who build on the "givenness" of social conditions like "the distribution of income and wealth . . . as though it were some kind of geological cir-

---

63 J.B. THAYER, JOHN MARSHALL 106–107 (1974).
64 *Supra* note 55.
65 *Supra* note 12, at 187 (emphasis added).

cumstance."[66] Yet, by refusing to consider or imagine a world without courts, Tribe commits exactly the same error; he has designed his critical drill so that it is not sharp enough or long enough to penetrate the bedrock of constitutional adjudication. As Tribe knows, but refuses to admit (to himself or others), in matters of social geology there is no solid ground on which to stand; "it's turtles all the way down."[67]

Of course, we are not free to choose as we wish. We are part of all that has come before. Yet the choice is not between the idolatry of existing arrangements or the madness of unmitigated solipsism. We must begin to take responsibility for what we have and begin to renegotiate and reconstruct the world. Insofar as the social world and ourselves have been made, they can be remade. The world is a coral reef of the mind; living metaphors that have crystallized and been forgotten, later to be (re)discovered as real and natural. If we are to begin the noble task "of replacing arrogant certitudes about our often unshared pasts with a more open search for a shared future",[68] we must rethink and rework the whole paraphernalia of law and statecraft; so-called free speech is a good place to begin. A complacent wringing of hands is an unaffordable and unpardonable indulgence. Legal doctrine and judicial review are intellectual constructs. They are ours. We are richer when we give them away. Divestment must begin at home.

---

66 *Supra* note 19, at 159.
67 *See* Singer, *Radical Moderation*, [1985] A.B.F. RES. J. 329 at 330.
68 *Supra* note 12, at 267.

6

Derek and Charles
v.
Anne and Martin

The Supreme Court of Canengaustrus*

Judgment: September 31, 1986

DOCTRIN C.J.: This appeal arises from a road traffic accident near Ottloncanwash on 31st April, 1980 in the late evening. The accident has given rise to several causes of action that have been consolidated for the purposes of this appeal. There are four central issues to be decided: whether Derek can recover damages for Anne's negligence; whether Derek was contributorily negligent; whether Martin was responsible for his failure to rescue Derek; and whether Charles can recover damages for emotional distress, and if so, against whom.

---

* Canengaustrus is a small, little-known island in the mid-Atlantic. Something of a geographical enigma, its capital, Ottloncanwash, is equidistant from Ottawa, London, Canberra and Washington. Coincidentally, it is a common law jurisdiction and its law is a unique blend of Canadian, English, Australian and American sources.

The facts of the case are relatively clear and are not in dispute. Derek was driving home along a quiet, narrow and winding country road that was unpaved, unmarked and unlit. As he rounded a sweeping bend, he saw a single headlight approaching close to the other side of the road; he assumed this to be a motorcyclist. Unfortunately, the light was that of a sports car driven by Anne: the off-side headlight was not working. At the last minute, Derek realized his mistake and applied his brakes. Regrettably, his braking system did not function properly. The car swerved, left the road, and came to rest in a shallow ditch at the side of the road. Anne, who had also taken avoidance action, was unaware that a serious accident had occurred and continued on her journey home.

The accident occurred near the isolated farm of Martin. At the time of the accident, he was standing on his front porch, calling in his dog for the night. Although he saw and heard the accident, he did nothing to ascertain whether anyone was injured or in need of help. For reasons best known to himself, he closed the door and retired to bed. Derek was trapped in his car. His right leg, stuck under the dashboard, was broken in two places. Reliable medical evidence indicated that if Derek had received immediate assistance, for example, by having the pressure on his leg relieved, the further complications which arose could have been averted. Sadly, he remained trapped for over half an hour and the blood flow to his leg was irreversibly impaired. As a result, his leg has been amputated.

Approximately thirty-five minutes after the accident, Jane came upon the scene. She was driving from Ottloncanwash to her home in the village of Tormanyork. She immediately went to Derek's aid, dragging him from the wreckage after levering away the dashboard. She administered artificial respiration; this probably saved his life. Jane then ran to Martin's farm and persuaded Martin to telephone for an ambulance. Derek was rushed to hospital where an emergency operation was carried out. His life was in the balance. A telephone call was made by the police to Charles, who lived with and apparently enjoyed a homosexual relationship with Derek. Charles' answering service advised them that Charles was away on business. The police succeeded in locating Charles and left a message for him. Charles telephoned the hospital and was told by the staff that it would be some time before there would be any definite news, but that Derek was presently in the intensive care unit. Fortunately, through the skill of the hospital staff, Derek's life was saved. But this experience has left its tragic mark on Charles. The psychiatric evidence establishes that Charles has suffered severe shock, organic depression and a change of personality as a direct result of the injury suffered by his friend. Also, the relationship between Charles and Derek has ended. After spending three months in hospital, Derek moved back to his parents' home. He is confined to a wheelchair.

The trial judge held that, as Derek was fifty percent to blame, his damages should be reduced accordingly. The third party proceedings brought by Anne against Martin was dismissed. The judge concluded that there was no legal duty to rescue. Charles' claim against Anne for compensation for his emotional distress was allowed. Anne's application to the Court of Appeal was dismissed and Derek's cross-appeal on the question of duty to rescue was also dismissed. Anne now appeals to this court and Derek cross-appeals.

The case raises a number of moral issues. However, I should make it clear from the outset that my concern is with the legal aspects of this case alone. Of course, the law, as a social force, overlaps with religion and morality, but it is incumbent upon me to resolve the issues presented in accordance with the law as it is, and not as some would like it to be. Like Sir George Baker, "my task is to apply the law free of emotion and predilection"; see *Paton* v. *Trustees of British Pregnancy Advisory Services*, [1978] 2 All E.R. 987 at 989. In blunt terms, "with purely moral obligation the law does not deal"; see *Buch* v. *Amory Manufacturing Co.*, 69 N.H. 257 (1897). Furthermore, as has been constantly emphasized, the desirability and continued existence of any particular law is for the legislature and not for the judiciary to decide. There is a clear separation of governmental powers in Canengaustrus. The legislature has the constitutional responsibility to enact laws designed to achieve substantively just results; the judiciary has the task of interpreting, applying and dispensing this received wisdom. As Kitto J. said, to discuss cases "in terms of 'judicial policy' and 'social expediency' is to introduce deleterious foreign matter into the water of the common law—in which, after all, we have no more than riparian rights"; see *Rootes* v. *Shelton*, 116 C.L.R. 383 at 387 (1967). In this way, the fundamental democratic demands of consensus, as sought in the political process, and rationality, as embodied in the legal process, are met. The formal and neutral application of the rules infuses the law with a central integrity and ensures that the law is insulated from political or moral controversy; see *Duport Steel Ltd.* v. *Sirs*, [1980] All E.R. 529 at 551.

WAS ANNE NEGLIGENT?

The issue of negligence can be dealt with expeditiously. The task for the Court is to determine whether Anne owed Derek a duty of care, whether that duty was breached and whether the breach led to cognizable damages; see *Donoghue* v. *Stevenson*, [1932] A.C. 526. There is, of course, no general duty of care. In order to be successful, a plaintiff must show that he was a foreseeable plaintiff; see *Palsgraf* v. *Long Island Railroad Co.*, 162 N.E. 99 (1928). The court must be persuaded that there are no considerations of policy which dictate that this *prima facie* duty of care be circumscribed so as to deny the liability of the defendant; see *Anne's* v. *Merton London Borough Council*, [1978] A.C. 728 at 751–752. The essence of the law has been succinctly captured by Macdonald J. In *Nova Mink* v. *Trans Canada Airlines* (1951), 2 D.L.R. 241:

> The common law yields the conclusion that there is a duty only where the circumstances of time, place and person would create in the mind of a reasonable man in those circumstances such a probability of harm resulting to other persons as to require him to take care to avert the probable result.

That a road user owes a duty of care to other road users is without question. The issue is whether Anne, in failing to have her car in proper working order, breached the standard of care to which a reasonable man would adhere.

It is well established that a breach of a statutory duty, while not conclusive evidence of liability, raises a *prima facie* case that the standard has been breached; see, for example, *Queen* v. *Saskatchewan Wheat Pool* (1983), 143 D.L.R. (3d) 9 and *Clinkscales* v. *Carver*, 22 Cal. 2d 72 (1943). It was argued by counsel for the respondent that the *Highway Traffic Act*, R.S.C.E.S., c. 198, being a regulatory statute and carrying its own penalties for violations, was not designed to determine the standard of care in civil suits. It seems to me that if the legislature, in its wisdom, has seen fit to enact legislation to ensure safety on our nation's highways, this Court ought not to treat such a pronouncement lightly. The legislature is in the best position to decide what the appropriate standards should be. Though let it be clear that, by accepting such a definition, this Court is in no way fettering its judicial discretion.

In *Sterling Trusts Corp.* v. *Postma*, [1965] S.C.R. 324, Cartwright J. considered the effect of a statutory duty in the context of a civil action for negligence. He settled on the following rule (at 329):

> I think it is plain that once it has been found (i) that the respondents committed a breach of the statutory duty . . . and, (ii) that the breach was an effective cause of appellants' injuries, the respondents were *prima facie* liable for the damages suffered by the appellants.

In the present case, the evidence satisfied this two-fold test. A defendant can rebut the *prima facie* case by showing that the statutory breach occurred without any negligence on his part. I agree with the trial judge that the malfunctioning headlights could reasonably have been discovered.

Accordingly, negligence on Anne's part has been established.

WAS DEREK CONTRIBUTORILY NEGLIGENT?

The more contentious question is whether Derek was also negligent and, if so, to what extent his negligence reduces Anne's liability. Although Anne's negligence may have increased the likelihood of an accident, the realization of that risk was in large part the responsibility of Derek who was also in breach of the relevant statutory provisions. The duty on Derek is aptly summed up by Lord Justice Buckley in *Lee* v. *Lever*, [1974] R.T.R. 35 at 39:

> It is not the law that a driver is entitled to assume that all other users of the road will in all respects and at all other times obey the Highway Code or otherwise drive with all due care and circumspection or use the road in every way in which it should be used. It is incumbent upon any driver to be prepared for foreseeable hazards, including hazards resulting from the foreseeable bad driving of other drivers or a foreseeable breach . . . [I]t is incumbent upon upon every user of such a roadway to drive in a way which enables him to meet an emergency or a hazard presented [by other drivers].

The failure of Derek to ensure that his car was maintained in a roadworthy condition, such that it would be able to negotiate the normal hazards of night driving in the countryside, is strong evidence of his contributory negligence; see *Parish* v. *Judd*, [1960] 3 All E.R. 33. Accordingly, the Court of Appeal was quite correct in refusing to disturb the trial judge's reduction in damages by fifty percent under the *Negligence Act*, R.S.C.E.S., c. 315, ss. 2 and 5.

DID MARTIN HAVE A LEGAL DUTY TO RESCUE?

The issue of whether there is a legal duty to rescue Derek raises one of the most sensitive and heated academic debates in tort law. Indeed, counsel for the appellant presented a most able and humanistic argument that this Court should give legal effect to what all agree is a clear moral obligation to one's fellow citizen. Appellant's counsel went on to argue that the law of tort itself was based on society's conception of right and wrong. In fact, the "neighbour principle" itself was said to stem from the biblical duty to love one's neighbour; see Luke, ch. 10, v. 29.

I am not persuaded, however, that we should vest this moral duty with legal sanction. The opinion of the court in *Union Pacific Co.* v. *Cappier*, 72 P. 282 at 282–83 (1903), is as relevant today as it was at the turn of the century:

> With the humane side of the question courts are not concerned. It is the omission or negligent discharge of legal duties only which come within the sphere of judicial cognizance. For withholding relief from the suffering, for failure to respond to the calls of worthy charity, or for faltering in the bestowment of brotherly love on the unfortunate, penalties are found not in the laws of men, but in that higher law, the violation of which is condemned by the voice of conscience, whose sentence of punishment for the recreant act is swift and sure.

A survey of early cases reveals no legal duty to rescue, even where the litigants had a particular relationship such as a business association or the like; *Osterlind* v. *Hill*, 160 N.E. 301 (1920) and *Yania* v. *Bigan*, 155 A. 2d 343 (1959). In *Yania*, the plaintiff was the widow of a business visitor, who had jumped into the water to aid the defendant. The plaintiff's husband subsequently drowned when the defendant refused to come to his aid. The court held that there was no legal duty unless the defendant places the plaintiff in peril. Likewise, in *Osterlind*, the defendant rented a canoe to the plaintiff which, in full view of the defendant, capsized and the plaintiff drowned. Once again, the court held no legal duty to effect a rescue.

Appellant's counsel pointed to a more recent decision which held that a ship's captain has a duty to rescue a passenger who falls overboard; see *Horsley* v. *Maclaren*, [1969] 2 O.R. 137. Counsel argued that the courts are expanding the duty to rescue and urged this court to do so in this case. It is true that there are now several specific relationships that will give rise to a duty to rescue. However, most of these are founded upon statutory duties, such as the obligations of parent to child, or upon some implicit agreement, such as between members of a social outing; see *Farwell* v. *Keaton*, 396 Mich. 281 (1976). This court is bound by a long line of eminent authority. Until the legislature deems it appropriate to introduce a general duty to rescue, we ought not to upset the delicate balance the common law has developed. Aside from the moral dimension, there exist very real technical and administrative difficulties associated with the introduction of such a general duty. What would be the extent of Martin's liability? And to whom would he be liable? Would Anne benefit from Martin's misfeasance? These problems combine to support the existing rules. Consequently, Martin cannot be found legally liable for his failure to rescue Derek.

CAN CHARLES RECOVER FOR EMOTIONAL DISTRESS?

Recovery for nervous shock caused by negligence is a relatively recent arrival on the tort scene. Prior to 1925 and the decision of *Hambrook* v. *Stokes Bros.*, [1925] 1 K.B. 141, courts were most reluctant to allow plaintiffs to recover for nervous shock without any bodily injury to themselves. This reluctance was founded upon the view that such awards were difficult, if not impossible, to determine, and that nervous disorder and emotional upset was easy to feign. The remarks of Mitchell C.J. in *Huston* v. *Borough of Fremansburg*, 61 A. 1022 at 1023 (1905), are pertinent:

> It requires but brief judicial experience to be convinced of the large proportion of exaggeration and even of actual fraud in the ordinary action for physical injuries from negligence; and if we opened the door to this new invention the result would be great danger, if not disaster to the cause of practical justice.

Since the turn of this century, the marvels and advances of medical science have come upon us with great speed. The field of psychiatry has grown to a point where diseases of the mind can be diagnosed and treated with a confidence that approaches certainty. And it is with matters of certainty that the courts of justice deal. As a result, courts have now begun to award redress to plaintiffs who have suffered recognizable psychiatric illness as a result of the defendants' negligence; see *Hinz* v. *Berry*, [1970] 2 Q.B. 40 and *Brown* v. *Brice*, [1984] 1 All E.R. 997. Initially, it was only admitted in cases where the plaintiff personally was in peril of physical harm; see *Dulieu* v. *White and Sons*, [1901] 2 K.B. 669. But the *Hambrook* case (*supra*) recognized that in certain specific relationships, such as between a mother and child, serious injury to another could be the basis for recovery; see *King* v. *Phillips*, [1953] 1 Q.B. 429.

There has been a gradual widening of liability. The general trend has been to allow recovery where the plaintiff has come upon the immediate aftermath of an accident; see *Marshall* v. *Lionel Enterprises*, [1972] 2 O.R. 177. Perhaps the best test is the one laid down by Torbriner J. in *Dillon* v. *Legg*, 29 A.L.R. 3d 1316 at 1326–27 (1968):

> In determining, in such a case, whether defendant should reasonably foresee the injury to plaintiff, or, in other terminology, whether defendant owes plaintiff a duty of due care, the courts will take into account such factors as the following. (1) Whether plaintiff was located near the scene of the accident as contrasted with one who was a distance away from it. (2) Whether the shock resulted from a direct emotional impact upon plaintiff from the sensory and contemporaneous observance of the accident, as contrasted with learning of the accident from them after the occurrence. (3) Whether plaintiff and the victim were closely related, as contrasted with an absence of any relationship or the presence of only a distant relationship. The evaluation of these factors will indicate the degree of the defendant's foreseeability.

In the present case, Charles was nowhere near the scene of the accident and did not even come upon the aftermath. He was some 250 miles from the scene. Secondly, while he may well have experienced true emotional disturbance rather than mere grief (which is not recoverable; see *Duwyn* v. *Kaprielian* (1978), 2 O.R. (2d) 736), it was not from the "sensory and contemporaneous observance of the accident" as is required; see, for example, *Hathaway* v. *Supreme Court*, 112 Cal. App. 3d 728 (1980). Furthermore, I am not persuaded that there existed the necessary relationship between Derek and Charles to warrant an extension of the rule. In *McLoughlin* v. *O'Brian*, [1983] A.C. 410, where a mother was two miles away from the accident and only heard of it two hours later, the lack of immediate physical proximity was counterbalanced by the fundamental nature of their relationship as mother and family and her arrival at what amounted to the "immediate aftermath" of the accident when she visited the hospital. Notwithstanding this, it was argued that the facts of the present case were sufficiently analogous to existing doctrine to warrant recovery. Although it is true that the law must develop from case to case, we must also strive to maintain certainty and generality so as to avoid a doctrinal wilderness of single instances. As Lord Wilberforce said, "there remains a . . . a real need for the law to place some limitations on the extent of admissible claims"; *id.* at 423. That limitation must be drawn where "the good sense of the judges decides"; see *Bourhill* v. *Young*, [1943] A.C. 92 at 110 per Lord Wright. In *Spade* v. *Lynn & B.R. Co.*, 47 N.E. 497 (1897), Allan J. offered an appropriate warning:

> The law must be administered in the courts according to general rules. Courts will aim to make these rules as just as possible, bearing in mind that they are to be of general application. But as the law is a practical science, having to do with the affairs of life, any rule is unwise if, in its general application, it will not, as a usual result, serve the purposes of justice. A new rule cannot be made for each case . . . One may be held bound to anticipate and guard against the probable consequences to ordinary people, but to carry the rule of damages further imposes an undue measure of responsibility upon those who are guilty only of unintentional negligence.

In conclusion, therefore, I hold that, although Derek is entitled to recover from Anne, his damages will be reduced by fifty percent as a result of his own contributory negligence. Further, Charles has no claim against Anne or Martin for his emotional distress and Martin, while worthy of our moral opprobrium, is not liable to anyone for his failure to rescue Derek.

★   ★   ★

MILL J.: This appeal requires this Court to decide the proper basis of liability for physical harm, whether the law of civil wrongs should be extended to impose legal liability for nonfeasance (the so-called "duty to rescue") and, finally, the extent of liability for negligently inflicted emotional distress.

Reading the judgment of Doctrin C.J., it readily becomes apparent that her conception of the judicial role is confused, schizophrenic, and altogether too restricted. It involves an ineffectual sleight of hand which a moment's mature reflection reveals as self-contradictory. I say this more by way of clarification and introduction to my own judgment than as vindictive criticism of much of the doctrinal substance of her view of the common law. Indeed, I hope that it will become clear that I am in broad agreement with some of her conclusions. My concern here, however, is to clear away the rhetoric behind which her cloak-and-dagger approach to public policy lurks.

Concepts such as duty, reasonable foreseeability and causation are veiled terms through which the courts formally express the choices they have made. They operate as a convenient screen behind which the real social drama is played out. As Lord Denning bluntly noted, "common law adjudication is . . . at bottom a matter of public policy which we, as judges, must resolve"; see *Home Office* v. *Dorset Yacht Co. Ltd.*, [1969] 2 Q.B. 412 at 426. This sentiment gained the express approval of Lords Dilhorne and Diplock; see [1970] A.C. 1004 at 1051 and 1058 respectively. The common law is a vast and intricate doctrinal edifice, but its chief architect has been policy and not logic. In practice, judges have been reluctant to expand the ambit of liability other than by analogical reasoning; see *McLoughlin* v. *O'Brian*, [1982] 2 W.L.R. 982 at 988–89. Whenever a court decides that compensation is payable only for loss that was "reasonably foreseeable," it *reaffirms* a policy decision taken years or decades ago. The appeal to "policy" is unavoidable and judges ought now to acknowledge this. There is obviously potential danger in this course of action. What strikes one judge as a suitable "policy risk" may appear to another to be the height of folly. But the threat of such idiosyncratic appeals can be diminished by a systematic theory of civil liability.

For too long we have lacked an adequate theory to explain the social function of negligence liability and of the fault system of liability that is built upon it. The true test of any theory, of course, is its ability to predict or account for the full diversity and complexity of life. Without the capacity to formulate some general hypothesis, we cannot have a system of law which people can confidently base their expectations on and plan their behaviour. To reply with Aristotle, as my colleague Justice Wright is wont to do, that the real purpose and only proper effect of tortious liability is to restore to a person what has been wrongfully appropriated—the concept of "corrective justice"—offers no insights into the source of the norms by which the conduct was judged wrongful. Thus, the experiential basis of my proposed theory confounds any critics who suggest that the theory rests on unrealistic behavioural assumptions. It is open to criticism only insofar as its postulates seek to explain the totality of those conditions. The behavioural consequences of the tort rules which this theory produces are beyond the scope of this Court to examine, beyond even the bounds of the theory to predict *in the individual case*.

My model is premised on the fact that the world is finite, an aggregate of scarce resources. Choices must be made, for example, as to the use, conservation and distribution of fossil fuel. So too must difficult choices be countenanced everywhere in our society. In torts, we must recognize the continuing force of Lord Atkin's dictum that "acts or omissions which any moral code would censure cannot, in a practical world, be treated so as to give a right to every person injured by them to demand relief"; see *Donoghue* v. *Stevenson*, [1932] A.C. 562 at 580. Ours is a practical world and "the law aims at practical justice rather than logical consistency"; see *Caltex Oil* v. *The Dredge "Willemstad"* (1976), 135 C.L.R. 529 at 545 per Gibbs J. It is for this reason that I find Justice Lefft's abdication of the judicial task so distasteful and unjustified.

This concentration on the practical world, with its scarce resources, further leads me to reject the constitutional separation of powers doctrine so rigidly adhered to by Chief Justice Doctrin. To believe that the legislature, with its tightly constrained timetable, can accommodate law reform at the drop of this Court's hat is to live in some other world. Political indifference and its legislative ally, inertia, are facts of life. Unless we properly appreciate the effects of these forces, we close our eyes to the distributive consequences of the law and fail in our political and social duty to ensure that the law meets the demands of contemporary society. The true measure of common law adjudication is the extent to which it can resolve today's problems in a fashion that will allow for both the predictive certainty of the law and the optimalization of accident costs and resources.

In order to keep the law in step with the march of modern society, judges must look beyond the letter of the law to its motive force and spirit. Unlike Doctrin C.J., we must not remain "timorous souls", but become "bold spirits"; see *Candler* v. *Crane, Christmas and Co.*, [1951] 2 K.B. 164 per Lord Denning. It is my honest and firm conviction that the notion of "allocative efficiency" is the golden thread which weaves together into a fine garment the seemingly disparate strands of the common law. Hitherto, this has only been vaguely glimpsed and partially grasped. Accordingly, although the theory of tort law suggested here has a clear political dimension, it does not represent a naked and personal political choice on my part. Indeed, a judge who follows and substantiates the logic of "allocative efficiency" more closely satisfies the democratic ideal of adjudication than the unthinking formalist.

As in life, two unavoidable facts dominate the law of tort: risk and uncertainty. As agents of the law, the courts must select doctrines that minimize both. By creating precedents, the courts promote efficient resource allocation by optimizing these two related concepts. It is not without significance that the response to uncertainty has occupied the forefront of human endeavour. Many of the distinctive institutions of primitive society, like polygamy and extended family groups, can be understood as such a response. With the recognition of the institution of private property came the related doctrine of contract. Of course, all contracting is risk-shifting; see *Photoproductions Ltd.* v. *Securicor,* [1980] 1 All E.R. 556 and *Globe Refining Co.* v. *Landa Cotton Oil Co.*, 190 U.S. 540 (1903). As a society develops, its wealth increases. Moreover, as the opportunity for interaction expands, there will be a corresponding rise in the probability of interfering with or harming others' interests. More state-imposed control is demanded. But, unless we are watchful, this increased protection could interfere with the market's ability to ensure that voluntary exchanges result in resources gravitating toward their most valuable uses. The goals of private and social allocative efficiency may be lost.

Undoubtedly, the desirability of social efficiency as a goal requires a value judgment as to the justness of the underlying distribution of income and property rights. But the modest ambition of my proposal is to optimize the use and exchange of whatever rights people start out with; this respects the proper bounds of political and judicial action. There is no longer general optimism concerning governmental intervention in the economic system. Tort law, dealing as it does mainly with accidents, does not lend itself well to state intervention to redistribute wealth. It is unrealistic to think that interest groups will overly concern themselves with redistribution through the tort system or will place accident compensation reform on their agenda for legislative action anyway. This point is perhaps not fully grasped by Justice Prudential, whose well intentioned, but misguided energies may now become a real cost in the world of imperfect information. My judgment attempts to come to terms with this precise problem.

Rules of tort law must be designed and implemented so as to facilitate and simulate the operation of a free and competitive market. If there were no barriers to effective bargaining, the assignment of legal rights would not affect the social efficiency of the final outcome. For example, Dexter lives next to a cricket ground, owned by Cowdrey, and is frequently assailed by hard-hit balls. Dexter could take adequate precautions at $500, but it would cost Cowdrey $1,000. If Cowdrey was legally liable, he would bargain to pay Dexter $500 to take the necessary precautions. If Cowdrey was not legally liable, Dexter would have to spend $500 on precautions. Either way, the *socially* efficient level of precautions would be taken.

In a world in which bargaining is often prohibitively costly, the initial assignment of rights is of crucial importance and has a fundamental impact on the allocative efficiency of societal resources; see *Miller* v. *Jackson*, [1977] Q.B. 966. The practical implementation of my thesis must, and does, take account of this fact. The rule of liability is relevant and will determine whether resources are used in an economically efficient manner. In most accident situations, private bargaining is not feasible. The necessary information may be unavailable, imperfect or too expensive, there may be too many parties to the potential transaction or there may be the problem of excluding free riders—those who do not pay for the benefits they receive—from the bargain. This, of course, is the case with Anne and Derek. Consequently, the rules of liability must as closely as possible approximate the apportionment of risk that would have been arrived at by the litigants *if they had been able to bargain*. Any dispute which reaches a court is, after all, only a case in which the bargaining process—settlement out of court—has broken down.

The economic logic of the competitive market must become the unifying force of the common law. The market and the legal system are similar operational institutions. Like the market, the legal system is a competitive process in which the pursuit of self-interest serves to promote an efficient allocation of resources. If the invisible hand of the market is replicated by the pen of the impartial judge, inefficient rules will be litigated out of the system. The adversary system would substitute for marketing strategies; the judge acting as a consumer in choosing between two fiercely promoted products. Legal rules could be cast as economic incentives to encourage individuals to maximise efficiency. Like the economic actor, the legal actor could be presented with the costs of any course of action in order to decide whether to incur those costs. The common law of tort, therefore, should ensure that the joint value of interacting activities is maximized and that joint cost is minimized. More particularly, the law must seek to encourage individuals to achieve a level of safety at which the value of the risks involved in an activity is equal to the cost of the precautions necessary to maintain that degree of safety. As Lord Macmillan said, "the law exacts a degree of care commensurate with the risk created"; see *Read* v. *J. Lyons Co. Ltd.*, [1947] A.C. 156. In short, individuals must be persuaded to "internalize" the costs of accidents in the cause of improved social justice. As such, the central task of tort law is to design rules of liability which will provide a sufficient incentive to achieve an efficient level of safety by deterring carelessness and rewarding care. As the Court summarized in *Losee* v. *Buchanan*, 51 N.Y. 476 at 484 (1873):

> By becoming a member of civilized society, I am compelled to give up many of my natural rights, but I receive more than adequate compensation from the surrender by every other man of the same rights, and the security, advantage and protection which the laws give me . . . We must have factories, machinery, dams, canals and railroads. They are demanded by the manifold wants of mankind, and lay at the basis of all our civilisation. If I have any of these upon my lands . . . I am not responsible for any damage they accidentally and unavoidably do to my neighbour. He receives his compensation for such damage by the general good in which he shares and the right which he has to place the same things upon his lands. I hold my property subject to the risk that it may be unavoidably or accidentally injured by those who live near me; and as I move about upon the public highways and in all places where other persons may lawfully be, I take the risk of being accidentally injured in my person by them without fault on their part. Most of the rights of property, as well as of person, in the social state, are not absolute but relative, and they must be so arranged and modified, not unnecessarily infringing upon natural rights, as upon the whole to promote the general welfare.

The centerpiece of negligence law is the seminal judgment of Judge Learned Hand in *U.S.* v. *Carroll Towing*, 159 F. 2d 169 (1947). The test for liability developed by him has a long and impeccable pedigree; see, for example, *Mackintosh* v. *Mackintosh*, 36 Jur. 678 (1864), *Chicago, Burlington & Quincy Rly. Co.* v. *Krayenbuhl*, 65 Neb. 889 (1902) and *Conway* v. *O'Brien*, 111 F. 2d 611 (1940). The beauty of this test is its elegant simplicity and sweep. With subtle adjustments that remain loyal to Learned Hand's ambition, this algorithm can be made to resolve all the problems of accident liability, like causation, contributory negligence and rescue, that so vex Doctrin C.J. and others.

In *U.S.* v. *Carroll Towing, supra,* an unattended barge had slipped its moorings and collided with another ship. In holding the barge owners liable, Judge Learned Hand stated that:

> [T]here is no general rule to determine when the absence of a bargee or other attendant will make the owner of the barge liable for injuries to other vessels if she breaks away from her moorings . . . It becomes apparent why there can be no such general rule, when we consider the grounds for such a liability. Since there are occasions when every vessel will break from her moorings, and since, if she does, she becomes a menace to those about her, the owner's duty, as in other similar situations, to provide against resulting injuries is a function of three

variables: (1) the probability that she will break away; (2) the gravity of the result-ing injury, if she does; (3) the burden of adequate precautions. Possibly it serves to bring this notion into relief to state it in algebraic terms: if the probability be called P; the injury, L; and the burden B; liability depends upon whether B is less than L multiplied by P; i.e., whether B⟨PL . . . In the case at bar the bargee left at five o'clock in the afternoon of January 3rd, and the flotilla broke away at about two o'clock in the afternoon of the following day, twenty-one hours after-wards. The bargee had been away all the time . . . At the locus in quo . . . barges were being constantly "drilled" in and out. Certainly it was not beyond reasonable expectation that, with the inevitable haste and bustle, the work might not be done with adequate care. In such circumstances, we hold—and it is all that we do hold—that it was a fair requirement that the [barge owners] should have a bargee aboard (unless he had some excuse for his absence), during the working hours of daylight.

Following from this, a basic presumption operates that losses will lie where they fall unless there are compelling reasons for their realloca-tion. This will only occur if it would have been cheaper for the defendant to have avoided the accident than to make good the expected losses. The accident cost is the magnitude of the loss if an accident occurs reduced by the probability of the accident occurring. If the defendant were to compensate the plaintiff under any other circumstances, it would lead to an economically inefficient result. It would be a waste of societal re-sources to require the defendant to spend a greater sum to avoid an acci-dent which would result in losses of a lesser amount. The Learned Hand test encourages cost-rational actors to modify their behaviour by taking cost-justified precautions to avoid liability; see *Watt* v. *Hertfordshire C.C.*, [1954] 1 W.L.R. 535 and *Wyong Shire Council* v. *Shire* (1980), 46 C.L.R. 40. As such, carelessness per se does not result in actionable negligence for "it is only the requirement that the care be commensurate with the risk and danger"; see *Nussbaum* v. *Lacapo*, 27 N.Y. 2d 311 at 319 (1970).

Two examples will suffice to illustrate the efficacy and desirability of this approach. In *Hedricks* v. *Peabody Coal Co.*, 115 Ill. App. 2d 35 (1969), a child was drowned and the negligence was the failure to prevent the use of an inherently dangerous waterhole by children known to play there. Damages to the child were assessed at $200,000, but the cost of fencing off the waterhole would have been between $12,000 and $14,000. The defendant was found liable as the prevention "cost was slight com-pared to the risk to the children involved"; *id.* at 45. Also, in *Bolton* v. *Stone*, [1951] A.C. 850, plaintiff was struck by a ball from the defendants' cricket ground. There was a twelve foot perimeter fence and a ball had only been hit out of the ground six times in about thirty years. The House of Lords refused to impose liability. The risk of injury was neglig-ible and the cost of further precautions immense. As Lord Reid said:

> In the crowded conditions of modern life even the most careful person cannot avoid creating some risks and accepting others. What a man must not do, and what I think a careful man tries not to do is to create a risk which is substantial . . . In my judgment, the test to be applied here is whether the risk of damage to a person on the road was so small that a reasonable man in the position of the appellants, considering the matter from the point of view of safety, would have thought it right to refrain from taking steps to prevent the danger.

An application of the Learned Hand test to the facts of the case at bar is instructive. Interestingly, Doctrin C.J. failed to mention some of the more pertinent facts. As we know, the loss to Derek was estimated at $1 million, but we also know from the evidence that Anne could have repaired her headlight for $250 and that there was a relatively significant possibility that an accident would have occurred, say .001 or a one in a thousand chance. Translating these into "economic" terms, it means that, as the accident cost is $1,000 (.001 x $1 m.) and the avoidance costs were $250, Anne ought to be held liable. It would have been more efficient for Anne to take precautions than to have allowed the accident to occur. It is an economically efficient use of society's resources to require an expenditure of $250 to save a loss of $1,000. However, this finding does not conclusively dispose of Anne's liability. As the objective of the law is to maximize overall social welfare, it is important to consider Derek's actions.

In general terms, where the cost to the plaintiff of avoiding the accident is less than the cost to the defendant, the impetus for shifting the loss disappears. Indeed, it would be efficient to do so. Consequently, the loss should shift only where expected accident costs and the defendant's avoidance costs are less than the plaintiff's. Under such a straightforward regime, optimal safety would be achieved as each party would have a powerful incentive to minimize accident costs and maximize avoidance costs. In the present case, as Derek could have repaired his faulty brakes for $200 ($50 less than Anne's avoidance costs), the loss will remain with Derek. Anne will not be liable. Derek should have taken the safety measures as they cost less than the predictable accident costs.

To interpret the *Negligence Act* as requiring a distribution of loss based on the proportionate fault of the parties, as Doctrin C.J. does, undermines the clarity and deterrent effect of that law. Such an apportionment of liability would be inefficient for the parties would be obliged to spend, jointly, more than an efficient amount on accident prevention. Where each party is liable for fifty percent of the loss, that is $500 each in this case, Anne would have an incentive to spend $250 to avoid the accident and Derek would have an incentive to spend $200. This means that either a total of $450 will be invested in accident avoidance (an increase of $250 over the cheaper avoidance cost) or nothing will be invested, on the basis that, knowing the other to have an incentive to prevent the accident, each might make no investment at all. This would result in an avoidable cost of $800; that is, the loss less the cheaper avoidance cost. The attempt to achieve an efficient level of accidents and safety can only be undermined by liability rules which enjoin the judge to assess the individual and relative culpability of the parties' conduct in each case.

Before leaving Derek's claim against Anne, a word ought to be said about causation. This issue has created considerable consternation for Doctrin C.J., if not in this particular case, certainly in other cases. Also, Justice Wright, by making causation the fulcrum of liability, has had to grapple continually and inconclusively with this traditionally perplexing problem. All of this is unnecessary. Once the Learned Hand test is accepted as the basis for liability, the puzzles of causation can be solved with confidence. As Lord Reid observed, causation exists when the defendant's act increases the risk of injury to the plaintiff; see *McGhee* v. *N.C.B.*, [1973] 1 W.L.R. 1 and *John Pfeiffer Pty. Ltd.* v. *Canny* (1981), 36 A.L.R. 466. In *McGhee*, the fact that an employer's failure to provide showers added to the risk that the plaintiff's dermatitis might develop was held to be a sufficient ground for liability. In strict terms, therefore, the probability of harm in the Learned Hand formula is the difference between the probability that the accident will occur if the defendant is negligent or not. For instance, in *Berry* v. *Sugar Notch Borough*, 191 Pa. 345 (1899), the fact that the plaintiff was speeding when his car was hit by a fallen tree during a violent windstorm was not a cause of the accident as the probability of the accident occurring was the same whether he drove slowly or speedily. In the present case, Anne's failure to repair her headlight undoubtedly increased the chance of an accident by at least .001, as did Derek's failure to fix his brakes. This latter fact seems to elude Wright J. and undermine his whole fragile "background theory of rights."

Another dilemma for my judicial colleagues has been the duty to rescue. The "efficiency" account of the law offers a convincing and moral response. As the courts are slowly beginning to accept, there is no significant or meaningful difference between misfeasance and nonfeasance. Any set of circumstances can be so arranged and presented as to meet either definition; see *Rowland* v. *Christian*, 69 Cal. 2d 108 (1968) and *Spreacher* v. *Adamson Companies*, 30 Cal. 3d 358 (181). Furthermore, the courts and legislatures seem to be committed to extending the liability of potential rescuers; see *Farwell* v. *Keaton*, 396 Mich. 281 (1976) and Utah Code Ann. § 41–29 to 31 (1953). The natural and obvious next stop is to establish a general duty to rescue. This advance will reflect and respect the moral and economic underpinnings of the common law. It is both inefficient and immoral for a good swimmer to be free to ignore the cries of a drowning person; see *Gautret* v. *Egerton* (1867), L.R. 2 C.P. 371. In such circumstances, the costs to the swimmer are slight compared to the tragic and high costs of the drowning person. Nevertheless, it would be counter-productive to impose an obligation to rescue in all circumstances. It might, for instance, discourage people from becoming good swimmers or visiting the beach. Also, the incidence of rescue might decrease as such acts would no longer be seen as motivated by heroic altruism, but by fear of legal liability. However, as Martin could have at least telephoned for an ambulance at little or no cost and certainly at less cost than Anne, Derek or Charles, he must assume liability.

Doctrin C.J.'s refusal to establish such a duty of "easy rescue" is indicative of her pusillanimity. Legislative inaction does not necessarily mean a desire to retain the *status quo*, but can be interpreted as an indication that the legislature feels it is more appropriate for the courts to change the law; see *Alvis* v. *Ribar*, 85 Ill. 2d 1 (1981). As regards the administrative problems, while they do present difficulties, they are of no greater magnitude than the initial question of liability under Doctrin C.J.'s approach. The most sensible distribution of losses is to have the original tortfeasor pay for the damages as if an early rescue had been effected and the "rescuer" pay for the remainder. In the present case, therefore, Martin would be responsible for the payment of a large portion of Derek's and Charles' damages.

Finally, Charles' claim for emotional distress can be easily and expeditiously disposed of. It is not so much a matter of liability as of proof; see *Molien* v. *Kaiser Foundation Hospitals*, 27 Cal. 3d 916 (1980). While it is difficult to imagine what cost-effective steps he could have taken to avoid injury, we can safely assume that they would outweigh the accident and avoidance costs of Anne, Derek or Martin. Liability, therefore, seems established. However, I do agree with Doctrin C.J. that we must be careful not to encourage or facilitate bogus claims. It is desirable that the law should march with medicine, "but in the rear and limping a little"; see *Mount Isa Mines* v. *Pusey* (1970), 125 C.L.R. 383 at 395. Nonetheless, in line with increasing medical sophistication, the courts have recently begun to recognize and accept broader recovery for nervous shock; see *McLoughlin* v. *O'Brian, supra* and *Sinn* v. *Burd*, 486 Pa. 146 (1979). Accordingly, as cogent medical evidence was led, Charles ought to recover for his emotional distress. His sexual orientation is no concern of the courts.

In conclusion, therefore, I hold that Derek cannot recover against Anne, but that he ought to receive a significant amount of damages from

Martin. Also Charles would be eligible for recovery of damages from Martin and Anne.

★   ★   ★

WRIGHT J.: As is often the case, I have the dubious distinction of following Justice Mill. It will come as little surprise to those who follow the proceedings of this Court that Justice Mill and I do not see eye to eye on the proper basis for compensation for injuries. Our bone of contention is that compensation matters are intrinsically questions of the moral entitlement of individuals in particular circumstances and not impersonal measurements of social utility. As Cicero said, "the study of law must be derived from the depths of philosophy"; see *De Legibus* i., 5. The resort to economic calculations does not take individual liberty seriously. When one person harms another, the injured has a moral right to demand and the injurer a moral duty to pay compensation.

The utilitarian ethic, espoused by Mill J., is incapable of furnishing sufficiently compelling reasons to deserve people's allegiance and support. It demands that individuals' wants, desires and projects be submerged or discarded in the interest of utility maximization; they are to be treated as mere entries on the debit side of society's moral accounts. Yet such tastes and preferences constitute an individual's moral integrity. Without these, individuals would cease to exist morally. Under such utilitarianism, individual projects are simply resources for use in the general welfare and are liable to be acquired by others. Utilitarianism seeks to maximize benefits, regardless of their distribution throughout society. Individuals are robbed of any intrinsic merit or importance. Indeed, the sacrifice of individuals is not only permissible, but is often demanded and sanctioned.

The recent Pinto affairs illustrate the callousness of life under such an "efficient" regime; see *Grimshaw* v. *Ford Motor Co.*, 174 Cal Rptr. 438 (1981). As a result of the explosion of Pinto fuel tanks in rear-end, low-velocity collisions, people died or were injured. Ford carried out a cost-benefit analysis of whether to recall and reinforce the cars:

Benefit

> Savings – 180 burn deaths, 180 serious burn injuries, 2,100 burned vehicles.
> Unit Cost – $200,000 per death, $67,000 per injury, $700 per vehicle.
> Total Benefit – 180 x ($200,000), 180 x ($67,000), 2100 x ($700) = $49.5 million.

COSTS

>Sales – 11 million cars, 1.5 million light trucks.
>Unit Cost – $11 per car, $11 per truck.
>Total Cost – 11,000,000 x ($11) 1,500,000 x ($11) = $137.5 million.

Under Mill J.'s theory of liability, Ford not only made a good commercial decision not to recall the cars, but adopted a morally commendable course of action. To have recalled the cars would have been to squander social resources. That corporations rest their business decisions and safety strategies on cost-benefit analysis is deplorable enough. For the courts to sanction and clothe such operations with moral legitimacy is intolerable.

Fortunately, the courts are not so irresponsible as Mill J. would have them. In *Grimshaw*, the plaintiff received $3.5 million and $125 million in punitive damages. Unfortunately, the punitive damages were reduced to $3.5 million on appeal. Nonetheless, the courts openly condemned such reprehensible conduct. Importantly, the court applied the principles of strict liability rather than the negligence standard. This points up a fatal flaw in Mill J.'s arguments. Not only does his liability scheme lead to a perverse decision, but it confounds his central claims that "economic efficiency" is the structural framework of the common law. On the contrary, it is his own personal political preference and an unjust one at that.

Clearly, information costs undermine and reduce the potential internalization of accident costs. How are Derek and Anne to discover the avoidance costs of the other? His whole scheme assumes that everyone has information about everyone else's costs. Indeed, even Learned Hand J. conceded that "care is the only one ever susceptible of quantitative estimate, and often that is not"; see *Moisan* v. *Loftus*, 178 F. 2d 148 at 149 (1949). At best, all risk quantifications are more impressionistic than precise. Moreover, at least in a theoretical sense, all risk is necessarily foreseeable and, therefore, one can place no limits on liability. No greater a supporter of utilitarian arguments than Posner J. has opined, while speaking of assessment of damages, that "the exactness which economic analysis rigorously pursued appears to offer is, at least in the litigation setting, somewhat delusive"; see *O'Shea* v. *Riverway Towing Co.*, 667 F. 2d 1194 at 1201 (1982). Indeed, the whole operation is artificial and counter-factual. The retrospective evaluation of the probability of something happening which has already happened is fanciful. The problem of applying the pseudo-scientific standard of "efficiency" to real-life problems is amply revealed in *Union Oil Co.* v. *Oppen*, 501 F. 2d 558 (1974). Furthermore, economic welfare is so protean a concept as to be able to justify as "efficient" a regime which determined beforehand the most likely cheapest cost avoider in particular activities and held them strictly liable whatever the actual costs.

Also, although attitudes to risk in our society are not uniform, Mill J. seems to assume widespread risk-neutrality. But there exists an asymmetrical distribution of risk-aversion and risk-preference. For instance, large-scale manufacturers can afford to be relatively indifferent to risk as they can effectively spread and pass on anticipated losses. On the other hand, individuals tend to be risk-averse and are less able to calculate and off-set future losses. Mill J. seems to overlook entirely the maldistribution of both attitudes and exposure to risk. At the very least, the Learned Hand test would need substantial adaption to affect these realities. The very act of allocating and settling risk favours the risk averse. For instance, he offers no account of why we ought not to have a reverse Learned Hand test in which loss would be carried by the person who caused it unless there are sufficient reasons to shift it. As the Pinto fiasco demonstrates, this would effect a complete change in patterns of compensation. Furthermore, according to Mill J., the law provides incentives to individuals to organize their behaviour in accordance with the dictates of economic efficiency; they will be rational maximizers of their resources. In order to do this, of course, a necessary piece of information will be knowledge of what that law is. There is nothing to suggest that people do take the law into account in actually planning their daily lives. The available information suggests that individuals do not consult legal materials before planning their activities.

A case that Mill J. relies on to support and substantiate his analysis, when read properly, exposes his disingenuousness. In *Bolton* v. *Stone*, [1951] A.C. 850, the plaintiff failed to recover after being hit by a cricket ball from the defendant's ground because the risk of such an accident was not sufficiently substantial. However, as the later case of *Miller* v. *Jackson*, [1977] Q.B. 966, makes clear, there is a hidden ordering of the social utility of the respective activities. Cricket occupies a special place in the hearts of Englishmen. It is not so clear that the courts would have reacted similarly if the cricket ground had been a water sports center; see *Kennaway* v. *Thompson*, [1981] Q.B. 88. Under Mill J.'s scheme, all activities are accorded equal significance; the playing of cricket is considered at least as important as the right of individuals not to be injured.

These difficulties strike at the root of any utilitarian argument. Although its rationale is to enhance and promote individual freedom, its operation reduces and neglects that liberty; it forces individuals to concern themselves with the projects and plans of others. Individuals deserve and merit respect simply as individuals. They are autonomous: they possess certain rights that cannot be overridden by appeals to general utility.

Rights are trumps over social welfare. Individuals are not to be conceived of as a means by which to maximize social utility, but instead are to be treated as ends in themselves. What is needed is not a maximizing and collective standard, but a distributive and individualizing principle. As Stephen J. so well put it, "the task of the courts remains that of loss fixing rather than loss spreading"; see *Caltex Oil Pty. Ltd.* v. *The Dredge "Willemstad"* (1976), 136 C.L.R. 529 at 558. The law must control the market, not be controlled by it. Individuals count. Although rather over-stated, Lord Scarman in *McLoughlin* v. *O'Brian*, [1982] 2 W.L.R. 982 at 987, emphasizes the priority of principle over policy:

> The distinguishing feature of the common law is this judicial development and formation of principle. Policy considerations will have to be weighed: but the objective of the judges is the formulation of principle. And, if principle inexorably requires a decision which entails a degree of policy risk, the court's function is to adjudicate according to principle, leaving policy curtailment to the judgment of Parliament. Here lies the true role of the two law-making institutions in our constitution. By concentrating on principle the judges can keep the common law alive, flexible and consistent; and can keep the legal system clear of policy problems which neither they, nor the forensic process which it is their duty to operate, are equipped to resolve. If principle leads to results which are thought to be so-cially unacceptable, Parliament can legislate to draw a line or map out a new path.

The imposition of legal liability ought to depend on moral entitlements as determined by causal enquiries. "Efficiency" is to be deplored for its casual nihilism. A deep sense of morality and rights pervades the common law. The Learned Hand test is, at best, a crude and misguided device to compromise and concretize individual rights. People are completely free to act, except when they cause harm to others; see *Beshada* v. *Johns-Manville Prods. Corp.*, 447 A. 2d 539 (1982). This moral principle is the driving force behind the common law: any system of tort must respect and implement such a moral notion. Tort law is a private ordering that articulates the immanent rationality of immediate personal interactions. Causa and culpa are intimately connected. As Lord Dunedin said, liability is "to be determined by common-sense principles. What is the cause of the loss?"; see *Leyland Shipping Co.* v. *Norwich Universal Fire Insurance Co.*, [1918] A.C. 350.

It would, of course, be ridiculous to pretend that negligence did not once form the backbone of accident liability. Yet, over recent decades, there has been a gradual movement from negligence to strict liability. The negligence principle was firmly established in *MacPherson* v. *Buick Motor Co.*, 217 N.Y. 330 (1918), notwithstanding decisions like *Rylands* v. *Fletcher* (1868), L.R. 3 H.L. 330. Strict liability began to reassert itself in *Escola* v. *Coca Cola Bottling Co.*, 150 P. 2d 436 (1944). On holding that a soda bottle manufacturer was absolutely liable for injury caused by a defective product, Traynor J., *id.* at 440–441, articulated the rationale for strict liability:

> Even if there is no negligence, however, public policy demands that responsibility be fixed wherever it will most effectively reduce the hazards to life and health inherent in defective products that reach the market. It is evident that the manufacturer can anticipate some hazards and guard against the recurrence of others as the public cannot. Those who suffer injury from defective products are unprepared to meet its consequences. The cost of an injury and the loss of time or health may be an overwhelming misfortune to the person injured, and a needless one, for the risk can be insured by the manufacturer and distributed among the public as a cost of doing business. . . . Against such a risk [of injury from defective products whether negligently manufactured or not] there should be general and constant protection and the manufacturer is best situated to afford such protection.

Since that seminal judgment, strict liability has begun to colonize accident liability; see *Greenman* v. *Yuba Power Products*, 377 P. 2d 897 (1963) and *Shaffer* v. *Victoria Station Inc.*, 588 P. 2d 233 (1978). Those cases which speak in the rhetoric of negligence achieve results more consistent with the dictates of strict liability. For instance, in *Hughes* v. *Lord Advocate*, [1963] A.C. 837, the defendants were liable for injuries caused by an explosion which the court accepted to be "so unlikely as not to be foreseeable." Throughout the law of tort, there has been a subtle, but profound shift in the structural foundation of the law; see *Bankstown Founding Pty. Ltd.*v. *Breisting* (1986), 60 A.L.J.R. 362 at 364 per McHugh J.A. and *Buchan* v. *Ortho Pharmaceutical (Canada) Ltd.* (1984), 8 D.L.R. (4th) 373. As early as 1936, in *Grant* v. *Australian Knitting Mills*, [1936] A.C. 85, a manufacturer was liable even though it had sold without complaint almost 5 million similar products over 6 years. To recognize the change from negligence to strict liability is to take a step much smaller and less controversial than that in *MacPherson, supra*, or *Donoghue* v. *Stevenson*, [1932] A.C. 562. As Murphy J. concluded, "what is reasonable care often becomes such a high standard that it amounts virtually to strict liability. In one sense, strict liability is but another aspect of negligence, both being based on responsibility for the creation of an abnormal risk"; see *Cartwright* v. *McLaine* (1979), 143 C.L.R. 549.

All of this, of course, is as it should be. The common law must move forward, but in so doing it must retain a principled integrity with the past. So it is with the incremental progress in tort law. As Windeyer J. in *Benning* v. *Wong* (1969), 122 C.C.R. 249 at 271 expressed it:

> We need not doubt, nor need we disguise, that this movement and development

of the law is the result of the creative work of courts making at times a conscious choice between allowing or disallowing a remedy and thus creating or denying a right. Nevertheless those who insist that the common law is still on the move should remember that it must always march in step. Decisions in cases passing at the moment must be in step with those which have just gone past, although not necessarily with those at the head of the column. Moving the metaphor from the parade ground to the field, it is as sound a maxim for law as for war that operations should be from a firm base. That an advance must be from a position which has been securely established. . . .

The political morality that explains and shows the doctrinal materials in their best light is one founded upon the right of individuals to be secure against non-consensual invasions of their personal integrity. Fault amounts to an interference per se. The focus is rightly placed upon the activity rather than the defendant's conduct: the *what* happened is more important than the *how* or *why*. Within such a regime, causation becomes not *a* basis for liability but *the* basis. It is the fulcrum of liability. Not only does it make strong ethical sense, but accords with common sense and intuitive notions of fairness. While this might give rise to the occasional penumbral puzzle, it is clear that Anne was the cause of the accident in the present case. But for Anne's failure to repair her headlight, the accident would not have occurred.

No doubt, Doctrin C.J. and Mill J. will complain that this ignores Derek's contribution to his own misfortune. Yet it is surely a foundational principle of the common law that defendants take their victims as they find them; see *Smith* v. *Leech Brian & Co.*, [1962] 2 Q.B. 405 and *Watts* v. *Rake* (1960), 108 C.L.R. 158. While the condition of Derek's car may well have extended the causal chain, it does not alter the primary fact that Anne was responsible for setting the chain in motion. Such a determination is as simple as it is fair. It also avoids another doctrinal swamp into which Doctrin C.J. and Mill J. have been lured; see *Daly* v. *General Motors Corp.*, 20 Cal. 3d 725 (1978) and *Overseas Tankship (U.K.) Ltd.* v. *Morts Dock and Eng. Co. (The Wagon Mound)*, [1961] A.C. 388. Further, the acceptance of a defence of contributory negligence would admit through the back door the very same utilitarian constraints on individual rights that were refused entry at the front. To use Derek's conduct to reduce Anne's liability is to set in motion a process that would ultimately erode Derek's rights. Although a sleeping passenger is more susceptible to serious injury than an alert one, it is ludicrous to reduce the defendant's liability on this account; see *Sloan* v. *Flack*, 150 So. 2d 640 (1963).

Both Derek's and Charles's injuries were caused by Anne's activities; if she had not acted as she did, there would have been no harm. The fact that Charles's injuries are emotional rather than physical is irrelevant. Once the court is satisfied, as Burke J. in *Battalla* v. *State of New York*, 10 N.Y. 2d 237 (1960), put it, of "the quality and genuineness of proof," there need be no further argument. It is illogical and unfair to hinge liability, as Doctrin C.J. seems to do, on whether the damage suffered is physical or emotional.

The wise refusal of the common law to recognize a general duty to rescue supports the arguments used to justify strict liability and illustrates the perversity and uncertainty of Mill J.'s "efficiency thesis." Moreover, contrary to what Doctrin C.J. states, it is because of the law's concern with morality not in spite of it. As Jessup J. succinctly expressed it, "no principle is more deeply rooted in the common law than that there is no duty to take positive action in aid of another, no matter how helpless or perilous his position is"; see *Horsley* v. *MacLaren*, [1970] O.R. 487. The imposition of a duty of care rightly depends upon the existence of some special relationship or the creation of risk which amounts to a positive acceptance of responsibility; see *Racine* v. *C.N.R.*, [1923] 1 D.L.R. 924 and *South* v. *National Railroad Passenger Corp.*, 290 N.W. 2d 819 (1980). In other circumstances, there is no promise or commitment to act and, therefore, no expectation of rescue. To require gratuitous acts of rescue flaunts individual freedom. As Deane J. noted, the common law has not "embraced the embarrassing moral perception that he who has failed to feed the man dying from hunger has truly killed him"; see *Jaensch* v. *Coffey* (1984), 54 A.L.R. 417 at 439. A similar principle animates other areas of the law. In contract, there is no general duty to co-operate, unless it is necessary in order to effectuate the exchange; see *Seaman's Direct Buying Service* v. *Standard Oil*, 181 Cal. Rptr. 126 (1981). In a very real sense, the "rescuer" ought not to be liable as she did not cause the plaintiff's dilemma or damages.

A glance at the solution offered by Mill J. betrays the muddled and dangerous nature of his thinking. In general, the imposition of a duty to rescue underlines the fact that a person's own welfare is of no special interest; it must be discarded for the social good. The pauper might have to sacrifice his life to rescue the president, but the president might be acting irresponsibly to attempt a rescue of the pauper. Apart from its obvious iniquity, such a rule is unworkable as the rescuer must first ascertain the "worth" of the plaintiff before knowing whether there is a social obligation to perform or refrain from a rescue. Further, a rescue rule is a form of conscription into social service; the rescuer becomes an insurer for the fool-hardy, risk-preferring or powerful. An obliged rescue is tantamount to a tax, a forced exchange exacted by government. Whereas a rescue rule leads to unjust results and renders it uncertain where liberty ends and obligation begins, a no-rescue rule is consistent with both moral and economic principle; see *Hargrave* v. *Goldman* (1963), 110 C.L.R. 40 at 66. In the present case, Martin would be free to engage in any rescue attempt he chose, but he would not be obliged to attempt any rescue. At least in my conclusion, I fully agree with Doctrin C.J. on this issue. However, I disassociate myself entirely from Mill J.'s decision. He has sown the wind and, unless we respond promptly, we will reap the whirlwind. He has contrived a decision that places almost exclusive responsibility upon Martin for the losses to Derek and Charles. The logic or fairness of such a decision completely eludes me.

I would like to conclude my judgment with some general remarks on why strict liability is preferable to a no-fault compensation scheme, so ably and fondly espoused by Prudential J. I believe that strict liability comes out on top in any comparison of the two major objectives of any scheme of compensation, its effectiveness in reducing accidents and its administrative costs. As Mill J. states, any system of accident liability must create incentives that minimize the sum of accident costs and avoidance costs. In general, as everyone is a potential plaintiff or defendant, a move from one scheme to another will tend to shuffle incentives around rather than reduce the overall level of accidents. What a no-fault system loses in incentives can be made up for by the rigorous enforcement of a robust criminal law. But, and Mill J. is at least right in this, the ideal world is not the practical world. Unless a change is made in the criminal law and its enforcement, the introduction of a no-fault system will actually reduce the incentives. Although other legal systems, like Sweden's, may manage to enforce vigorously and effectively the criminal law, Canengaustrus has neither the appropriate substantive criminal law nor, it seems, the will to enforce it fully. Accordingly, a decentralized system of private actions, based on strict liability, provides the most self-contained and realistic method to maintain and enforce the norms of optimal behaviour.

Prudential J. astutely notes that the costs of administering any tort system are considerable. Certainly under a negligence regime as proposed by Doctrin C.J. and Mill J., the uncertainty of the standard generates immense costs; see, for example, *Hammontree* v. *Jenner*, 97 Cal. Rptr. 739 (1971). A scheme of strict liability is not so vulnerable. Its focus of inquiry is narrow and clear; therefore, the frequency of litigation and its cost will be reduced. If the litigation process is streamlined, the cost of the reduced litigation can be pared down. Finally, under any scheme, the cost of hiring a physician to determine the actual damages in each individual case remains uniformly high.

In conclusion, therefore, I hold that Anne is responsible to Derek and Charles for the full extent of their damages. Martin is under no legal obligation at all.

★   ★   ★

PRUDENTIAL J.: The late F.R. Leavis wrote in his *New Bearings in English Poetry* (1932) at 17, that:

> [P]oetry can communicate the actual quality of experience with a subtlety and precision unapproachable by any other means. But if the poetry and the intelligence of the Age lose touch with each other, poetry will cease to matter much and the age will be lacking in finer awareness.

I have read in draft the opinions delivered by my colleagues. Whereas Mill J., Doctrin C.J. and Wright J. allow intellect to operate unmitigated by poetry, Lefft J. indulges in a poetry that drifts free from intellect. My own solution to this appeal lies in forging a rapprochement between the actual quality of experience (partially, but cynically demonstrated by Justice Lefft) and the intellectual fervour of Justice Wright. It will become clear that I reject the sentiments espoused by Doctrin C.J. whose formalistic inquiry into the conduct of the parties is misplaced. It is the plight of the injured plaintiff and not the conduct of the defendant that deserves our attention. The pseudo-intellectual rigour of Mill J. and his indifference to the fate of individuals in the march to improved social welfare fill me with despondency and horror.

The judgment of Wright J. has intuitive appeal; it seems ethical, practical and efficient. Yet, his principle of "causative responsibility" is thoroughly unequal to the massive task he sets it. In practice, it amounts to a crude and cumbersome norm by which to allocate compensation. Justice Wright still lives in the Platonic cave of abstract justice. He is not only naive, but dangerous. Common sense is a notoriously unreliable source of guidance for practical affairs. In the pluralistic society of Canengaustrus, its identity is vague and indeterminate. Causation is a labyrinth for which Wright J. offers no realistic through-route. At bottom, he has to smuggle in substantive value judgments as formal causal criteria. Recall the memorable words of Andrews J. in *Palsgraf* v. *Long Island Rly. Co.*, 248 N.Y. 339 at 352 (1928):

> Any philosophical doctrine of causation does not help us. A boy throws a stone into a pond. The ripples spread. The water level rises. The history of that pond is altered to all eternity: it will be altered by other causes also. Yet it will be forever the result of all causes combined. Each one will have an influence. How great only omniscience can say. You may speak of a chain, or, if you please, a

net. An analogy is of little aid. Each cause brings about future events. Without each the future would not be the same. Each is proximate in the sense it is essential. But that is not what we mean by the word. Nor on the other hand do we mean sole cause. There is no such thing. . . .

As we have said, we cannot trace the effect of an act to the end, if end there is. Again, however, we may trace it part of the way. A murder at Sarajevo may be the necessary antecedent to an assassination in London twenty years hence. An overturned lantern may burn all Chicago. We may follow the fire from the shed to the last building. We rightly say the fire started by the lantern caused its destruction.

A cause, but not the proximate cause. What we do mean by the word "proximate" is that, because of convenience, of public policy, of a rough sense of justice, the law arbitrarily declines to trace a series of events beyond a certain point. This is not logic. It is practical politics. . . .

Causation is and must always remain a choice; see *Kinderavich v. Palmer*, 127 Conn. 85 (1940). If we are to abide by general rules, we must be prepared for arbitrary results. Each accident is unique and demands a unique causal inquiry—"cause and effect find their beginning and end in the limitless and unworkable . . . , [h]ence arbitrary limits have been set"; see *Atlantic Coastline Rly Co.* v. *Daniels*, 8 Ga. App. 775 (1911). Indeed, in the present case, which Wright J. labels simple and straightforward, it is unclear why "common sense" would burden Anne with the whole cost of the accident. Surely Derek was an "active" factor in the accident and Martin might have been. In any fault-based compensation scheme, the conundrum of causation represents an insuperable barrier to the achievement of personal or social justice. Only a shift to a no-fault regime can overcome this impasse.

As for a "negligence" regime, blindly adhered to by Doctrin C.J. and zealously championed by Mill J., it is unclear why rules laid down in the days of the horse and carriage should continue to govern us today. Having witnessed a phenomenal increase in the scale and gravity of destruction which modern technology can wreak, Baron Bramwell's decision "to put up with such mischief as reasonable care on the part of others cannot avoid" is no longer acceptable; see *Holmes v. Mather* (1875), L.R. 10 Ex. 261 at 267. As we enter the third millenium, the victims of society's collective progress deserve more protection. Our society is dominated by subservience to neither a thoroughgoing holistic nor an atomistic ideology. The law of torts may indeed be the paradigmatic law of the mixed society. It is our responsibility as Justices to ensure that the balance is the best we can make it. Unfortunately, the present mixture is in need of titration. We should add a hefty dose of concern and compassion for our fellow human beings to the tort system. The hotch-potch of add-on or modified plans used to bolster up the private tort action needs comprehensive reconsideration and amendment. The time for makeshift tactics is well passed. In the age of mass torts and toxic devastation, it is perverse to model accident compensation around "snails in ginger beer bottles" and "exploding parcels". My judgment today should be read as a set of guidelines for a long overdue experiment in social reform.

We now have an overwhelming body of data that catalogues in precise detail the litigation lottery. The cost of accidents is astronomical. In Canada, for instance, out of a population of 25 million, 3.5 million sustain product-related injuries annually, 4,000 are killed and 11,000 permanently disabled. Losses are over $2 billion in product-related injuries alone. Of these victims, forty-five percent never recover anything. Further, only one percent reach the courts and most of those are settled on the courthouse steps. Over fifty percent of the compensation ultimately paid out is lost in administering and financing its recovery, mainly to lawyers. These statistics are repeated in every common law jurisdiction. But, revealing as they are, they are even more disturbing when it is remembered that "negligence" is a feature endemic to modern life. For instance, strong evidence suggests that a "good driver" makes about nine mistakes every five minutes. Against such statistics, the efficacy of tort law as a compensatory or deterrent device is illusory.

Dissatisfaction with existing tort law is now a universal phenomenon. Committees, commissions, courts and commentators have railed for long enough. Unhappily, this court still does not speak with one voice. I refrain today from moving in advance of the legislature only after long, hard and sustained reflection. I have kept in mind what was said in the related context of vicarious liability by Lord Wilberforce in *Launchbury* v. *Morgans*, [1973] A.C. 127 at 136:

> I do not know on what principle our Lordships acting judicially can prefer one of these systems to the others or on what basis any one can be formulated with sufficient precision or its exceptions defined. The choice is one of social policy. . . . Whatever may have been the situation . . . in the youth of the motor car, it is very different now, when millions of people drive for a vast variety of purposes and when there is in existence a complicated legislative structure as to insurance—who must take it out, what risks it must cover, who has the right to sue for the sum assured. Liability and insurance are so intermixed that judicially to alter the basis of liability without adequate knowledge (which we do not have the means to obtain) as to the impact this might make on the insurance system would be dangerous, and in my opinion, irresponsible.

Today, I hesitate to remind the legislature that we are all better informed; the evidence is clear and overwhelming. Yet even some of my enlightened judicial colleagues, who recognise the thoroughly decrepit character of the common law of torts, still insist that only the legislature can step in. This is impractical and unnecessary. The difficulties of legislative action, of weighing and balancing competing political forces, is so great that even urgent law reform may be frustrated. Throughout our legal system, legislation overtakes and overwhelms the common law. The age of statutes is upon us. The judiciary must respond or, at least, belatedly acknowledge this shift. This does not mean an unthinking obeisance to legislative wisdom. Judges must become constitutional partners in keeping the law in tune with contemporary society; see *Jaensch* v. *Coffey* (1984), 54 A.L.R. 417 at 456 per Deane J. The judicial timidity evidenced in cases like *Maki* v. *Frelk*, 40 Ill. 2d 193 (1968) does not befit our democratic responsibilities. The common law must grow and develop with society. As the court concluded in *Alvis* v. *Ribar*, 85 Ill. 2d 1 (1981):

> We believe that the proper relationship between the legislature and the court is one of cooperation and assistance in examining and changing the common law to conform with the ever-changing demands of the community. There are, however, times when there exists a mutual state of inaction in which the court awaits action by the legislature and the legislature awaits guidance from the court. Such a stalemate exists and the legislature has, for whatever reason, failed to act to remedy a gap in the common law that results in injustice. It is the imperative duty of the court to repair that injustice and reform the law to be responsive to the demands of society.

With their training and experience, the judiciary may properly be entrusted with this democratic responsibility to prompt and, ultimately, to cajole the legislature to action. While greater power correctly lies with the legislature, this does not mean that the judiciary is relegated to the role of constitutional ciphers. As such, my judgment today is a clarion call for action. It may give the legislature the opportunity for a second look, not a passive glance, but an active investigation. Canengaustrus must embrace and implement a thoroughgoing and comprehensive scheme of accident compensation.

The implementation of such a scheme is not a revolutionary move. It simply universalizes the relief that underpins the present world of accidents. Through a combination of compulsory and voluntary insurance schemes, society has generally considered it appropriate to spread the economic consequences of accidents over the whole community. The search for negligent or strictly liable defendants is fictional; a vain attempt to control the aggregate sum payable by society. If loss-distribution is our goal, the patchwork of tort actions, private insurance and public relief is a grossly inefficient way to proceed. They are fundamentally incompatible and hostile. Indeed, the resort to insurance undermines the "rationality" assumptions of Doctrin C.J., Mill J. and Wright J. People lack sufficient ability to make rational judgments about accident prevention and, therefore, they insure. Behaviour in the face of danger is not motivated by concern for person safety, but for its financial consequences. To seek, as Mill J. might, to explain the distribution of accident insurance purchased as a function of individually optimal decisions is absurd: the demand for insurance refutes any assumption of risk neutrality. It reflects and corresponds to the maldistribution of information and resources. It is not enough to be "prudent", one must also be rich enough to carry insurance; see *Redding* v. *Lee*, [1983] 47 A.L.R. 241 at 284 per Mason and Dawson JJ. My plea is to introduce minimal levels of compensation below which it is morally unjustifiable to allow anybody to fall. Private insurance can still exist and prosper: market forces can provide a cushion for the wealthy who fall heavily or awkwardly on the state safety-net.

To introduce such a scheme of comprehensive accident compensation is a tall order for the Exchequer. Candour obliges us to recognize, as Justice Lefft does, that the notion of communal responsibility is a two-edged sword. Not only does the community have a duty to safeguard its members, but it must do so in a way that best suits the community at large. If the population is daily subjected to the dangers of modern technological life, it follows that its productive capacity is constantly at risk. Any injury to a human being is a loss to society. The loss occasioned to the injured person cannot be recouped; it is a net social loss. Once it is conceded that this loss can never be made good, the question becomes whether any one person should be required to bear that loss. For instance, Doctrin C.J. perceives the harm suffered one dimensionally; the harm inflicted is solely on Derek. But it seems to me that when a person suffers injury, so does the economy. There exists a *real* social cost. Moreover, by failing to recognise the full extent of these social costs by artificially transferring it to innocent victims, we reduce the demand for action to reduce injuries and avoidable causes; see *Todorovic* v. *Waller* (1981), 37 A.L.R. 481 at 563 per Murphy J.

Thus, the community has not only a clear duty, but a vested interest in hastening physical and fiscal rehabilitation. That is what maximizing social welfare truly means. It is not to be hedged with utilitarian calculations nor swamped by hedonistic fervour; it is a programme that eschews slogans and tokenism to encourage care and responsibility. If this proposal means some minor injuries go uncompensated so that the most serious, lasting and debilitating injuries are fully compensated, so be it. If it means that there are those whose pre-accident earnings cannot be fully reimbursed from the state fund and they must forego the last few drops in order to allow the blood to flow more freely to all parts of the body politic, so be it. There are no simple or perfect solutions, only difficult choices.

The most persistent argument made against "faultless" insurance schemes is that the deterrent effect of tort law is lost. I have never been persuaded that there is anything to be lost. For the law to act as an effective deterrent, there must exist a correlation between the sanction and an individual's behaviour. Yet, under the existing system, while there may be a massive award of damages based on a minor deviation from the behavioural norm, there will be no liability, no matter how heinous the breach, so long as no one is injured. The prevalance of insurance further diminishes the impact of tort law and the courts' failure to acknowledge this exacerbates the situation; see *Lamb* v. *Camden Council*, [1981] 2 W.L.R. 1038. Insurance, like an increase in oil prices, is merely another cost of doing business or owning a car. Anne knows this well. Furthermore, the existence of criminal regulation undermines the deterrence argument. Why would overworked legislators deliberate over the introduction of manifold regulations to control careless conduct, if this merely duplicated results under the civil law? The probability of criminal sanction better encourages pre-accident safety measures and possible post-accident liability in tort.

The vision of social justice I have argued for will offend my colleagues. Mill J. will recall those "eccentric principles of socialist philanthropy" which so fatally offended his judicial kin sixty years ago; *Roberts* v. *Hopwood*, [1925] A.C. 578 at 594 and *Bromley L.B.C.* v. *G.L.C.*, [1982] 2 W.L.R. 62. Lefft J. will be dismayed because an insurance scheme requires society, on behalf of injured persons, to enter the marketplace of compensation. But its strengths are that it makes some effort to recognize the levelling quality of injury and death. Within the structure of administrative bureaucracy, it seems to restore to the law of tort its paradigm nature in a mixed society and not, as would the despair of Justice Lefft and the agnosticism of Justice Mill, destroy it. They are equally in danger of losing sight of the mixed society which demands a mixed law. Our natural and proper feelings of compassion for injured persons must not bankrupt the strained resources of the Exchequer. Nor must our concern for fiscal logic eclipse our compassionate response to injury. We must take into the post-industrial age some incarnation of essential principles which have served us well, but whose present forms have now outlived their usefulness.

There must be an incentive to recover offered by effective rehabilitation. To encourage a return to productive and gainful employment, there must exist a fair margin of return on independent effort. This incentive must not be handicapped by the tendency for levelling state benefits or denying effective help for long-term incapacity. Real compensation must be the goal. Full and adequate financial assistance carefully tailored to the severity of injury and to the victim's financial status must be the aim. Such a system will provide a direction and an objective for individuals that will subvert charges of state paternalism. Redistribution is not a valid ambition in matters of accident compensation.

The coverage offered must be properly comprehensive. Injury, not cause, is at issue. I recognize that this raises in the most acute manner possible what is to be counted as an injury. Objectors will point to the potentially arbitrary lines which this formulation might require. While I am sensitive to such critics they do not carry the day. They are the intellectual Luddites of the litigation system. Their objections are based either, in good faith, on the redistributive anomalies which accident compensation throws up or, more mischievously, on a secret desire to return to the formalities of a system of pleading which operates to the satisfaction only of lawyers and to the glorification of none. Both are mistaken. A comprehensive accident insurance scheme is such an enormous leap forward from our present haphazard, arbitrary and capricious tort scheme that it cannot and ought not to be jeopardized by the sensibilities of radical reformers or conservative critics.

Why have such schemes not been introduced if they are so desirable and workable? The answer is simple: there are no votes in accident compensation. Legislators daily make rules with little expectation that they will have any substantial impact upon people's lives; they are directed towards future electoral prospects. Accident victims are a diffuse class and lack an effective lobbying voice. As has been astutely noted, "the average man is not greatly stimulated by potential difficulties: until they actually beset him he remains an optimist and a sturdy supporter of what is familiar"; see *Compensation for Personal Injury in New Zealand* (1967), s. 14. Like the New Zealanders, I believe the people of Canengaustrus have begun to realize that accidents regularly befalling large numbers of their fellow citizens are not so much due to human error as to the complicated and uneasy environment in which we live. It is the risk of social progress; its cost ought to be shared among society. As Judge Fuchs said in *Montgomery v. Daniels*, 38 N.Y. 41 (1975):

> I believe that the concept that the individual is the basic and ultimate unit in society must be supported by recognition of the value of one's physical, mental and emotional integrity, including freedom from pain and suffering and the ability to live an uncrippled life. The automobile, a modern bane and boon, daily threatens that integrity for millions of people.

Finally, there is the moral and legal dilemma of the rescue situation. Although the introduction of the proposed scheme ameliorates the plight of the injured, our concern must be to reduce the incidence of injury. The attempt to increase safety and reinforce moral standards of care through the tort system has been an unmitigated disaster. The appropriate device for such control is the criminal law. It focuses on the punished behaviour that is morally culpable. The offences of careless driving and unhygienic preparation of food are obvious illustrations. Similarly, the failure to effect an easy rescue can be dealt with in this way. As in Vermont and Czechoslovakia, it ought to be a criminal offence to fail to rescue someone who is in imminent and serious danger when there is no serious danger to the potential rescuer; see Vt. Stat. Anne. tit. 12, § 519 (supp. 1971) and C.S.R. 1964, Oblansky Zakonik, ss. 415–19.

Not only is criminal law a more efficacious deterrent than tort law, but it encourages us to take a more caring, less alienated attitude towards our fellow citizens. As such, it is a natural corollary to a comprehensive insurance scheme. Anyone who is injured in a rescue attempt will automatically be compensated. Also, it seems entirely proper, and accords with common law morality, that the "rescuer" ought to be criminally liable whether or not the victim is injured, if there existed a serious possibility of injury. Finally, we should not underestimate the moralizing power of the criminal law. Law must not only keep up with morality, but give moral guidance to the less sure or weaker among us.

My support for the early implementation of a new compensation scheme has created a dilemma for me in disposing of the present case. Do I act today as a legislator and introduce such a scheme or give the legislators one last chance? Reluctantly, I have decided to stay my hand. This is not for fear of upsetting the insurance markets or because all existing mechanisms for compensation would grind to a halt. Rather, out of deep respect for our constitutional traditions, I defer to the legislators this one last time. I will uphold the decision of the lower court. The patent absurdity and inequity of that result is not lost on me. I can only hope it is not lost on others too.

★   ★   ★

LEFFT J.: The writing of this judgment has been an occasion of very mixed blessings. It is very sad in that it is the last judgment I ever intend to give. It concludes a legal career that I now view as being an embarrassing and inexcusable dissipation of energy and time. Yet it is an occasion of happiness for me as well. I have finally come to accept the true nature of the enterprise that I have participated in as lawyer and judge for the past forty years. I have moved from the shadows into the light. Stepping through the veil of my ideological ignorance, I see the existing world for what it is—horrible, depressing and unnerving. Yet this is not a harbinger of despair, but a case for some small hope. The circumstances of my "conversion" provide some explanation and offer some encouragement to others.

While strolling through Memorial Park recently, my attention was caught by a young group of demonstrators who were distributing leaflets. Out of idle curiosity, I went over to listen. The pamphlet contained a battery of staggering statistics and information: every minute the world spends $1.3 million on military objectives and thirty children die through lack of food or health care; one nuclear submarine costs more than the annual education budget of twenty-three developing countries with 160 million school children; the United States government paid farmers to take over forty million hectares of land out of production while 450 million people in the world starved. These figures went on ad nauseam. As I left the Park, I walked through a run-down part of Ottloncanwash. Ragged children played in the dirty streets and asked me for money as I passed. Families lived in dilapidated buildings. People lined up at hostels for food and shelter. Deprivation and degradation were everywhere. The contrast with my own pleasant neighbourhood was stark and sickening.

That night and over the following days, I agonized over that experience. Whichever way I looked at it, I could not avoid the conclusion that I had previously rejected, but always feared; that the judicial process is a major force in creating, sustaining and justifying our social situation. As organs of state power, the courts must accept their share of responsibility for the plight of the homeless and the poor. Judges hold in place the deep structure of society that sacrifices people for profits.

The vast paraphernalia of legal rights and entitlements amount to nothing more than a sugar coating on a bitter pill. Although suffering and domination are rife within society, the ideal of governance according to the Rule of Law masks these offensive facts. Far from being a vehicle for social justice, the law represents a formidable barrier to significant social change. Lord Scarman is correct in stating that "the law . . . operates not in Utopia, but in the world as it is"; see *Sidaway* v. *Bethlehem Royal Hospital Governors*, [1985] 1 All E.R. 643 at 665. But more is the pity for that.

The ideological potency of the law is subtle and profound. It contrives to be both friend and enemy. It persuades us that contemporary life is almost rational and just. Although there are blemishes and sores, this is the best there is. Certainly better than the anarchy that would thrive in the absence of law. It is the natural and, therefore, inevitable form of an ordered social life. Distinct from the naked power play of party politics, the judicial process is a passive conduit of an elusive rationality. The law claims to be neutral between individuals who self-interestedly determine their own social universe. Yet this simplistic process hides substantial and manifest injustice. The legal process places society in a condition of bondage. A powerful instrument of mystification, it breeds a false sense of moral security and political resignation. Yet its continued success depends on our acquiescence. Like Canengaustrusian Railways, the legal and political process is sustained in bankruptcy by a sinister combination of naivety, self-interest and fear of alternatives; see, for example *Bromley L.B.C.* v. *Greater London Council*, [1982] 2 W.L.R. 92.

Of course, judges are not neutral or neutered political agents. Judgments are rationalizations of our ideological prejudices. The legal order is not a coherent moral scheme, but an elaborate shell to facilitate and protect concrete economic interests dressed up in doctrinal gibberish; see *Rondel* v. *Worsely*, [1969] A.C. 191. Accidental death and injury are not only individual psycho-medical problems, but are components of a pervasive socio-economic system. They are not conditions that can be isolated and cauterized, like non-malignant tumours, from the body politic. The problem is more rooted and bespeaks a cancerous society. It is the very structure of social relations that must be attacked, if we are to achieve any meaningful and effective change.

Although the judicial function is carried on in diverse, ingenious and sophisticated forms and often with genuine and well-intentioned sincerity, as the judgments of my former colleagues amply demonstrate, the judiciary cannot escape indictment in this grand affair. Doctrin C.J., Mill and Wright JJ. may be the chief culprits, but Prudential J. is fully implicated. Her criticisms of the others are valid as far as they go, but she remains firmly within this unfortunate tradition. Although variously expressed and disguised, their judgments are nothing more than a crutch for a terminally ill society. Each one legitimates the tragic toll of human life in our industrialized society. They present accidents and injuries as an inescapable and natural feature of modern life. But I do not think that there can be any real improvement unless there is a crucial shift in the way people think about themselves as members of a community. Individuals must comprehend that life in a community entails mutual obligations and interdependence. The present attitude toward health and misfortune reveals its impoverished sense of community and its modern tendency to bureaucratic solutions. Society is institutionally incapable of imagining alternative modes of social life other than an anarchic individualism or a bureaucratic collectivism; organisational parasites locked in a destructive embrace that is crushing contemporary society. Although there has been a general movement from charity to citizen rights, from special to universal schemes, from minimal to optimal payments, from private to public sources, the efficiency dictates of a market economy have always constrained this progress. So profound is their commitment to the status quo that one judge has gone so far as to condemn enterprise liability as "socialistic"; see *Markle* v. *Mulholland Inc.*, 509 P. 2d 529 at 546 (1973).

While they disagree about the redistributive role of the state, all the judges envision a similar kind of just society. The basic dynamic is individualistic and competitive. The only shared experience is one of isolation and fragmentation. However, although feting the individual and celebrating personal freedom and action, the law recommends a set of social organizing principles that rest on a pessimistic notion of human personality. Individuals are, at best, ambivalent to others; at worst, they are distrustful of others. By expecting the worst of human nature, a collective lifestyle is entrenched that stifles the full potential of each person to care for others and instead treats others as foes, not friends.

The attitudes of all my colleagues toward compensation exemplify the full force of this wretched situation. The common law task is to restore individuals to the position they were in before the accident. In its more grandiloquent moments, tort insists on the "general underlying principle . . . that whoever unlawfully injures another shall make him whole;" see *Bullerdick* v. *Pritchard*, 8 P. 2d 705 at 706 (1932). Prudential J. does not object to this standard: he wants all of society to bear this burden and to make compensation available regardless of the injury's particular cause. Clearly, these proposals represent a substantial improvement over prevailing arrangements. Yet, they are much too limited in their remedial and distributive ambitions. Prudential J. shares with his colleagues the same objective: to ensure through the payment of money and the provision of institutional health care that victims are reconstituted. Victims can then resume their roles as rugged operatives in the bruising market of individual competition. Where the misfortune is too great to allow such reconstruction, the aim is to ensure that the individual is able to live out her days in reduced physical discomfort, at a minimal level of material satisfaction; see *Sharman* v. *Evans*, [1977] 138 C.L.R. 563 and *Lim* v. *Camden H.A.*, [1980] A.C. 174. Economics and efficiency always temper care and concern. Health has been converted into another commodity to be traded for and traded off in the market. Human life and suffering represent just one more variable in the production-consumption equation. As the court put it in *Helene Curtis Inds. Inc.* v. *Pruitt*, 385 F. 2d 841 at 862 (1967), "the balancing [between the need for adequate recovery and viable enterprises]. . . . involves a determination of the most just allocation of the risk of loss *between members of the marketing chain*". The victim is reduced to a weak link.

This obscene reduction of people to a piece of property reaches its most egregious form in the arguments of Mill J. His bottom line is that it does not pay to be too careful. Indeed, he seems committed to the view that the taking of certain safety precautions would be unjust as they will squander valuable social resources. Even if we took such ludicrous and despicable talk of a market in accidents seriously, the law is concerned with particular accidents and, if "efficiency" has any value, it is only over the totality of accidents; see *O'Shea* v. *Riverway Towing*, 677 F. 2d 1194 at 1201 (1982). Of course, the very notion of "efficiency" is anathema. We would not contemplate using "efficiency" to justify tortured confessions, slavery or baby markets, so why rely on it to determine the incidence of death and injury? While characteristically extreme, Mill J.'s supposedly rational scheme shows the political bias of his colleagues. Rationality is not a formal device, but embodies a deep structure of values. Although the courts would not enforce a $1 million bargain to undergo a .000001 chance of death, they would enforce the payment of a $1 bus ride which, statistically, offers a far higher risk of injury.

Nonetheless, the excesses of Mill J. must not be allowed to deflect criticism from his colleagues. All combine in their treatment of injury and death as economic events. Each accident is considered remedial by the payment of money. People are simply their property; their worth is measured by the value of that "capital asset"; see *Graham* v. *Baker* (1961), 106 C.L.R. 340. As Oscar Wilde might have said, "the law knows the price of everybody, but the value of nobody." For instance, the bulk of a damages award consists of a sum for discounted future earnings; see *Andrews* v. *Grand & Toy Alta. Ltd.*, [1978] 2 S.C.R. 229 and *Seffert* v. *Los Angeles Transit Lines*, 56 Cal. 2d 498 (1961). This means that, for exactly the same injuries, an infant may get $100,000, a young adult $250,000, and a senior citizen $30,000. A victim's worth is her or his income loss.

Indeed, the whole law of damages is not only based on "unprovable predictions, metaphysical assumptions and rationalized empiricism", but on a vicious conservatism; see *Skelton* v. *Collins* (1966), 115 C.L.R. 94 at 118 per Windeyer J. With bare-faced condescension, the courts sanction the child of an unemployed plasterer receiving substantially less in damages than one similarly injured who's father owns a prosperous business. The reason is that the children will likely "follow in father's footsteps"; see *Connolly* v. *Camden & Islington A.H.A.*, [1981] 3 All E.R. 250 and

Arnold v. *Teno*, [1978] 2 S.C.R. 287. Furthermore, not only does the law of damages, by preserving the income of claimants, perpetuate the existing maldistribution of wealth, the rules on collateral benefits extend the gap between rich and poor. For instance, whereas private insurance need not be brought into account, some public provisions, like unemployment benefits, reduce the plaintiff's recovery; see *Bradburn* v. *G.W. Rwy* (1874), L.R. 10 Ex. 1 and *Redding* v. *Lee* (1983), 47 A.L.R. 241. Mindful that it is the richer among us who carry private insurance and the poorer who depend on public benefits, the law manages to exacerbate economic inequality in even tragic circumstances.

In all its guises, the whole process of accident compensation serves to dehumanize. It encourages the maker of Pintos to act as it does and, more, to claim moral and political legitimacy for its economic endeavours. Compensation for injury simply pays off our collective conscience. We add insult to injury by offering cold cash instead of communal support. We can ignore the injured by pretending to have taken care of them. It escapes me why "the common law has . . . not embraced the *embarrassing* moral perception that he who failed to feed the man dying from hunger has truly killed him"; see *Jaensch* v. *Coffey*, [1984] 54 A.L.R. 417 at 439 per Deane J. If the judges identified more with the hungry than with the moralist, the law might become socially relevant. Accident victims must become moral subjects involved in their own rehabilitation and not administrative objects of state-enforced benevolence. Our law reflects a profound indifference to life and suffering: its crassness dents further the already battered self-esteem of the injured victim. The sentiments of Esher M.R. in *Le Leivre* v. *Gould*, [1893] 1 Q.B.491 at 497 that "a man is entitled to be as negligent as he pleases towards the whole world if he owes no duty to them" still inform the law. In 1969, Breitel J. in *Tobin* v. *Grossman*, 24 N.Y. 2d 609 (1969) held that a mother who did not see, but heard and came upon the aftermath of a bad accident to her son could not recover; "this is the risk of living and bearing children."

No matter how comprehensive or generous, compensation schemes only address part of the problem. They are all cure and no prevention. Compensation must be subordinated to safety and health. The overriding objective of the law must be to equalize risk throughout society and restore control of those risks to those who undergo the dangers flowing from such risks. Of course, it will never be possible to eliminate risk in our lives. But the second-best alternative is to ensure that all persons can decide the risks to which they are individually exposed. We must share risk collectively and equally. Achieving this objective demands a complete restructuring of all aspects of social life. The time to begin such an heroic effort is well past. As well-intended as they are, Prudential J.'s proposals will function as much as a crutch for crippled society as a means for social improvement. Instead of simply treating individual symptoms, our response to injury must take in the total environment in which people live, work, play and die. The democratic control of risk must be of at least the same importance as the treatment of injury and misfortune.

The first step must be to redistribute knowledge and information. The corporate elite hold a monopoly on knowledge which comprises the foundation and guarantee of its power. Indeed, this very assumption of information-deprivation is the motive force of Mill J.'s "efficiency" scheme. He treats transaction costs as a natural given rather than a political choice. The debacle of the Ford Pinto case illustrates the pernicious operation of a system based on an unequal distribution of knowledge. The possibility of bargaining with a manufacturer over the safety of a car you wish to buy is fanciful. What does a consumer know of a product compared to its manufacturer? For instance, the purchaser of the thalidomide drug lacked adequate resources to discover information about it in order to make a truly informed choice about using it. The fact that the manufacturer possessed, but concealed the available information compounds the injustice; see H. Teff and C. Munro, *Thalidomide: The Legal Aftermath* (1976).

Throughout our lives we are constantly exposed to risk, but starved of proper information as to the extent of that risk. Moreover, exposure to risk is thoroughly maldistributed. White and blue collar workers do not face the same risk of injury. Whereas a manager of a quarrying company has a .004 chance of injury, a quarryman has a .098 chance; see 2 *Royal Commission on Civil Liability and Compensation for Personal Injury* (1978). Furthermore, the quarryman does not receive compensation for this exposure in his wages, but earns substantially less than the manager. The reliance on choice as a justification is, of course, hopelessly unrealistic. As the court in *Green v. Sterling Extruder Corp.*, 471 A. 2d. 15 at 21 (1984) said, "the practicalities of the workaday world are such that . . . the employee works 'as is' or he is without a job." As regards domestic injuries, incidence of injury depends on the quality of the product bought which, of course, is a function of wealth. In the instant case, Derek is more exposed to injury in his old jalopy than is Anne in her expensive sports car. Also, the level of environmental pollution to be endured is higher in poorer residential areas than in richer ones; there is a strong inverse relationship between smog levels and property values.

Finally, the notion of risk-sharing proposed is neither novel nor radical. Although its pervasive implementation would revolutionize society, its general validity is recognized and upheld by existing doctrine. Only the English courts have refused to incorporate it into the law; see *Sidaway* v. *Bethlehem Royal Hospital Governors*, [1985] 1 All E.R. 643. Although artificially confined to medical situations, a clear feature of tort law is "informed consent"; see *Cobbs* v. *Grant*, 8 Cal. 3d 229 (1972) and *Reibl* v. *Hughes*, [1980] 2 S.C.R. 880. Doctors are required to supply their patients with all the necessary and available facts of the material risks of a procedure in order for there to be intelligent consent. As the court declared in *Canterbury* v. *Spence*, 474 F. 2d 772 at 780 (1972):

> The root premise is the concept . . . that "every human being of adult years and of sound mind has a right to determine what shall be done with his own body . . . " True consent to what happens to one's self is the informed exercise of a choice, and that entails an opportunity to evaluate knowledgeably the options available and the risk attendant upon each.

This requirement rests upon a person's right of self–determination. Founded on the need to promote individual responsibility and to encourage informed decision–making, it is impliedly defended and espoused by all of my former judicial colleagues. Yet it remains arbitrarily and illogically confined to peripheral situations. If it were not held in check, it would consume the whole of the tort law. Its present constriction highlights the arbitrary character and deep indeterminancy of the law and reveals the illegitimate hierarchy of power its confinement serves to sustain.

In taking my leave of this court, I implore you to follow my lead. I dedicate my remaining years to this struggle. Humanity stands on the edge of the abyss. We must regroup and make good on our commitment to ourselves. Love and power must converge. We must give voice to the inarticulate speech of the heart. Victims of the world unite. In the eternal words of John Donne:

> No man is an Island, entire of itself;
> Every man is a piece of the Continent, a part of the main.
> Any man's death diminishes me,
> Because I am involved in Mankind;
> And therefore never send to know for whom the bell tolls;
> It tolls for thee.

7

CHARTER CUTTINGS

FORWARD TO THE PAST

(16.X.85)

Canada . . . Notwithstanding
Roy Romanow, John Whyte and
Howard Leeson
Carswell-Methuen, 286 pages

"Once upon a time, in a snowy land to the North . . . " So should begin this new book on the most recent chapter in the long-running saga of Canadian constitutional history. Except for the occasional skeptical note, the book's thematic chord is essentially lyrical and romantic. In the ceaseless process of national self-discovery, the powers of Good triumph over Evil and the "miracle of Canada's existence" is maintained. The "Gang of Eight" and the "Northern Magus" finally get their act together. The Charter is born in a cathartic moment of national self-discovery.

The ambition of the book is to flesh out the skeletal understanding that most people have of the immediate events that led up to the patriation of the Canadian Constitution. As they played an active role on behalf of the Saskatchewan Government, each author is well placed to do this. As such, it is a major success and contains a wealth of colorful detail: the major personalities are introduced; the crucial events described; and the critical deals explained. Especially interesting is the account of the NDP's ambivalent role in the drama and the temporary relocation of the struggle to London's

Westminster. It is a good reference work, richly detailed and popularly styled. Few will not benefit from reading and reflecting upon this book and the history it chronicles.

Yet the book is not without faults. There are a couple of small, but irritating stylistic objections. The book reminds one of the story about the camel's creation—it is really a horse put together by a committee. The writing is uneven and sometimes obtrudes into the narrative smoothness. Also, the authors write about their own involvement in the events in a ridiculously strained impersonal way. They opt for detachment when intimacy is required and would be the making of the book. Although a kiss-and-tell technique would be inappropriate, they play down their own not inconsiderable part, especially Roy Romanow's as Saskatchewan's Attorney General. In so doing, they waste the very expectations about the book's likely quality, pertinence and instructiveness.

However, its major problem is that, although it thoroughly and convincingly fleshes out the political skeleton, it does not tell us what makes it move and do the things it does. It is a bloodless tale that is long on the how, but short on the why. For instance, in recounting the crucial events that led up to the breaking of the log-jam at the First Ministers' Conference in early November, 1981, they are content to attribute it to "raw bargaining" without more. Moreover, the whole occasion is presented as almost mystical in its performance and unfolding, with an invisible hand leading the participants to the inevitable denouement: "The whirling events . . . took on the characteristics of the aurora borealis on a clear win-

ters' night on the prairies, as positions shifted and danced through the conference room, each displaying a multitude of shades and hues." Within this scenario, it is not surprising that because of their affiliations, the authors emphasize the importance of Saskatchewan's visible hand.

Inadvertently or otherwise, this book does convey graphically how the whole process was deeply undemocratic; constitutional participation was an exercise in high politics. Although supposedly for the benefit of all Canadians, the "People's Charter" took on a governmental life of its own. Constitutional reform became simply another venue for the continuing power-play between Ottawa and the provinces. For Prime Minister Pierre Trudeau, whatever his original motives, an entrenched Charter of Rights became an end in itself. In an important sense, even only a couple of years after this "momentous watershed," it should already be clear to Canadians that everything has changed, but nothing has really altered. Why would such a canny politician as Trudeau give away power, unless he knew that it was a shell game?

To talk, as this book does, of a "profound change" in Canada's self-image from a salad bowl to one in which it is seen as "a single political unit" with the responsibility and will to represent all is the stuff of fairy tales. At best, this can only be wishful thinking. The tension between East and West and English and French remains unabated. The Charter of Rights is a conservative document which will need more than a conscientious, but also naturally conservative judiciary to breathe radical life into it. If the past is any guide, the Supreme Court will have to surpass itself and confound the historical record.

Economic power and deprivation remain grossly maldistributed. The Charter does little to confront such problems. If there is to be a real transformation in the Canadian ethos and way of life, there must be a massive change in the way we think about ourselves, our relations with others and the state. This cannot be brought about through the symbolic tools of constitutionalism, by rewriting and shuffling around the documents of our nationhood. Change must take place in the hearts and minds of Canadians, along with an honest commitment to act upon and remain faithful to those personal and collective ideals.

When all the hoopla of the opening acts diminishes, we might recognise the emptiness of the Charter circus. The time to take up Robert Fulford's challenge is already upon us: "The Charter was the great legal project of Trudeau's generation; undoing it may turn out to be the great legal project of the generation following him."

CHARTER RHETORIC

(1.V.84)

The second anniversary of the introduction of the Charter of Rights has been used as another occasion to celebrate and reaffirm the Charter's significance and importance for Canadians. As the Supreme Court of Canada begins to grapple with the document's interpretation, we are reminded that great changes are likely and that the Charter will really begin to bite. Such rejoicing is misplaced. The entrenchment of the Constitution and Charter litigation are much overrated exercises.

At one and the same time, we take the Charter both too seriously and not seriously enough. It is a grave error to think that the Charter is going to change the quality or structure of life for the average Canadian; millions remain unemployed, poverty-threatened and socially frustrated. If we do want to effect such changes, we have to take those freedoms and rights that are embodied in the Charter much more seriously than simply passing a document through Parliament. Established through a profoundly undemocratic process, the Charter's promise of "a free and democratic society" cannot be achieved through the courts. The judicialization of politics is a retrogressive and harmful step in Canadian constitutional and social history.

There is a massive discrepancy between social life as depicted by the law and as actually lived. Legal change does not amount to social change. Charter rights are abstract and procedural rather than concrete and substantive. Civil and procedural rights are emphasized at the expense of economic and social rights. Yet any scheme of civil rights is useless without the economic ability to take equal advantage of them. Indeed, the introduction of such civil rights can serve to exacerbate the already vast inequalities of wealth and power in Canadian society.

For instance, around Christmas,

the Globe and Mail's front page carried two headlines. The first heralded "Anti-Metric Dealers Awarded $42,000"; two garage owners, fighting against metric legislation, had recovered the costs of vindicating their rights. The other headline proclaimed "Homeless in Record Numbers Seeking Shelter"; Toronto hostels were unable to accommodate the bag-carrying down-and-outs. Those two headlines, same page, same day, speak eloquently to the effect of the Charter. Certain people will win under the Charter and certain people will lose. But nothing will change.

Another example is the political struggle in British Columbia, especially its austerity and anti-union programs. The Government sought to enact legislation that would permit it to dismiss employees without cause and that would make it criminal for people to withhold their labor. Of course, those people are free—they are free to vote in the next election, to demonstrate, to protest and, if arrested, not to be unfairly treated or given cruel or unusual punishment. But none of this will help them obtain or keep a job and take care of their families. What price the Charter for them?

The cases on the Supreme Court's docket tell a similar tale. Although the cases on police powers likely will force the police to rethink their procedures, the effect will be of limited practical value. Most arrests result in guilty pleas and there is respectable empirical evidence to suggest that, on the basis of the U.S. experience, police activities may not change, even minimally, for the better. Also, the success of an appeal against legislative restrictions on election advertising will not necessarily be a victory for free speech, except

those rich enough to afford advertising; who you can get to listen is as important as being free to speak. Similarly, protection against random Revenue Canada searches of financial consulting firms will hardly work to the benefit of the average Canadian taxpayer who has little wealth to hide.

A preliminary comment worth making is that Charter litigation has provided incontrovertible evidence that resort to the courts is an extremely costly business. Like the Ritz hotel, the courts are available to anyone who can pay the going rate. This not only puts litigation well out of the reach of most citizens, but means that an unrepresentative preponderance of cases will concern the interests and problems of wealthy individuals or, more realistically, corporations.

To say the Charter has no impact is, of course, not quite accurate. It has had two effects: one rhetorical, the other negative. It will change the Canadian culture of argument. Political dialogue may restructure itself. "Rights" talk will become a staple of Canadian legal argument. All this will be grist for the lawyers' mill. Second, the Charter's introduction and the hype surrounding it has given the false impression that things are better or will soon become so. This merely raises hopes in order to dash them. More important, the Charter deflects valuable energy and attention away from the real challenge, making Canada into the democratic society it aspires and strives to be.

Democracy is not just about processes or elections. It is about a substantive way of life: the cultivation of a form of social life that maximizes the opportunity for individuals to control their own lives. The judicialization of politics under the Charter eschews that ideal. To hand over basic political issues to a predominantly male, middle-class and middle-aged group of judges is a mistake. No matter how sincere or conscientious, the same judges that administered the law before the Charter are unlikely to suddenly change their approach and breathe revolutionary life into the Charter. Their performance under the old Bill of Rights does not give cause for great hope or confidence.

What ought those genuinely committed to social justice and a truly democratic Canada do? First, greater efforts ought to be made to expose the peripheral nature of the Charter and its largely rhetorical functions. Second, armed with this awareness, Charter litigation might be used as a platform from which to develop a more caring and egalitarian society. Cases might be brought to try and persuade judges that basic rights to welfare, jobs, health and housing ought to be read into the Charter.

But third, the major resources of social activism must be deployed in more concrete and central concerns. The ramshackle nature of Canadian democracy must be renovated. Concerted efforts must be made to organize political life so it best enables individuals to participate and realize their own potential. A transfer of the energy, expenditure and intelligence presently devoted to litigation strategies to efforts to improve the legislative process would be a major first step.

If Canada is to become "a free and democratic society", the Charter and its judicial enforcement are not the answer. Democracy is about popular, not privileged power.

SUBSTANTIVE JUSTICE

(8.II.85)

In recent months, there has been a raft of Charter decisions. While many have received considerable coverage in the media, the more technical cases have understandably been given less attention. A couple of weeks ago, the Supreme Court of Canada handed down one of these apparently "technical" decisions, the *Motor Vehicle Reference*. Couched in the arcane language of constitutional law and centring on a narrow issue, the judgments of the Supreme Court amount to one of the most potentially important and socially significant rulings under the Charter to date.

Whereas most sections of the Charter spell out specific rights, such as freedom of religion, speech and the like, s. 7 is much more general. It states that everyone has the right not to be deprived of their life, liberty and security of the person except "in accordance with the principles of fundamental justice." At the time of the Charter's enactment, conventional wisdom in the legal and political community took the view that this placed only a procedural obligation on government.

The understanding was that, if fair procedures were insisted upon, there would be a greater likelihood of better substantive decisions being made; it would enhance rather than inhibit government policy-making. A secure base for rational discussion of the pros and cons of a policy issue would exist. It was not anticipated that the "principles of fundamental justice" requirement gave the courts a general mandate to invalidate the content of government policy even though it respected all the other specific rights enumerated in the Charter.

The overwhelming evidence of parliamentary hearings and debate is that the Charter was not intended to introduce some vague, but judicially-enforced "reasonableness" check on government activity. As Wayne MacKay of Dalhousie Law School has noted, if the courts have any expertise, it is "in designing the appropriate procedural structure and not in second guessing the legislators on government policy." However, in its recent decision, the Supreme Court has managed in one fell swoop to deal a body blow to those parliamentary and popular intentions.

Under the constitutional reference procedure, the British Columbia government asked the courts to rule on the constitutional validity of a section of its *Motor Vehicle Act*: it made it an offence, punishable with a mandatory period of imprisonment, to drive a motor vehicle without a licence or while under suspension. Further, this was a so-called "absolute liability" offence; drivers were to be convicted whether or not they were aware of the prohibition or suspension. The central question was: does a law that demands the automatic imprisonment of someone who is, "morally innocent", offend the principles of fundamental justice and violate a person's right to liberty under the Charter?

For many, the B.C. law will be draconian and deserve to be struck down. Both the B.C. Court of Appeal and the Supreme Court of Canada agreed and held that the law is constitutionally invalid. While offences of absolute liability are not in themselves unconstitutional, they become so when they are combined with a mandatory term of imprisonment.

Mr. Justice Lamer gave the leading opinion of the Supreme Court. Relying on the general rights-protecting purpose of the Charter to justify an expansive interpretation of s. 7, he chose to place "minimal weight" on the Parliamentary evidence. In order to ensure adequate protection for people's liberty, he maintained that "the principles of fundamental justice" must be applied to the wisdom and content of legislation as well as to the fairness of the procedures through which it was formulated and enforced.

However, Lamer J. refused to offer any vaguely definitive account of its extent or character. He left this crucial task for future judicial development and refinement. Whatever this "reasonableness" standard was, the B.C. legislation fell foul of it.

The problem with this decision is that it uses a sledgehammer to crack a nut. Although more limited, less expansive interpretations were available to dispose of the particular point in issue, the Court made a self-conscious decision to transform and extend considerably the reach and scope of the Charter. For instance, with only a little ingenuity and imagination, the Charter's provisions against "cruel and unusual punishment" could have been deployed to arrive at the desired decision. Instead, Lamer J. has opened up a whole Pandora's box.

In short, any law which affects

people's life, liberty and security of the person (what law might not?) must conform to an as-yet-unknown standard of "reasonableness" or be struck down as unconstitutional. Although ostensibly justified in the name of the Rule of Law, the Court's introduction of such a nebulous standard, over and above the other specific requirements of the Charter, jeopardises the traditionally cherished ideals of certainty and opposition to arbitrariness.

The American experience, unconsidered and unheeded by the Court, is frighteningly illuminating. Beginning in the last quarter of the nineteenth century, American courts began to nurture a constitutional doctrine of "substantive due process". They struck down a variety of public health and market regulation statutes. This conservative attack on the substantive validity of legislation reached its zenith (nadir?) in 1905 in the notorious case of *Lochner*. The U.S. Supreme Court invalidated legislation which limited the employment of bakery employees to 10 hours a day and 60 hours a week as interfering with persons' general liberty and, in particular, their freedom to contract.

Between 1890 and 1924, the Supreme Court alone struck down almost 200 statutory and administrative regulations; this was relatively restrained compared to the zealous activism of the state courts. Although the courts began their doctrinal retreat from "substantive due process" in the early 1930s, they still managed to stymie the introduction of New Deal social policies. Only in the face of Roosevelt's court-packing plan did the Court drop its libertarian opposition to progressive legislation.

The doctrine still comprises part of American constitutional law, but its modern manifestation has been put to much more liberal ends. The courts have used it to develop a limited set of rights based on privacy and personhood. Through such devices, the courts have struck down laws making abortion and the use of contraceptives a crime. Despite the change in judicial values since the 1930s, the problem remains that social justice depends on the substantive wine that the judges choose to pour into the constitutional bottles: ephemeral standards of judicial taste remain determinative.

Of course, it would be fanciful to suggest that, armed with Lamer J.'s judgment, the Supreme Court will spearhead a reactionary campaign to dismantle the welfare state; its ideas and practices are too much part of the Canadian ethos. However, while "reasonableness" is sufficiently protean to harbour a range of political philosophies, the history of judicial decision-making and the individualist thrust of the Charter do not presage a judicially-crafted socialist revolution!

What the courts could realistically do is to check the further development of socially progressive policies and encourage debilitating attacks on specific limbs of the body social. The message that the Court's decision sends to its different constituencies and the responses it will invoke are deeply troubling. The recent statements by the doctors suggesting they could use this decision to challenge any legislation banning extra-billing is an early illustration.

The legislators will begin to look over their shoulders more than ever at the brooding and shadowy presence of the courts; the decision will have a chilling effect on the democratic process of policy-making and the capacity of elected representatives to respond to popular sentiment. Although legislators are far from perfect, they do not view social life through the keyhole of litigation. Also, unlike the political process, the judicial process is exceedingly tardy at correcting its mistakes, even when it acknowledges its error.

While the reaction of the judicial community is difficult to assess in any detail, the decision sends out clear signals of the Supreme Court's intention to take an extremely active posture in the judicial review of government activity. The Court itself might envisage a very limited role for this "reasonableness" review, but there is no guarantee that lower courts will utilise this new interpretive device with restraint or responsibility. Experience shows that handing out a blank check often leads to it being filled in not only for extravagant amounts, but also in wildly different kinds of political currency.

Finally, if we ever doubted it, the decision confirms the shift in constitutional power from Parliament to the courts. The Court has taken a massive step in entrenching and extending the judicialisation of politics and the politicisation of adjudication. Further, the

nature of that politics is extremely dubious if the existing decisions under the Charter are any guide.

The most egregious of these decisions involves the almost unthinking acceptance that a corporation enjoys the same rights as humans, independent of and in addition to those of its shareholders and officers. In a few short pages, Chief Justice Dickson went from talk about "human rights" and "the inherent dignity of the person" to the equal protection that the Charter bestows on corporations.

Only four years after the introduction of the Charter, the Supreme Court has laid out its constitutional gameplan. Its tactics are varied, but its overall strategy is plain: Parliament has (mis)-handed the political ball to the judges and they intend to not only run with it, but to rewrite the rules of the constitutional game as they go along.

With the Charter, we sowed the wind and now we will have to reap the judicial whirlwind. We can only hope that the storm will blow itself out or confine its damage to relatively out of the way spots on the Canadian political landscape. Unfortunately, the Court's decision is much more than a storm in a teacup.

AN AGE-OLD PROBLEM

(30.X.85)

(with Andrew Petter)

Like the Pythia of Delphi, the Canadian Charter of Rights and Freedoms is fast becoming the political oracle of our time. When confronted with complex questions of public policy, Canadian politicians no longer feel obliged to consult their constituents. Instead, they have the Charter to guide them.

A case in point is the recent decision of the federal government to abolish mandatory retirement in the federal public sector and in federally-regulated industries. The decision was taken after little public consultation and with only cursory consideration of its social consequences. Such consultation was apparently thought unnecessary because, to paraphrase Justice Minister John Crosbie, "the Charter made us do it."

Some, of course, will welcome this shift from political to legal norms as the controlling force in our constitutional future. Their enthusiasm may wane, however, once they realize that Charter rights carry with them a hidden agenda: an agenda that, left unchecked, threatens to undermine notions of collective responsibility upon which so many of our social and economic programs are founded, and to stymie the further development of a socially just Canada.

The rights of the Charter strongly favour the interests of individuals over those of the community. Moreover, the assumption underlying Charter rights is that government, not disparities in wealth or concentrations of private power, is the major enemy of individual liberty. If politicians knuckle under to this assumption—if they abdicate their responsibility to defend collective values in the face of Charter claims—the ultimate losers will be those who lack wealth and power, those who most depend upon the state for protection and social benefits.

Consider mandatory retirement. At first blush, the issue seems simple and straightforward. Viewed from the perspective of the affected individual, a rule which requires people to retire upon reaching the age of 65 seems to limit freedom and to discriminate on the basis of age. Surely a 65-year-old schoolteacher should be permitted to continue teaching provided she has the will and the ability to do so? If it were only the teacher whose interests were at stake, it would be hard to disagree. But it is not the teacher alone who is affected by the mandatory retirement rule. While the rule stands in the way of her desire to continue teaching, it provides a measure of protection and security to many others in the community.

The teacher's liberty is just one value among many that must be considered. Any assessment of liberty must look to the social whole. For example, the elimination of mandatory retirement will limit job opportunities for younger people, particularly in those desirable job categories in which older workers are likely to continue working beyond 65. Ontario Labour Minister William Wrye has estimated that abolishing provincial laws on mandatory retirement could increase the number of unemployed by about five per cent, adding 20,000 people to the unemployment lines in Ontario alone.

Furthermore, the choice is not between mandatory retirement and nothing. It must always be asked—mandatory retirement as compared to what? If mandatory retirement is eliminated, employers will be motivated and perhaps obliged to institute job evaluation schemes. The prospect of such schemes will cast a long shadow over Canadian industry. They are notoriously difficult to apply. At a time when there is already general bitterness and tension between management and workers, introducing such programs will fan, not smother, the industrial flames.

Typically, such schemes are only introduced for non-managerial employees. The potential for abuse is large and may be used by unscrupulous companies to eliminate difficult or troublesome workers. Moreover, for employees engaged in physically demanding labour, the institution of job evaluation schemes could reduce the effective retirement age to 55 or younger.

The operation of such schemes among professional groups is also fraught with problems. Peer groups find it very difficult to pass judgment on their colleagues. In the universities, for instance, professors will be loath to conclude that older professors have passed their prime and are no longer competent in their craft.

An interesting problem will be the stage at which such job evaluation schemes are to commence. Presumably, if there is to be some consistency of principle, any scheme that is triggered by the age of an employee will be condemned as discriminatory. For this reason, job evaluation may have to be used on an annual basis for all employees. This will rightly be considered an intolerable burden by workers and an administrative nightmare by management.

Another issue will be the pension eligibility of those people who are "retired" in their 50s. If we do not change the pension provisions (and the federal government has given no indication that it intends to do so), these people will be thrown back onto welfare programs. They will suffer the double stigma of being labelled unfit for work and of being cast onto the welfare scrap heap.

At the same time, age-based social benefits currently available to those 65 and over will be placed in jeopardy. In the absence of mandatory retirement,

the various tax and other concessions made to the elderly will be open to challenge as discriminating against those under 65. For instance, travel concessions and housing benefits to seniors will become suspect as depriving non-seniors of similar benefits.

To expose these benefits to challenge by abolishing mandatory retirement is to let the tail wag the dog. Moreover, by ensuring that people retire over a broader and less focused period of time, the government will relieve itself of any sustained pressure for pension reform. Some people will now continue to work not out of a desire to exercise their democratic rights of free choice, but out of the economic necessity to keep body and soul together. At the same time, the government will be able to deflect demands for improved social security benefits by shifting responsibility to those seniors who "choose" not to work. Over time, those who cease work at 65 may come to be regarded as a drain on the community, further hampering their difficult task of adjusting to a different style of life.

All of this adds up to the conclusion that, by abolishing mandatory retirement, the many will be paying for the privilege of the few. In general, blue-collar workers will have to suffer the indignity of being pushed off the job as their manual ability decreases in order that white-collar workers can indulge their taste for further remuneration beyond the age of 65.

Clearly, it would be wrong to exclude people from social activity at 65. But this is not what mandatory retirement does. On the contrary, it frees people to make their social contributions in new and different ways. For instance, the retired schoolteacher could make a valuable contribution in a voluntary sector which is crying out for persons with her skills. If the challenge is one of principle over profits, then such voluntary alternatives should be taken enthusiastically and not dismissed derisively.

In light of such considerations, the claim that the abolition of mandatory retirement will promote individual liberty and freedom of choice seems transparent and difficult to justify. At best, this decision is misguided and, while there is still time, ought to be rescinded. At worst, the government's action reflects its willingness to use the Charter as a pretext for promoting economic efficiency at the expense of social justice.

Progressive Conservative MP Patrick Boyer, who was the head of the parliamentary committee that initially proposed ending forced retirement, may have let the political cat out of the Charter bag recently when he said: "We have got to look at anything and everything that can cause Canadian industry to be more productive. Companies that have been carrying employees who are really much retired on the job will have to make a decision." As if this was not enough, he went on to conclude that it is a greater indignity to postpone the day of reckoning and let employees drift than to "discuss" their performance with them.

Those concerned with social justice will recognize the abolition of mandatory retirement for what it is; a thinly-veiled attempt to clothe the urge for productivity at any price with the spurious and ubiquitous garments of individual rights.

The danger with all oracles is that, ultimately, they are no better than those who interpret their delphic phrases. The Charter and the judges are no exception. We must not allow their mystic allure to seduce us. In a democracy, we ought to celebrate ourselves and abandon our homage to false gods.

GOING INTO OVERRIDE

(3.V.86)

(with Andrew Petter)

It is fast becoming an article of Canadian constitutional faith that questions of social justice are best resolved by the courts. Although section 33 of the Charter permits government to override certain of its rights and freedoms, many consider such action to be high-handed and tantamount to political heresy.

The recent move by the Saskatchewan government to use section 33 to exempt back-to-work legislation from Charter review, following an adverse court decision, was almost universally condemned. The government invoked the override in response to a Saskatchewan Court of Appeal ruling that the right to strike was protected by the Charter's guarantee of freedom of association. A coalition of labour and other groups charged that the Saskatchewan action "was an abuse of process that threatens the newly gained rights of all Canadians". Now the Saskatchewan Government Employees Union has commenced court action to have the government's use of section 33 itself declared unconstitutional.

Such a response is misconceived. The override provision of the Charter is a central pillar in the new constitutional structure. Its use by government is not only thoroughly legitimate under present constitutional arrangements, but is more likely to promote than to undermine the establishment of an improved and socially progressive polity. Unions who lift the Charter to aim for the stars will only succeed in shooting themselves in the foot.

The irony of a union going to court to argue in favour of constitutional limits on legislative power will not be lost on those with a sense of history. The victories that have been won by organized labour have come in the legislative arena. The powers of the state have been harnessed to displace the unbridled individualism of court-made law with a legislative regime that emphasizes collective social responsibility. Workers rights' are creatures of statute; they have replaced the common law dinosaurs that protected employers' unfettered liberty of contract and treated unions as illegal combinations.

Governments, of course, are not always kind to unions. But what is clear, is that, where there has been progress, it has invariably come from legislatures—in spite of, not because of, the courts. This pattern is unlikely to change under the Charter. The rights and freedoms in the Charter are predicated on the same hostility to state action and the same reverence for individual autonomy that animated the common law.

Contrary to what critics suggest,

the override power is as much a part of the Charter as are free speech and equality rights. The inclusion of section 33 was not an oversight in drafting. The section was a key element of the federal-provincial accord that gave rise to the Charter. Without it, the Charter might not have seen the constitutional light of day.

Further, the existence of the override provision has been used by the courts as a pretext to strengthen their political hand. It has enabled them to justify their activism on Charter issues. In giving expansive readings of the various individual rights sections, the courts have reminded their critics that legislatures are still free to insulate laws against judicial review if they so choose: courts only become "super-legislatures" with the acquiesence of elected legislative bodies. Indeed, in the Saskatchewan case that prompted the government to invoke its override authority, the key judgment of Justice Cameron made explicit reference to section 33 to justify his forceful interpretation of the right to "freedom of association".

As if this were not enough to rebuff the opposition to using the override power, the way the courts have played their strengthened hand in Charter review of legislation gives further cause for concern. In a series of judgments, the Supreme Court of Canada and provincial appellate courts have tended to interpret the Charter in favour of corporate and established interests. This traditionalist stance jeopardizes socially progressive legislation or, at best, will stymie its further enactment. The courts are pushing Canada towards an Americanized version of political justice; an ideological credo that allows the individual to hold the public interest to ransom.

Looking at the Saskatchewan decision, labour groups might question this point of view: Didn't the Saskatchewan Court of Appeal in fact protect the right to strike? Indeed it did, but the Saskatchewan case is hardly typical. Three other provincial courts of appeal have rejected arguments that the Charter protects a right to strike. Moreover, even if the right to strike were upheld by the Supreme Court of Canada, the benefit to unions would be marginal as compared to the damage that they could suffer as a result of other Charter claims. A multitude of Charter challenges are already being mounted against the present regime of collective bargaining and union rights. In case upon case, the Charter is being used as a weapon to attack union security agreements, first contract legislation, compulsory dues check-off, and all aspects of the collective bargaining system.

In short, the very groups who labelled the use of section 33 in Saskatchewan an abuse of power are most likely to need the override in the future. This does not mean that unions should not have opposed the decision to use the override in the Saskatchewan circumstances. But it is one thing to attack the political judgment of the Saskatchewan government, it is quite another to suggest that the use of section 33 is illegitimate or that the power to invoke it ought to be subject to judicial restraint.

Further, the need to preserve section 33 is not peculiar to unions. It is a need shared by all those in society who look to government as a means for advancing social justice. Women's groups, for example, are currently fighting a rearguard action to preserve certain recently enacted sexual assault provisions of the Criminal Code: protecting victims of sexual assault from having their identities disclosed and from cross-examination in court concerning their sexual histories. Already, these provisions have been struck down by a number of courts for violating Charter rights to freedom of the press and to a fair trial. Unless the court decisions are reversed, the only avenue left will be section 33.

Democracy is better served by the continuation of political debates in the legislative arena than through the imposition of so-called "right answers" by the courts. It is notoriously difficult to reverse judicial decisions on Charter issues; constitutional amendment would be the only and improbable solution available. Legislative decisions often signal the beginning and not the end of political debates. The final opinion ought to remain with the people of Canada, not its judicial proconsuls.

Social justice cannot be a gift of judges; it can only come from the sweat of our own democratic brows. As an American jurist once remarked: "Liberty lies in the hearts of men and women; when it dies there, no constitution, no laws, no court can save it; no constitution, no law, no court can even do much to help it."

The Canadian system of government has always recognized this basic truth. That is why section 33 confers upon the people through their elected representatives final responsibility for the protection of human rights in our society. Legislatures ought not override the Charter with reckless abandon, but neither should they feel timid or apologetic in doing so.

Unions who seek to limit this democratic guarantee do so at their own peril. If they succeed in persuading the courts to place restrictions and conditions on the use of section 33, it is they who are likely to be the ultimate losers. Like those who seek power by riding the back of a tiger, they may soon find themselves in the belly of the beast.

DE-MANNING THE CHARTER

(1.IX.86)

(with Andrew Petter)

In his tirade in *Canadian Lawyer* (May 1986) against legislation that would ban doctors from charging more than Ontario Hospital Insurance Plan rates, Manning sketched out his personal vision of Canada's new constitutional order. Manning's Charter is one that is firmly committed to a society founded upon the dubious ethic of laissez-faire capitalism—a society in which the only right worth preserving is the right to be free from government regulation.

The thrust of Manning's argument is that preservation of the private economy is the Charter's core value. The government's attempt "to end free enterprise in the physician–patient relationship" is seen as a monstrous invasion not only of doctors' political rights, but of their legal just deserts. In short, the Charter entitles doctors to insist that the government stay out of the medical *business*. Manning suggests that interference in the doctor-patient relationship may deprive the parties of their "liberty" or "security of the person" and may also infringe upon their freedom of association and equality rights.

Our objection to Manning's interpretation of the Charter is not that it is incredible. Unfortunately, he may well be correct in supposing that the Charter will be interpreted according to his libertarian likings. In academic articles and popular journals, we have argued—albeit with less enthusiasm than Manning—that the Charter's overall impact will be likely to favour established interests at the expense of others. It is a document that places questions of social justice in the hands of an elite few. Further, it translates those questions into issues of individual entitlement rather than of civic concern.

What we do strongly object to, however, is Manning's suggestion that his reactionary vision of Charter freedom is inevitable and legitimate. The Charter is a barrel capable of holding all variety of political brew. Ascertaining the meaning of the Charter text is more a matter of speculation and political choice than it is of objective insight or moral certainty.

For instance, plausible Charter arguments can be put forward to justify a position that would require, or at least protect, legislation against extra-billing. It takes little imagination to recognize that "liberty" and "security of the person" can be read to guarantee a patient's access to a decent level of health care. Also, government efforts to make the distribution of health care depend upon need rather than wealth could be viewed as a fulfillment, not a negation, of the equality guarantee under section 15.

Underlying Manning's entire argument is the crass belief that property is a natural entity and entitles its owner to rights and powers that are proportionate to the extent of his or her property-holding—"What we have, we hold."

Yet for all his insistence that government "stay out of our lives," he would no doubt be only too happy to demand the government's help and protection should his or the doctors' property come under threat. Like other free marketeers, he conveniently forgets that private property is a creature of the state, and its protection is neither more or less politically neutral than its confiscation.

What Manning's vision of freedom amounts to is the entrenchment of the right of the privileged "haves" in society to exploit the more numerous "have-nots." Taking this to its logical conclusion, he would presumably favour dismantling Ontario's entire public health-care system. Further, if Manning's constitutional arguments were accepted at face value, governments would be obliged to do away with laws establishing minimum wages and imposing unemployment insurance schemes upon employers. According to Manning, the Charter makes it "questionable whether a province can fix prices in any field where the freedom to contract supposedly prevails."

Finally, Manning's conclusion that the government's "only reasonable course of action . . . is to seek a constitutional reference" again reflects his prejudice. There is no need to bring the courts into this debate. If he is wrong about the Charter, litigation would be fruitless. If he is right, then all the more reason to keep the courts from imposing his perverse vision of freedom upon the rest of us.

The United States went through a period of judicially imposed freedom of the kind that Manning so cherishes · in the first part of this century. During the so-called Lochner era, the U.S. courts struck down everything from maximum hours of work legislation to laws prohibiting anti-union activity. That period finally ended when President Franklin Roosevelt, in an effort to save his New Deal legislation, threatened to pack the Supreme Court with his own appointees. We hope it will not take a similar crisis in Canada to convince our courts that the claims put forward by the Mannings of this world on behalf of owners, employers and doctors occupy no higher place in the theoretical firmament than the claims of those who are poor, unemployed or in need of medical care.

Rather than submit its legislation to the courts, the Ontario government would do better to invoke the section 33 override clause to keep the extra-billing dispute well away from the judicial arena. Such an action would spare the province and the courts the inconvenience of protracted litigation. It would also serve to reassure the disadvantaged that government will not permit the Charter to be used to sabotage movements towards social justice.

Last, and least, it would also spare the good doctors of Ontario the prohibitive cost of *Manning* the Charter barricades.

CHARTER REACH

(1.I.87)

Charter litigation is a boom industry. There is no hint of a productivity decline here. But like all industries, its products vary in quality. While some are sleek and sophisticated, others are shoddy and disreputable. Yet most of them are simply ignored as being too technical for popular consumption. However, it is these very technical goods that often wreak the most havoc.

Good examples of this are the recent decisions of the Supreme Court of Ontario concerning the Charter and the workplace; one on mandatory retirement and the other on compulsory union dues check-off. It will be remembered that, while the former was held to be constitutional, the latter was struck down as being in breach of the Charter. The media concentrated on the substantive merits of these decisions, but failed to pick up on their deeper significance. This lay in the more "technical" issue of what types of activities are governed by the Charter.

In both cases, the court held that the Charter only covered government action. Section 32 of the Charter states that the Charter only "applies to the Parliament and government of Canada . . . and to the legislature and government of each province in respect of all matters within [their] authority." Affirming other decisions, the court stated that private action was not caught within the Charter's net. Only "private" action exercised under statutory power or delegated by government can be considered within the

court's catch. Because the Law Society regulates the legal profession on behalf of the government, it is covered by the Charter's demands; but the Ontario Hockey Association is not as government has no responsibility for its operation.

The Supreme Court of Canada has independently confirmed the general thrust of these decisions. The Charter does not stretch to cover the picketing of workers at a private business. Not only does this evidence further the courts' antipathy to workers, but the Supreme Court's judgment is formalistic and technical: it gives no extra-textual defence of its decision and hopes that adding together enough academics' conclusions will amount to a chain of reasoning. Considering the Court's own urging of purposive reasoning and the acknowledged importance of the question, its pusillanimity is revealing and suspect.

The important threshold question, therefore, is whether allegedly unconstitutional behaviour falls within the governmental or private sphere. As the history of American constitutional law demonstrates, the difficulty of drawing a clear line between the two is notorious. Indeed, those recent decisions of the Ontario Supreme Court illustrate this. Whereas a community college was thought to fall within the sphere of government responsibility, universities did not as, even though over 75% of their funding comes from the government, they were sufficiently autonomous in tradition and decision-making to be private bodies and, therefore, outside of the Charter's reach. The logic and wisdom of this distinction is tenuous at best.

The implications of this decision are both trivial and vast. The decision is trivial in the sense that it merely confirms what many lawyers had always thought and anticipated; namely, that the Charter only applies to truly public action and does not invade the private sphere—for instance, blatant discrimination between private persons cannot be a breach of the Charter, but, of course, can still be regulated by human rights codes, statutes or the common law.

Its implications are vast in that this will come as news to most people who probably thought that the Charter covered most aspects of Canadian life. If a university is not considered to be covered by the Charter, then many other institutions in our society will fall outside the reach of the Charter. All private business and individual activity will be exempt from Charter control unless the government chooses to step in and regulate them. Yet, paradoxically, efforts to regulate business or the work place in the name of greater social justice for consumers or workers has been seriously hampered by the Charter.

In earlier decisions by the Supreme Court of Canada, corporations have been interpreted as possessing many of the rights of ordinary Canadians; for example, they have freedom of speech, freedom of religion and the right to be free from unreasonable search and seizure. Adding these formal weapons to their existing privileges and economic powers gives the corporations very effective means to resist government regulation. This

seems contrary to the "People's Charter" that was promised; the Charter effectively insulates vested interests from popular scrutiny rather than opens them up to popular control.

This lamentable state of affairs is compounded by the fact that, under a "government action" doctrine, these corporations can act without fear of breaching the moral injunctions contained in the Charter. An individual who is adversely affected by corporate behaviour has no remedy under the Charter. Such a distinction is ludicrous if the real protection of individual freedom or the attainment of full social justice is sought. Why is the source of injustice considered so important as to justify a dual scheme of institutional response?

The ability to cause personal or collective injustice is the same whether the relevant bureaucracy is an Ontario ministry or IBM; they both can deploy massive resources and influence the lives of thousands of Canadians. We at least exercise some democratic control over the Ontario government, but IBM are left to the invisible hand of the market—a market which, in the case of huge conglomerates, is more controlled by than in control of those it supposedly controls. The courts' decisions under the Charter exacerbate this situation.

What is the appropriate solution or, at least, the best immediate response? For those enamoured with the Charter and who see these developments as aberrational, the challenge is two-fold; an ambivalent strategy of withdrawal and extension. First, there must be a concerted attempt to persuade the courts that their decisions to extend Charter rights to corporations were ill-advised and ought to be reversed; Charter litigation is not so entrenched yet as to make this a futile gesture. Nevertheless, remembering the strength of corporate opposition there will be to this change, the size of the task should not be underestimated.

The second and related response might be to urge the courts to extend the reach of the Charter to all activity, both governmental and private. One possible line of argument is that as all matters fall within, as section 32 puts it, the potential "authority" of at least one level of government, the decision not to intervene and regulate is as much governmental responsibility as the decision to do so. Under such a proposal, acquiesence and action are merely flip-sides of the same constitutional coin. Success on this front would mean that all private activity could be scrutinized and sanctioned for Charter violations.

For those like me, however, who believe that the Charter and its political ethos are part of the problem rather than tools for its solution, such a "withdrawal and extension" response is unconvincing. Protection of vested interests like corporations is not aberrational, but provides the bedrock on which the Charter stands. Accordingly, a vigorous and consistent policy of Charter withdrawal must be pursued.

This means that as well as working toward omitting corporations from the Charter's protection, there must also be simultaneous efforts to circumscribe as closely as possible the Charter's reach over private activity. If we are to have a Charter, then we must work to confine its judicial interpretation and enforcement to the most limited range of actors and action. Over the long haul, the judiciary will not act as a bulwark, but more as an obstacle to the achievement of social equality and the expression of popular justice.

For those whose every thought is conditioned by the iron grip that the Charter seems to have over their political imagination and democratic sensibilities, this proposal will be rejected out of hand. Nonetheless, I believe that it is the right decison. We need less, not more judicial activism. Although it carries with it many risks, it is the best course of response.

In a Canadian world that is already dominated by the Charter, any indication that some part of social life is not covered by the Charter will raise the presumption that actors within that sphere need not concern themselves with matters of equality and individual rights. This need not be the case. Such an arrangement puts the responsibiity for action where it should be. It leaves it for the individuals involved to debate and take action to bring about social justice.

The decision that the Charter does not apply ought to be the beginning and not the end of popular debate. Indeed the decision that the Charter does apply prevents debate by rendering it irrelevant. We can talk all we want, but the courts will tell us the "right answers". This is a debasement of democracy and not its apotheosis.

The essense of democratic justice is that people should be engaged in the process that brings about the decisions and conditions that affect their personal life. Social justice cannot be administered like a course of chemotherapy by avuncular judicial doctors. Such treatment only cures by killing the patient.

JUDICIAL APPOINTMENTS

(4.III.87)

Judges have become our new philosopher monarchs. These black-robed, secluded figures hand down solutions to society's problems from the Olympian detachment of the Supreme Court. Under the Charter, they have increased their already considerable power and reponsibility. On the judges' own admission, politics and law are now inextricably linked and their fates joined.

The recent death of Julien Chouinard has created a vacancy in the ranks of the Ottawa Nine. Speculations about his likely successor has brought to public light some usually unseen aspects of the judicial process— Who are these Platonic guardians? Where do they come from? Why and how are they selected for such privileges?

Like most democracies, Canada manages to confer enormous prestige and authority on its judicial proconsuls and, at the same time, insulates them from political and popular scrutiny. The belief is that judicial independence and power will be legitimated and assured by institutional anonymity, but compromised by public debate. This state of affairs is antithetical to democratic instincts and is precariously maintained. Consequently, the appointment of judges and the temporary spotlighting of their identity and background is crucial to its constitutional justification and acceptabililty.

The appointment process is secretive and uncontrolled. It boils down to a case of "when Brian nods." The formal structure is that Supreme Court judges are appointed by the federal cabinet on the recommendation of the Minister of Justice. In practice, the Prime Minister decides. The candidate for this highest judicial office need only have been a lawyer for ten years to qualify. The selection is constrained by no consultation requirements nor independent ratification procedure.

Indeed, attempts to look behind the inscrutable public masks of judges is fraught with risk. Not only do extant rules of political propriety counsel deference by the press, but the common law of contempt discourages any unconventional efforts to dig too deep or criticise too briskly à la Harry Kopyto.

In effect, one of the Prime Minister's most significant and far-reaching decisions is effectively free from public censure and rigorous scrutiny. Against a dismal and generally-accepted history of judicial appointments in which party political affiliations and personal ties have been influential, the scope for abuse is manifest. At best, the appointment of party faithful like Sterling Lyon can only confirm such suspicions.

The villain of the piece is the idea of "judicial independence." This is deployed as a huge and ubiquitous blanket to throw over the judiciary to discourage and impugn attempts to inquire about and rouse these slumbering sentinels. Of course, independence is important, but we need to develop a more selective and critical appreciation of its valid reach and application. The claim that judges not be politically independent does not mean that they must (even if they could) be apolitical or neutral in their views and values.

If by "independent" we mean that they must be above and beyond the day-to-day shenanigans of partisan politics, this is an undeniable and desirable demand that presumably has universal approval. Nonetheless, the present process of appointment seems designed to permit this state of affairs; it arouses rather than allays fears of crude politicking and feather-bedding.

If by "independent" we mean the aspiring judge must be completely free from ideological assumptions and political preferences, then we are surely deluding ourselves. People are a bundle of values and ideas; it is what makes them "them" and what makes them distinctive. Without such standards and attitudes, the critical faculty is blunted and personal judgment becomes whimsical or haphazard. Unless, as we seem to pretend, we want our judges to imitate a neutered and lobotomized political animal, we must recognise those values and not ignore them. It is not ideology that is the crime, but the silence that hides it.

The classic profile of a Supreme Court judge is a white, middle-aged, Christian, male, middle-class professional. To believe that this is somehow representative of Canadians is nonsense. To believe that such persons are more "neutral" than others is an ethnocentric arrogance that we would do well to abandon smartly. Judges are honest, diligent and act in good faith for the most part. But to suggest that they hold a monopoly on impartiality and political balance is a middle-class myth.

The fact that we recognise regional considerations in the appointment of judges hints at the understanding that not all Canadians share the same perspectives or bring to the judicial task the same experience; they are presumably valued because *they are different*. Moreover, the drive to have more women elevated to the bench reflects a similar and laudable concern. But, once conceded, the recognition that regional ties and gender bring desirable and neglected qualities to the judical process undermines the whole traditional defence and understanding of "judicial independence." If judges are to rule and reason for us, they ought to reflect the proud and rightly touted diversity of Canadian life.

Short-term solutions to the problem of judicial homogeneity are difficult to conceive or implement; it requires a thoroughgoing reappraisal of political attitudes and institutional arrangements. Nevertheless, some small, but important reforms can be made. In this regard, the American approach offers some interesting possibilities. Supreme Court candidates are nominated by the President and submitted to the Senate for approval by a simple majority.

Although the appointment is usually ratified, 26 nominations have not been approved; this amounts to a rejection rate of about 1 in 5. Although Senate and presidential decisions are made for all manner of reasons, not exclusively related to the ability and ethics of the candidate, the relatively open process does check crass partisan ambitions and goes some of the way to satisfying democratic ideals.

For Canada, this process could be adopted and supplemented. A more organised and wide-ranging procedure for generating the names of suitable candidates should be introduced; the Canadian Bar Association might facilitate a community-wide consultative search. After cabinet selection, the appointment would be submitted for approval by a parliamentary committee. This would serve to curb the patronage instincts of government, publicise the identity of the presently faceless bureaucrats and give the judicial arm of government a more democratic warrant and legitimacy for its exercise of power.

It is not coincidental nor without significance that the major opposition to these types of reforms has come from lawyers. They complain already about the poor financial incentives to enter the judicial life. This says much about the social concerns of the profession: they are more preoccupied with matters financial than "justice through law". Many leading lawyers think such open procedures would discourage "suitable" candidates from coming forward for fear that they would suffer possible public humiliation.

Such a response reveals much. Of course, some parliamentarians will choose the public turning over of private stones to revel in the political lowlife. But this is insufficient a concern to suspend democratic demands and to rob people of the only real opportunity to vet the custodians of judicial power. It should not be forgotten that once appointed, Supreme Court judges can be removed only by a resolution of both Houses of Parliament; this has never occurred.

The American judicial commentator, Anthony Lewis said that the character and appointment of a country's judges is "one test of its civilization." If that is true, Canadian civilization is marked by a miserable combination of institutional secrecy, political expediency and public naivety. It is in the interest of all Canadians, including and especially lawyers, to let the bracing winds of publicity and scrutiny blow down the corridors of constitutional power to dispel the unhealthy fog of secrecy and the stale, but unavoidable whiff of patronage.

STRIKE OUT

(16.IV.87)

It never rains, but what it pours. So goes the old saying. Dark Charter clouds have been gathering over the unions for the last few years. Last week, the judicial heavens opened and labor was thoroughly soaked. As such, the Charter's fifth anniversary was a sobering occasion for those concerned with social justice, especially those intoxicated by its promise to improve the lot of disadvantaged Canadians.

Nevertheless, the darkest legal clouds can have a silver lining, even if it might be a little tarnished and thin. The labor movement and other social groups with positive change on their agenda might actually realize that the Charter is a canard. Whatever the motives of its creators, it will make social change more difficult, not easier to achieve. Except for the occasional sop, the courts have never been nor ever will be a forum or force for deep social change; they are institutionally unprepared and unable to play such a role.

To begin with, the unions should take Shakespeare's advice—"the first thing we do, let's kill all the lawyers."

Or, at least, those who advised the unions. It is nothing short of a criminal act for those lawyers to have persuaded them in 1982 that the inclusion of "freedom of association" in the Charter was sufficient to protect their interests and activities. The fact that other countries, like France and Japan (and the United Nations), thought it necessary to enumerate specific protections in their constitutions ought to have tipped them off. Moreover, the continuing willingness of some unions to turn to the courts, instead of the legislature, to further their ambitions is an act of naive complicity.

Nonetheless, for all this, the Supreme Court of Canada's announcement that there is no constitutionally protected right to strike or bargain collectively needs to be put in perspective. It does not make strikes or collective bargaining unlawful nor does it prevent the federal or provincial governments from extending or reinforcing by statute those rights. To be sure, however, it does mean that any union successes in the legislative arena will be all the more difficult to win and, if won, will be all the more precariously held.

By announcing that "the modern rights to bargain collectively and to strike are not fundamental rights and freedoms," as Le Dain J. put it, the Supreme Court has sent out strong messages to the Canadian people that the interests of workers are not deserving of special protection. In a world in which law, and not religion, has become the new opium of the nation, these judicial musings will have an addictive appeal and narcotic effect on the Canadian moral conscience.

More importantly, when labor legislation is challenged by various anti-union groups, the unions will have no effective rights to place on the constitutional scales to balance against competing claims by employers based on free speech, liberty or equality. By refusing to interpret "freedom of association" to include striking or bargaining, the Supreme Court has rendered its protection nugatory. Workers are now free to form and join unions, but to do none of those things that make the forming or joining of a union a desirable objective in the first place.

The Supreme Court's insistence that it is unnecessary to extend the right to strike and bargain collectively in order to give unions a meaningful existence is wrong; it confounds the historical record and reality of industrial relations. The whole idea and existence of a union is to establish a collective solidarity and presence which can overcome workers' vulnerability to the greater power of employers. By limiting the rights of the union to those that can be exercised by the members individually is to subvert the whole *raison d'être* of the union. The refusal to recognise such rights is a punishing betrayal of the hopes and opportunities of working people for an improved life.

As if this were not bad enough, it must be remembered that employers have been doing particularly well under the Charter. The courts have shown little timidity in extending human rights and freedoms to corporations—which is what most employers are. They have included corporations in the meaning of "everyone" and, in case after case, protected their "free speech" and "liberty" from government regulation. Yet what is a corporation but an artificial entity to allow individuals to combine, often anonymously, to strengthen their economic position and standing? What is sauce for the union goose ought surely to be sauce for the corporate gander.

Furthermore, in an earlier decision, the Supreme Court held that most workers' rights to picket were not protected under the Charter as it only applied to those situations involving government action. Therefore, such rights, and other *fundamental* freedoms, are not available to private employees; that is, the vast majority of workers. Consequently, while employers (corporations) are scoring on nearly every legal shot, the unions and the workers they represent are having trouble even getting onto the ice, let alone the scoreboard.

An immediate, and understandable, reaction of the labor movement to these deeply troubling turn of events has been to call for an active campaign to amend the Charter to include such specific rights as that to strike and bargain collectively. While this should be part of any overall strategy, it must not become its exclusive or even main ambition. The obvious problem is that the amendment process is notoriously difficult to invoke. Moreover, such a tactic seems to be premised on the notion that the failure to include pro-union rights was some sort of official oversight. There is no evidence to suggest this and recent events seem to point to quite the opposite concusion.

A more profound problem is that the inclusion of such rights will not in itself change much. It certainly will strengthen the bargaining hand of labor, but it will not in itself improve in any substantive or substantial way social conditions. If there is to be a concerted attempt to amend the Charter, it would be more productive to seek the entrenchment of basic socio-economic rights to adequate shelter, food and health care.

Nevertheless, it is important to neither under-nor over-estimate the impact of a Charter right to strike or bargain collectively. The minority view of Chief Justice Dickson and Madam Justice Wilson that "freedom of association"· does include such rights is to be applauded: they acknowledge the historical need for such rights and their protection in the name of social justice. However, they also maintain that those rights can be legitimately curtailed under s. 1 of the Charter when it is demonstrably justifiable "in a free and democratic society."

For instance, the Chief Justice thought that the right to strike could be withdrawn when the workers were engaged in the provision of "essential services", like the police or fire services. While this might seem appropriate to some (but by no means all), it does demonstrate that any rights the unions obtain will be thrown into the s. 1 hopper and balanced against other interests. Indeed, the Chief Justice's dissenting judgment offers a glimpse at what might be considered to be a sufficient interest to outweigh such rights: the prospect is not a comforting one for the unions. What he gives with the "left" hand, he takes with the "right" hand.

In the Saskatchewan case, dairy farmers stood to be seriously affected if the dairyworkers went on strike. Accordingly, restrictions on the right to strike were justifiable as "the effect of a strike would be especially injurious to the economic interests of a third party." However, it is surely the case that *all* strikes will result in some economic harm to somebody; this is the reason that it can prove to be an effective weapon against the greater economic clout of employers.

As disturbing is the placing of "economic interests" on the scales as a counterweight to the right to strike. Little or no mention of "economic interests" has been mentioned by the Supreme Court when dealing with the protection of other Charter rights, like free speech and equality. Further, will the courts be equally assiduous to protect the interests of third parties, such as local businesses and workers, when a corporation decides to re-locate or shut-down for reasons of so-called "economic rationalisation"?

The unions should be surprised by none of this. Any gains that the labor movement have made have been the result of constantly struggling against long odds and an unsympathetic establishment. As in the past, that struggle will not be won through the courts, but in spite of them. The most positive message of the Supreme Court decision is that unions will have to (re)turn to the political arena and take their case to the people of Canada, and not their judicial surrogates.

8

AND LAW
(or Further adventures of the Jondo)

"Leave Truth to the police and us; We know the Good;
We build the Perfect City time shall never alter;
Our Law shall guide you always like a cirque of mountains."—W. H. AUDEN

Grandmother didn't talk much about the future. When she did, she compared it to catching the last bus. It always left early. And you had to run to try and catch up with it. Time and buses wait for no one, she said. All too quickly the present became the past and the bus of the future had already turned the corner out of reach. She talked more about the past though. That was like the first bus, she used to say. Everyone somehow managed to catch that. Yet, even when you got to where you were going, it was like you couldn't remember where the bus had been or started from. Anyway, she said, time was just a state of mind or a number 76 bus—you paid your money and you took your chances. Enjoy the journey: sit back and savour it, she kept telling me. Even if you catch the last bus, there's always the last train or the last plane to chase and miss. Count your life by the happy beats of your heart and not the cold chimes of the clock or the bus schedule—that was Grandmother's creed.

Grandmother didn't talk very much at all. But I knew she had much to tell. Behind those watery eyes, her thoughts ran deep. But what she lacked in talk, she made up for by telling stories. She could spin tales as easily as a silkworm could do its stuff. She came to life when she cast her narrative spell. Her stories rekindled a bright flame within her: it burned away the years and lit up life in all its vulnerable hues. The world in her stories, as out of kilter as it was, made more sense than my daily round of existence. Still, they were just stories; weren't they? But there were so many tales. From that vast treasure-chest of storied memories, I remember one that you might like. I can do little justice to her magical tellings. But my prosaic translation might convey, however poorly, something of the warm wit and uncommon wisdom of Grandmother and her tale.

Much had happened to the Jondo in the intervening years. Fish and maize were no longer their food staples nor their totems; they were reduced to a lesser, but still important dietary and symbolic significance. Diversification now seemed such a natural way of life that the younger Jondo found it difficult to understand the resistance and resentment these changes had brought. The autumnal and vernal harvests were still celebrated, but more as simple holidays than as ritualistic reaffirmations. And the Sacred Hermaphrodite remained venerated, but only as a convenient heraldic figure. The symbolic side of life was still central to the Jondo: *cosmos* had given way to *nomos*. Ideas and argument had become the new idols and icons. The wordsmith and philosopher had replaced the fisher and farmer as the embodiment of Jondo achievement and maturity. No longer did the young strive to learn the practical skills of the rod and plough. Instead, they honed their intellectual talents on the philosopher's stone, struggling with the mysteries of the normative universe and thrilling to their recherché challenge. Homage was paid to Truth, Justice and other lesser deities. Spectacular ceremonies still occurred each year. At these, the purveyors of untruths were symbolically sacrificed at the Altar of Rationality. The high priests were metaphysical masters of analytical arcanities and ontological obfuscations, a canny bunch.

In this single-minded pursuit for philosophical fulfilment, existence had become secondary to enlightment. Many perished as willing hostages to intellectual progress. Yet, as with their ancestors, existence tempered enlightenment: the unmitigated hedonist and the spartan aesthete found their way to the intellectual altar. The perpetual challenge was to discover a set of intellectual principles that were sufficiently concrete to give guidance to the daily rote of existential dilemmas and to be sufficiently abstract so as to offer guidance beyond the immediate context of any particular problem. This dilemma haunted our Jondo ancestors and cast a long shadow over their future contentment. It still does.

The neighbouring Usa had also changed, but events had worked more subtly. *Homo ludens* remained their dominant tribal icon, but there had been two major developments. Although Usa society continued as a sprawling and robust sporting contest, the vast majority played little active part. Life had become a spectator sport. The Usa experienced the game of life vicariously, often third- or fourth-hand. Everyone had to snatch voyeuristic pleasure where and when they could: it became a desultory game of catch-as-catch-can. Most Usa were not so much playing the game as having the game play them. The fate of whole lives rested on the pitcher's fastball or the market's swing. The ordinary Usa played no part in the selection of players or the tactics to be used. Secondly, the Law Game had slowly become almost the only game in town. Other contests flourished and faded, but only with the blessings of the legal quarterbacks. Athletes played their most important innings or fought their most crucial rounds in Law's stadium. No victory was more final nor more important than in the Super Bowl of Law. The small and elite squad of legal agonists ran a demanding schedule. But no gamesters were more consummate in the ludic nuances. They elevated law-sport to a unique status in which causal and metaphoric effect combined irresistibly to shape the destiny of Usa society. If life was a game, then law was their game of life.

Over the years, of course, the Usa and ourselves had come into contact. Neither was particularly enamoured of the other or its values and lifestyle. Our high-minded kin considered the Usa's ludic lust and thirst for spectacle to be shallow; they preferred to engage in more worthy cerebral contests. On the other hand, the hard-headed Usa had little time for what they called "Mumbo-Jondo". But they maintained cordial relations with us. Like everything the Usa did, their dealings with us were part of an elaborate game-plan. Apart from the immediate gratification of such ludic scheming, the Usa were tribally committed to extending the venues and schedules for the performance of the Usa game of life. At that time, we seemed to offer easy pickings. However, the experience and intuition of the Legal-Usa told them that the patient ground-game was preferable to the long bomb.

Among the Legal-Usa, there existed a privileged coterie who were adept at the most baffling mind-games. They deployed this odd facility in the coaching of legal initiates and, coincidentally, for the betterment and aggrandisement of the Law Game itself. One such elder was Chafri. Although once infatuated by the pure intellectualism of his Jondo neighbours, he had cultivated a suitable scepticism. He was sent as a pioneering emissary. With his knowledge and understanding of our idealistic tradition, he was given a generous Jondo welcome. Soon, he was inaugurated as an honorary tribal elder, A Man of Learning. Using his ample rhetorical talents which had been so finely tuned in years of lawyerly cut-and-thrust, Chafri began to unveil his master strategy and to turn us to his way of thinking. His central argument was simple and appealing. Conceding the apparent superiority of philosophical endeavour, he proposed to bring it within physical reach with a minimum of pragmatic compromise. In his measured tones, he spoke with assurance and authority:

> The picture I have . . . is of philosophy proposing an elaborate structure of arguments and considerations which descend from on high but stop some twenty feet above the ground. It is the peculiar task of law to complete the structure of ideals and values, to bring it down to earth; to complete it so that it is seated firmly

and concretely and shelters real human beings against the storms of passion and conflict. That last twenty feet may not be the most glamorous part of the building—it is the part where the plumbing and utilities are housed. But it is an indispensible part. The lofty philosophical edifice does not *determine* what the last twenty feet are, yet if the legal foundation is to support the whole, then ideals and values must constrain, limit, inform and inspire the foundation—but no more. The law really is an independent, distinct part of the structure of value.

Envisaging lasting fame and fortune in Jondo history, the fickle tribunal elders endorsed this project and guaranteed its expeditious completion. With much trumpeting, it was announced that a Tower would be built. At first, most of our countryfolk were shocked at the enormity of this project and its apparent conflict with the central article of our constitutional faith—that Jondo was to be governed by the Rule of Philosophy, not men. But, when they were assured that they must at times forego philosophy in order to attain PHILOSOPHY, resistance lessened. People were reminded of the psychic satisfaction in a physical job well done. With the completion of the Tower, it would be possible to finally reach and know the Truth. Each Jondo would be able to climb the Tower and experience the serenity of complete self-knowledge which would surely be there.

It is reported that some remained unconvinced and marched in protest against the project. They rallied behind the cry, "Which of you, intending to build the Tower, has first sat down and counted the cost?" With bloated indignation, the tribal elders dismissed such questions. They responded that, not only does the Devil read the scriptures for his own purposes, but that economic and ontological calculations of an exquisite complexity sanctioned such a construction. As protest waned, the Sacred Hermaphrodite announced with due solemnity that the Tower was to stand as a mega-monument to Jondo's philosophical prowess; a magnificient obelisk of pride and achievement and a beacon to light the way for other less fortunate nations and neighbours. Temporary hubris would lead to lasting humility.

Before the building could begin, much preparatory work had to be undertaken. Because we were untutored in the many facets of Tower-building and previously content to inhabit more modest dwellings, foreign expertise had to be imported. The first task was to locate the best site for the Tower. When the visiting geologists arrived, our forebears took an immediate shine to them. Never leaving their comfortable quarters, they pored over the sheafs of maps, charts and reports they had brought with them; these papers only related to and were based on surveys of their own country. After intense and technical discussion, it was announced that the Tower would be built equidistant from the two largest settlements. This was not, as the elders were quick to point out, a solution of expediency, but was demanded by the rational application of geological knowledge. As few Jondo knew anything about geology, but were predictably impressed by the geologists' intelligence and learning, the consecration of the site by the Sacred Hermaphrodite soon followed.

The next step was to draw up plans for the construction of the Tower. An edificial committee of tribal elders was struck. In typically decorous tradition, debate was lengthy and heated as the elders thrilled to the intellectual give-and-take. This was the stuff of Jondo legend. Against his lawyerly will, but in line with his Usa instincts, Chafri found himself also caught up in the excitement of the architectural-game. Grappling with the cryptic possibilities of edificial imagination, opinion tended to divide into three main thrusts. One group of elders argued strenuously that it would be necessary to draft the most detailed of plans before work could commence; the placing of each brick and every spreading of mortar would have to be plotted and graphed beforehand. However, the supporters of this position were themselves divided into two fractions. One took the view that the appearance of the Tower was extremely important; its design and structure must reflect the majesty and grandeur of its purpose. After all, it was intended to be an enduring monument and not simply a rudimentary ladder. The other faction would have no truck with this. For them, the Tower's form was subordinate to its function. They claimed that it would be indulgent to delay and increase the cost of the project because of the ephemeral standards of architectural elegance: the Tower was an instrument, not an ornament. With equal force, the other major group contended that the work should proceed cautiously and incrementally. Once the building began, the Tower would begin to take on a shape of its own and develop an immanent structure. In short, the Tower would be its own architect.

The deadlock was for our scholastic brethren—for they were all men—more sublime than troubling. Calling on all the fabled Usa negotiating techniques in his legal locker, Chafri barely managed to secure a deal between the competing factors. Backrooms were redolent with the stench of midnight oil and horse-trading. The resulting "agreement" was to become a document of truly historic proportions. It came to be known as The Bill of Works. Framed in the most sweeping terms, it was long on generalities and short on details. There was much space between the lines. It called for elaborate facades and brickwork, demanding the most intricate and exacting craftsmanship. But there was little guidance on its interior structure and construction; these were to be decided upon as circumstances demanded and resources allowed. Before anyone had much chance to reconsider their consent to the fragile compact, work on the Tower was begun. As seemed fitting, the Bill of Works was set in stone.

Work on the foundations commenced immediately, but the progress was slow and deliberate. Our inexperience in the building crafts and our tendency to engage in disquisitions over the finer points of architectural protocol ensured that. Also, much of the work demanded hard physical labour. This was felt to be below the dignity of most Jondo men. Consequently, a brisk trade soon developed in the importation of Blanco labour. Blanco was a neighbouring land which was inhabited by large, ivory-skinned, but primitive people; they knew nothing of the civilised Jondo life-style and remained enslaved to the subsistence economy of rod and plough. The elders felt that, by working on the Tower, they might be introduced gently to the liberated world of Jondo society. Blanco resistance and reluctance was construed as a forgivable ignorance that must not be allowed to weaken the proselytizing resolve and responsibility of the superior Jondo. Anyway, they came cheap and kept Jondo hands clean.

Years passed before the foundations were complete. This was of no consequence. It was accepted that it was better to build on solid rock than on the shifting sand of Jondo. Unfortunately, the rock had to be imported at great expense from Usa. At last, though, the Day of Dedication arrived. Already, Chafri and many of the tribal elders had died. Nonetheless, missed, mourned and—if truth be told—cursed as they were, there was no shortage of people willing to assume their responsibilities. All were present to witness the Towering Hermaphrodite, as s/he was now known, lay the ceremonial stone. A pure chunk of lexite, it was inscribed with the great Turris Creed:

> We the People of Jondo, in Order to reach a perfect Truth, establish Justice, insure intellectual Tranquility, provide for a common Epistemology, and secure the Blessings of Philosophy to ourselves and our Posterity, do erect and establish this Tower.

After a fresh spurt of enthusiasm occasioned by the festivities of the Day of Dedication, the building of the Tower settled back into its more languid and accustomed routine. At first, there had been a scarcity of sufficiently willing or capable workers. You will understand, of course, that Blanco labour did not count—were they not resources more than "workers"? Few qualifications were expected; the Jondo skills were learnt on the scaffolding and at the lathe. But, after many years, there developed a glut of builders. This was for a combination of reasons. Fathers had passed on their trades to their sons and a tradition of craftsmanship was established. Also, the Tower had begun to have a substantial impact on the fragile economy of Jondo. The burgeoning demands of the building and the need to import foreign materials placed a heavy burden on the overdrawn coffers of the Treasury. Work became scarce, wealth was thinly spread, and many were drawn toward the Tower as a place where fortunes could still be made and reputations forged. Finally, the Tower had begun to exude that scentless, but unmistakeable whiff of power which caught in Jondo nostrils and went straight to their heads.

In order to preserve their own improving wealth and position, the builders formed a guild. Its first actions were to control entry to the ranks of the Tower-builders, to clamp down on unauthorizd building and to formalize the training of apprentice builders. Along with these official moves, the builders began to develop a special vocabulary and to embed their professional skills in a technical patois. A common form of dress was assumed and a sombre accent affected. Within a few years, what had once been the most tedious of occupations became an exclusive calling that was accessible to only the most gifted and expert; the prosaic heaping of brick upon brick had begun to displace the divinations of the tribal elders as the most worthy and revered of vocations. Yet the Builders were not so naive as to flaunt their new-found power and prestige. Each new builder was taught—and some often believed—that he existed to serve the Tower and to hasten its rendezvous with Truth and Justice. In this way, building became the very highest and most humble commitment to the people; the Builder was the quintessence of the Jondos ethos. Who would begrudge wealth and status to those of such selfless devotion?

For a number of decades, the progress of the Tower went on without any real incidents or disturbances. Architectural disputes were muted as the Builders' guild recognized the need to maintain a common and united front. Yet broad disagreement over the design of the Tower festered. In time, the engineers and surveyors broke ranks and affiliated with competing guilds. Each had their own quarters in the building. Communication between the groups went quiet and they only met at formal confrontations. Past great Builders were honoured and their portraits hung on the walls of the respective guilds. Exhibitions of their architectural sophistication were regularly given in the hope of attracting fresh recruits and of demonstrating their supposedly superior artisanship. Exegetical pamphlets began to appear and oaths of architectonic allegiance were sworn. Yet, for all this internecine rivalry and emblematic falling-out, the actual building of the Tower seemed to proceed much as it had always done.

While one guild spent much of their time contemplating and working on the West Side of the building, the other guild devoted their efforts to the East Side. However, both sets of Builders followed a very similar modus operandi. They did not draw up any plans or work schedules until after a section of the Tower was complete. Occasionally, a particular structural innovation would be completed, the blueprints would be duly made available and then that part of the building would be demolished or simply collapse. Unfazed by this edificial turn of events, a Rationalization Program was immediately developed and announced. This was accompanied by stacks of detailed documents and sheaves of supporting calculations. Indeed, a couple of years were spent in constructing suitable annexes to house this prolific body of professional literature.

Although many neophyte Builders were initially disturbed by these happenings, they soon recognized the wisdom of this way of proceeding (or, at least, of not asking too many questions about it). Nevertheless, there was a significant group of renegade Builders who had become so disenchanted with the architectural machinations and shenanigans that they began to establish an Alternative Style of Building. At first, they worked to expose these daily facts of life to other Builders and anyone who would listen. Soon, however, they began to criticize the whole Tower project. They sought to show how it was not only a waste of valuable time and money, but was a vast diversion from the central challenge that faced Jondo society—to make Jondo a better and more just place to live. In keeping with their iconoclastic instincts, they offered a variety of alternative ways of thinking about and actually being a Builder.

A popular line of critique concentrated on the extent to which the warring factions of Tower-Builders were hopelessly and fundamentally dependent on each other. The West face of the Tower was different to the East, but without the East to prop it up the West side would collapse. They both were built to eclipse the other, but relied upon the other for vital support. And, of course, if you viewed the Tower from the north or south, they each merged into the other to form an appearance that was neither East nor West, but both East and West. All the renegade Builders combined to insist that there was no immanent or instrumental rationality of architecture that inheres beyond the historical and geographical confines of Jondo: Tower Rationality was no less constructed than the Tower itself.

Colloquially known as "The Deconstructors"—"it is better to deconstruct for our generation than to construct for eternity" was their logo—they carried out a series of geological tests, using the tools and techniques of the Tower Builders. These studies concluded that the Tower was far from being built on the most stable of foundations. In fact, close inspection of the Tower's footings revealed that there was an almost perfect balance between the annual increase in the Tower's height and its sinking back into the terra not-so-firma of Jondo. Yet some among the Deconstructors accepted that, while "undermining" was fun, the Tower would not collapse nor its Builders relinquish their vision by a demonstration, no matter how convincing, that the Tower was monumentally unsound in theory and practice. Consequently, concerted efforts were made to offer alternative visions and architectural projects. Campaigns were organised to persuade the Jondo that the future lay not up in the clouds, but down on the ground: salvation lay in making the best buildings they could out of the warm earth of Jondo. By lowering their gaze from the always-in-sight-but-forever-out-of-reach philosophical heavens, the Tower Builders might better see the conditions of their present enslavement and the possibilities for future liberation.

After some initial bemusement and structural tolerance, the Building guilds and the tribal elders began to close ranks and work to discredit these architectural down-starts. Some responded by letting the beauty and symmetry of the brickwork speak for itself, others began to engage in a spirited refutation of this architectural heresy; and still others argued that the existence of such "rebels without a Tower" served to keep the true Tower-Builders honest. A small, but influential group of Building Elders started to hurl all shapes and sizes of brickbats. Ridicule was a favoured tactic. But the most traditional demanded nothing less than their complete banishment from the environs of the Tower and, preferably, from Jondo itself:

> Even the Deconstructor must recognize that Building students are infertile ground for the seed of destruction: within institutions like the Tower, Deconstruction is a doomed testament. Elsewhere, such teaching may find an audience, but not among those who have set their hands to perform the Tower's work. Seeing her blemishes (they are many) and knowing her perfidies (which are not few), true Builders can love the Tower. We love the Tower not because reason requires it, but because our commitment to our discipline serves the needs of the Jondo public to whom, and for whom, we are responsible.

This struggle between the Building Constructors and the Deconstructors ebbed and flowed. Yet, even as it did, work continued and the Tower went up or, more accurately, went up-and-down to the same place. Building disputes inevitably arose. While many were of a minor technical nature, an important few raised issues of major architectural substance, such as the Tower's appearance and elevation. These matters received considerable coverage in the Jondo Gazette. Public opinion was often sharply divided and many, remembering the simple philosophical pleasures of days gone by, savoured the intellectual niceties of these controversies. In order to resolve these disputes, a Tower Commission was established. The difficulty, of course, was to know who to select and appoint to this crucial institution. There was a strong lobby to the effect that, as the problems of the Tower touched on the lives of all Jondo, the Commission should contain a representative cross-section of the Jondo community. While most disputes had a clear Building dimension which required specialised knowledge, the future of the Tower and its aesthetic development, it was argued, fell outside the exclusive authority or expertise of Architectural Science.

With calm assurance and learned patience, the Builders demonstrated that the view that Tower-Building was little more than applied common sense had become accepted only because the great learning and erudition of the compleat Builder made possible the effortless sophistication and apparent simplicity of the Building Craft. It was not so much that people were convinced by these arguments, but that they could think of no effective response. Like most of us Jondo, they could make no sense of the proposition that the Building argument which could withstand all deconstructive attacks might not be true. Accordingly, the most esteemed of the Builders duly took their seats on the Tower Commission. Across the portals of the modest tower that was erected for their deliberations was emblazoned their one basic truth: "It is a Tower We are Building".

At the inauguration, at which a ceremonial meal of fish and maize was taken, the Towering Hermaphrodite announced that the Commission was, like the Tower itself, open to everyone. As the Bill of Works itself stated, "All Jondo must be treated according to the Principles of Tower Justice". However, as a purely administrative matter in order to expedite and standardize proceedings, all submissions were to be presented in the language of Building Terminology and one non-returnable tonne of bricks had to be deposited with the Commission as a sign of serious intent—a commodity in short and valuable supply.

Many cases went before the Tower Commission. Whereas some raised novel questions, most required clarification of the full meaning of earlier pronouncements. One celebrated complaint captured the style of the Commission's workings. After many generations of building, a new system of utilities was proposed for the Tower. A dispute arose over the appropriate way to install and maintain it. After many years of bitter wrangling which brought all building operations to a halt, the problem fell to be resolved by the Tower Commission. As things turned out, the decision was more important for the methodology it established than the actual result reached. It was held that, although such a system of utilities had not been developed or even thought about when The Great Tower Plan was completed, it was vital to discover what the Basic Builders would have concluded if they had thought of such a system. The Commission insisted that it must not be forgotten that the building and completion of the Tower was a sacred trust; its lofty purpose cast a long shadow of responsibility over the transient interests of all future generations. As the chosen builders of the Tower, the Jondo had to keep faith with the past if they were to fulfil the promise of the future. The Basic Builders provided the metric and it was for the Jondo to measure up to its standards.

For a number of years, there had been developing a strong voice of protest among Jondo women. They objected to the fact that they were not able to contribute to the building of the Tower. They wanted some choice over whether to build families or towers. For a long time, the men were able to fob them off with excuses about the harsh physical demands of Tower-Building—most of which, of course, was done by the Blanco. Also, the men made predictable noises about the valuable contribution women already performed in caring for the next generation of Builders and sustaining the present Builders. There was much talk of "Tower-envy" and of how women were not unequal, just different; men possessed a greater facility for the logical disciplines of trigonometric calculation and mechanical design. Women, on the other hand, had an innate aptitude for domestic arrangements and emotional understanding. This seemed to placate many, but a few persisted and changes were slowly made. At first, only the most direct forms of discrimination were banned. Women became eligible to be tribal elders (although none were actually selected) and a woman was appointed to the Building Commission. In time though, more indirect forms of discrimination were proscribed; conditions of Tower employment, such as working hours and leave entitlement, were amended to better accommodate the female Builders and quotas for female Builders were established.

All of this, of course, was not achieved without struggle. At the same time, Blanco men began to gain begrudging entry to the Building guilds and to rise through the ranks of the Tower-Builders. But, although there had been many changes, in a deep sense nothing changed at all. The Tower still continued to go up-and-down to the same place and its overall appearance remained a relatively stable structure of chaotic construction. Many male Builders still rankled at having to work shoulder-to-shoulder with female Builders and grumbled about the effect this would have on Jondo children. And most of the higher architectural posts remained a largely Jondo male preserve. The bulk of manual labour was still performed by Blanco men and now women as well. Enlightened men still complained that "We would love to use more women as Tower Builders, but we just can't find enough women of the necessary calibre."

One wag responded that it wasn't calibre they offered or that was needed—"Equality will occur when there are as many incompetent and third-rate Blanco Builders as there are Jondo." That seemed to hit the proverbial nail bang on the head.

For some women, this continuing state of affairs confirmed their ambivalence about the much vaunted reforms. Especially when a proposed new E.R.E. (Equal Rights Etching) to the Bill of Works was narrowly, but consistently defeated. Although the status of Women had improved, these women insisted that equality meant more than simply becoming Builders: the ambition was to alter the whole Jondo ethic, not simply extend it across the gender board. Women had been given an equal opportunity to experience and play the hierarchical game of Jondo life in which the "Towers" came out ahead of the "Tower-nots". At bottom, such radicals saw the Tower as no more than a phallic manifestation of Jondo malehood; a crude erection that celebrated nothing but its own potency. Combining with the Deconstructors, they sought the demolition of the Tower. This does not mean, they said, that future generations would be condemned to a life of crawling and stumbling through its ruins for fear that any new constructions would become more Towers for future enslavement. In order to reach Truth through the Tower, Jondo had renounced life. In place of the urge to build and climb towers, the exploration and reinforcement of social webs had to be encouraged. Life was to be reclaimed.

Although work on the Tower continued, commitment and enthusiasm waned. Truth, Justice and The Tower Way remained the heraldic totems of Jondo life, but they had lost much of their inspirational immediacy and symbolic vigour. This is not to say that the Tower did not continue to dominate and pervade the daily regimen of life. It did. The whole of the social and political economy was organized to meet the demands of Tower construction. All life was lived in the shadow of the Tower. Resources and energy were slowly, but surely being exhausted in this magnificent obession: the Tower was Jondo and Jondo was the Tower. Finally, with its completion seemingly further away than the long-ago day that it was first commenced, the Tower simply collapsed of its own enormous weight. Thousands were killed and even more were injured. The Tower was in ruins. The few survivors, destitute but somehow invigorated, left for more welcoming lands. Jondo was no more.

Millenia came and went. The inexorable weather inscribed its lasting signature on the land, transforming it beyond recognition. In a distant year, a lone space traveler came upon what was once Jondo. It became fascinated by the ample debris that seemed to be strewn across the desolate wasteland. In time, it returned and began to excavate these "rude, enormous monoliths" which stood in as splendid and inscrutable silence in history as they did on the vast wilderness that once was Jondo. After the first wave of explorations, many returned to examine these mighty megaliths and cryptic cairns. And, as seemed people's wont, theories were proposed and suggestions made on the origins and purpose(s) of this huge quarry of serene detritus. Was it a Metropolis of the Dead? A Lunar Temple? A Pagan Sanctuary? Or The Playground Of a Behemoth Brood? Speculation abounded and a new interpretive discipline, along with a freshly minted currency of hermeneutical argot, took its first faltering steps to intellectual respectability. In what became an epochal discovery, several fragments of rock containing strange markings were unearthed. They. . . . —But that's another story for another day.

★   ★   ★

Noble the Tower built with stones of Will
on the rock of law; eternal that habitation.
In the House of the One may dwell the multitudes.
But the heathen are cast out to die as animals.

So we said, very well then,
and came away from the Kingdom
to the fields of grass, where we made small houses.
We build with dirt and wood and water.
We live with the animals and plants,
eating and praising them and die with them;
their way is our way made mindful,
a river running over stones and rocks.
We live in the low places
like water and shadows.
Our houses do not last long.
We have lost sight behind us
of the spiritual Tower.
We go on down along the river.

9

WORKING THE SEAM: TRUTH, JUSTICE AND THE FOUCAULT WAY

The story of the Tower of Babel has had many different tellings and tellers.[1] Yet, although there are almost as many interpretations as there are iterations, it still seems relevant to the practice and plight of modern life and legal theorising. Traditionally, it has been told and heard as a cautionary tale of conceit and come–uppance, impiety and imperfection, and destiny and despair. Yet, as I interpret it, it is not a curse from which we must deliver ourselves, but a blessing that we seem unwilling to accept. We live in a Post–Collapse Age. Although modern jurisprudence recounts a begrudging escape from the crumbling garrison of Absolute Truth and Formalism, modern scholars still live in the neighbouring fields and work in its capacious shadow; a grim pageant of conformity and acquiescence, based on superstition and fear. Any exploration or expedition that pushes beyond the immediate horizon will, so the story goes, result in such heretics dropping off the rational world and landing in an anarchic nihilism where only might is right and chaos has full reign.

This simple allegory still manages to hold legal scholarship in its iron(ic) grip: there lingers a mystic belief in some objective certainty, even if it remains perennially out of sight and out of reach. As if confirm-

---

1 *See* M. OAKESHOTT, ON HISTORY 165–194 (1983).

ing Koestler's belief that we might be genetically pre-conditioned "to carry bricks to Babel",[2] lawyers continue to design and erect these baroque towers. While most of these modern constructions are less awesome in size and scope, they are no less grand in their ambitions and pretensions. Hubris remains the singular quality of the modern jurist. The legal establishment continues to build monuments to its achievements and fortresses for its acolytes: some even harbour visions of empire.[3] Internecine struggle is commonplace and seems to represent the lifeblood of its political economy. Yet, behind the theoretical clamour and personal antagonism, there is a not-so-surprising homogeneity of philosophical interest and ideological commitment. These juristic barons and warring factions unite in their opposition and resistance to any subversive factions that challenge the terms and conditions of this warfare. It is one thing to fight over the meaning and enforcement of "the entrenched clauses of the constitution of the republic of [legal] knowledge",[4] but it is entirely another thing to decry the need for any constitution at all or to call for the disbandment of the republic itself.

Critical Legal Studies is such a subversive faction.[5] In exposing these latter-day bastions as so many "castles in the sky", its members are playing a crucial role in challenging the structures of domination and hierachy that characterise and comprise modern North Atlantic countries. The particular target of their critical energies has been the central distinction between law and politics; or, to be more precise, the alleged contrast between the open ideological nature of political debate and the bounded objectivity of legal reasoning. Despite its modernist protestations, mainstream legal thought remains in thrall to an ideal of legal rationality. Critical scholars have ruthlessly attacked this "foundational" thinking: there is no privileged ground for legal argument to stand or build on. Traditional theorising is a clumsy and repetitive series of bootstrap arguments. Doctrinal understanding is more a matter of professional familiarity and political partiality than moral insight or technical correctness. Legal rationality is no less constructed than the courts of law themselves. Objective interpretation, bounded or otherwise, is oxymoronic.

In effecting this critique, Critical scholars have achieved a considerable measure of success. Yet success comes with its own responsibilities

---

2 *See* A. KOESTLER, FROM BRICKS TO BABEL (1982).
3 *See supra* ch. 3.
4 Magee, *Sandcastles and The Search for Certainty,* 99 THE LISTENER 567 at 570 (1978) (An interview with Ernest Gellner).
5 *See* CRITICAL LEGAL STUDIES (A. Hutchinson ed. 1987).

and further challenges. The deconstructive tools of the Critical trade are not only extremely delicate and volatile, but they are limited in their utility and reach. Deconstruction does not do away with that which it deconstructs; it impugns the validity of all metaphysics by exposing and undermining its inescapably metaphorical roots. A demonstration of systemic incoherence, internal contradiction and endless circularity is only fatal within a tradition of rationalist epistemology.[6] Although it can serve to de-legitimate and de-mystify the authority of legal reasoning, to be fully convincing and successful, critique must suggest an alternative way of proceeding. It is naive to believe that the jurisprudential castles will crumble and their overlords will lose authority by a demonstration, no matter how convincing, that these edifices are not built on the solid rock of Necessity, but on the shifting sands of History. Moreover, even if these jurisprudential strongholds could be razed to the "ground"—whatever that would mean!—is there nothing more to social life than an unmitigated crawling and stumbling through the ruins of some architectural indulgence of earlier hegemonic imaginings that we have demolished for fear of constructing new palaces for our future enslavement?

The thrust of this essay will be to fashion a tentative answer to that Critical dilemma. I will endeavour to suggest that Deconstruction is not simply a weapon of destruction, but is a double-edged sword that can be turned to reconstructive tasks. It can be wielded not only to smite the decaying culture of contemporary society, with its continued obeisance to the false gods of Necessity and Objectivity, but also to cut a path through the intellectual jungle and its historical undergrowth to a more satisfying and egalitarian society. While there is no form of society, utopian or otherwise, that approaches perfection—even assuming the ambition was somehow desirable—there are some kinds of social arrangements that can be less intolerable than others. Notwithstanding the appetite of deconstruction to consume all before it, we must still live and struggle to make the best of our finite existence. The collapse of the belief in an overarching Rationality that can integrate and harmonise the buzz of divergent dialects must be turned to social and political advantage. The task is to imagine and establish a form of life that can accommodate those voices without recourse to a universal Language. This apparent necessity of "translation" arises at the very moment of its seeming impossibility.[7] Within this dynamic of "necessary impossibility", we

---

6 *See* Hunt, *The Theory of Critical Legal Studies*, 6 Ox. J. OF LEGAL STUD. 1 at 33 (1986) and *supra* ch. 2.

7 *See* Derrida, *Des Tours de Babel* in DIFFERENCE IN TRANSLATION 171 (J. Graham ed. 1985).

must learn to catch its vital rhythms and work its thematic possibilities. The ambition is not to compose and perform the perfect fugue, but to facilitate and inspire a series of jam sessions.

Deconstruction need not lead to moral despair or political quietism: it can be incorporated within a mode of political life that is organised in accordance with a radical form of democracy. Deconstruction is not the advance guard of nihilism, but, in revealing the fabrication of social life and thought, it creates openings for reconstructive action. By seizing those moments, we can *truly know* that there is more to life than Knowing and Truth. The challenge is to conceive of a social structure and political lifestyle that respects the dictates of social contingency and resists the temptation to see solid ground where there is only sea and sky, while, at the same time, providing the possibility of a communal context in which people can experiment and experience fulfilling intersubjective relationships. In short, "a world in which choices are more than an invitation for endless *actes gratuites* and bonds are more than painful restrictions of individual development".[8]

Any effort to turn the deconstructive urge into a reconstructive impulse is fraught with difficulties: it must operate simultaneously at the levels of thought and action. Yet, encouraged by the pioneering work of others,[9] I maintain that the project is not doomed to failure. There are many chasms to be avoided and many bridges to be built and crossed. To accomplish this adventurous journey, I have chosen to enlist the extravagant services of Michel Foucault as my guide and mentor. For many this choice of an "all-purpose subversive"[10] *par excellence* will seem as baffling as it is self-defeating. Insofar as it will go anywhere, a Foucaultian-inspired exploration will either wander off into other dense forests of dementia or charge headlong into some bottomless pit. Needless to say, I remain more optimistic, if guardedly so. In a very real sense, we all look into and make the future by standing on the shoulders of intellectual giants. But we must ensure that our chosen colossus has not already been cut off at the knees. Although Foucault has been dealt some savage blows, I believe that his ideas are still sufficiently intact to justify and bear the onerous burden I intend to place upon them. In what follows,

8 R. DAHRENDORF, LIFE CHANCES: APPROACHES TO LEGAL AND POLITICAL THEORY 33 (1979).

9 *See* Frug, *The Ideology of Bureaucracy in American Law*, 97 HARV. L. REV. 1276 (1984) and RYAN, MARXISM AND DECONSTRUCTION: A CRITICAL ARTICULATION (1982).

10 C. GEERTZ, LOCAL KNOWLEDGE: FURTHER ESSAYS IN INTERPRETIVE ANTHROPOLOGY 4 (1983).

I will attempt to show how a particular form of discursive practice is an appropriate complement to a vigorous application of deconstructive critique. "Dialogic democracy" offers the best chance of turning the deconstructive dynamic to constructive advantage:

> We have to move beyond the inside-outside alternative: we have to be at the frontiers. Criticism indeed consists of analyzing and reflecting on limits. . . . [T]he critical question today has to be . . . : in what is given to us as universal, necessary, obligatory, what place is occupied by whatever is singular, contingent, and the product of arbitrary constraints?[11]

I.

Michel Foucault is an enigma. His work is always provocative, often paradoxical, frequently baffling and invariably disconcerting. The sense of disorientation is exacerbated by his seemingly deliberate cultivation of a self-image and reputation as an *enfant terrible*: "Do not ask who I am nor ask me to remain the same: leave it to our bureaucrats and our police to see that our papers are in order. At least spare us their morality when we write."[12] For many critics, this studied precocity is sufficient grounds for dismissing Foucault as the worse kind of intellectual poseur. His affectation is thought to undermine any claim he may have to being a truly important and radical thinker. Like a grotesque side-show on the academic fairground, his appeal is to our dark fascination with the bizarre and menacing; he trades in deviations and conundra, not in answers and anthems. Moreover, for most readers, his preference for oracular pronouncements, misty metaphors and prophetic apostrophe serve to conceal the profound emptiness of his work. The verdict of professional opinion is that Foucault is more distracting than didactic.

A few critics concede that Foucault's work is significant and makes an important contribution to our understanding of individuality and human agency, especially as a counterpoint to the naive humanism of much modern theorising. Yet these critics ultimately reject his ideas. His radical credentials are fatally undermined by his pessimistic (and inconvenient?) refusal to offer any politically relevant critique of present practice and any suggestions about the possibility of a "good-er life". In short, Foucault's negative politics of destruction condemn us to travelling the

---

11 M. Foucault, *What is Enlightenment?* in THE FOUCAULT READER 45 (P. Rabinow ed. 1984).

12 THE ARCHAEOLOGY OF KNOWLEDGE 17 (A.M. Sheridan-Smith trans. 1972).

abysmal spiral of Nietzschean nihilistics. This critical stance is succinctly represented by David Fraser:

> The fundamental difficulty with any attempt to resurrect Foucault for a practical, leftist critique is that his views lack a coherent starting point. While Foucault may have shared, by intuition, many goals with the left, his mistrust of all ideology prevented him from developing a coherent framework on which others could build. . . . In Foucault, there is neither a normative base nor a political theory from which we might draw practical guidance. All relationships are oppressive, all forms of interaction involve subjugation and power. In the end, there is no ground for criticism or for preferring one form of freedom over another because there is no freedom. . . . If we need more political theory, we will not find it in Foucault.[13]

Although I acknowledge that these interpretations of Foucault's ouevre are entirely plausible, I do not believe that they are the only ones. More to the point, I am not fully persuaded by them. Of course, I do not offer my reading of Foucault as the "best" or "true" interpretation; that would be a ridiculous pretension. To so do would be to miss completely the critical insight and thrust of the deconstructive tendency.[14] In the spirit of Foucault himself, I have come to some conclusions and ideas that a reading of and reflection on his books has suggested to me. To offer a traditionally "rational" reading of Foucault would be to miss completely the deeper message of his critique—*Le savant est le style*. In effect, I have accepted his own invitation and assessment that his writings "are, in the final analysis, just fragments and it is up to you and me to see what we can make of them."[15] In a celebratory and, perhaps, lyrical mood, I have adopted a style of reading that responds to the injunction to "walk through the text as you would through the streets of a city, or on a beach or in fact anywhere. If something attracts you, stop and look; if not, walk on."[16] What follows is the result of my beachcombing along the Foucaultian shores, a cobbling together of archaeological flotsam and genealogical jetsam.

Accordingly, this short essay is not so much an interpretive essay on Foucault as an essay about the problematic of human agency after a reading of Foucault. I maintain that Foucault's work is the most useful

---

13 Fraser, *Truth and Hierarchy: Will The Circle Be Broken?*, 33 BUFFALO L. REV. 729, 771 (1985). See, also, C. LEMERT AND G. GILLAN, MICHEL FOUCAULT: SOCIAL THEORY AS TRANSGRESSION 108 (1982).

14 *See supra* ch. 2.

15 POWER/KNOWLEDGE 79 (C. Gordon ed. 1980).

16 *See* Mohr, *Post-Cartesian Transformation: The Cloud of Knowing*, 2 CAN. J. OF POL. & SOC. THEORY 5 (1978).

available for grasping and diagnosing the condition and plight of the modern world and its residents. Further, I do not think that Foucault's insistence that we can never be outside the historical regimes of power relations leads to despair or resignation. Criticism à la Foucault is an engaged act of political commitment and social involvement. I maintain that his writings, especially in his later years, contain "some tremulous hint of emancipating the oppressed."[17] It is the major ambition of this essay to take that hint and to develop the constructive possibilities of Foucault's arguments by contributing to the development of a political theory of discursive practice as the ends and means of a fully democratic polity.

The title of the essay, "Working the Seam", is intended as a double metaphor through which to understand the interpretive position I take on the reading of Foucault's texts and, also, on his own style of "interpretive terrorism". For me, Foucault's texts comprise a vast and rich terrain which is ribboned with seams of precious intellectual metals. The reader's task is demanding, but exciting: to map these seams, to mine the minerals, to work the ore into interpretive artifacts and to utilize them to study the history of the present, including the study of the artifactual process itself. To understand Foucault's own interpretive techniques, the idea of "working the seam" is also instructive, but the metaphorical context is that of sewing and not mining. The Foucaultian interlocutor is an epistemological seamster: the challenge is to locate the conventional seam between the rational and the irrational, the political and non-political, and the like, to pick at that seam and to show how the seam does not join separate pieces of cloth, but merely closes an historical fold in one "seamless" piece of cloth. In this way, we might be better able to effect "an unfolding of space in which it is once more possible to think."[18]

My interpretation of Foucault emphasises and focuses on him as an un-sewer rather than as a sewer, what he unmakes rather than what he makes. He does not stitch together grand theoretical costumes, but works their seams. He advocates a continual questioning that searches out the intolerable and identifies possible strategies for transformation. When nudge comes to push comes to shove, as W.B. Yeats puts it, "things fall apart; the centre cannot hold".[19] He is a committed op-

---

17 A. Quinton, *Michel Foucault* in THE FONTANA BIOGRAPHICAL COMPANION TO MODERN THOUGHT 235 (A. Bullock and R.B. Woodings eds. 1983).

18 M. FOUCAULT, THE ORDER OF THINGS: AN ARCHAEOLOGY OF THE HUMAN SCIENCES 343 (A. Sheridan-Smith trans. 1970).

19 *The Second Coming* in LATER POEMS OF W.B. YEATS (1924).

positionist, forever searching out the shadows in order to shed more light. It is crucial to remember that Foucault is not suggesting that we can stand naked and dispense with the rational clothes of the historical present. What we can do, however, is to recognize the historicity of those garments and work to create and recreate new epistemological and ideological wardrobes from the protean fabric of social experience.

II.

At the heart of Foucault's work is the attempt to understand the nature, scope and operation of POWER for it serves as the heart, muscle and mind of political theory and practice. Without a full understanding of the intricate historical relation between power and knowledge, the body politic is a game of squash played without walls. The traditional Baconian view is that power and knowledge are ontologically separate entities. Knowledge can only arise and exist outside the sphere of power's corrupting influence. Yet, when knowledge is valid, it can engender and sustain power. With characteristic perversity, Foucault challenges this critical separation and strives to demonstrate how power and knowledge are mutually constitutive and supportive: power is as much the generator of knowledge as its result.[20] The phrase "think tank" evokes the Foucaultian idea perfectly. While power cannot be exercised or be effective without knowledge, the production of knowledge impinges on and nurtures power. The hidden agendas of power are secreted within the interstices of "scientific" codes of knowledge.

In pursuing this project, Foucault does not seek a general theory of power, but rather the development of an analytical grid through which to examine how, in particular historical locations, certain conceptual techniques and devices have been isolated and privileged so as to make people's action intelligible; in terms of the squash game of life, where the walls have been sited generally and in relation to one another. By revealing how these social practices take on a life of their own beyond the conscious intentions of their practitioners, Foucault hopes to trace the procedures that create and forge our own identities. Throughout, he insists on the contingency of such processes. There is no universal pattern to the power-knowledge relation; it is situated within the dynamic field of political struggle. He is alive to and resists the constant temptation to confer on these routines the spurious status of "historical laws" or imbue them with a transcendental logic of necessity.

---

20 *See* M. Foucault, Discipline and Punish 27 (1977).

The realization that power is the engineer and engine of history is nothing new. Although some deny that it is an essentially contested concept and prefer to see it as "an essentially messy concept",[21] most agree that power is a fundamental category of analysis in political theory and have striven to understand its multi-faceted operation. Both political "right" and "left" have tended to view it as the ability possessed by persons or organisations to manipulate others in compliance with their will or design; disagreement has been over the use to which power has and ought to be put. The prescriptive challenge that traditional theorizing has set itself is to suggest and justify a fair distribution and exercise of power. But such accounts of power have been relatively crude and decidedly humanistic. They emphasize the agential, negative and programmatic aspects of power's operation as an intentional attempt to dominate. While such an analytical framework helps to highlight the overt effects of power, it serves to obscure its more subtle and pervasive dimensions. For Foucault, power also functions in an anonymous, positive and localised manner. It comprises the enabling network within which the agent arises and is able to act intelligibly. Whereas the traditional inquiry is into the philosophical limits that the discourse of truth places on the rights of power, the more concrete and instructive Foucaultian focus is upon the rights which "are implemented by the relations of power in the production of discourses of truth".[22]

The foundations of the prevailing wisdom can be traced to the work of Max Weber. He characterised power as "the probability that one actor within a social relationship will be in a position to carry out his will despite resistance."[23] Much modern scholarship has simply amounted to a set of extended footnotes to this definition.[24] The more unimaginative work has viewed power as a general resource or ubiquitous tool to be passed around and possessed at will. The power relation is identified by a simple causal dynamic and can be measured in terms of simple behavioral responses. It is a type of political currency, a negotiable coin of the political realm. The more inventive writing has concentrated on the relational and context-specific quality of power. It construes power not as a personal attribute or facility, but as the property of particular rela-

---

21 Barry, *Is it Better to be Powerful or Lucky?*, 28 POL. STUD. 338, 349 (1980) and Mac-Donald, *Is "Power" Essentially Contested?*, 6 BRIT. J. OF POL. SCI. 380 (1976).

22 Foucault, *supra* note 15, at 93.

23 A THEORY OF SOCIAL AND ECONOMIC ORGANIZATION 152 (T. Parsons ed. 1957).

24 *See* Dahl, *Power* in 12 INT. ENCY. SOC. SCI. 405 (1968); R. GOODWIN, MANIPULATORY POLITICS (1980); D. WRONG, POWER: ITS FORMS, BASES AND USES (1980); and J.K. GALBRAITH, THE ANATOMY OF POWER (1983).

tions. Unlike currency, it is not "a circulating medium . . . , [b]ut has only limited liquidity."[25] Power can only exist if it becomes localised and inhabits specific relational apparati.

Within this genre, Stephen Lukes' work is seminal and radical. Emphasizing the conflictual nature of power, he goes deeper than the usual enquiries which explore the attempts by some to make others act against their own experienced preferences; his focus becomes "power over" rather than "power to". Lukes explores the artful way in which power installs personal wants. For him, power is exercised when "A affects B in a manner contrary to B's interests, . . . interests being defined as what men would want . . . if they were given the choice, not what they actually do want."[26] Despite its relative sophistication, Lukes' account still seems trapped within the traditional confines of theorizing about power. He imagines anteriorly and objectively existing patterns of interests within which human agents act and have adverse effects on others. Even in his relational theory of power, Lukes manages to retain the individual as the crucial catalyst in the power reaction. Like most of his humanistic and "non-radical" predecessors, he still clings to the need for some individual intentionality, a repressive affecting and teleological measurement.

In contrast, a Foucaultian-inspired account of power emphasizes its non-subjective dimension, productive capacity and localised operation.[27] It is non-programmatic and works from the ground up by ascending the hierarchical ladder rather than descending it. Power consists of a mobile multiplicity of force relations which, continually disaggregating and coalescing, shape themselves into strategic patterns. These matrixes help to create the individuals who use and are used by power, the needs power feigns to satisfy, and the Truth in whose name power claims to speak. In this way, power is not merely negative in its effects, but is an essential enabling force. As such, it sustains itself by establishing discursive economies of truth through which individuals must make and defend their claims. In modern society, constitutional law is a fine example of such a discursive regime. What is important is not the effect of a particular piece or series of constitutional litigation, but the very existence of the whole adjudicative process as a privileged mode of social ordering. In short, constitutional litigation and adjudication are special social activities that do not cause or condition, but comprise and are constitutive

---

25 Martin, *The Concept of Power: A Critical Defence*, [1971] Brit. J. of Socl. 244.
26 Power—A Radical Analysis 34 (1974).
27 *See, especially*, The History of Sexuality: Volume 1, An Introduction 92–98 (1979), Power/Knowledge 78–145 (1980) and Language, Counter-Memory, Practice 205–217 (1977).

of extant social conditions: "[it] is not so much that the court is the natural expression of popular justice, but rather that its historical function
is to ensnare it, control it and to strangle it, by re-inscribing it within
institutions which are typical of a state apparatus".[28]

To participate in the litigation process as lawyer or litigant, however
radical the claim or cause, runs the risk of hindering rather than enhanc-
ing social change and of entrenching rather than overthrowing the
dominion of the status quo. Litigation occurs *within* the limits of existing
social structures and arrangements. Accordingly, constitutional litigation
must not be thought of, as mainstream jurists do, as an independent variable in society and as sharing a complicated and, perhaps, unfathomable
cause-and-effect relation with that society. Litigation and other social
phenomena are part and parcel of the same thing; law, courts, property
regimes, civil rights and the like interpenetrate in manifold ways. Social
power and legal knowledge are two sides of a political coin. In this sense,
therefore, constitutional litigation and adjudication are not important because they cause anything to happen, but because they form part of an
integrated and rhetorical system of social control and ordering.
Nevertheless, the fear of co-optation must not lead to paralysis. The first
step to enlightenment is the recognition that there is no available "outside" from which to engage in revolutionary action: all struggle is already
sited within the very mechanisms to be resisted and reworked. The only
available strategy is to develop legal tactics that politicise the courts and
litigation. Strategies for social change must disrupt the very process in
which they engage; "as in judo, the best answer to the opponent's manoeuvre never is to step back, but to re-use it to your own advantage as
a base for the next phase."[29]

Although many areas of the law continue to articulate power in the
anachronistic language of sovereignty, with its invocation of loyal obedience and ritual aggression, this persistence merely serves to obscure the
more pervasive and profound disciplinary techniques in which power
thrives. Although law does rely on crude coercion and naked authority,
it is much more than a "code of organized public violence"[30] or a barely
disguised process of ideological inculcation. These claims do not deny

---

28 Foucault, *supra* note 15, at 1.
29 *Interview with Foucault*, LES NOUVELLES LITTERAIRES, 17 March 1975 as quoted
in Gambal, *Intellectual Work as a Political Tool*, 2 HIS. OF THE PRESENT 6 at 21 (1986).
For a power-oriented rather than a rights-oriented approach to law practice, see
Gabel and Harris, *Building Power and Breaking Images: Critical Legal Theory and the
Practice of Law*, 11 N.Y.U. REV. L. & SOC. CH. 369 (1983).
30 N. POULANTZAS, STATE, POWER, SOCIALISM 77 (1978).

or trivialize the extent or experience of "naked force," but serve to illuminate the broader context in which acts of naked force gain their leverage and authority. Again as a sub-activity of law, constitutional litigation and adjudication are important activities through which society generates and maintains "collective goods", such as the institutions of contract, private property and the family unit.[31] The particular range and quality of collective goods a society possesses and relies on are one of its major distinguishing features: a society would be a different place if it had a different set of collective goods. Insofar as constitutional litigation and adjudication manufacture the social institutions of government authority, civil rights and the like, they make a valuable and valued contribution to the retention of the present social arrangements. As water is to fish, adjudication is to the contemporary regime of political life. It does not make anything happen, but it is a vital part of existing arrangements and their continued vitality.

Of course, law is itself part of other more embracing regimes of discourse and economies of truth. These discursive practices allow the possible realization of an intelligible world, but, at the same time, lay down the parameters of that world. Importantly, therefore, it is in the nature of discursive regimes that they do not allow for the existence of "objective interests", in the sense of being exterior to the historical actuality of extant power relations. Consistent with such an epistemological and historiographical account, intentionality is as much discursively manufactured as individually conceived. Furthermore, within this radical de-centring of individuality, the traditional idea of "repression" loses much of its critical bite:

> By power, I do not mean, either, a mode of subjugation which, in contrast to violence, has the form of the rule . . . , a general system of domination exerted by one group or another . . . . The analysis, made in terms of power, must not assume that the sovereignty of the state . . . or the over-all unity of a domination are given at the outset; rather these are only the terminal forms power takes. . . . [P]ower must be understood . . . as the multiplicity of force relations immanent in the sphere in which they operate and which constitute their own organization; as the process which, through ceaseless struggles and confrontations, transforms, strengthens, or reverses them; as the support which these force relations find in one another, thus forming a chain or a system, or on the contrary, the disjunctions and contradictions which isolate them from one another. . . . Power's condition of possibility . . . as a grid of intelligibility of the social order, must not be sought in . . . a unique source of sovereignty . . . ; it is the moving substrata of force relations, which by virtue of their inequality, constantly engender states of power, but the latter are always local and unstable.[32]

---

31 *See* Griffiths, *Is Law Important?*, 54 N.Y.U. L. REV. 339 at 363–369 (1979).
32 M. FOUCAULT, THE HISTORY OF SEXUALITY 92–93 (1979).

Before leaving this preliminary introduction to Foucault's analysis of power, it is useful to compare and contrast it with similar ideas that are fashionable among fringe elements in the mainstream tradition of legal scholarship. The work of Thomas Kuhn has exerted a strong influence on jurisprudence.[33] The history of legal thought is considered to be a succession of paradigms, essentially oscillating between variations of Formalism and Realism. As anomalous situations occur, revisions are made to the paradigm. However, once the anomalies reach endemic proportions, the paradigm collapses and a revolutionary paradigm installs itself. These different paradigms represent "incommensurable ways of seeing the world and of practicing [legal science] in it":[34] they determine what counts as data, as the agenda of legitimate problems, as the range of plausible answers and the like. There is not so much a Whiggish progression as an enforced shift in professional sensibilities.

Similarly, but coming from the direction of literary theory, Stanley Fish argues that all interpretations are convention-bound, including the meta-debate over the prevailing conventions of the interpretive community.[35] Fish's brash entrance onto the jurisprudential scene has ruffled many feathers and has done much to expose the positivistic commitments that remain at the heart of the traditional juristic project. Yet, like Kuhn's, Fish's arguments are clearly incomplete: there is no attempt to explain the forces at work in determining why paradigms collapse when they do and why one particular paradigm follows another. Unless they are content to embrace some mystical theory of change, it is essential to offer some suggestions about the relation between the political conditions and structure of society and the timing and substance of paradigm-shifts. The difference with and appeal of Foucault's way of proceeding is that the task he sets himself and the analysis he offers is intended to encompass those very problems. For instance, the rise, fall and renaissance of Legal Formalism are closely tied to and form part of the economic and structural reorganisation of contemporary society. They are much more than the results of the ebb and flow of intellectual fads and fancies: the prestige and standing of any legal theory is as much a matter of political fit and convenience as intellectual cogency and perspicacity. Legal knowledge and political power restrain and reinforce each other.

---

33 *See* Hutchinson and Monahan, *Law, Politics and the Critical Legal Scholars: The Unfolding Drama of American Legal Thought*, 36 STAN. L. REV. 199 at 202–213 (1984).

34 T. KUHN, THE STRUCTURE OF SCIENTIFIC REVOLUTIONS 4 (2d ed. 1970).

35 *See supra* ch. 5.

III.

Although my main ambition is to offer and justify a "liberating" reading of Foucault, it is necessary to give some explanation of his basic arguments about the historical functioning of power-knowledge relations. To do this, I will locate his work within the traditional debates of social and historical theory. The central problematic is the need to come to terms with and resolve the perplexing interaction between human agency and socio-historical structure. A committed humanism maintains that the individual's own subjective experience can transcend and break free from the social conventions that often come to mediate the individual's confrontation with social reality. Freedom consists of individuals rupturing the constraints of social structure so as to realize and retrieve their own suppressed identities and substantive selves. At the other extreme, an uncompromising structuralism dismisses subjective individuals from their privileged position at the centre of the history-making process. It replaces them with the pervasive and ineluctable structures of social forces. Individuals become the creations rather than the creators of history, empty and transparent bottles to be filled with an intoxicating and full-bodied historical wine.[36]

Expressed in such stark and unsubtle terms, neither naive humanism nor structural determinism offers a plausible account of social history. Whereas one underdetermines the individual by denying the past, the other overdetermines the individual by obliterating the future. Indeed, both alternatives rely on the possible existence and threat of the other for their own viability and intelligibility. The humanistic version has to posit the menace of a structural leviathan, while the structuralistic account has to assume the vague prospect of a god-like individual to be overwhelmed or displaced.[37] Accordingly, modern scholarship has sought to colonise and defend one of the many staging-posts between the humanistic and structural alternatives; different theories are distinguished by the strength of their tendency to gravitate towards either

---

36 I am not insensitive to the fact that much of Foucault's own earlier work can be plausibly read to support such a "structuralist" characterisation of him. However, as I stated at the beginning of the essay, *supra* pp. 266–267, I intend to concentrate on his latest writings in which he moves away from that restricted position and its paralyzing consequences.

37 James Boyle provides an excellent study and critique of how the leading Critical Legal Scholars, particularly Duncan Kennedy, Peter Gabel, Robert Gordon and Roberto Unger, navigate these dangerous shoals of legal and social theory. *See* Boyle, *The Politics of Reason: Critical Legal Theory and Local Social Thought*, 133 U. PA. L. REV. 685 (1985).

pole. The critical challenge of Foucault is to reject the claims of both
humanists and structuralists and to suggest an alternative way of thinking
about and resolving the problem of human agency. Furthermore, he
seeks to undermine the validity and value of this whole polar analysis
and suggests a different style of political critique and proposal.

For Foucault, the "individual" is a modern invention; the subject is
not a fiction, but an artifact. Over vast stretches of history, people did
not think of themselves as free, self-defining and independent contributors to that history. They considered themselves as little more than
specks of dust in a huge cosmic sandlot: "the threshold of modernity is
situated . . . by the constitution of an empirico-transcendental doublet
which was called *man*".[38] Around the sixteenth and seventeenth century,
people became a posited object of a self-conscious scientific inquiry.
Foucault's inquiries attempt to reconstruct the complicated and extended
process by which this modern subject was fabricated as a cultural, historical and economic artifact. Relying on subversive historiographical
tools,[39] he uncovers the disciplinary and discursive devices through
which power invests, constitutes, objectifies and transforms individuals.
Through its norms, power establishes an ideal of normativity and effects
a thoroughgoing normalisation. Unlike traditional anthropological and
humanistic studies, Foucault decentres and displaces individuals from the
driving-seat of history by denying them epistemic or moral privilege.
Looking to the concrete conditions and detailed operations of power, he
rephrases the classic questions of modern thought—not Who am I, but
Where am I?: not What am I, but When am I?

Through the carceral archipelago of asylum, hospital, prison, courtroom and psychiatrist's couch, power has managed to discipline and control individuals. Further, these foyers of power have been the breeding
ground for the modern person as an object and subject of knowledge
and as a moral agent. In this sense, *subject* has two meanings; "subject
to someone else by control and dependence, and tied to his own identity
by a conscience or self-knowledge".[40] For Foucault, the spectacle of ritual
terror has simply been replaced by the more subtle, but nonetheless disciplinary techniques of "bio-power". Although there have been periods
and stages of change, contemporary humanism is a form of social control
and comprises the prevailing strategies of power.[41] Indeed, these tactical

---

38 Foucault, *supra* note 18, at 319. On his sexism, *see infra* p. 288.
39 For a good introduction to Foucault's "archaeological" and "genealogical"
   techniques, *see* B. SMART, MICHEL FOUCAULT 47–70 (1985).
40 Foucault, *The Subject and Power* in H. DREYFUS AND P. RABINOW, MICHEL
   FOUCAULT: BEYOND STRUCTURALISM AND HERMENEUTICS 212 (1982).
41 *See infra* ch. 10.

alignments are all the more effective as they present themselves as forces of "liberation". For instance, we are bombarded by images of the fulfilled libidinous being. Foucault explains this as an example of how the relations of power-knowledge have been inscribed in the body, including the repressed sexuality that is purportedly straining for liberation:

> I don't agree at all with this talk about "recuperation". What's taking place is the usual strategic development of a struggle. . . . [S]exuality, through . . . becoming an object of analysis and concern, surveillance and control, engenders at the same time an intensification of each individual's desire, for, in and over his body.
>   The body thus became the issue of a conflict. . . . The revolt of the sexual body is the reverse effect of this encroachment. What is the response on the side of power? An economic (and perhaps also ideological) exploitation of eroticisation from sun-tan products to pornographic films. Responding precisely to the revolt of the body, we find a new mode of investment which presents itself no longer in the form of control by repression but that of control by stimulation. "Get undressed—But be slim, good-looking, tanned!"[42]

Like Derrida, Foucault accepts the futility and misguidedness of trying to use deconstructive techniques to sculpt an anthropological reconstruction.[43] But, while Foucault has no truck with any form of humanism, he is equally assiduous to reject the totalising and global claims of many structural accounts. He eschews the worth of any grand theories or holistic frameworks which claim universal applicability and validity. Highlighting serious lacunae in the traditional accounts, he rejects any form of "theoretical reductionism" and maintains that the operation and effects of power cannot be compressed into any simple formula. Accordingly, although power relations are pervasive, they are only discoverable by appreciating the oppressive minutiae and routines of everyday life.[44] Although, for obvious practical reasons, he tends to focus on marxism, his critique applies to similar imperialistic theories of social explanation.

Foucault argues that, in all its various shapes and sizes, marxism is flawed as an analytical tool. It tends to characterize power relations as the epiphenomena of a capitalist system, ideologically shaped and substantiated by economic forces. For Foucault, history is much too varied and complex to fit such relations into the general pattern of working

---

42 *Supra* note 15, at 57.
43 *See* J. DERRIDA, THE MARGINS OF PHILOSOPHY 109 (A. Bass trans. 1980).
44 For an interesting and sophisticated application of this kind of theorizing, *see* A. BRITTAN AND M. MAYNARD, SEXISM, RACISM AND OPPRESSION (1984).

class oppression or other capital-based arrangements like feudalism. "Class" implies a homogeneity of interests and experience, but the daily practices of discipline show that it cuts across traditional categories. Local domination is not fully explainable in terms of these global categories. Sexism and racism cannot be compressed into the crude relations of productive forces. Even in marxist terms, labour is being displaced by knowledge and information as its major organising unit. Instead, these local "rapports de force" constantly coalesce and disaggregate. Forming themselves into fragile and unstable webs of power, they react upon and condition local confrontations. It is a dynamic, ceaseless and unstructured process of fission and fusion. Power is multi-dimensional and -directional. Nevertheless, this does not mean that marxism as an explanatory theory must be jettisoned entirely. Some forms of economic oppression are broadly experienced, even if locally generated, and contemporary marxism can provide a major insight into its operation; it can comprise one dimension or strand in the overall web of power relations:

> No "local center" . . . could function if, through a series of sequences, it did not eventually enter into an over-all strategy. And inversely, no strategy could achieve comprehensive effects if it did not gain support from precise and tenuous relations serving, not at its point of application or final outcome, but as its prop and anchor point. There is no discontinuity between them, as if one were dealing with two different levels (one microscopic and the other macroscopic); but neither is there homogeneity (as if the one were only the enlarged projection or miniaturization of the other); rather, one must conceive of the double conditioning of a strategy by the specificity of possible tactics, and of tactics by the strategic envelope that makes them work.[45]

Further, according to Foucault, marxism emphasizes the oppressive aspects of power to the exclusion of its enabling capacities and operation. Like humanism, it imagines the possibility of an ahistorical "human nature", presently incarcerated and awaiting future release. Both view power as an economic commodity. Whereas humanism looks to justify its allocation through freely-entered and binding contracts, marxism condemns its illegitimate use by one class over another. Foucault is implacably opposed to any pseudo-humanistic belief in the ontological or ethical status of individual subjectivity. History cannot be reduced to the collected biographies of particular people nor can it be ascribed to the structural teleology of an historico-scientific evolution. As such, "individuality is neither the real atomistic basis of society nor an ideological illusion of liberal economics",[46] but is generated through and in the his-

---

45 *Supra* note 32, at 99–100.
46 *Supra* note 20, at 194.

torical technologies of local power-knowledge relations: individuals flourish and wilt in their inter-subjective connections. Domination is not produced through the propagation of ideological falsehood which can be ultimately cast aside in favour of "reality". Oppression is effected through an historical regime of truth which trivialises or eschews the important potential of dialogic growth and democratic truth-making.

Importantly, different technologies of power not only formalize and organize knowledge, but ensure its possibility, intelligibility and parameters. As the study of legal reasoning shows, power finds different ways to produce and hide in the discursive regimes and practices of knowledge-making. Like Nietzsche, Foucault insists that knowledge is only a spatio-temporal perspective and works as a tool of power. This, of course, radically undercuts any notion of a "universal truth". Indeed, Foucault proclaims that "to reveal truth . . . [is] a ridiculous preten-sion".[47] There is no available independent or exterior ground between the extant protocols of power and the validating procedures of knowl-edge, no timeless plateau to which we can escape to pursue universal interests. Truth has no meaning or intelligibility outside the historical complex of power-knowledge relations. We must pull the curtain down on the melodramatic comedy of scientific manners that presents the pur-suit of truth as an attempt to achieve an ever closer approximation to reality. For Foucault, there is nothing beyond interpretation except more interpretation; the lingering belief in the possibility of a direct confronta-tion with "reality", unmediated by the perspective of power, is a roman-tic *divertissement* and the curtain ought to be pulled down on it.

Truth is a historical mask. The past differs from the present by the mask it wears. Behind these "truth-masks", there are only other masks. We only change masks when we have fashioned and fabricated a suitable replacement for the transparent and worn old mask. These masks are socially imposed and individually assumed. We can never stand naked or maskless; we have no face to save nor to turn against the biting winds of history. History is a masquerade of power. At best, unmasking can only destabalize because truth is always inside power. As such, it is not "the reward of free spirits, the child of protracted solitude nor the privilege of those of who have succeeded in liberating themselves."[48] By accepting truth as an experienced thing of this world, life can be grasped as something more than "a mobile [Nietzschean] army of metaphors,

---

47 *Preface to Transgression* in LANGUAGE, COUNTER-MEMORY, PRACTICE (M.F. Bouchard ed. 1977).
48 *Supra* note 15, at 131.

metonyms, and anthropomorphisms"[49] marching to the beat of a conventional drum. Truth is that, but it is much more as well:

> [T]ruth is pain and effort and dirt and sweat and blood as well. Wince if you will, object if you will, make a point or two if you will. Truth isn't an argument or a correct phrase, that's all words, that's lawyer's truth—and who knows a greater liar than a lawyer? There's city truth and there's country truth. There's lawyer's truth and there's human truth. Thought-up truth and lived truth.[50]

All this seems to present a depressing prognosis. Foucault offers little optimism to those political theorists and activists who seek a cure to the power contagion or want to know where to sweat. Understandably, this has lead some critics, like Mark Philp, to conclude that as Foucault does not believe "that there is anything better (in any sense of the word) for others in the future . . . , this makes his status as a radical somewhat questionable".[51] Like Joyce's Stephen Daedalus,[52] they begin to despair that history *is* a nightmare from which, however hard we try, we cannot awake; there are only other nightmares to enact and experience. Having come all this way, the (de)pressing question still remains as to whether Foucault's work suggests any way to judge or choose, in any meaningful way, between different ways of life. In Foucault's own words, "how can the growth of capabilities be disconnected from the intensification of power relations?"[53] In terms of my own agenda, can "the hint of emancipating the oppressed" overcome its quivering timidity and make itself felt in a more positive and tangible manner? Can nightmares at least become daydreams?

IV.

Although Foucault rejects any belief in a universal human nature or a primitive vivacity, he does not succumb to a deterministic dogma that reduces individuals to the whimsical playthings of history. Such a scenario is as anti-historical as it is ludicrous. If people were exhaustively dictated by the regnant conventions of power and destined to become

---

49 Nietzsche, *On Truth and Lie in an Extra-Moral Sense* in the PORTABLE NIETZSCHE 46 (1954).
50 F. RAPHAEL, THE GLITTERING PRIZES 147 (1976).
51 Philp, *Foucault on Power: A Problem in Radical Translation*, 11 POL. THEORY 29 at 48 (1983).
52 *See* Joyce, *Ulysses* in THE ESSENTIAL JAMES JOYCE 475 (H. Levin ed. 1948).
53 Foucault, *supra* note 11, at 48.

fleeting ciphers in a cosmic script, history would ossify; individuals would become fossils in the accumulated sediments of a timeless history. The clock would tick, but no one would hear it. Foucault has no truck with such deterministic dalliances. He follows and acts on the Nietzschean insight that "the will to power can manifest itself only against resistances; therefore it seeks that which resists it".[54] Although subjectivity is conceived and concocted by the bio-technologies of power, it does not mean that the individual is a mythic phantom or fabulous chimera. The individual subject is always in the process of being overwhelmed, but is never completely overwhelmed. There is only history because of the individual's need, capacity and desire to resist. As E.M. Forster so succinctly put it, "a perfectly adjusted organism would be silent"[55] and, I would add, be "dead".

The same applies to societies. While we live in a disciplinary society, we are not a disciplined society. All situations are staged by the protocols of power and, as such, dominate the individual actors and participants. Yet, while always pressed to the margins and barely detectable, there is always some chance of escape and potential for individual resistance. Although we often seem trapped within Weber's "iron-cage", there are small, often hidden gaps between the bars through which we can occasionally slip and elude the control of power; even if the escape is temporary and only into another cage. Every victory contains the seeds of its own future defeat. Like Frankenstein, power's strategies bring into play a cast of individual "monsters" who take on a life of their own and threaten the continued efficacy of those same strategies. Our uneven history charts our passage through these countless and crucial episodes. The normative message of Foucault is to confront and confound the regime of truth/power and work its manifold seams—"all of my work consists in showing that history is traversed by strategic relations that are consequently mobile and that we can change."[56]

This reading of Foucault leads to the conclusion that history is not simply the reeling from one "monstrous" situation to another: "my point is not that everything is bad, but that everything is dangerous".[57] This is not cause for deep despair or dark fatalism. It tells us that we should renew the social struggle with a revitalised energy and sense of purpose. By making felt certainties uncertain, openings and seams are

---

54 F. Nietzsche, The Will to Power 656 (1947).
55 E.M. Forster, A Passage to India 133 (1924).
56 *Interview de Michel Foucault*, Actes, June 1984 as quoted in Gambal, *supra* note 29 at 6.
57 *On the Genealogy of Ethics* in Michel Foucault: Beyond Structuralism and Hermeneutics 343 (H. Dreyfus and P. Rabinow eds. 1983).

displayed for struggle and transformation. The present is not a secure vantage-point from which to survey the past and ponder the future, but a narrow and precarious ledge between the yawning past and the gaping future. It is not a home, but a battleground. The individual-in-society is a confrontational site on which the traditional forces of the past and the untold imaginings of the future clash in unresolved and ceaseless encounters to conquer and inhabit the present. Hannah Arendt put it well when she said that the past "does not pull back, but presses forward, and it is . . . the future which drives us back into the past".[58] Our present selves are partly *being*, in the sense of what we have become, and partly *becoming*, in the sense of what we will be: domination thrives when the being eclipses and squeezes out the becoming.

We, and the counterfeit necessity of our canons of rationality, have emerged from a network of contingencies. Our rationality was and will become another period's irrationality. Therefore, since we must realize that these rational practices "have been made, they can be unmade, as long as we know how it was that they were made".[59] These canons of rationality are not simply intellectual window-dressing, but constitute the practical context for the intelligible possibilities and limits of our present activities. It is our responsibility to write the history of the present and disclose the dubious and power-full origins of these so-called rational practices. In this way, the normative and radical edge cuts deep and sharpens itself in the process:

> [T]he real political task in a society such as ours is to criticise the workings of institutions, which appear to be both neutral and independent; to criticise and attack them in such a manner that the political violence which has always exercised itself obscurely through them will be unmasked, so that one can fight against them.
>
> This critique and this fight seem essential to me . . . because political power goes much deeper than one suspects; there are centres and little-known points of support; its true resistance, its true solidity is perhaps where one doesn't expect it.[60]

V.

In meeting this challenge, "justice" is not a standard or ideal by which to direct and evaluate social struggle. Instead, justice lives its life

---

58 H. ARENDT, BETWEEN PAST AND FUTURE 10 (1968).

59 Raulet, *Structuralism and Post-Structuralism: An Interview with Michel Foucault*, 55 TELOS 202 at 206 (1983).

60 Chomsky and Foucault, *Human Nature: Justice versus Power* in F. ELDER, REFLEXIVE WATER 170 (1974).

within the struggle itself; it is born in and dies in struggle. For instance, Bruce Ackerman's declaration that "so long as we live, there can be no escape from the struggle for power"[61] reveals the fundamental difference between Foucault's analysis and that of traditional political theory. Ackerman puts struggle and power in the service of justice, whereas Foucault critically reverses that relation and makes justice the result of struggling against and within power. Any theory of justice must arise from and can never sever its roots in the very conditions of power that social struggle is intended to overthrow. There is not so much a battle "for truth", but "around truth". It is more of a detachment than an emancipation; the power of truth must be disengaged from the strands of economic, social and cultural relations that are woven together to form the heavy and often suffocating blanket of the status quo. Instead, they must be re-woven in the popular hands of those who depend on its sustaining warmth: weavers and wearers must become one.

The concrete implications of these abstruse arguments can best be appreciated in the context of particular disagreements in jurisprudence. Recently, Drew Fraser has taken Roberto Unger to task. While there is much of value in Fraser's indictment of Unger's post-modernist position, his own championing of the republican tradition seems to trap him in the structuralist snare. Unger's superliberalism is devoted to defending the notion of a "context-revising self" and developing a form of collective life that provides the maximum opportunities for individuals' "irresistible capacity for transcendence and revision."[62] Although the Ungerian individual is formed through and is never outside communal connections, the fulcrum of his social theory is the perfected individual who can master and better him or herself by becoming more open to revision. In seeking to make good on the reneged promise of liberalism, Unger retains the individual as the primary source and judge of value. It is a theory of personal development based on an asymetrical and non-reciprocal view of human relations and driven by a condemnation of "anti-modernist fantasies of communal integration and permanent civic mili-

---

61 B. ACKERMAN, SOCIAL JUSTICE IN THE LIBERAL STATE 3 (1981).
62 R. UNGER, PASSION: AN ESSAY ON PERSONALITY 36 and 161 (1984). For my own criticism of Unger, see Hutchinson and Monahan, The "Rights" Stuff: Roberto Unger and Beyond, 62 TEX. L. REV. 1477 (1984). In that essay, I remained committed in part to an Ungerian-type notion of personality: I have now sought to shake off that lingering commitment. However, there is much in Unger that is highly insightful and powerful. In rejecting his ontological claims, it is important not to throw out the baby with the bathwater. For instance, his deconstructive critique is seminal in its thoroughness, suggestiveness, and depth. See The Critical Legal Studies Movement, 96 HARV. L. REV. 563 (1983).

tancy:"[63] the "republic" is another species of mythic consciousness.

Fraser contends that Unger's critique only deepens rather than re-solves the crisis of modernity and "seems bent on destroying the few remaining institutional and cultural obstacles to the ongoing capitalist rationalization of everyday life."[64] Unger's superliberalism is nothing more than the glorification of subjectivity as the normative basis of social life taken to higher, less compromising and more romantic levels of gen-erality. Whereas Unger capitulates to the modernist contagion, Fraser wants to find solace from its political contamination in the tradition of republican virtue.[65] In contrast to Unger's futile modernist peregrina-tions, Fraser argues that republicanism is not about the vain attempt to reconcile the different interests of private persons, but to transcend them in the search for a common ground and the establishment of civic unity through a virtuous public life. Self-interest is juxtaposed to communal virtue and the locus of moral authority moves from the subjective life to the republican polity itself; the modernist individual is replaced by the mature citizen. Instead of collapsing the barrier between public and pri-vate life, the public sphere would become the nursery for private action and responsibility.

As with Unger's ideas, there is much to commend Fraser's republi-can alternative. Yet Fraser seems to replace Unger's wide-eyed amnesia with his own misty-eyed nostalgia. Insofar as there ever was a genuine period of republican life, it was an intensely hierarchical and elitist society in which the privileges and benefits of civil life were jealously guarded; its invocation today as a worthy and realistic ideal seems dubious. Moreover, Fraser's attempt to utilise Alasdair MacIntyre's account of "practices"[66] as an alternative vision of lawyering runs into an already familiar set of objections. The A.B.A. or C.B.A. is an improbable en-clave for radical insurgence. In particular, the definition of practices is so thin and insufficient as to incorporate and dignify all manner of objec-

---

63 *Id.* at 31–32.
64 Fraser, *Legal Amnesia: Modernism versus The Republican Tradition in American Legal Thought*, 60 TELOS 15 at 19 (1984).
65 This tradition is presently enjoying a fashionable revival. *See* Michelman, *Foreword: Traces of Self-Government*, 100 HARV. L. REV. 4 (1986) and Sherry, *Civic Virtue and the Feminine Voice in Constitutional Adjudication*, 72 VA. L. REV. 543 (1986). The most concerted attempt to revitalize this tradition in legal thought is by Cass Sunstein. *See Naked Preferences and The Constitution*, 84 COLUM. L. REV. 1689 (1984) and *Interest Groups in American Public Law*, 38 STAN. L. REV. 29 (1985). Drawing on a neo-Madisonian strand, unlike Fraser, he relies on popular sovereignty through a representative constitution of the modern nation state.
66 A. MACINTYRE, AFTER VIRTUE 187–188 (2d ed. 1984).

tionable activities. Indeed, as Richard Bernstein notes, "the types of practices that Foucault analyzes . . . and which he claims constitute the "disciplinary society" or the "carceral archipelago" appear to satisfy MacIntyre's definition of a practice."[67] In the context of a republican notion of legal practice, there seem very real problems with how the shared norms operate as principles of inclusion and exclusion; the cult of the expert contributes to an inegalitarian sense of cognitive and moral superiority which is hardly the stuff of the civic good life. What seems to be envisaged is a Salem without the witches, the Ku Klux Klan without its racism or a Moral Majority without its bigotry; that is, much wishful thinking and no cause for realistic confidence.

Some of these fears are brought out in Fraser's unease about the criminalisation of marital rape. He views such developments as problematic because they jeopardise the possibilities for nurturing nuclear families which exist as one of the rare institutions for public commitment and mutual dependence; its further decay threatens to escalate the desperate atomisation of human relations.[68] Yet, if Fraser is keen to resist the growing fragmentation of social life, his turn to the family is surely misguided. For many women and children, the family has been as much the site of oppression and subordination as a "haven in a heartless world".[69] Indeed, the division of social life into public and private compartments seems to be more the problem than the solution to social alienation. The "family" is not so much good or bad in absolute terms, but will depend on the quality particular individuals in particular circumstances give to their inter-subjective relationships. Consequently, Fraser, in attempting to save the baby, contrives to retain the bathwater and lose the baby.

At bottom, both Unger and Fraser, in their different ways, indulge in the anthropological conceit of neo-Aristotelianism. They assume that *man* has an essential nature or purpose and that we must organize ourselves so as to be better able to realize our true species being. They remain deep in "anthropological sleep."[70] Like so much intellectual debate, Unger's and Fraser's disagreement is impoverished because they trap themselves in an either/or dilemma, a choice between an over-socialized fate or a splendid anomie. Any meaningful reconstruction of ethics must

---

67 Bernstein, *Nietzsche or Aristotle?: Reflections on Alasdair MacIntyre's After Virtue*, 67 SOUNDINGS 6, 13 (1984). *See, also,* Gutmann, *Communitarian Critics of Liberalism*, 14 PHIL. & PUB. AFFS. 308 at 319 (1985).
68 *See* Fraser, *Feminism and Marital Rape*, 46 ARENA 14 (1977).
69 *See* C. LASCH, A HAVEN IN A HEARTLESS WORLD (1977). For an unqualified critique of this view, *see* MacKinnon, *Feminism, Marxism, Method, and the State: Toward Feminist Jurisprudence*, 7 SIGNS 635 (1983).
70 Foucault, *supra* note 18, at 340.

go beyond the negativity of Ungerian politics, but not as far as the communal saturation of Fraser's republicanism. For Unger, freedom is the freedom to be a conscript in a continual state of social war. At worst, relations with others are seen as hostile contexts to be smashed; at best, as temporary respites to refuel for future battles. For Fraser, virtue becomes an enforced solidarity in which failure to identify completely with others is an act of civic treason; you are with the community or against it. Both possibilities traduce any realistic achievement of "love". Whereas one reduces it to the by-product of transactions in the market economy of anomic morality, the other devalues it by obliging us to treat strangers as intimates and intimates as strangers.

A further difficulty is that, although the notions of "individual" and "community" stand in supposed opposition, they are interdependent and mutually-reinforcing; they exist as the mirror-image and condition of the other. Each uses the perceived threat of the other to ensure its own unity. The flawed "metaphysics of presence" that individualism relies on to deny difference by implying the sameness of all has been sufficiently rehearsed.[71] Communalism resorts to the same device and is part of, not an alternative to, contemporary political theory and practice. The search for community overwhelms difference in its dangerous drive toward uniformity. By reducing everything and everyone to a lowest common denominator, communalism includes by exclusion and achieves shared values at the expense of diversity; what is "inside" is implicated in that which it places "outside".[72] The obvious challenge is to break out of this either/or—neither/nor dialectic and to conceive of the multi-dimensional relations between subject and structure in different terms. By deconstructing the morphology of social thinking, it might be possible to reconstruct social relations.

Rather than worry about falling between the two stools of subjectivism and structuralism, it is better to take the fall and explore the neglected spaces of inter-subjective relations. By thinking about and understanding our personal and social lives as complex and overlapping accumulations of such relations, political theory and practice can cut across the traditional organising dichotomies; it can borrow and combine innovatively much from each without succumbing to the excesses and sterile options of either. An acceptance of intersubjectivity helps us to come to terms with our vulnerability to and dependence on others, our commitment to and responsibility for others. Unlike communalism, it

---

71 See supra ch. 2.
72 See Young, *The Idea of Community and the Politics of Difference*, 12 SOC. TH. & PRAC. 1 (1986).

recognizes and allows a real difference between self and other. But, unlike individualism, it does not turn that difference into a divisive barrier. Intersubjectivity suggests a relation between self and other that is based on fragility and need rather than on suspicion or suppression.

A commitment to intersubjectivity allows us to reach flexible and contingent balances of negative and positive liberty, a freedom *from* and freedom *to*. In the current search for absolutes, we deny our finitude and, therefore, our humanity. We overlook what we can discover in the hopeless search for what we can never find: "by coming to terms with our finitude, we gain the humility necessary to overcome the hubris of individualism".[73] By viewing the individual self as constituted in and through its intersubjective connections, the notions of autonomy and solidarity can be better and differently understood: criticism and commitment, innovation and connection can be mutually supported. As Mark Taylor so aptly summarizes it, "the decentering of the subject . . . does not issue in the simple disintegration of the self. Neither completely undifferentiated nor entirely separate, the deconstructive subject is situated in the midst of multiple and constantly changing relations."[74]

Intersubjectivity is not a novel state of affairs to be exalted, but is a standard feature of human history that has always been under our noses, if we only bothered to lower our gaze from the enticing horizon of absolutes that seem daily in sight, but forever out of reach. In this shift in focus from the identity between self and other to their relational context, the work of feminist writers is especially insightful and important. Feminism is the cutting edge of social theory and change; it offers itself as a revolutionary alternative to contemporary practice and ideas. Although there are many shades of opinion in the feminist movement, there exists the basic deconstructive belief that knowledge and gender are not mutually exclusive categories: metaphysical commitments operate to conceal the man-made and man-serving construction of reality by making women's experience and standpoint invisible or trivial. At the top of the feminist agenda is the need to rethink and rework not only the human drama, but the way we think about the idea and experience of what is and can be the human drama. As well as multiplying the number of

---

73 Cornell, *Toward a Modern/Postmodern Reconstruction of Ethics*, 133 U. PA. L. REV. 291, 338 (1985). The following pages owe a great deal to this excellent article. It is an Hegelian-inspired attempt to show how "dialogism can serve as a powerful regulative ideal" in the development of an ethic for political practice. Although her essay does not deal directly with the work of Michel Foucault, I believe that her findings are not inconsistent with his ideas, at least as presented here.

74 M. TAYLOR, ERRING 435 (1984).

female actors and authors, the drama and performance themselves must be made on a wider, more popular front and by virtue of a different ethic and voice. At the heart of this enterprise is the understanding that self-definition is a function of intersubjective experience; it is the relation and not the relating entities that should be protected and nurtured. As Carol Gilligan puts it, the ambition is "a world comprised of relationships rather than of people standing alone, a world that coheres through human connection".[75]

Political life is like music. Collectivist musicology aspires to the ultimate composition and performance of the great fugue. Society would be orchestrated as an indivisible melody in which each individual is a single note harmoniously related to every other note and the work as a whole; there is no space for or tolerance of improvisation and experimentation.[76] In contrast, the individualists envisage almost as many ensembles as there are individuals. Each player is either single-earedly devoted to composing and striking the "right" note, even if they have a tin-ear or the note is beyond human hearing, or else each is in competition to produce the best solo; improvisation becomes the melody and experiment the rule. At the risk of blandness or cacophony, the intersubjective musicologists stimulate and listen for the sounds of exciting and fluid jam sessions; local networks that are constituted by and constitutive of individual musicians who easily move between point and counterpoint, carry the melody or explore a thematic variation, are comfortable as a sideperson or a soloist and the like.

VI.

In recognizing the centrality of intersubjectivity, we are inevitably thrown back onto the difficulties of language and discourse. Individuals work upon and make language and history, but are themselves worked upon and made by history and language. Insofar as the individual consciousness needs to become articulate, it must do so within the pre-existing domain of linguistic relations and discursive practices. Language, thinking and being are inextricably linked. Our language is the raw material from which our world and reality are forged; they are a cultural artifact of the first order. Language is not a transparency through which

---

75 C. GILLIGAN, IN A DIFFERENT VOICE: PSYCHOLOGICAL THEORY AND WOMEN'S DEVELOPMENT 29 (1982).

76 See M. KUNDERA, THE BOOK OF LAUGHTER AND FORGETTING 62–68 (M. Heim trans. 1981).

we observe the world nor a catalogue of labels to be attached to the appropriate contents of the world. There is no form of pure communication that merely represents instead of creating. The world is within the language and the language within the world. The world cannot speak for itself; it must be spoken for. Social reality and our place in it is constantly being negotiated and constructed, re-negotiated and re-constructed. Language is not a system of static symbols, but is a form of social action. To acquire and exercise a language is to engage in the most profound of political acts: to name the world is to control it. Accordingly, as language-users, we are unwitting gamblers in life. We make a critical wager: in return for the privilege of living in *any* world, we are committed to living in *one* world. The nature of that world will depend on the language in which we speak for each mode of discourse consists of a whole package of foundational beliefs and assumptions about reality. By using a language, we accept its unspoken values and commitments.[77]

The acquisition of discursive literacy is a step of immeasurable consequence; to become linguistically competent and to inhabit society's stories is to take a stand in the world and to accept a matrix of assumptions and beliefs about the world *and our position in it*. To talk like a lawyer is to be a lawyer. A familiar example illustrates this point. Language provides us with images of ourselves and others as men and women. It constructs the "natural" categories of masculinity and femininity. It interposes itself in and structures gender encounters. Discursive practices have established and maintained the hierarchical differentiation between men and women. "Male" is the grammatical and semantical norm that relegates "female" to a deviant and derivative status. As a mere, albeit necessary, foil for masculinity, femininity occupies a secondary status through a subterranean process of exclusion. Moreover, sexist language uses men and women as much as it is used by them. It nurtures and conditions its speakers to their roots and, in the process, persuades them of their autonomy. Inasmuch as language is "man-made," "man" and "woman" are also made by language.[78]

The turn to dialogue as the locus of intersubjective development is

---

77 *See supra* chs. 1 and 5.

78 Although profoundly concerned with sexuality, Foucault fails to address male power as systemic and hegemonic. Men define gender and femininity to such an extent that "women have little choice but to *become* persons who freely choose women's roles." MacKinnon, *Feminism, Marxism, Method, and the State: An Agenda for Theory*, 7 SIGNS 515 at 542 (1982) (emphasis in original). MacKinnon criticizes Foucault for failing to appreciate gender "as a primary category for comprehending [power]." *Id.* at 526 n. 22. Domination operates not through physical constraints, but by controlling the way women think about their lives and possibilities.

fraught with difficulties. By abandoning the search for foundational truths, we enhance the possibilities for the powerless to engage in the essential dialogue of world re-making. But, at the same time, ample opportunities arise for the powerful to dominate that conversation. As conversationalists, we are front-line combatants in the daily struggle to resist, reproduce or change the world. We can never escape the historical context of our efforts in narrative reconstruction. But, armed with that knowledge, we can guard against its hegemonic impulses. Within the bonds and options of intersubjective connection, people might better be able to engage history. We must stretch and enlarge the discursive resources at our disposal so that we can go beyond the traditional boundaries of social life and bring back linguistic records of our imaginative adventures. We must resist the seductive melody of liberal pluralism and, instead, work together so that we can "oppose humanity in different songs of joy".[79] To this end, democratic dialogue will chart its own dialectic trajectory and propel its participants along the path to a substantive democratic life.

While touted as a conversational idiom *par excellence*, the dominant patois of liberal pluralism constricts the range of dialogic fulfilment in the name of greater choice; it preserves the status quo and induces an uneasy conformity. For instance, in a very Habermasian vein,[80] Bruce Ackerman looks to replace purposive rationality with a rational ethic of "neutral conversation". He posits a form of political dialogue in which no person can lay claim to moral insight intrinsically superior to others nor to intrinsic personal superiority over others.[81] Yet, by imposing such conversational constraints, he trivialises dialogue by removing from the agenda the most vital of topics—our developing visions of the good life and the nature of good citizenship. Neutrality is always a blind for sectarian interests. By failing to confront and change existing structures of power, Ackerman disables dialogue and fails to elevate it from desultory chatter to a potent medium of world-making. Moreover, not only is conversation to be regulated by an ahistorical, transcendent and artificial mode of communicative rationality, but it contrives to incorporate the

---

79 J. O'NEIL, ON CRITICAL THEORY 32 (1976).
80 *See* J. HABERMAS, TOWARD A RATIONAL SOCIETY (1970) and *A Philosophico-Political Profile*, 151 NEW LEFT REV. 75 (1985).
81 *See* B. ACKERMAN, SOCIAL JUSTICE IN THE LIBERAL STATE 11 and 43–44 (1980). In his scheme of things, law-talk still manages to achieve a special privilege and to dominate social conversation. See RECONSTRUCTING AMERICAN LAW (1984). For a critique of this privileging, *see supra* ch. 5. From the ample critical literature on Ackerman, the best work can be found in Hyde, 57 N.Y.U. L. REV. 1031 (1982) and Singer, [1985] A.B.A. FD. RES. J. 329.

individualist logic of market economics. For the Ackermaniac, "autonomy . . . [is] the best thing there is" and market failure is the metewand for collective intervention. In such a world, it will come as no surprise that economic actors will speak in an economic voice and economic contestants will run an economic race. If, as Ackerman rightly demands, "the first meaningful reality we must create . . . is the idea that you and I are persons capable of giving meanings to the world",[82] we will have to look somewhere other than Ackerman's own liberal version of power-talk.

The spirit and practice of this "reciprocal elucidation" can be best fostered in a radical form of dialogic democracy. Unlike Republicanism or Superliberalism, democracy does not rest on any metaphysical foundation or rely on any un-deconstructed privileging of individual or community. The essence of democracy is that it denies closure or, at least, recognises fully the provisional and historical nature of all judgments and standards for political action; choice and decision-making are necessary, but contingent. In the sense that there cannot be "a pure and simple landing into a beyond of metaphysics",[83] democracy offers the possibility of accomodating the fact that, while we can never erase or deny the existence of an inside/outside limit, we can be alive to its constructedness and work to keep it on the move. It is in this sense that "politics is epistemology."[84] Determinacy and indeterminacy are polarities on the plane of praxis. While theory has to disentangle them, our existential condition means that we cannot reject their difference. Democracy enables us to embrace both, and at the same time, grapple with and rework them. It allows politics to cease being the forcing-ground of overwhelming orthodoxy and conformity and, instead, to become a fairground in which there can be experiments with the experience of *normality*.

Democracy is the appropriate institutional complement to deconstruction. As deconstruction provides the subversive philosophy to loosen the tenacity of an oppressive culture of rationality, democracy looks to situated interrelationships and represents a form of life that allows the optimal options for transformative politics without losing sight of the sustaining intersubjectivity of social life. Within such a scenario, political knowledge becomes a matter of practical and shared judgment that works to re-cast the world in its own developing and experimental image. This form of democracy is antithetical to traditional styles of political theory and practice. Traditional theorists misguidedly seek to

---

82 *Id*.
83 J. DERRIDA, POSITIONS 12 (1981).
84 B. BARBER, STRONG DEMOCRACY 131 (1982).

entrench a dominion of Truth that makes "debased slaves" of its citizens.[85] The ethic of democracy guarantees that we manufacture truth and knowledge through the sweat of our own democratic brows; philosophy would be but one voice in an open and continuing conversation. As such, democracy is not only a philosophy and politics of everyday life, but everyday life becomes its own philosophy and politics. As Amelie Rorty puts it, democracy would enhance "our ability to engage in continuous conversation, testing one another, discovering our hidden presuppositions, changing our minds because we have listened to the voices of our fellows. Lunatics change their minds, but their minds change with the tides of the moon and not because they have listened, really listened, to their friends' questions and objections."[86] Dialogue is as much about listening and responding as it is about talking and asking.

The ambition must be to induce and develop a self-conscious "agonism" which is "less a face-to-face confrontation which paralyzes both sides than a permanent provocation".[87] On this radical Foucaultian agenda, there is a crucial switch from the problem of authenticity to that of intersubjective creativity: the challenge is less to do with false consciousness than it is to do with civic unconsciousness. Efforts to think out and install institutional devices which best guarantee the liberation of individuals so that they can better find and realize their own unique selves or which best ensure communal harmony tend to dissipate valuable radical energies. The focus of endeavour must be realigned. Each person must individually and collectively encourage themselves and others to promote and experience new forms of inter-subjectivity.

To effect such changes, however, we must refrain from the familiar attempt to think in total and global terms. The response must be much more local and domestic. By working at ground level, transformative action becomes a real possibility for disaffected citizens. Foucault himself took his own advice and was instrumental in setting-up Group On Prisons, a clutch of intellectuals devoted "to creating conditions that permit the prisoners themselves to speak".[88] Through intermediate, non-hierarchical organisations like mental health advocacy groups, people become involved as the potential relievers of their own victimisation; self-help and -improvement are the tools of democratic justice. Resort to the

---

85 See J.J. ROUSSEAU, THE SOCIAL CONTRACT, bk II (G. Cole trans. 1950).
86 Rorty, *Experiments in Philosophic Genre: Descartes' Meditations*, 9 CRIT. INQ. 545 at 562 (1983).
87 *Supra* note 40, at 222.
88 *Interests and Power* in LANGUAGE, COUNTER-MEMORY, PRACTICE 206 (D.F. Bouchard ed. 1977).

courts can only be a pragmatic and occasional strategy for change. By engaging in such popular action, the dangers of bureaucracy and paternalism are not only avoided, but are challenged; dependency is replaced with self-respect, alienation with solidarity and impotence with empowerment. For instance, rape crisis centres are democratic microcosms in action—they provide emotional and physical support, challenge and change the institutional responsibilities of hospitals and the police, and attack the structure of male domination.

In line with localised politics, the lingering image of the intellectual as the Delphic sage or guru who deals in universal pronouncements must be exorcised. Instead of inculcating a program of "correct" values, they should strive to cultivate a critical cast of mind and aspire to "creating problems that we badly need."[89] Academic study must become more politically immediate and specific. Philosophy is not a spectator sport. Instead, we must cultivate a philosophy-as-life. Efforts to work in the foyers of power and to expose the historicity of their technical claims to legitimacy must increase. It is essential to nurture a new "politics of power" in the university classroom, the factory floor, the lawyer's office, the doctor's consulting room, the political committee rooms, the science laboratory and the like. Criticism must become an instrument of struggle and not continue as a reactive reflection on that struggle:

> [The intellectual must] no longer . . . place [himself or herself] "somewhat ahead and to the side" in order to express the stifled truth of the collectivity; rather it is to struggle against the forms of power that transform [her or him] into its object and instrument in the sphere of "knowledge", "truth", "consciousness" and "discourse".
>
> In this sense theory does not express, translate or serve to apply practice: it is practice.[90]

VII.

In this essay, I have sought to adumbrate and defend a theory of political practice that incorporates and supports a deconstructive approach to social reality and thinking. The emphasis has been on the interpenetrating dimensions of intersubjectivity and dialogue. The ambition has been to show that the crucial theoretical underpinnings of contemporary political life are not cut from whole cloth. By toiling in local and specific conditions, it might be possible to work the seams in the histor-

---

89 Gambal, *supra* note 29, at 18.
90 *Supra* note 88, at 207–208.

ical fabric of rationality and to reveal its contingency, its threat and its opportunities. Also, this constant unstitching of the dominant garments of power-knowledge offers the chance to work towards a new, but always temporary, outfit of self-created social clothing. In this way, deconstructive theory becomes reconstructive practice; it is a mutually supportive and productive method of engaging in the discursive practices of social life. Further, it is only through such local critiques that it becomes even vaguely possible to grasp and hold together the immediate experience of individual subjects and the overarching structures of modern rationality. Although this moment may be elusive and evanescent, it might be sufficient to allow us to act critically and constructively in the social world and on the history-making process.[91]

In keeping with Foucault's critical imperative, a radical form of democracy means that the future is always open, but always dangerous. It is not that we have nothing to lose but our chains and a world to win, but that in winning that world we may forge new chains for our enslavement. Like all challenges, where there is hope, there is hazard; where there is potential, there is peril. The price of freedom is eternal struggle. "Working the seam" is one way of assuming and beginning to meet that responsibility. Democracy is the way to nurture that state of affairs as a personal fulfilment, as an intersubjective undertaking and as an organizational ethic.

> One day in a nuclear age
> They may understand our rage
> They build machines that they can't control
> And bury the waste in a great big hole
> Power was to become cheap and clean
> Grimy faces were never seen
> But deadly for twelve thousand years is carbon fourteen
>
> We work the black seam together.[92]

---

91 *See* Boyle, *supra* note 37, at 773–778.
92 Sting, *We Work The Black Seam* on THE DREAM OF THE BLUE TURTLES (1985).

10

BEYOND NO-FAULT

Deconstructive criticism is a valuable source of enlightenment and therapy in itself. Without removing the intellectual and material conditions of domination, the search for social justice is "condemned to be idolatrous or utopian, or both at once."[1] By unfreezing the world as it now appears, new possibilities for meaningful and innovative social interaction can be imagined and grasped. However, while something cannot be replaced by nothing, the replacement of one form of domination by another must be studiously avoided. The challenge is to ensure that the deconstructive imperative connects up with and, at the same time, checks the reconstructive impulse.[2] In charting such a course, it is important to devise tangible and viable programs that can be realised in the near future by exploiting the loose seams in present arrangements. A problem that is ripe for analysis and transformation is the issue of whether to retain the fault system as a major mode of accident compensation and control.

---

1 R. UNGER, KNOWLEDGE AND POLITICS 252 (1975).
2 *See supra* ch. 9. These proposals, like much of the earlier critique, fall within the intellectual parameters of the Critical Legal Studies movement. In response to recent allegations and condemnations, I want to suggest that these proposals are not "nihilistic" nor are they likely to "result in the learning of the skills of corruption, bribery and intimidation." *See* Carrington, *Of Law and The River*, 34 J. LEGAL EDUC. 227 (1984).

The heated debate between the "faulters" and the "no-faulters" continues unabated.[3] In the last few years, discussion has become even more furious and partisan. Only recently in retreat, the faulters seem to have experienced something of an unexpected renaissance. Taking advantage of the supposed crisis in insurance coverage, they have regrouped and launched a fresh defence of the fault status quo. This articulation of tort theory represents a major part of contemporary legal scholarship and is a microcosm of its ideological conflict.[4] Unfortunately, there is little new on offer. The debate seems well past the point where further argument or evidence might affect its resolution. Its participants cannot agree on what systemic aims the law should pursue, let alone on the relative priorities of those aims.

As with most legal debates, the problem is as much ideological as intellectual. Both the faulters and no-faulters can claim some analytical and statistical support for their interpretations of the arguments and the evidence. At bottom, the categories of "fact" and "truth" cannot be divorced from the ideological presuppositions of the categorizer. Ideological presuppositions cannot be discarded to achieve some ahistorical or universal standpoint. Each view, no-fault and fault, depends on rarely articulated assumptions and beliefs about the nature of human personality, social organization and moral responsibility. Proposals to provide health care and income support to the injured and unhealthy reflect a commitment to deep normative principles and raise important questions about social justice and political obligation. How we take care of the social victims of bad fortune is an integral part of our collective and individual self-image and self-understanding. It speaks to the kind of people and community we aspire to be. The tort system is a part of a larger societal problem—entitlement to and provision of health care and income support benefits—and this itself is part of more global concerns about domination and inequality. A lasting solution to the former demands a response to the latter.

Insofar as the debate has dealt with these issues, the faulters adopt a conservative ideology of individualism. Their ambition is to facilitate

---

3 By "faulters," I mean those who favour retaining the torts system, albeit in some reformed state, whether under a negligence or strict liability regime. These include Epstein, Posner, Priest, Rosenberg, Shapiro, and Weinrib. By "no-faulters," I mean those who would abandon the tort system, at least in part, and introduce some no-fault accident scheme, whether comprehensive or tailored, in its place. These include O'Connell, Keeton, Calabresi, Henderson and Havinghurst. I do not *necessarily* include those who favour a universal disability scheme, such as Ison, Abel, Franklin and Sugarman.

4 *See supra* ch. 6.

individual freedom and choice; their self-regarding premises only have room for social responsibility as an afterthought. On the other hand, the no-faulters are depicted as supporting a more collectivistic political morality. They emphasize the universalization of compensation benefits. In this essay, I contend that, contrary to the conventional wisdom, these characterizations are misleading.[5] *Both* groups are beholden to a liberal credo; they share an individualistic vision of social arrangements and political justice. Although there are degrees of orthodoxy within each group, the difference between them is much less than meets the eye. We should not mistake their social accoutrements and political trappings for their substantive views.

I agree with Holmes' belief that "[t]orts is not a proper subject for a law book".[6] Between the two, I would undoubtedly prefer a move to some no-fault scheme of accident compensation. But I do not think that there can be any real improvement unless there is a crucial shift in the way people think about themselves and their constitutive relation to and responsibility for others. Social life necessitates and entails mutual obligations. Liberals recognise this, but are intellectually powerless to act; they are trapped within the impoverished confines of an individualistic worldview. The existing maldistribution of risk, injury and care is far too high a price to pay for a misguided ideological fidelity. This essay outlines that liberal approach to welfare and criticises its normative ambivalence and practical inadequacy. In its place, I offer an alternative approach to health that is based on a strong theory of social democracy.[7]

I. THE LIBERAL APPROACH TO WELFARE

While there is relatively little political theorizing that directly and overtly connects up with the compensation debate, there is a vast literature on the right to well-being. If there does exist a related right to compensation embracing some provision of income security and health care,

---

5 *See* Englard, *The System Builders: A Critical Appraisal of American Tort Theory*, 9 J. LEG. STUD. 27 (1980) and J. FLEMING, THE LAW OF TORTS 369–377 (6th ed. 1983).

6 Holmes, *Book Note*, 5 AM. L. REV. 340 at 341 (1871). Of course, Holmes' opinion as to why that is the case and what ought to replace tort is very different from my own. See O.W. HOLMES, THE COMMON LAW 94–96 (1881).

7 This essay owes much to the influence of Richard Abel's work. *See* Abel, *A Critique of American Tort Law*, 8 BRIT. J. L. & SOC'Y 199 (1981) and *A Socialist Approach to Risk*, 41 MD. L. REV. 695 (1982). However, my thesis and conclusions are different from Abel's and ought not to be confused with his. Nevertheless, my debt is a substantial one and I gladly acknowledge it.

it would demand the same type of moral and political justification as the right to well-being itself. Theorists have begun to accept the need for *some* scheme of welfare support. Discussion centers on the questions of how much and to whom. Nevertheless, it is worthwhile to canvass the foundational arguments used to justify even a minimal right to well-being. Within the liberal paradigm, the central issue is one of political legitimacy—when is the state justified in coercing one person to alleviate the distress or suffering of another? If liberalism is to make a convincing claim that it provides a workable and principled program for social justice, it must offer a coherent, and not simply an expedient, explanation for any rights to well-being. I will sketch the kind of arguments that a utilitarian, rights-theorist, and libertarian, representatives of three different strains of liberalism, might plausibly make to ground a claim by one person against another for her support. Although these are highly stylised arguments, I have tried to avoid caricature and present them in their most credible form.[8]

For utilitarians, no state of affairs is intrinsically better or worse than another. Its moral rightness depends on the extent to which it maximises social utility. Social justice is evaluated by the optimality of consequences as determined by the felicific calculus. Thus, a right to well-being is derivative; society will acknowledge it only if it improves rather than reduces overall social utility. Nonetheless, some states of affairs so frequently maximise social welfare that they achieve a preferred status and amount to "rights". Assuming the declining marginal utility of wealth and money,[9] a shift of resources from the rich and healthy to the poor and unhealthy would arguably result in benefits to the latter that would outweigh the costs to the former. In overtly moral language, this would allow society to alleviate what is bad without sacrificing anything of comparable moral significance.[10] In making this calculation, the greater

---

8 In writing this section, I have benefitted from the materials and writings of others. *See* D. BEATTY, PERSONAL INCOME SECURITY IN A LIBERAL DEMOCRACY (1982) and Weinrib, *The Case for a Duty to Rescue*, 90 YALE L.J. 247 (1980). Neither would necessarily subscribe to my presentation of liberal arguments. Another set of influential essays is contained in INCOME SUPPORT: CONCEPTUAL AND POLICY ISSUES (P. Brown et al. eds. 1981).

9 *See* W. BLUM AND H. KALVEN, THE UNEASY CASE FOR PROGRESSIVE TAXATION 56–63 (1953). Not all utilitarians would agree with this assumption. For instance, Posner seems to make no distinction between the "value" of a dollar in the hands of a billionaire or a beggar. *See* R. POSNER, THE ECONOMICS OF JUSTICE ·60–61 (1981).

10 *See* P. SINGER, PRACTICAL ETHICS 158–181 (1979) and D. REGAN, UTILITARIANISM AND CO-OPERATION 83–93 (1980).

productivity of the many individuals who would be restored to working health would offset the putative disincentive effects of unearned income and the cost of those "free riders" who hitch on the social locomotive.

Notwithstanding the positive outcome of the welfare equation, the utilitarian ledger must balance all the costs and benefits. While individualized transfer payments would strike this balance ideally, such a delivery system would itself have prohibitive costs. Accordingly, society would do better to establish a general taxation-welfare scheme. Importantly, however, within such a regime of well-being rights, "transfers . . . [would be] undertaken for the sake of a maximizing interest ascribed to the populace as a whole, and not for the sake of any acknowledged claim of justice or right on the part of the disadvantaged claimant as an individual."[11] Accordingly, utilitarians could acknowledge a right to well-being, but, like all utilitarian calculations, it would be typically protean and pragmatic. While it might be revoked, it could as easily expand to assume a dominant feature in the social landscape.

The rights–theorists reject the accounting mentality of the utilitarians. They insist on taking the individual seriously and not as a costing item on a political ledger. They argue that life and health cannot be reduced to one more set of goods allocated or expended in the name of increased social efficiency. For the rights–theorists, life and health are constitutive of the person. Each individual is entitled to be treated with dignity and as an entity of intrinsic moral worth. Insofar as a society is best organized to allow individuals to design and pursue their own life plans, it is axiomatic that physical well-being is a vital precondition to that goal.[12] All healthy persons, therefore, have a duty to contribute to the well-being of the less healthy in society. However, that duty of benevolence is not bounded. The universal concept of personhood also encompasses healthy people who have no obligation to forego their own welfare. To expect benevolence is not the same as to demand a self-defeating commitment to selfless altruism. Like the utilitarian, however, the rights–theorist recognizes that as a matter of efficiency *and* fairness, it is necessary to coordinate these rights and obligations through a generalized welfare scheme.[13]

---

11 Michelman, *Constitutional Welfare Rights and A Theory of Justice*, in READING RAWLS: CRITICAL STUDIES ON RAWLS' A THEORY OF JUSTICE 319, 326 (N. Daniels ed. 1975).

12 *See* I. KANT, THE DOCTRINE OF VIRTUE 112 (M. Gregor trans. 1964) (Part II of *The Metaphysic of Morals*).

13 These arguments do not exhaust the fecundity of the rights–theorists' arguments. For instance, although Rawls does not list health care as a primary social good, a plausible argument can be made for its inclusion in such a category. For a discussion

Although libertarians are but a special kind of rights-theorist, their case merits separate discussion. The basic libertarian stance opposes all forms of distributive justice. Libertarians advocate absolute and inviolable moral entitlements to property, provided it was not obtained by force or fraud. While some moral obligation of philanthropy may exist and be encouraged, the government must leave the provision of welfare benefits to private charity. However, even these apparently uncompromising precepts do not preclude the establishment of some right to well-being. Indeed, one writer has gone so far as to argue that, under a libertarian ethic, a system of welfare rights is "morally required."[14] There are a number of philosophical avenues available to reach this counter-intuitive, but compelling conclusion.

For instance, Robert Nozick argues that the use of property is subject to the Lockean proviso that absolute rights can be exercised only so long as there be " 'enough and as good left in common for others.' "[15] He accepts that a person cannot acquire exclusive title to "the total supply of something necessary for life."[16] Yet, once this concession is made, moral intuition suggests that a right to a relatively healthy life justifies strong qualifications to property use. Further, if individual liberty is taken *very* seriously, it becomes clear that there are in fact two competing liberties at stake—the liberty to do with property as one wishes and the liberty to take property for life-sustaining needs. In default of a meta-principle of ultimate liberty, a reasonable assessment has to be made as to which sacrifice is greater and this, at least, tilts toward the latter liberty. This reduces rights-talk to a quasi-utilitarian calculation about the net cost of public appropriation being less than the expected costs of private self-protection for the haves and the benefits of public welfare being greater than publicly unrestrained, but privately resisted acts of expropriation for the have-nots.[17]

---

of Rawls' notion of a primary social good, *see* J. RAWLS, A THEORY OF JUSTICE 90–95 (1971). Also, those in the Rawlsian original position would more than likely agree to a universal welfare scheme. For further arguments, *see* Daniels, *Health-Care Needs and Distributive Justice*, 10 PHIL. & PUB. AFF. 146 (1981) and Buchanan, *The Rights to a Decent Minimum of Health Care*, 13 PHIL. & PUB. AFF. 55 (1984).

14 Sterba, *A Libertarian Justification for a Welfare State*, 11 SOC. TH. & PRAC. 285 at 295 (1985).

15 R. NOZICK, ANARCHY, STATE AND UTOPIA 175 (1974) (quoting J. LOCKE, TWO TREATISES OF GOVERNMENT, Second Treatise, s. 27 (P. Laslett 2d ed. 1967)).

16 *Id.* at 179. For a development of this line of argument, *see* Grey, *Property and Need: The Welfare State and Theories of Distributive Justice*, 28 STAN. L. REV. 877 at 888–891 (1976).

17 Sterba, *supra* note 14, at 289–295 and J. BUCHANAN, THE LIMITS OF LIBERTY: BETWEEN ANARCHY AND LEVIATHAN 53–73 (1975).

II. LIBERALISM EXPOSED

A. INDETERMINACY AND INDIVIDUALISM

The liberal response to the needs of the poor and "unhealthy" reflects liberalism's moral ambivalence, political plasticity and enduring individualism. As with any attempt to apply its theoretical precepts to concrete situations, liberalism's approach to well-being founders on the reefs of indeterminacy and contingency. In all its forms, liberalism begins and ends with the individual; a thing or state of affairs is only estimable if it is valuable to a particular individual as actual human experience. Liberalism maintains that the self-interested actions of individuals represent the most appropriate and effective principled basis for society's economic and political organization. Indeed, the whole structure of the liberal debate over welfare is ideologically loaded; the question it poses and the answer it suggests are already fully penetrated with liberal values. By asking in what circumstances one person can claim assistance from another, the terms of any discussion resist acceptance of our basic sociability. There is a foundational reliance on the understanding of people as pre-social ethical agents who view connection with and responsibility for others as a matter of voluntary choice. There is an almost wilful refusal to recognise the extent to which people are socially situated; we shape and are shaped by others and, therefore, have a mutual responsibility toward each other. We are all in this together and, as Lysias put it, "all fortune, good and bad, is to be shared in common."[18]

Notwithstanding this distinct ideological orientation, liberalism cannot fulfill its promise to provide a neutral or objective algorithm by which to mediate the contradictory forces of individual interest and collective concern.[19] Liberal theory is at a crossroads. Indeed, liberal theory is always at a crossroads. This quality is what identifies a theory as liberal. In the context of rights to well-being, liberalism suffers from its general and irremediable failure to establish any rational criterion for deciding between claims based on want and those based on need. Most social arrangements can generate a liberal theory of justification. Even a libertarian variant of liberalism can be consistently used to ground a strong welfare state; this is merely further evidence of its expedient status as a mode of rationalisation. For instance, James Buchanan maintains

---

18 Quoted in K. FREEMAN, THE MURDER OF HERODES AND OTHER TRIALS FROM THE ATHENIAN LAW COURTS 167 (1946). For further discussion of sociability, *see* *supra* ch. 9.

19 For a fuller discussion, *see* *supra* chs. 4 and 5.

that minimal rights to well-being can be established based on the need to reduce blatant inequalities in the effective opportunities to exercise libertarian rights. He prefers to characterise these rights as accruing through a person's status as citizen and not as a victim.[20] Although he argues that the foundational right to property acts as a powerful fetter on the tendency to enlarge such rights so as to effect a total redistribution of wealth, his characterisation moves the debate away from a theoretical engagement to an endless empirical controversy over the contingent weighing of social necessity and individual liberty. Even under libertarian logic, a Reichian regime becomes a distinct possibility.[21]

While they disagree about the redistributive role of the state, both faulters and no-faulters envision a similar kind of just society. The basic dynamic is individualistic and competitive. Alienation is the only shared experience. Although liberalism fetes the individual and celebrates personal freedom and action, it recommends a set of social organizing principles that rests on a pessimistic notion of human personality. People are, at best, ambivalent to others; at worst, they are distrustful of others. By expecting the worst of human nature, liberalism establishes a collective lifestyle that stifles the ameliorating potential in people and its limits become "the limits of the self-preoccupied imagination."[22] In a liberal regime, people unite only in their separateness and self-interest. They become exiles in their own society. The dominant motif of liberal society is its tendency towards anomie and communal disintegration; an accumulation of individuals divided by a common politics of hierarchy and inequality. Bereft of any sense of community, "our society may have become so anomic that explicit occasions for mutual recognition among strangers on public streets are more feared than sought."[23]

The attitudes of both faulters and no-faulters toward compensation exemplify the full force of this political scenario. The common law task is to restore individuals to the position they were in before the accident. The no-faulters do not object to this standard. However, they want all of society to bear this burden and to make compensation available regardless of the injury's particular cause. In short, they seek to universalize the compensation standards of the faulters. The traditional requirements of an accident and some identifiable and isolatable cause remain central. Clearly, the no-fault proposals represent a substantial improvement over

---

20 *See* Buchanan, *Deriving Welfare Rights From Libertarian Rights* in INCOME SUPPORT, *supra* note 8, at 236–245.
21 *See* Reich, *The New Property*, 73 YALE L.J. 733 (1964).
22 B. BARBER, STRONG DEMOCRACY 18 (1984).
23 R. BURT, TAKING CARE OF STRANGERS 41 (1979).

the prevailing "fault" status quo. Yet, even these proposals are much too limited in their remedial and distributive ambitions. The no-faulters share with the faulters the same liberal objective and rationality: to ensure through the payment of money and the provision of institutional health care that victims are reconstituted. Victims can then reassume their roles as rugged operatives in the bruising market of individual competition. However, economic logic and productive efficiency always temper communal care and human concern.[24]

Like their fault counterparts, most no-faulters fail to address the root cause of the problem. Operating within the rationality of liberal economics, they do not confront the pervasive correlation between wealth and health. Enforcing stricter rules on collateral benefits and placing a ceiling on compensation payments might effect marginal improvements. However, it is possible that they might actually aggravate the existing maldistribution of wealth.[25] Nonetheless, even if these measures are useful, they do not tackle the problem directly. In societies which are marked by an inegalitarian pattern of wealth distribution, any genuine attempt to improve the quality of health and health care must direct its attention to the economic structure of society. Without such a commitment, the ambition of establishing a democratic program for the control of health risks and the provision of health care will never be achieved.

B. HEALTH AS A COMMODITY

The statistical correlation between health and wealth is plain. Not only does it present a compelling picture of an intolerable social situation, but it reveals efforts to explain away this correlation as more apparent than real to be based on equally troubling ways of thinking about social problems. At its starkest, government data show that top-income Canadian men and women can expect to live 6 and 3 years respectively longer than their low-income counterparts. More dramatically, top-income Canadian men live 14 more disability-free years than low-income men.[26] For many Canadians, therefore, while they can expect a longer life than their parents, they can also look forward to living in worsening health. In America, the situation is even more polarised and is also exacerbated by racial disparities. Across the whole range of diseases and disabilities,

---

24 *See supra* at ch. 6.
25 *See Abel, supra* note 7, at 696, n. 3.
26 *See* J. EPP, ACHIEVING HEALTH FOR ALL 4 (1986). For a general study of the health-wealth correlation, *see* L. DOYAL, THE POLITICAL ECONOMY OF HEALTH (1979).

"affluent white America is as healthy as Sweden, . . . [but] the health of the black poor American nation is comparable to such nations as Venezuela, Romania and South Vietnam."[27]

The traditional rebuttal of this correlation is revealing. The claim is that the wealth–health connection is too crude. It is mediated by diverse factors, such as diet, exercise, work and environment. Such a sweeping and systemic conclusion, it is claimed, fails to acknowledge the considerable effect that individual decisions and propensities have upon the occurence and distribution of ill-health. But this response confirms more than it challenges. While those mediating factors are important, they themselves are closely correlated with wealth. The way and where people live, work, play and die is heavily influenced by their income and wealth status. Individual choice is constrained by economic standing.[28] Daily diet and regimen are as much socially patterned as individually chosen. The willingness, however reluctant, to "blame the victim" is a lamentable consequence of a liberal way of thinking: it flows from its individualistic account of human action and responsibility. Contrary to liberalism, ill-health is not an individual state of mind or body. Nor is it a social symptom to be isolated and treated. It is an integral and lasting condition of the extant structure of social arrangements and thinking.

The cancerous heart of this social milieu is the treatment of health and health care as a commodity. Like almost everything else in our society, health has been converted into one more commodity to be traded for and traded off; demand for health care is treated as another preference to be satisfied in line with the economic logic of the market. Human life and suffering represent one more variable in the production–consumption equation and a not particularly important one at that. It is indicative of prevailing social mores that we see the choice between arms and alms as a "tragic choice" and construct ever more complex institutional structures to obfuscate the moral nature and political consequences of such choices.[29] Health is business and health care is big business. Drug manufacturers are some of the wealthiest corporations and doctors one of the

---

27 W. RYAN, BLAMING THE VICTIM 324 (1976).

28 For a cogent gathering of the relevant data, see M. FRENCH, BEYOND POWER: ON WOMEN, MEN AND MORALS 356–397 (1985).

29 See G. CALABRESI AND P. BOBBITT, TRAGIC CHOICES (1978). It was, of course, Marx who emphasised the degrading tendency to reduce humanity to an economic resource. As Marx asks, "if money is the bond binding me to human life, binding society to me, binding me and nature and man, is not money the bond of all bonds? Can it not dissolve and bind all ties? Is it not, therefore, the universal agent of separation?" See K. MARX, THE ECONOMIC AND PHILOSOPHIC MANUSCRIPTS OF 1844, 167 (D. Struick ed. 1964).

highest-paid professions. Indeed, as medicine becomes less of a social calling and more of an enterpreneurial opportunity, a mutually sustaining medical-industrial complex thrives.[30] Yet, *surely* profiteering from ill-health reflects "exploitation in its most egregious form."[31] The rapid growth of public health-care programs has created increased opportunities for the private health care industry to exploit. The expansion of social compensation schemes will almost certainly exacerbate that situation.

In recent years, of course, there has been an apparently concerted attempt to take health care out of market. The so-called welfare state is intended to modify the play of market forces by ensuring a floor of basic benefits. The public provision of private assistance covers basic economic necessities and medical care and, more indirectly, legislation regulates working conditions and remuneration. However, although the value of these steps cannot be impugned, they still operate within a basic commitment to a market economy; the objective is limited and remedial. If health care, why not food, clothing and shelter? Beyond a certain threshold, health remains a good that is distributed according to economic ability to pay and not human need. Indeed, the origin and rise of the welfare state is closely related to the demand to increase production and facilitate capital accumulation. If it has improved standards of public health, it has been equally, or more, successful at oiling the wheels of industrial progress and economic growth.[32] The welfare state has also devoted most of its attention and resources to care and cure, not prevention and avoidance. These remain largely a matter of "private choice" and, therefore, reflect the social imbalance of information, power and wealth. Moreover, treatment of health as an economic commodity is not only offensive, but there does not exist any "market" even by the already minimal criteria of economic theory. Victims lack the regular attributes of consumers and doctors operate a largely unregulated monopoly. Finally, and perhaps most importantly, people who live within such a social structure assume its materialistic values; they begin to see others as competitors in the race for scarce resources and to stifle any instinct for generous altruism or common affection.

The attitude of health as a commodity is reflected throughout society. The victims of bad fortune face severe systemic and personal obstacles to a full integration into communal life. The victim's agony is not

---

30 Relman, *The New Medical-Industrial Complex*, 303 NEW ENG. J. MED. 963 (1980).
31 H. WAITZKIN AND B. WATERMAN, THE EXPLOITATION OF ILLNESS IN CAPITALIST SOCIETY 108 (1974).
32 *See* I. GOUGH, THE POLITICAL ECONOMY OF THE WELFARE STATE (1979).

merely the physical pain, but the frightening realization that she has been destroyed as a person. Accident victims' self-esteem and confidence in the community "become as ashes in [their] mouth[s]."[33] People's responses to the disabled and unfortunate compromise a mixture of contradictory feelings, combining pity and compassion with embarrassment and revulsion. Disability forces persons to face some uncomfortable facts about their own fragile vulnerability and the aleatory unpleasantness of their environment. Yet this insecurity also inhibits others from offering the communal support victims so vitally require to come to terms with their bad fortune. As a result, people close their eyes, if not their hearts, to the plight of the disabled, who become " 'a hidden population . . . unknown to the communities and individuals around them.' "[34] Even the relatively sensitive and sophisticated New Zealand scheme spends less than 1% of its budget on social rehabilitation programs.[35]

These deep-seated attitudes to disability explain the persistent and systemic discrimination that works against disabled people. In North America, the unemployment rate among the disabled exceeds the general average of 10% more than fivefold.[36] Also, many disabled who do work are part-time employees who receive low pay. Those who become disabled while in full-time employment often have a reduced earning capacity and face imposed early retirement.[37] However, evidence shows that, if given the chance, the disabled can and do work extremely well.[38] They are more often refused jobs because they are disabled rather than because they cannot perform the job satisfactorily.[39] Unless and until there is a substantial change in society's attitude to the disabled and unfortunate,

---

33 R. Lewiston, Hit From Both Sides 32 (1967).
34 United States Comm'n on Civil Rights, Accommodating The Spectrum of Individual Abilities 17 (1983) (quoting 118 Cong. Rec. 3320–3321 (1972) (statement of Sen. Williams)). For a powerful examination of the plight of the disabled child, see J. Gliedman and W. Roth, The Unexpected Minority: Handicapped Children in America 380 (1980).
35 See T. Ison, Accident Compensation 156 (1980).
36 See United States Comm'n on Civil Rights, supra note 34 at 29 (1983) and Canada House of Commons Special Comm. on the Disabled and the Handicapped, Obstacles 31 (1981).
37 See D. Harris, M. MacLean, H. Genn, S. Lloyd-Bostock, P. Fenn, P. Corfield and Y. Brittan, Compensation and Support for Illness and Injury 270–272, 274–278 (1984).
38 See United States Comm'n on Civil Rights, supra note 34, at 30.
39 See McGarity and Schroeder, Risk-Oriented Employment Screening, 59 Tex. L. Rev. 999 at 1008–1013 (1981).

the situation will remain bleak. This change will have to include a fundamental reassessment of the "work ethic". Although the opportunity to engage in productive activity is important, it ought not to dominate social thinking and organization. To expect people to work, while the opportunities are lacking, creates the worst of both worlds and is a significant source of distress among disabled people.

C. THE POLITICS OF HEALTH

A related, but neglected dimension of the tendency to treat health as a commodity is the ideological nature of "health" and its definition in terms of ability to work. A liberal society thinks of health in the familiar context of an instrumental rationality and not a constitutive ethic. Health is defined in terms of a fitness for economically productive work and not as a personally experienced and socially integrated sense of well-being. Even no-faulters, like Bernzweig and Conard, talk in terms of restoring individuals to their fullest usefulness. They indirectly present the unhealthy and unfortunate as defective goods.[40]

The concepts of "need" and "welfare" have a very full and varied history.[41] Modern society distributes its resources through a combination of schemes. Two of the major ones are structured around need—welfare—and productivity—work. Liberal rhetoric would have it that these are the only schemes, but the reality is that resources are primarily distributed in line with existing patterns of capital-holdings. Nevertheless, the primary criteria for distributing income (not wealth) is determined by the uneasy combination between work and need. Although presented as independent schemes, their relation is of one-sided dependence. Need is defined by the inability or lack of opportunity to work. Its boundaries are constantly shifting and are largely determined by the profitability of the industrial economy. Accordingly, disability is as much an economic function as a scientific category.

Not only is the provision of health care inseparable from the socioeconomic struggle to regulate individual and social conduct, but the categories of "health" and "unhealth" are the site of political conflict. Disability is a moving administrative boundary and not an objective clinical concept; health is not a naturally given condition, but a socially-constructed state of personal and collective consciousness. The health–disability axis

---

40 See E. BERNZWEIG, BY ACCIDENT, NOT DESIGN 163 (1980) and Conard, *The Economic Treatment of Automobile Injuries*, 63 MICH. L. REV. 279 at 294–295 (1964).
41 *See* D. STONE, THE DISABLED STATE 3-117 (1984).

is a mobile line that intersects political, technical, economic and cultural sectors of power and sustains shifting coalitions of influence. In this sense, disability is as much about social relations as the individual experience of illness and injury. Moreover, while its economic character offers a cogent account of disability and its organisation, there is another side to its definition and deployment. The accepted meaning of disability formulates and fixes ideas of normality; it instructs people in those inconveniences and afflictions that comprise the "natural" tribulations of living to be endured. As such, the whole health system forms part of the control framework through which society effects "the universal reign of the normative."[42] It generates many of the needs it administers to or feigns to satisfy and, in the process, maintains a semblance of social cohesion and order. For instance, although reproductive and contraceptive technology has increased women's autonomy, it has also extended the capacity of others (men) to control sexual and procreative activity.

If ill-health is a type of deviancy, the medical profession has eagerly assumed a role as the high priests of absolution. Their God-like aura and prominence in contemporary society is based on fear and awe as much as respect and gratitude. Their power was obtained and is exercised not through force, but through a careful cultivation of an image as practitioners of a scientific craft. The crucial encounter between doctor and patient reflects the destructive and hierarchical tendencies of the contemporary regimes for health care and general welfare. What should be an intimate occasion often becomes a clinical and remote exchange. As health care becomes increasingly technological and bureaucratic, medical treatment reduces individuals to "limp and mystified voyeur[s]"[43] of the treatment of their own bodies. The medical establishment expects patients to be the passive objects of therapy rather than active participants in their own well-being. The demise of home visits ensures that consultation occurs on the doctor's own professional turf. The whole asymmetrical relation between doctor and patient depends on the patient's continuing ignorance. Yet, more than most sciences, medicine is an art that looks to professional norms for guidance rather than to any objective body of medical information.[44]

An important aspect of doctors' power is not only their ability to control and manipulate technical knowledge, but also their success at

---

42 M. FOUCAULT, DISCIPLINE AND PUNISH: THE BIRTH OF THE PRISON 304 (1977) and *supra* ch. 9.

43 I. ILLICH, MEDICAL NEMESIS: THE EXPROPRIATION OF HEALTH 53 (1975).

44 *See* Edelman, *The Political Language of the Helping Professions*, 4 POL. & SOC'Y 295 (1974).

extending the reach of "medical matters". Taking advantage of the growing cult of expertise, they have managed to medicalise social problems.
This is very similar in strategy and effect to the legalisation of politics.
Not surprisingly, lawyers have been willing accomplices in this trivialisa-
tion and marginalisation of lay competence. The recent case of *Gillick*[45]
is illustrative of both trends. A mother of five girls challenged the legality
of a Health Department memorandum which permitted doctors to prescribe contraceptives to children under 16 without parental consent. Although the Court of Appeal found for the mother, the House of Lords
narrowly denied her challenge. It held that contraceptive advice and treatment was essentially a medical matter and that it was for the doctor to
decide what was in the best interests of the patient. In short, doctors can
refuse to prescribe contraceptives if they are of the opinion that the girl
does not "have a sufficient maturity to understand what is involved."[46]
As Lord Fraser put it, "the medical profession have in modern times
come to be entrusted with this further responsibility *which they alone are
in a position to discharge.*"[47]

At a general level, *Gillick* evidences the increasing trend to turn administrative and political issues into legal questions and to extend the
judicialisation of practical politics.[48] A more focused effect is to reinforce
the medicalisation of social problems and to underline the "control" dimension of medical technology. For all its doctrinal huff and puff,[49] the
Gillick case was actually about "who makes decisions for young
women?" The House of Lords fell back on its usual response—"doctor
knows best". Also, and typically, it was a decision by men about
women. All the judges were men, the doctors were predominantly men,
the administrative officials were mostly men, and the only woman directly involved was the young Gillick herself. Matters of female reproductive choice seem a particularly inappropriate area for decisions by
men. Indeed, there was only one question for the doctor in *Gillick*: "If
this woman is going to have intercourse, how soon can I give her the
contraceptives?" Discussion about whether she has "sufficient maturity
to understand what is involved" is condescending and misses the point.
If the doctor comes to the opinion that she is going to have intercourse,

---

45 [1986] A.C. 112.
46 *Id*. at 189 per Lord Scarman.
47 *Id*. at 174 (emphasis added).
48 This is dealt with at length, *supra* ch. 4.
49 An amazing aspect of the decision was the serious discussion about whether a doctor
who provides contraceptives to women under 16 is criminally liable for aiding and
abetting unlawful intercourse. *Id*. 174–175 and 190–191.

and there are no *serious* physiological difficulties, the doctor must proceed to prescribe the pill. We have to get away from professional elitism. That somehow professionals know best. Because they do not.

As *Gillick* makes clear, lawyers and doctors seem to be engaged in a professional alliance to separate people from control over their own lives and their bodies. The medical profession are educated and socialised to be commercial carers who are as interested in their own professional well-being as in the welfare of people. Their resistance in Canada to socialised medicine and, more recently, to bans on extra-billing are typical. Their energies and prestige are tied to the furtherance and refinement of acute health care. As an organised group, they do relatively little to oppose the environmental devastation of industry or to challenge dietary trends. The greater part of their talent, for instance, is devoted to curing cancer rather than working to eliminate the largely human-made sources of its incidence.[50] As always, the problem is primarily one of mind-set; "fragmented in mind, [doctors] apply themselves to sickness as a problem to be solved, rather than to health as an ideal to be reached by everyone, wholly—in mind, body and emotion."[51] No real progress will be made in confronting and responding to disability until we begin to contemplate it differently: we must see it as part of an overall social malaise and not an individual failing.

To this end, we must inculcate a greater appreciation that health and welfare are as much socially caused as individually experienced. To develop this appreciation we must foster a more holistic approach to well-being. Health care should not merely treat individual symptoms. It should concern itself with the total environment in which people live, work, play, and die. The control of risk would be of at least the same importance as the treatment of injury and misfortune. The objective must be to combine as full a social health coverage as possible with as much individual control of risk. Restorative arrangements would not be tied to the socio-economic status of victims or the cause of their misfortune, but would be related to maximising their potential for social rehabilitation. In a vigorously democratic society, citizens would determine the assumption and allocation of risk democratically. The presumption would be that all of society should share risk collectively and equally.[52] In short, the maxim that an ounce of prevention is better than a pound of cure would be taken seriously and acted upon.

---

50 *See* Doyal, *supra* note 26, at 60–80 and J. STAPLETON, DISEASE AND THE COMPENSATION DEBATE (1986).
51 French, *supra* note 28, at 368.
52 *See* Abel, *supra* note 7.

III. A DEMOCRATIC PRESCRIPTION

A. THE BUREAUCRATIC OPENING

A prerequisite for the successful accomplishment of a radical agenda for social transformation is a thoroughgoing acceptance and willingness to act on the fact that people only exist in and are constituted by a social milieu. Any plausible theory for political action must incorporate two related insights about what people share and binds them to one another: a common vulnerability to injury and a common capacity to envisage a better life beyond their present condition. The only way for people to respond to these human traits is to move beyond an inward-looking individual interest to other-regarding social solidarity. Our shared vulnerability and frustrated potential are the basis for hope, not despair. These frailties present an occasion for expressing and showing our common humanity. By developing a moral sense and practical experience of community, people could better contribute to the growth of a shared set of values in accordance with which social and individual life would be organised. By establishing an informed and democratic balance between the availability of personal choices and the existence of communal bonds, people would be respected as people, and not simply as rights holders. In this way, society could develop a modus vivendi that encourages caring and sharing and actualises the possibility for meaningful connection with others. Social concern would help assuage anxiety over personal vulnerability, ensure that risks were distributed equally, begin the shift from care to prevention, detach the meaning of "health" from the work ethic, and provide care for the "unhealthy". Communal support would maximise the genuine opportunities for individual freedom of action within a context of social stability.

The growth of the welfare state has been a clumsy attempt to meet some of these modern exigencies. However, whatever the good intentions of its no-fault proponents, they suffer from a certain liberal myopia. They do not seem to grasp that the universalization of health care carries with it the very real threat of increased bureaucratization and the further institutionalization of human values. Even when a compensation and care scheme is sufficiently comprehensive and adequately financed,[53] it requires a massive regulatory structure to administer the available be-

---

53 The British system suffers in exactly this way. *See* F. FIELD, INEQUALITY IN BRITAIN 68–911 (1981). Also, it should be remembered that the private cost of drugs and medical care exacerbate the need for greater public funding.

nefits. In this regard, the experience of the last two decades strongly suggests that the growth of a sprawling welfare bureaucracy has created a troubling paradox. A health bureaucracy relieves individuals of the anxiety borne of the struggle to maintain a basic standard of health and living. However, they still suffer the debilitating effects of powerlessness, dependence, and loss of self-respect. The modern welfare state places individuals in a state of "bondage to the bureaucratic machine."[54]

As individuals become enmeshed within the ample embrace of the welfare system, they lose a sense of their own individuality and see themselves as administrative charges on the common purse. Existing arrangements serve to demean and dehumanize recipients of state assistance. Moreover, the pervasiveness of the welfare bureaucracy discourages self-help and communal support: dependency breeds further dependency. The bureaucracy tends to buttress the hierarchical structure of modern society and to engender hostility to the "undeserving poor."[55] The hopeful ethic of social work has succumbed to the intrusive ideology of law and bureaucracy:

> The concerns of law and management have converged in the three basic themes of the recent literature and practice of welfare administration: first, the formalization of entitlement, by which I mean the formulation of the eligibility norms as rules; second, the bureaucratization of administration, by which I mean the intensification of formally hierarchical organization; and third, the proletarianization of the work force, by which I mean the diminution of the status, skill, education, and reward associated with the frontline welfare worker's job.[56]

The goal must be to establish an appropriate decisional distance between the vital institutions of care and the recipients of that care. At present, that gap is too large; people experience too little direct involvement by themselves and too much indirect control of themselves. If no-fault schemes are grafted on to the contemporary organisational and economic conditions of liberal society, they will be as much a crutch for a crippled society as a radical means for social improvement. There still thrives the either-or mentality that is trapped within a narrow choice between a wholesale deference to individual liberty and an unqualified submission to bureaucratic authority. Not only need the choice not be so polarised, but the options are more mutually-sustaining than mutually exclusive.[57]

---

54 M. WALZER, RADICAL PRINCIPLES 33 (1980).
55 See J. HANDLER AND E. HOLLINGWORTH, THE DESERVING POOR: A STUDY OF WELFARE ADMINISTRATION (1971).
56 Simon, *Legality, Bureaucracy, and Class in the Welfare System*, 92 YALE L.J. 1198 at 1199 (1983).
57 See supra ch. 9.

This insistence on viewing and organising the world as naturally divided between the government and the governed must be rejected. There must be a shift from government-as-bureaucracy to government-as-governed. In short there must be a "revolution in democratic consciousness"[58] and a concerted attempt to fracture the boundaries between bureaucracy and citizens.

It is clear that the increasing public and private bureaucratisation of life—and there must be no distinction between public and private spheres in diagnosis or remedy—distances people from the very decisions that pervasively affect and shape their lives. As people encounter non-democratic institutions at every turn, there is a prevalent feeling of alienation, impotence and helplessness. The bureaucratic structure stands in place of a communal web based on intersubjective relations and social co-operation. Yet, although we must resist Lenin's vision in which "the whole of society will have become a single office and single factory",[59] we must also avoid a naive romanticism in which we imagine ourselves engaged in a Thoreauean pond-life.[60] Our complex and technological society requires a more generalised scheme of organisation. Governmental regulation is not the enemy per se, but it is the lack of individual control of and participation in that regulation. To condemn it out of hand is almost as bad as to revere it unreservedly. Accordingly, the democratization of bureaucracy, both public and private, must be at the top of any realistic agenda for radical change.

B. BEYOND LIBERAL DEMOCRACY

The practice and theory of contemporary democracy is in a lamentable state. There is a growing distance between people and power. In popular usage, democracy represents rule by representative government; citizens vote for decision-makers rather than make decisions for themselves. Our rulers are the winning competitors in the electoral race.[61] Political equality is achieved by providing for equal opportunity of access and influence over decision-makers. The focus is on form and process. Democracy is reduced to "consumerism in a controlled marketplace of prepackaged political ideas."[62] Sustained popular participation in politics

---

58 C.B. MACPHERSON, DEMOCRATIC THEORY: ESSAYS IN RETRIEVAL 184 (1973).

59 V.I. LENIN, STATE AND REVOLUTION 84 (1932).

60 See H.D. THOREAU, WALDEN (1854).

61 See J. SCHUMPETER, CAPITALISM, SOCIALISM, DEMOCRACY (1950) and R. DAHL, PREFACE TO DEMOCRATIC THEORY (1956).

62 Mensch, *Freedom of Contract as Ideology*, 33 STAN. L. REV. 753 at 771 (1981).

is not encouraged as this would escalate conflict and destabilize the system. Consequently, the contemporary democratic scene is dominated by interest-group politics. Citizens are free to vote and can align themselves with a pressure group between elections.

Yet this "pluralist model" represents a travesty of the democratic ideal. The supporters of such a system are merely apologists for the prevailing maldistribution of power. Participation is reduced to a formal and sporadic ritual. Democracy's pale and perverse contemporary performance is anathema to its full-blooded possibilities.[63] Political equality is rendered meaningless by economic inequality. Moreover, such notional participation is confined to government activity. Politics is not seen to embrace the exercise of private power in corporate decision-making. Insofar as government is suffocated by corporate and private power, popular participation has no impact on the real decision-makers. It merely allows contemporary social arrangements to be presented as the outcome of citizen choice rather than the imposition of elite preference. Democratic practice constitutes an accommodating screen behind which the political drama of private power is played out: "democracy is the most prostituted word of our age, and [anyone] who employs it in reference to any modern state should be suspect either of ignorance or of bad motives".[64] The forums of popular choice—legislature and market—are deadlocked.

The offensive symbolism and injustice of modern democracy must be replaced by a substantive and just vision of democratic society. Democracy is much more than a formal theory of political organization; it is a potent way of daily life. It is not about process and method, but about social action and individual experience. Democracy means the greatest possible engagement by people in the greatest possible range of social tasks and public action. Participation is not desirable as a means to self-expression, but because it ensures people an active role in their own constituting and re-making of themselves and their social context. Democratic politics is generative and experiential. A genuine commitment to an unadulterated democratic practice will represent the most powerful challenge to the hierarchical elite. In a flourishing democracy, "true authority is not frozen in hierarchy, but is continuously recycled back through the society from which it emanates."[65] For domination arises and thrives

---

63 *See* C. PATEMAN, PARTICIPATION AND DEMOCRATIC THEORY (1970) and J. MANSBRIDGE, BEYOND ADVERSARY DEMOCRACY (1980).
64 Schaar, *Legitimacy and the Modern State* in POWER AND COMMUNITY: ESSAYS IN DISSENT 288 (P. Green and S. Levinson eds. 1970).
65 M'Gonigle, *The Tribune and the Tribe: Toward A Natural Law of the Market/Legal State*, 13 ECOLOGY L.Q. 233 at 297 (1986).

when people lose the sense that society and its institutional paraphernalia are created by people and can be changed by people. Furthermore, participatory democracy is addictive; it educates the political mind. As people begin to reclaim control over their own lives, they will develop an appetite and talent for more. Increased political engagement will create and sustain its own momentum. A system of democratic participation in *all* communal life exploits the vast untapped resources of popular power.

Some critics argue that the attempt to transform and radicalize democracy is doomed to failure because "nothing risks killing democracy more than having too much of it".[66] The central argument is that liberal individualism and democracy are so related that when they fall, they will fall together. While it is true that democratic governance has been historically associated with liberal states, it does not follow that they share any necessary or mutually-entailing relation. Although some form of democracy has become an almost indispensable component of modern government, its history reveals that it is more of an optional extra than an essential condition. The liberal state has been with us for centuries, but universal suffrage is a decidedly modern phenomenon. Democracy is the by-product of a pre-occupation with private autonomy and enhanced individual liberty.[67] As a subsidiary feature of a liberal constitutional order, the radical possibilities of democracy are not exhausted by its present annexation.

If democracy is elevated to the central organising principle of the constitutional order, the whole dynamic of socio-political change and action will be transformed. Instead of giving ontological priority to individual interest, participatory democracy enables people to participate and re-work the profound and sensitive dialectical tension between self and others; it enhances the opportunities for the continuous negotiation of the multiple interplay between the unique and the individual, and the common and the communal. It is an engaged, not an abstract, rapprochment between particular and general concerns. In this way, democratic arrangements meet the challenge of historical contingency. They respect its imperative, but do not become enslaved to it: the possibility and importance of normative discourse is retained and invigorated. The agenda of political debate and action is constantly being redrafted. Of course, the stakes will be high and there are no guarantees. But strong democ-

---

66 Bobbio, *The Future of Democracies*, 61 TELOS 3 at 6 (1984).
67 For an account of this history, *see* Hutchinson and Monahan, *Democracy and the Rule of Law* in THE RULE OF LAW: IDEAL OR IDEOLOGY (A. Hutchinson and P. Monahan eds. 1987).

racy offers a chance that its stunted contemporary practice can never imagine or realize. The design is not to develop a romantic or utopian harmony, but a political order which facilitates direct participation in the
continuing social deliberation over political ends.

The benefits and freedom that come with democratic solidarity are
not costless. Apart from demanding a gracious humility and an unrelent-
ing magnanimity, democrats must make a major personal commitment
to the maintenance and improvement of the participatory structure and
process. The required commitment is an exhausting, but exhilarating experience. However, individuals would defeat the purpose of social
change if they engaged in mindless masochism, expending all their energies in perfecting the democratic process without living the life it is intended to make possible. Accordingly, it will be necessary to explore
intermediate forms of institutional organisation.[68] In establishing such
structures, people will have to guard against the temptation to allow
them to ossify and impair the vitality of a truly democratic life. While
the deconstructive impulse must check the reconstructive instinct, it need
not obliterate or paralyse that instinct. Gerald Frug captures this idea of
a temporary stopping place:

> This would be reached when people abandoned abstract arguments that seek to
> defend some form of life as a structure than can protect human individuality—
> when people jointly recognize that no structure can protect us from each other
> given the variable, intersubjective, interdependent nature of human relationships.
> The forms of organization that would then be created would not be understood
> as an answer to the human predicament. They would be transparently open to
> transformation (no form of organization is necessary) and always in need of trans-
> formation (all forms of organization create forms of domination that need to be
> combatted.)
>   . . . Only by creating these forms together can people confront the intersubjec-
> tive nature of social life. . . . In this view, the term "participatory democracy"
> does not describe a fixed series of limited possibilities of human organization but
> the ideal under which possibilities of joint transformation of social life are col-
> lected.[69]

C. PLANNING FOR SOCIAL CHANGE

The problem facing any radical program is to translate its theoretical
postulates into attainable dimensions of concrete human experience. This

---

68 A valuable and suggestive list of possibilities can be found in Barber, *supra* note 22.
69 Frug, *The Ideology of Bureaucracy in American Law*, 97 HARV. L. REV. 1276 at 1295–
   1296 (1984). The idea of stopping places fits in nicely with the "nomadic" depiction
   of social life. See *supra* ch. 2.

task must not be overlooked or underestimated. Yet, in dealing with questions of health care and income support, the challenge is perhaps not as hopeless as it might first appear. Indeed, the present state of affairs manages both to highlight the limited record of liberal democratic practices and to suggest the exciting possibilities for democratic participation. The centralized bureaucratization of welfare places a divisive barrier between individuals and distances people from the making of decisions about their own lives: it dulls the democratic imagination and suppresses the participatory initiative. Yet this very process opens up opportunities for democratic involvement. As *both* the powerful and the powerless come to rely on the state provision of welfare, there emerges a shared focus for their opposing claims and objectives. As long as care is taken to avoid replicating the competitive and elite pluralism of representative democracy, popular involvement in the administrative process is the shortest and most effective route to a more just and caring society.

At every turn, citizens presently encounter non-democratic institutions. Strenuous efforts must be made to elect all policy-makers and gain effective popular control of policy-making. Instead of social policies being imposed by social administrators, no matter how beneficient, citizens must be entrenched within local centres of bureaucratic power; they must experience and control social programs as an integral part of their local and personal life.[70] In this struggle, the work of the environmental and anti-nuclear movements exemplifies the present despair and the future hope. Excluded from the decision-making process, such activists testify to the true democratic spirit which, repressed and subdued for so long, strains for recognition and fulfillment. Aroused and unleased, its power is sufficient to dismantle the debilitating barriers between citizens and those that separate people from the management of risk and recovery.

In the context of compensation schemes, the actual and potential victims of bad fortune (i.e. everyone) must seize responsibility for their own exposure to harm and be able to participate fully in their own treatment and recovery. The strict division and characterization of medical and nonmedical roles must be broken down. Individuals need to educate themselves as to the value of personal preventive medicine and the contribution they can make to their own healing. Patients must involve themselves in the formulation of any rehabilitation or treatment program. We must not relegate the welfare recipient to the status of client or

---

70 Glennerster, *The Need for a Reappraisal,* in THE FUTURE OF THE WELFARE STATE 1 at 8 (H. Glennerster ed. 1983).

claimant. The need for a sense of belonging is never more urgent than when misfortune strikes. Although society will continue to maintain a corps of professional carers, each individual must become a "welfare worker" who contributes to her own personal health and to that of the overall community. As Alastair Campbell rightly warns, "the notion of health *care* involves mutual learning, mutual help and mutual responsibility. A society which ignores this may stave off, for a time, the effects of illness and injury, but only to pave a better road to ill-health."[71]

When people begin to realize the benefits of active participation and acquire a taste for further communal involvement, they will appreciate the contingent character of social life. Communal attention will turn toward setting appropriate standards for health and health care. Even the fully democratic society will have to make "tragic choices" about the allocation of scarce resources.[72] Yet the visible and personal hand of democracy is preferable to the invisible and impersonal hand of the market. Altough the community of informed individuals will decide the issue, they might think it appropriate to designate health care as a non-market good, taking it out of the distributive forum of competitive choice. Moreover, this might prompt other questions: if health, why not food and clothing? Why not housing? Why not education? On the medical front, at least, neighborhood boards of doctors, patients, and local residents will govern hospitals and local clinics. Medical research funding can be wrested from the exclusive control of medical experts and private corporations, and placed under greater public scrutiny. Although there has been a significant increase in medical knowledge, there has not been a corresponding improvement in general health standards or care. While medical technology advances apace, its direction is not presently open to direct public control. For instance, much medical research has been devoted to the reduction of mortality, but this has meant an increase in morbidity, especially among the elderly.[73]

In all this, a central villain of the piece is the general tendency to professionalize the policy-making process and devolve decisional authority to "experts".[74] In particular, as a society, we have made the choice for continuance of life over quality of life more by default than anything

---

71 A. CAMPBELL, MEDICINE, HEALTH AND JUSTICE: THE PROBLEM OF PRIORITIES 88 (1978).

72 *See* Calabresi and Bobbit, *supra* note 29.

73 *See* D. HORROBIN, MEDICAL HUBRIS: A REPLY TO IVAN ILLICH 24 (1977) and Hacker, *"Welfare": The Future of An Illusion*, N.Y. REV. BOOKS, February 28, 1986 at 37 at 39.

74 *See supra* at pp. 309–310.

else; doctors have been allowed to appropriate such issues under the rubric of medical competence. Yet the treatment and care of defective babies, geriatrics, paraplegics and other afflicted individuals is as much a question for so-called lay opinion as for medical experts. Answers must come through a wide-ranging and informed public debate. For instance, technology has "advanced" to the stage where we can keep almost any person alive indefinitely—death is no longer natural. In this Brave New World, questions of when to give, withhold or terminate treatment are the daily fare of hospital life: the answers are doubly difficult to give when the patients are new-born children and incapable of speaking for themselves. Whether we like it or not, the invisible hand of the market indirectly flicks the on/off switch of medical treatment. But particular instances are almost exclusively controlled by doctors. In a world of wonderful successes and spectacular failures, doctors engage in *ad hoc* decision-making, only consulting parents as a matter of courtesy. The giving or withholding of treatment is dependent on a whole host of non-medical factors—an unwed mother's child has less chance of treatment as does a large family's.[75] With benign arrogance, doctors assume a Jovian responsibility; medical ethics becomes the ethics of medics.

Yet, once certain technical and prognostic questions have been answered, the nature of what tragic choices to make on behalf of the newborn child becomes an issue of general social and moral competence. Apart from entrusting well-informed parents with ultimate authority, local health boards might decide that the major criteria for whether to give, continue or withhold treatment should be the quality of expected life, and not simply its extension. Indeed, it may be that a quick and painless death is the most humane response; to simply let a child die is a course of action tht may be less painful for doctors, but especially cruel to the child. Difficult as these matters and choices are, society owes it to itself and the unfortunate victims to confront and respond to them in the practical context and moral spirit of the democratic life. By deferring to the pseudo-expertise of doctors and lawyers, our ideals are compromised and popular apathy is reinforced. Democracy has no easy answers, but it can empower and galvanise those who share in its obligations and rewards.

Society must aim for social health care services which work toward a local supportive environment for rehabilitation. Of course, some pro-

---

75 *See* J. MAGNET AND E. KLUGE, WITHHOLDING TREATMENT FROM DEFECTIVE NEWBORN CHILDREN 21–25 (1986). This book offers a stimulating and suggestive discussion of the problem and the democratic possibilities for its resolution.

vision for domestic health care already exists, but these programs receive inadequate funds and half-hearted community support. Furthermore, in an individualistic society, these programs place a heavy burden on family care-givers, especially women kin.[76] Lacking any real democratic support, carers and cared-for become locked in a mutually suspicious and destructive relationship. Existing social and home-care programs utilise their idealistic image in order to justify and excuse limited public action.[77] Before any substantial improvement can take place, society must thoroughly change its thinking about health and health maintenance. An urgent commitment to strong democracy is the only place to begin.

IV. CONCLUSION

In this short essay, I have sought to expose and criticize the individualistic foundations of both the fault and no-fault contributions to the modern compensation debate. Only by struggling to establish a democratic community of respectful beliefs and shared practices can society develop a humane response to death and injury. My basic credo is that "there is a difference . . . between what we would do as individuals competing in a market and what we would do as members of the public building a conception of ourselves as a community."[78] Whereas the democratic society takes an integrated and coherent stance on risk and well-being, the liberal society adopts a divided and contradictory position. Many will no doubt deride and dismiss my suggestions as hopelessly utopian. But, since these suggestions only involve making good on our pre-existing commitment to democracy, such criticism reveals liberal theory's fearful lack of vision and the extent of its enslavement to the status quo. Of course, theorizing is insufficient by itself; it must be accompanied by appropriate action. Yet efforts to change our ways of thinking about ourselves and efforts to change society "are profoundly interconnected, if for no other reason than that [theorizing] is a *part* of the social world as well as a *conception* of it."[79] By theorising a problem, we take the first practical steps towards its resolution.

---

76 *See* Note, *Home Health Care for the Elderly: Programs, Problems and Potentials*, 22 HARV. J. ON LEGIS. 193, 213–215 (1985).

77 Some countries have progressed in this area. On the available evidence, Sweden *seems* like a good example. *See* Liljestrom, *Sweden*, in FAMILY POLICY 19 (S. Kamerman and A. Kahn eds. 1978).

78 Sagoff, *On Markets for Risk*, 41 MD. L. REV. 755, 773 (1982).

79 A. GOULDNER, THE COMING CRISIS OF WESTERN SOCIOLOGY 13 (1970).

APPENDIX

CHAPTER 1 ACKNOWLEDGMENTS

Works referred to in the play include, in order of appearance; W. Blake, *Auguries of Innocence* in THE POETRY AND PROSE OF WILLIAM BLAKE 481 (D. Erdman ed. 1965); Toronto Globe and Mail, June 15, 1985, at B5, cols. 3–6; L. Carroll, *Through the Looking Glass* (1871), reprinted in C. DODGSON, THE COLLECTED VERSE OF LEWIS CARROLL 15 (1929); A.C. Doyle, *The Adventure of Silver Blaze in* THE MEMOIRS OF SHERLOCK HOLMES 7 (1894); J. FOWLES, MANTISSA 118–120 (1982); J. JOYCE FINNEGAN'S WAKE 219 (1939); and The Police, *De Do Do Do, De Da Da Da*. Taken from ZENYATTA MANDATTA. Copyright 1980 Virgin Music (Publishers) Ltd. Used by permission. All rights reserved.

CHAPTER 3 INDEX SOURCES

1. UNITED STATES DEP'T OF COMMERCE, BUREAU OF THE CENSUS, STATISTICAL ABSTRACT OF THE UNITED STATES 1985 455 (105th ed. 1984) (1982 data) [hereinafter 1985 ABSTRACT]. **2.** T. SMITH. A COMPENDIUM OF TRENDS ON GENERAL SOCIAL SURVEY QUESTIONS 169–70 (1980) (1977 data). **3.** Of 751 white respondents, 434 agreed "strongly" or "slightly" to the statement. NATIONAL OPINION RESEARCH CENTER, GENERAL SOCIAL SURVEY (Question 126, Feb. 4, 1985). **4.** 1985 ABSTRACT at 170 (10.4 per 100,000; 1981 data). 5. *Id.* (64.8 per 100,000; 1981 data). 6. *Id.* at 407 (1984 data; comparable figure for whites is 7.4%). **7.** *Id.* (1984 data; comparable figure for blacks is 27.3%). **8.** *Id.* **9.** *Id.* **10.** *Id.* (8.5/4.3 in 1965; 17.2/7.2 in 1984). **11.** JOINT CENTER FOR POLITICAL STUDIES, BLACK ELECTED OFFICIALS 11 (1985). **12.** Clauss, *Keynote Address*, 13 N.Y.U. REV. L. & SOC. CHANGE 225 (1985). **13.** 1985 ABSTRACT at 456 (1983 data). **14.** *Id.* **15.** *Id.* at 71 (1981 data;

2165 blacks per 100,000; 1182 whites per 100,000). **16.** Clauss, at 227–238. **17.** *Id.*
18. *Id.* **19.** *See* Blumstein, *On the Racial Disproportionality of U.S. Prison Popula-*
tions, 73 J. CRIM. L. & CRIMINOLOGY 1259, 1260 (1982). **20.** *Id.* **21.** 1985
ABSTRACT at 446. **22.** *Id.* **23.** *Id.* (1970 black family income: $16,111; 1970 white
family income: $26,263). **24.** *Id.* **25.** *Id.* at 406 (1972 rate: 10.4%; 1982 rate
18.9%). **26.** *Id.* (1972 rate: 5.1%; 1982 rate 8.6%).

CHAPTER 6 BIBLIOGRAPHY

Abel, *A Critique of American Tort Law* (1981), 8 BRIT. J. LAW & SOC'Y. 199.
Abel, *A Socialist Approach to Risk* (1982), 41 MD. L. REV. 695.
Atiyah, *Accidents, Compensation and the Law* (3d ed. 1980).
Belobaba, 1 Products Liability and Personal Injury Compensation in Canada: Towards
Integration and Rationalization (1982).
Bernzweig, *By Accident, Not Design* (1980).
Boehringer, *The Death of Fault* (unpublished, June 1986).
Brown , *Towards an Economic Theory of Liability* (1973), 2 J. LEG. STUD. 323.
Calabresi, *The Costs of Accidents* (1970).
Calabresi, *Torts—The Law of the Mixed Society* (1978), 56 TEX. L. REV. 519.
Calabresi and Hirschoff, *Toward a Test for Strict Liability in Torts* (1972), 81 YALE L.J.
1055.
Cane, *Justice and Justifications for Tort Liability* (1982), 2 OXF. J. LEG. STUD. 30.
Chapman, *Ethical Issues in the Law of Tort* (1982), 20 U.W. ONT. L. REV. 1.
D'Amato, *The Bad Samaritan Revisited* (1975), 70 NW. U.L. REV. 798.
Dworkin, *Taking Rights Seriously* (1979).
Dworkin, *A Matter of Principle* (1985).
England, *The System Builders: A Critical Appraisal of Modern American Tort Theory* (1980),
9 J. LEG. STUD. 27.
Epstein, *A Theory of Strict Liability* (1980).
Epstein, *Automobile No-Fault Plans: A Second Look at First Principles* (1980), 13
CREIGHTON L. REV. 769.
Fleming, *The Law of Torts* (6th ed., 1983).
Fletcher, *Fairness and Utility in Tort Theory* (1972), 85 HARV. L. REV. 537.
Franklin and Rabin, *Cases and Materials on Tort Law and Alternatives* (3rd ed. 1987).
Fraser, *The Legal Theory We Need Now* (1978), 40–41 SOCIALIST REV. 147.
Freid, *Anatomy of Values* (1970).
Freid, *Right and Wrong* (1978).
Glasbeek and Hasson, "Fault—The Great Hoax," in Klar ed., STUDIES IN CANADIAN
LAW 395–424 (1977).
Golbert and Lowenstein, *The Court and the Market Place: Who Should Regulate Whom?*
(1981), 34 BAYLOR. L. REV. 39.
Griffith, *The Politics of the Judiciary* (2d ed. 1985).
Holmes, *The Common Law* (1881).
Hutchinson and Monahan, *Law, Politics and The Critical Legal Scholars: The Unfolding
Drama of American Legal Thought* (1984), 36 STAN. L. REV. 199.
Hutchinson and Monahan, *The Rights Stuff: Roberto Unger and Beyond* (1984), 62 TEX.
L. REV. 1477.

Ison, *Accident Compensation* (1980).

Kennedy, *Form and Substance in Private Law Adjudication* (1976), 87 HARV. L. REV. 1685.

Kennedy, *The Structure of Blackstone's Commentaries* (1979), 28 BUFFALO L. REV. 205.

Landes, *Compensation for Automobile Accident Injuries: Is the Tort System Fair?* (1981), 11 J. LEG. STUD. 253.

Landes and Posner, *The Positive Economic Theory of Tort Law* (1981), 15 GA. L. REV. 851.

Linden, *Canadian Tort Law* (1983).

Lowi, *The Politics of Disorder* (1971).

MacIntyre, *After Virtue* (2nd ed. 1985).

Marcuse, *One-Dimensional Man* (1974).

Mensch, *Freedom of Contract as Ideology* (1981), 33 STAN. L. REV. 753.

McClung, *In Defense of Reasonableness: A Critical Analysis of Monolithic Theories of Tort Law*, [1981] S. TEX. L.J.1.

NEW SOUTH WALES LAW REFORM COMMISSION WORKING PAPER, *A Transport Accident Scheme for New South Wales* (1983).

Noel and Phillips, *Torts and Related Law* (1980).

Note, *Stalking the Good Samaritan: Communists, Capitalists and the Duty of Rescue* (1976), 3 UTAH L. REV. 529.

Nozick, *Anarchy, State and Utopia* (1974).

Posner, *A Theory of Negligence* (1972), 1 J. LEG. STUD. 29.

Posner, *The Economic Approach to Law* (1975), 53 TEX. L. REV. 757.

Posner, *Economic Analysis of Law* (3d ed. 1986).

Posner, *Some Uses & Abuses of Economics in Law* (1979), 46 U. CHI. L. REV. 281.

Posner, *The Economics of Justice* (1980).

Posner, *Tort Law: Cases and Economic Analysis* (1982).

Priest, *The Common Law Process and the Selection of Efficient Rules* (1978), 6 J. LEG. STUD. 65.

Rawls, *A Theory of Justice* (1970).

AUST., REPORT OF THE NATIONAL COMMITTEE OF INQUIRY, *Compensation and Rehabilitation in Australia* (1974).

N.Y., REPORT OF THE NEW YORK DEPARTMENT OF INSURANCE, *Automobile Insurance: For Whose Benefit?* (1970).

Report of the Royal Commission on Civil Liability and Compensation for Personal Injury (Cmnd. 7054, 1978).

NEW ZEALAND, REPORT OF THE ROYAL COMMISSION OF INQUIRY, *Compensation for Personal Injury in New Zealand* (1967).

Sagoff, *On Markets for Risk* (1982), 41 MD. L. REV. 755.

Steiner, *Justification and Social Vision in Modern Tort Law of Accidents* (1987).

Steiner, *Economics, Morality and the Law of Torts* (1976), 26 U. TORONTO L.J. 229.

Steiner, *Putting Fault Back Into Products Liability: A Modest Reconstruction of Tort Theory* (1982), 1 LAW & PHIL. 419.

Sugarman, *Doing Away With Tort Law* (1985), 73 CALIF. L. REV. 642.

Thompson, *Whigs and Hunters: The Origins of the Black Act* (1978).

Unger, *Knowledge and Politics* (1975).

Unger, *The Critical Legal Studies Movement* (1983), 96 HARV. L. REV. 561.

Ursin, *Judicial Creativity and Tort Law* (1981), 49 GEO. WASH. L. REV. 229.

Weinrib, *The Case for a Duty of Rescue* (1980), 90 YALE L.J. 247.

Weinrib, *The Insurance Justification and Private Law* (1985), 14 J. LEG. STUD. 681.

White, *Tort Law in America: An Intellectual History* (1980).

CHAPTER 8 ACKNOWLEDGMENTS

Works referred to and rephrased include, W.H. Auden, *It's No Use Raising a Shout*, The Collected Poetry of W.H. Auden (1961); Richard Rorty, Philosophy and the Mirror of Nature (1979); Paul Carrington, *Of Law and the River*, 34 J. Legal Educ. 222 (1984); Charles Fried, *The Artificial Reason of the Law or: What Lawyers Know*, 60 Texas L. Rev. 35 (1981); Arthur Allen Leff, *Law And*, 87 Yale L. J. 989 (1978); Ursula Le Guin, Always Coming Home 336 (1985).